*Stained glass window of St. Dominic by Jean Hugo, Chapel of St. Dominic's house, Fanjeaux
Photo by Austin Flannery, O.P.*

DEDICATED
to all the women and men
of the Kentucky Dominican family
named and unnamed
whose lives have been
a *Signadou* — a sign from God —
to all the people
who crossed their paths

The wilderness and the dry land shall be glad,
the desert shall rejoice and blossom;
like the jonquil it shall blossom abundantly,
and rejoice with joy and singing.

ISAIAH 35:1-2

Contents

— *Part Three* —

From Prioress to Mother General to President

— *Part Four* —

La Bella Brigata

Acknowledgements

THIS HISTORY of the Kentucky Dominicans was made possible by the collaboration of many persons. After the General Chapter of 1988 mandated that a history be written, Sr. Elizabeth Miles, president, commissioned me, Sr. Paschala Noonan, to undertake the task. The course of the writing was delayed twice when I had surgery, but Sr. Elizabeth was most supportive then and during the entire process. Her patience and kindness made the task easier.

One of the highlights of the project, was meeting Francis Furgang, a Maryland resident and descendant of the Sansburys. He and his delightful wife Dorothy had me as their houseguest and toured me all over the Maryland territory where the settlers of Cartwright Creek originated. I owe a debt of gratitude to Francis, an ardent genealogist who generously shared Sansbury history and put me in touch with other Sansbury researchers.

Grateful acknowledgement is made to the editorial committee: Srs. Sheila Buckley, Marie Francesca Cameron, Ann Miriam Hickey, Joan Monica McGuire, Elizabeth Miles and Eleanor Tierney. Thanks to over 200 persons who granted interviews whenever I called on them and to my Dominican sisters whose support and enthusiasm were invaluable.

I have been blessed to have as readers who critiqued each chapter as it was written: Ms Catherine Bowser, a friend with a proofreader's eagle eye; Sr. Ann Miriam Hickey, our dedicated archivist; Sr. Mary Eva Kimbel, a companion from novitiate days whose clarity, precision and balance enhanced the manuscript; and to my brother John D. Noonan, professor of Communication Arts. Also, I am indebted to my brother for proofreading the galley sheets of the entire book with his trusty red pencil.

Thanks to Ms. Diane Rezendes, my computer scribe, who transcribed the entire book and was a godsend for one who is computer ignorant. Ms. Eleanor Shea and Sr. Rose Vincent O'Brien helped with some computer lists. To translate documents from Latin, Italian, Spanish and French were Sr. Rose Irma Doyle, Ms. Mary Ciccolella, Sr. Amelia del Carmen Rivera and Sr. Sheila Buckley. Srs. Marie Cleary and Jean Delaney helped with pictures.

Countless sisters in the community sent information and helpful leads. Among those who did research were Srs. Ruth Anne Rezek, Margaret Philip Shaw and Louise Quinlan. One outstanding researcher was Sr. Marie Francesca Cameron whose meticulous methods and boundless enthusiasm were a constant inspiration. I regret that she died before the book was published. Sr. M. Nona McGreal, director of the OPUS PROJECT (Order of Preachers in the United States) was most generous in sharing information and documents, as was Sr. Loretta Petit, also of OPUS. Archives of Dominican communities — Ohio, Nashville, Houston, Sinsinawa, Illinois, New Jersey, Fall River (MA) and Kansas graciously supplied valuable data as did Nazareth Archival Center and Loretto Archives. Archives of the St. Joseph Province of Dominican fathers was one of the richest sources of primary source documents.

Srs. Maureen Flanagan and Jean Vianney Norris with whom I live supported and encouraged me through all the ups and downs during the writing process.

I am forever grateful to Thomas P. Sullivan, O.M.I., my mentor and editor for 40 years. Whenever I balked at rewrites he reminded me that Hemingway often rewrote a manuscript ten times. I am sorry Fr. Sullivan did not live to see the finished product.

Lastly, a big thank you to publisher Charles Roth, Executive Director of the Catholic Book Publishers Association, whose encouragement and constant patience will never be forgotten.

THE KENTUCKY DOMINICANS
— SISTERS OF ST. CATHARINE —
have a great story to tell. It is one of sac-
rifice and dedication, of fidelity and
achievement, the Church owes this
Congregation a great debt of thanks.

The beginnings were difficult, hardships great indeed. It is
painful for us now to realize that the Sisters were often hungry,
sometimes out of penance but more often because they were
undervalued. It is to our shame that the Sisters were often taken
for granted; it is to their glory that they rose above that pain
to give glory to God and to remain enthusiastic about their
mission.

The story is not confined to Kentucky, of course. Kentucky
Dominican missions to other areas of the country brought in
vocations rich in diversity, talent, and geographical background.
New foundations paved the way for new congregations, and
from St. Catharine there developed many of the great
Dominican motherhouses of this nation. When St. Catharine
celebrates its 175th anniversary, the Church in the United States
has much to rejoice over.

Sister Paschala Noonan has written this history with profes-
sional skill and much affection. She has proven once again that
history can be very exciting.

I first visited St. Catharine in 1952. It became at once an oasis
of solace and comfort. The motherhouse is still filled with the
good spirits of the past, leading us on with the prayers and
encouragement.

As a Dominican I am proud of what our Sisters have ac-
complished. As a bishop I acknowledge the Church's debt to
these women, and I offer to all of them thanks and deepest
appreciation.

✠ THOMAS C. KELLEY, O.P.
Archbishop of Louisville

THE DOMINICAN SISTERS of St. Catharine, Kentucky, have a long history as a congregation founded in the United States. An adequate and authentic update of this history had not been written until Sr. Paschala Noonan, O.P. undertook this daunting task in 1989. A Chapter Act from the 1988 General Chapter coupled with efforts of Sr. Nona McGreal, O.P. (Sinsinawa) to write a comprehensive history of the Dominican Order in the United States were the nudge needed to bring to focus the importance of recording our story. Sr. McGreal looked to the Kentucky Dominicans to research their roots, the roots of the first U.S. Dominican Congregation of religious women, to assist in her recording of U.S. Dominican Life named OPUS (Order of Preachers in the United States). The members of the Kentucky Dominican Family, looking toward their 175th anniversary for founding, are excited about Sr. Paschala's commitment to be the scribe of our story.

For six years, Sr. Paschala, a woman with broad educational background, varied experiences in ministry and a remarkable energy for this undertaking has done critical research to authenticate the facts and to record them in a style that is pleasing and as factually correct as possible. One critical source of documents was the archives of the St. Joseph Province of Dominican Fathers. Such a source was invaluable for two reasons: a fire in 1904 destroyed St. Catharine Motherhouse and most of its contents; and, it was the Dominican pastor of St. Rose who had issued an invitation to his parish for women who could educate the children. Nine women responded. This invitation and the response gave birth to Dominican religious life for women — the Kentucky Dominicans.

The history of the Kentucky Dominicans is woven into the history of the young and struggling nation. Wars, epidemics, social crises and natural disasters were endured while the determination to provide education in private and parish schools never wavered.

The evolution of other needs soon drew the Congregation into health care, social and pastoral services and other ministries in response to the needs of Church and society. This history authentically relates some decisions and policies that are regrettable, but these realities are well balanced by the overall determination to be faithful seekers of truth through commitment to mission and ministry.

As the Dominican Congregation of St. Catharine of Siena, Kentucky, approaches the new millennium, we, vowed members and associates, are confident that our journey as preachers of the Word, healers of the earth and creative interpreters of contemporary Dominican life will enable us to continue to be a "Sign from God"...SIGNADOU.

SR. ELIZABETH MILES, O.P.
President 1988-1996

Prologue

U<small>NLIKE SOME CONGREGATIONS</small>, we have no words of inspiration passed on to us from our foundresses to cherish and preserve. No diaries exist; no letters remain for us. This seems unfortunate. However, it is not surprising. It is typically Dominican: St. Dominic was a preacher, not a writer. To his faithful followers, he left only four compositions consisting of the first Constitutions of the Order and three other letters.

Like Dominic and his early colleagues, the Dominican Sisters of St. Catharine Congregation, Kentucky, were *do-ers*, not writers. In this book we try to capture the spirit which moved those young women to face the hardships of an unknown frontier and to inspire others to follow in their footsteps for 175 years. Their heritage from Dominic continues to be action coupled with contemplation. As Preachers, they "give to others the fruits of their contemplation."

Unfortunately, most of the records documenting the sisters' early days were lost in a devastating fire in 1904. Consequently, what we really know of the foundresses is limited, while apocrypha abound. Acknowledging those limitations, this book attempts to create as authentic an account as possible about the early history. Information about later years is preserved at the Motherhouse in Kentucky.

The archives of the Dominican Fathers of St. Joseph Province have provided a rich source of information. Those records, together with the reception/profession book rescued from the fire, furnish the basis of our early history. In time and with further research, other material may surface, which will require an update of this history of the first American foundation of Dominican Sisters in the United States.

SR. PASCHALA NOONAN, O.P.

Signadou

— Part One —

Bringing the Torch of Dominic to the United States

AN EASTER PEOPLE

Easter SUNDAY, April 7, 1822. The parish-
ioners of St. Rose who filled the Church came to Mass with hope
and expectation enkindled by the coming of spring and the
glories of Easter. The sacred season of Lent was over and new
beginnings were apparent everywhere: new lambs on the
Kentucky hillsides, an occasional colt following its mare, dog-
wood bursting into bloom and yellow trumpets of jonquils
blanketing the land. Excitement was high, most of all because of
a new undertaking about to be launched.

The Call

On February 28, 1822 (Sunday), Samuel Thomas Wilson, then
61 years of age, had preached one of the most fruitful sermons
of his life.[1] He appealed to the women of his parish to consider
becoming members of the Dominican Order. Their mission
would be the education of the youth of the settlement.[2] His
friend Fenwick had nurtured this idea ever since their days in
Belgium; it was part of their dream for an American foundation.
Together the two friars hoped to establish a community of
women much as St. Dominic had done 600 years previously
when he wanted women to collaborate with the friars in mission
and charism.

The women of St. Rose parish needed no introduction to

3

teaching the elements of faith to the children. There were periods in the early Kentucky settlements when a priest was seen infrequently, if at all. Rev. Stephen Badin, proto-priest of Kentucky, knew that he needed help if the church were to flourish.

> One of his first works was the training of women as catechists in teaching the faith. Their special charge was the teaching of the children and the slaves. Upon instruction of this last group, Badin made particular insistence.[3]

Badin had instilled these ideas among the faithful before the Dominicans arrived in Kentucky.

Fr. Charles Nerinckx founded a group of local women in 1812, commonly known as the Sisters of Loretto. A few months later in the same year in Bardstown, Kentucky, Fr. John Baptiste David (later Bishop) founded another group, the Sisters of Charity of Nazareth. These two congregations were in a rural area where the people knew each other, were interrelated and shared the same background.[4] Consequently, the idea of religious life was not new to the people of this area.

The Response

Nine women responded to Wilson's appeal and contacted him at St. Rose. Who were they? Did they know what they were getting into? How would they support themselves, since once a woman left her paternal roof, she was strictly on her own unless she married? What transpired when they met with Wilson? Did he interview them separately or in a group? While details are left to the imagination, there are some verifiable facts.

The first candidates were Mariah Sansbury, Mary Carrico, Severly Tarleton, Judith McMan, Molly Johnson, Rose Ann Boone, Ann Hill, Mary Sansbury and Rose Sansbury.[5] Five were teenagers, two were in their twenties and two went unrecorded as to age, perhaps exercising a woman's prerogative that age is a personal matter.

Of the nine, four were chosen to receive the habit on Easter Sunday. Mariah Sansbury received the habit from Wilson at St. Rose Church on the morning of April 7, 1822.

The beginning of the Third Order Dominican Sisters was definitely parish-based, with the parishioners as witnesses to the ceremony. Later in the day, Judith McMan, Mary Carrico and Severly Tarleton received the habit at St. Mary Magdalen Chapel with Frs. Miles and Wilson presiding.[6] The others were postulants, serving a period of probation before committing to the religious life.

Mrs. Judith McMan

Although there is no record of it, it is probable that Mrs. Judith McMan, was the oldest of the group. She was a married woman who, with her husband, had mutually decided to separate in order to embrace religious life. They had no children.[7] Wilson appointed Judith as Superior over the first candidates. In a letter about the McMans to Rev. Joseph O'Finan, OP, Wilson wrote: "By experience however I am prepossessed in favor of this McMahon (sic), his wife is a most worthy and well-qualified lady whom I have appointed over our Nunnery, he intends to follow her example as soon as he can wind up his business."[8]

John McMan may have been a professor at the Dominican college of St. Thomas Aquinas, and although he applied to become a novice at St. Rose, he did not realize his dream. Later, he was ordained for the diocese of St. Louis but lived only a short time after ordination before becoming a victim of cholera.[9]

It is this Judith McMan, a married woman, born in Cork, Ireland, who was the first head of St. Magdalen Convent. True, she was not a canonical prioress; later, another would assume that position, but she was the temporary leader. In a sense, Judith's contribution was an "outsider's view" to a group of kinfolk and neighbors whose roots were Maryland and Kentucky. She remained seven months as Sr. Magdalen before returning to Ireland where the Archbishop of Dublin entrusted to her care the Penitents' Asylum. No reason is given for her return to her native land, but a plausible explanation is that it would facilitate her husband's dispensation to enter the priesthood.[10] Hers may have been a temporary commitment to the Kentucky Dominicans, but she brought a richness not to be overlooked.

Mariah Sansbury

Mariah Sansbury[11] was born to Alexius and Elizabeth (Hamilton) Sansbury in March, 1794.[12] Alexius Sansbury married Elizabeth Hamilton on February 16, 1789 in Prince George County, Maryland.[13] Judging from census figures, they had nine children but only seven survived childhood — four boys and three girls. They lived on a farm near Croom Station, Maryland, not far from Boone's Chapel. Boone's Chapel was one of the satellites of the Jesuits serving that area.

Rev. John David, at the request of Bishop Carroll,[14] spent 12 years serving Catholics in the lower part of Maryland before coming to Bardstown. He lived with the Jesuits and worked in their missions. It is very possible that the Sansburys were acquainted with him when he was in Maryland, since Boone's Chapel was one of the Jesuit stations.[15]

A more remote possibility is that the Sansbury family may have met itinerant Dominican preachers before moving to Kentucky. Sometimes the traveling friars stayed with Jesuits who were based in Upper Marlboro. Again, since visiting priests usually assisted with the ministry, the friars may have served sporadically at Boone's Chapel.

Later, the Boone s Chapel area would be named Rosaryville to honor the Dominican Fathers.[16] Whether or not the Sansburys knew Dominicans in Maryland is moot, but the fact remains that the Kentucky Sansburys were faithful and devoted Catholics. Interestingly, not all Sansburys were Catholic. Some of the Maryland Sansburys recorded their religious affiliation as Methodist and some as Episcopal. This would indicate a family tree with an ecumenical background.[17]

When Alexius died intestate in 1816,[18] his widow Elizabeth became executrix of his estate. The estate appraisal lists horses, cows, sheep, house furnishings, farm implements, books, a spinning wheel and many other things.[19]

From the appraisal certain deductions can be made about Mariah's family. First of all, her mother was educated because she signed her name to documents with a strong hand at a time when most people signed with a mark.[20]

Secondly, there were books in the house besides the Bible, an indication that value was placed on education. Thirdly, they must have been reasonably wealthy if personal property, not including land and buildings, was valued at close to $6,000.[21] In addition to farming, they engaged in milling, some leather business, cloth weaving and raising tobacco, rye and corn. In short, Mariah came from an entrepreneurial family, an experience that would stand her in good stead when she became head of a pioneer community.

After Alexius died, his widow moved to Kentucky where other Hamiltons and Sansburys had already settled. Elizabeth (Hamilton) Sansbury appears as head of a household in the 1820 census of Washington County, Kentucky. In March of that year, she and her daughter Mariah purchased 106 acres of land from Elisha and Henrietta McAtee near the St. Rose Farm.[22] In time, this would become the site of the first foundation of the Third Order of Dominican sisters in the United States.

Mariah was the first woman in the United States to receive the habit as a member of the Third Order Dominicans. The ceremony took place in her parish church of St. Rose, Kentucky, with Rev. Samuel T. Wilson, OP, provincial, presiding. She took the name of Sr. Angela. She was 28 years old. As one of the foundresses of the Kentucky Dominicans, her influence would reach far beyond the confines of her adopted state.

Severly Tarleton

Severly Tarleton, daughter of Jeremiah and Eleanor (Medley) Tarleton was born in Fayette County, Kentucky. She was 23 years old when she received the Dominican habit in St. Magdalen's Chapel on Easter Sunday afternoon. Severly took the name Sr. Columba. After three months she left St. Magdalen's. Evidently she still longed for religious life, because a month later she entered the Sisters of Charity of Nazareth, still retaining the name Sr. Columba. However, she did not live long.

> ...death was threatening to take one of the most beloved Sisters at the Motherhouse — the young and beautiful Sr.

Columba Tarleton. Strong of soul, but delicate of body, this Sister could not stand the rigors of the life and like Sister Scholastica and Sister Molly had contracted tuberculosis.[23]

Sr. Columba died at Nazareth October 24, 1824, less than a year after her first profession.[24]

Mary Carrico

The fourth young woman to receive the habit on that special Easter day was Mary Carrico. Born in Washington County, Kentucky to Levi and Catherine (Osborn) Carrico, she was 18 years old when Wilson invested her that afternoon in the Magdalen Chapel. She brought with her one year's provisions and moveable property valued at twenty dollars. She took the name Sr. Margaret. Not much is known about her beyond the fact that she served the congregation for nine years during its difficult beginnings. She died at the age of 27 on June 7, 1831.

Other Early Members

Two others of the original Kentucky nine chose not to remain. There is no record of Molly Johnson ever being received. In trying to trace her through the Johnson surname in Washington County records, a marriage license was issued on January 12, 1839 to Mary Johnson and John Emerson.[25] This may or may not be our Molly.

Rose Ann Boone, daughter of Henry and Mary (Mudd) Boone received the habit on August 3, 1822. Her parents had opened their home to Wilson when he first arrived in Kentucky and had no place to go.[26] He gathered a group of boys and began a school in the Boone homestead until such time as a place was ready at St. Rose. There is no notation to show when or why Sr. Rose left the community, but the oral tradition is that she later married. A marriage license was granted to Rosan (sic) Boone and John Medley on May 25, 1835.[27] Rose Anne would have been 27. Through her mother she was a first cousin to Mary and Rose Sansbury.

Mary and Rose Sansbury, daughters of Nicholas and

Henrietta (Mudd) Sansbury received the habit at the August 3 investiture. Born in Washington County, they were not only first cousins to Rose Ann Boone, but also to the daughters of Alexius and Elizabeth (Hamilton) Sansbury. Their father Nicholas was one of the first Sansburys to migrate to Kentucky. He is listed in the 1800 census of Washington County. As yet, no records have been found to show that his brother Alexius ever reached Cartwright Creek. Nicholas was known as a staunch member of the church. Like other Maryland settlers, he did not follow the Church but importuned the Church to follow him. Nowhere is it better illustrated that the Church is not a building but rather the People of God living the Gospel message of Jesus.

Nicholas died soon after Rose was born. The widowed mother remarried but times were hard and there were debts to be paid. Their stepfather was not exactly a keen businessman and cash was scarce, but Mary (Sr. Catherine) and Rose (Sr. Frances) each brought one year's provisions when they entered the community.

Ten days after the first reception, two more women presented themselves for admission — Elizabeth Sansbury, Jr. and Teresa Edelen. They were formally received on August 3, 1822.

Teresa, daughter of Samuel and Mary (Smith) Edelen was born in Prince George County, Maryland. She was 26 years old when she entered the convent. She brought with her provisions for one year and moveable property amounting to $30.[28]

Sr. Angela's sister, Elizabeth, Jr. decided to join the community of St. Magdalen and became Sr. Benven.[29] Early on, recognition of her leadership qualities led her to other states and to responsible positions in her long career, even though she accepted them with reluctance.

Sr. Angela and Sr. Benven each brought with them one year's provisions and a "joint claim to a tract of land containing one hundred and six acres" valued at $2400. Before Sr. Angela entered religion, she and her mother had purchased this piece of property from the McAtees. Elizabeth Jr. inherited her share in the division of her mother's estate.[30]

Another candidate who was numbered among the foundresses of this first Dominican congregation was Ann Hill, daughter of Clement and Mary (Hamilton) Hill. One of seventeen children, Ann was 17 years old when she entered. She brought with her one year's provisions and $100 in moveable property or cash. Through her mother she was a first cousin once removed of Srs. Angela and Benven. In religious life she retained her baptismal name of Ann.

This first foundation of Dominican sisters in the United States could almost be called a family affair because of the interrelationships of sisters and cousins joining in the endeavor. Undaunted, they started religious life with very little of this world's goods. Some brought provisions, two brought a tract of land and altogether they had moveable property or cash in hand amounting to $150. Not an auspicious beginning when judged from a material point of view!

Chapter One Notes

1. SCA Copy of sermon preached by V. Rev. V.F. O'Daniel, OP, at St. Rose Convent, Kentucky, May 1924 (p. 5) on *Centenary of the Death of the V. Rev. Samuel Thomas Wilson*, OP, STM. O'Daniel says that Wilson was born in England in 1761.

2. Minogue, *Pages from a Hundred Years of Dominican History*, p. 43. (hereafter called Minogue, *Pages*.)
   Also Victor O'Daniel, OP, *A Light of the Church in Kentucky*, p. 246 passim. (Hereafter referred to as O'Daniel, *A Light*.)

3. Clyde Crews, An American *Holy Land*, p. 50. (Hereafter referred to as Crews, *Holy Land*.)

4. Misner, *A Comparative Social Study of the Members and Apostolates of the First Eight Permanent Communities*, 1981, pp. 264, 266, 267.

5. *SCA — Profession Book* — The Profession Book was copied from the original document in 1847. In the fire which destroyed the Motherhouse in 1904, this book was one of the few items rescued. In this chapter, facts about the foundresses are based on material in this book. Also Minogue, *Pages*, p. 44.

6. *SCA Profession Book I* — 1822-1919, unpaginated except for introduction.

7. Reginald Coffey, OP, *The American Dominicans*, pp. 111, 114. (Hereafter referred to as Coffey, *The American Dominicans*.)
   O'Daniel, *A Light*, pp. 249, 250.

8. Copy of letter from San Clemente Archives, Rome, from Wilson to O'Finan, July 4, 1822, p. 4. SJPA.

9. Minogue, *Pages*, p. 44.

10. Copy of letter from San Clemente Archives, Rome, Wilson to O'Finan. Wilson wrote: "....he wishes to enter among us and wishes to be under my direction, or in the same house which will be St. Rose's, but then his wife is 3/4 of a mile off. Can you Rev. have something settled about this business, that he may know what to depend on against his profession." It sounds as if Wilson wanted to make certain that no questions would arise about the propinquity of Mr. McMan as a novice at St. Rose while his wife was a novice at St. Magdalen.

11. Eighteenth and nineteenth century records present ambiguities to the researcher. Since everything was hand-written, some records are difficult to decipher because of penmanship. Others are faded, torn, disintegrated. Fire and floods often destroyed records of vital statistics, leaving only sparse information. Unfortunately, when writing about early settlers, writers sometimes embellished the facts or novelized the scarce data. In some cases, myths still prevail. Conflicting facts about Mariah Sansbury abound, but in this book an attempt is made to use only verified facts. Her given name is spelled in various ways. I have chosen to use the first spelling as it appears in the *Profession Book I.*

12. On Angela's gravestone in Columbus, Ohio, her birth date is given as 1794. In the *Profession Book I*, SCA, it is written that she was born in Prince George County, Maryland in March 1795. No birth record was found in Maryland.

13. Index of Marriage Licenses, Prince George County, Maryland, 1777-1886.

14. Ramona Mattingly, *The Catholic Church on the Kentucky Frontier*, p. 203. (Hereafter referred to as Mattingly, *Kentucky Frontier.*)

15. Benjamen Webb, *The Centenary of Catholicity in Kentucky*, p. 228, 229. (hereafter referred to as Webb, *Centenary.*) Bishop Carroll assigned Fr. David upon his arrival in the United States c. 1792, to some Catholic missions in the lower part of Maryland where he labored for 12 years. He later became Bishop David in Bardstown.

16. Sargent, *Stones and Bones*, p. 277.
See Part 2, *Episcopal Church Cemeteries* and Part 4, *Methodist Church Cemeteries.*

17. Prince George's County Genealogical Society, Maryland. Deeds AB#1, F8, Wills T#1F134, Deeds AB1F8.

18. The entire file of documents on Alexis Sansbury was photocopied from the files in the Prince George County Record Office. It includes appraisals, anecdotes and doctor bills.

19. Ibid.

20. Ibid.

21. Ibid.

22. Washington County, Kentucky, Deed Book F 356, dated March 18, 1822.

23. Spillane, *Kentucky Spring*, pp. 118, 119, 281.

24. Letter to author from Sr. Collette Crone, Nazareth Archivist, dated June 24, 1991.

25. Washington County, Kentucky Marriage Bonds, Book 2, p. 513.

26. O'Daniel, *A Light*, p. 108.

27. Washington County, Kentucky Marriage Bonds, Book 2, p. 137. In those days it was not unusual for a young woman to return home to care for her younger siblings if her mother died in childbirth after the girl had entered the convent. The mortality rate in childbirth was high and families tended to be large.

28. SCA — *Profession Book I.*

29. SCA — Letters from Sr. Aurelia Ottersbach, Loretto Archivist. Angela and Benven had a sister who entered the Sisters of Loretto. Her name was Sr. Maxima. She was professed on April 5, 1824 and died the same day.

30. Will Book C, Washington County Records, pp. 473-474.

MIGRATION FROM MARYLAND

BACK TO THE FUTURE! The reception or profession of anyone entering religious life is a momentous occasion because total commitment to a vowed life is a serious step. It was momentous on that Easter Sunday in 1822 and is still momentous to this day.

In the early 1960s, the Congregation of St. Catharine of Siena numbered over 800 members, but with the exodus following the Vatican II Council and the onslaughts of social changes, the total has dwindled to fewer than 350. This phenomenon was not particular to the Kentucky Dominicans; it was a sign of the times among congregations of women religious. Within a period of 17 years, the number of women religious in the United States plummeted from 181,421 to 120,000 in 1983, a drop of 33%.[1]

During the years from 1969 to 1984 seven young women were professed as Kentucky Dominicans but left in a short time. On July 8, 1984, there was great rejoicing and renewed hope when a young Vietnamese woman was accepted for profession. Hue Thi Le wanted to make a commitment to a life few people valued and even fewer understood. As a sister in her native country she had fled the oppression of Communism and now wished to transfer to the Kentucky Congregation. No wonder the

13

Kentucky Dominicans were celebrating!

Why would Hue choose a communal life of study, prayer and preaching in a new and strange country? True, she had belonged to a Dominican Congregation in Vietnam, but could she let go of the ties to that community she had left behind when forced to flee for her life? Would the Kentucky Congregation of St. Catharine of Siena be her new home, her new family? Could she adapt to American culture, to the language, the food and the customs? Would her new American sisters appreciate her Asian background, so different from their own? The important factor was that both she and the Kentucky Dominicans were willing to try.

There was some precedent in the background. This was not the first time in the history of the Kentucky Dominicans that collaboration with Vietnamese sisters came under consideration.[2] In the Register of Audiences of Pope Pius VII, on November 26, 1820, there is a special request of the Dominican Fathers.

> The Dominican Fathers of the Province of Kentucky in the United States of America, knowing the advantage for the good of religion that their confreres report for the Philippines, Tunquin and Chine through the establishment of Colleges of tertiaries who occupy themselves with the education of young girls, implore your Holiness to permit them to make equal establishments in the Provinces of Kentucky and Ohio, these being the States who have made offerings for such purpose. [3]

The Pontiff granted permission. Although this decision heralded a departure from the kind of congregations prevalent in Europe, Rev. Thomas Wilson, OP, had voiced some reservations in a letter to Rev. Francis J. O'Finan, OP.

> As for our sort of nunnery — Mr. Hill has procured leave for them to live as they do in Chine. I sincerely wish he had taken a trip hither to know how that is, or at least, to have inquired about it.[4]

With the transfer and profession of Sr. Hue Thi Le, the Kentucky Dominicans would learn firsthand what Wilson would like to have known over 170 years ago!

Preparing the Way

Three centuries after Columbus arrived at the shores of North America, the Commonwealth of Kentucky was admitted to the union of the United States. Eighteen years before statehood, the area had been a hunting ground for various Indian tribes who called it the "dark and bloody" ground. In 1775, permanent white settlements were made at Harrodsburg and Boonesboro. The Wilderness Trail, which Boone had blazed through the Cumberland Gap, soon extended westward and north, bringing families from the worn-out farms of Virginia and the Carolinas to the legendary fertility of the Blue Grass. Marylanders and Pennsylvanians, crossing the Appalachians to Pittsburgh, floated down the Ohio on rafts, transporting their belongings from the river to their homesteads with the aid of what animals they could bring. This was the route of Catholic migration largely from St. Mary, Charles and Prince George Counties, Maryland.[5]

What prompted these first migrants to abandon the comparative comfort and security of Maryland for the unknown stretches west of the Alleghenies? Historians differ as to why. Was it the economy? Was it a desire for religious freedom? Was it a spirit of adventure? Whatever the reason, they felt Kentucky offered what they could no longer find in Maryland.

Economy

Maryland's land was tired from overuse. Constant replanting of tobacco diminished the richness of the soil. As the quality of the soil lessened, so did the quality and quantity of tobacco, as well as the profit from it. As for other crops, wheat rust and the Hessian fly destroyed them when attempts were made to diversify.

Added to this loss in agricultural income, there was an economic crisis following the Revolutionary War. A superabundance of paper money had been issued. Much of it was backed by state-owned stock in the Bank of England. There was provision that if the stock were confiscated, the property of British subjects in Maryland would be substituted.[6] Barter was tried unsuccessfully. Rates of exchange for paper currency varied widely. Foreign countries refused to enter into commercial treaties with the United States. In short, there was little available cash locally or in the country at large.

Religion

Another factor causing unrest among Marylanders in the latter part of the 18th century was religion. The history of religious freedom in Maryland embraced a series of changes whenever the ruling power changed. In 1649, the Act Concerning Religion had been adopted, guaranteeing religious freedom to all except non-Trinitarians. Later, with the influx of Puritans who believed in religious toleration for themselves but not for anyone else, the Toleration Act was repealed. The second Lord Baltimore restored it, but when Maryland became a royal colony, the Toleration Act was again repealed. Catholics were disenfranchised and persecuted until 1776.[7]

None other than General George Washington himself issued a Commander-in-chief order at Cambridge, Massachusetts that there should be no discrimination in the Revolutionary Army because of a patriot's religion and in particular, Catholics.

After the Revolutionary War, the Church witnessed phenomenal growth as streams of immigrants came from many European lands. The church sought to incorporate these values in the Americanization of the church. Catholics prided themselves on their tolerance of other faiths and of being "inoffensive" in regard to their own practice of religion. Nativism was yet to come with the question: Can a good Catholic be a good American?[8]

Adventure

About this time, when the financial, agricultural and religious outlook of Maryland began to pale, along came a native Philadelphian who had adopted Kentucky as his home. Known as a fur trader in Louisville, John Filson was an entrepreneur par excellence. He settled on land in Kentucky granted to Virginia war veterans. At that time, Kentucky was still part of Virginia.[9] Filson loved Kentucky and was a born salesman. In 1784 he published a glowing account about the beauties of Kentucky and the adventures of Colonel Daniel Boone.[10] His description of the Bluegrass State was alluring as a TV commercial.

> The beautiful river Ohio, bounds Kentucke in its whole length, being a mile and sometimes less in breadth, and it is sufficient to carry boats of great burthen.
>
> The country in general may be considered as well timbured, producing large trees of many kinds ... the sugar tree which furnishes every family with plenty of excellent sugar ... the honey-locust is curiously surrounded with large thorny spikes, bearing broad and long pods in form of peas, has a sweet taste and makes excellent beer.
>
> The coffee-tree greatly resembles the black oak, grows large, and also bears a pod, in which is enclosed good coffee. The soil is very favorable to flax, and hemp, turnips, potatoes and cotton.[11]

He made it sound like the Eden of North America — transportation, sugar, coffee, beer and a variety of crops! His account of the adventures and misadventures of his friend Daniel Boone in blazing the Wilderness Road and founding Boonesboro, Kentucky, aroused the adventurous spirit of Marylanders. Only one thing was lacking — provision for their spiritual needs. They counted on an appeal to Bishop Carroll for priests to remedy this deficiency. That Ecclesiastic promised a priest as soon as one became available.[12]

From Maryland to Kentucky

Encouraged by the prospect of a better future, 60 Catholic families formed a league to plan the migration to Kentucky. Not all would leave at the same time, but all agreed to settle in the same area.[13] They believed there was strength in numbers. By traveling in groups, they would be able to defend themselves better against hostile Indians, should the occasion arise[14] and they could provide mutual assistance in the massive task of clearing land, building homesteads and managing emergency health care in illness or injury.

Under the leadership of Basil Hayden and Philemon Lee, the first group left Maryland in 1785 to settle on Pottinger's Creek, now Holy Cross. The following year the second contingent arrived at Hardin's Creek, now St. Charles. No priest reached Kentucky until two years later, and he stayed only two years. More years passed before there was a church building, and still more before the parish was formally established. Nevertheless, the bicentennial of Holy Cross Parish was celebrated in 1985, on the anniversary of the arrival of a group of People of God banded together as a Catholic community to practice, preserve and pass on their faith while importuning Bishop Carroll for priests.

St. Rose Foundation

Cartwright Creek settlement is of historical importance to Dominicans. It was on this spot that the cradle of Dominicans in the United States, the convent of St. Rose, was established.[15] In 1787, Catholics, a majority of whom came from Prince George County, Maryland, entered the richer lands near Springfield, Kentucky. Other families from St. Mary County joined them. After nearly two centuries of proximity in Maryland, they were not only friends and neighbors, but in many instances, they were "kin." Today their names still ring out there: Blandford, Boone, Cambron, Hill, Hamilton, Edelen, Mudd, Smith, Montgomery, Osborn, Carrico. These early families lost no time in begging Bishop Carroll to send them priests.[16]

John Carroll, the first Roman Catholic bishop (1789) and later first archbishop (1808) of the United States, had a diocese of staggering size. It embraced all of the eastern seaboard except Florida and vast uncharted regions of the south and midwest. The spiritual needs of 30,000 Catholics were committed to 25 priests, most of them aging itinerants and refugees from persecution in Europe.[17]

Among the clergy serving under Bishop Carroll in those early days were twelve Dominicans who were missionaries apostolic.[18] They spent most of their time in the saddle riding from one settlement to another to hear confessions, offer Mass and teach the people about the faith. In the absence of churches or chapels, these men relied on the hospitality of lay people who were only too happy to welcome them into their homes. These homes were called Mass Stations. Whenever a priest would come, the neighbors would gather together to pray, to listen, to confess and to celebrate. In between visits of the clergy, the laity did what they could — led the community in prayer, taught catechism to the children and the slaves, bought land for future churches. The women played the leading role in nurturing religious practices.

Some lay leaders were officially commissioned to preside over the community's religious services and catechetical instruction. With only one bishop in the United States and few clergy, the continuity of the faith depended on lay participation.[19] Collaboration between laity and clergy was a fact of life.

It is no surprise that Bishop Carroll joyfully welcomed the Dominican, Edward Dominic Fenwick, an American, who proposed founding a branch of the Dominican Order in the United States. Having Dominican priests would enable Carroll to partially answer the constant pleas for clergy.

Chapter Two Notes

1. Patricia Wittburg, *Creating a Future for Religious Life*, p. 34.
2. San Clemente Archives, Rome, *Register of Vatican Audiences* (Nov. 26, 1820 - Folio 36).
3. Ibid.
4. Excerpt from letter of Thomas Wilson, OP, to Francis J. O'Finan, OP, regarding the Foundation of Dominican Sisters in Kentucky. San Clemente Archives, Rome. Other documents of P. Fide demonstrate that Chine is an abbreviation for Indochina, i.e., present-day Vietnam — known to Dominicans also as the locale of the Tonkin martyrs. At that

time, religious congregations in Europe were cloistered, did not take solemn vows and worked among the people, particularly in education. The Mr. Hill mentioned was Rev. John Augustine Hill, OP. It was customary to use the title *Mr.* instead of *Fr.* at that time.

5. Crews, *Holy Land*, p. 30.

6. Webb, *Centenary, The*, p. 26. Cf Mattingly, *Kentucky Frontier*, pp. 4, 5, 6.

7. *Encyclopedic Dictionary of Religion*, p. 2286.

8. Nativism may be defined as a protective policy of favoring native-born inhabitants against immigrants and aliens who allegedly are objectionable for racial, social, religious, economic or political reasons.

9. Webb, *Centenary*, p. 158.

   Mattingly, *Kentucky Frontier*, p. 42.

10. John Filson, *The Discovery and Settlement of Kentucke*.

11. Ibid., pp. 12, 22, 23.

12. Mattingly, *Kentucky Frontier*, p. 23.

13. Webb, *Centenary*, p. 26.

    Mattingly, *Kentucky Frontier*, p. 81.

14. Samuel V. Lancaster, *The Lancaster Family of Maryland and Kentucky*. Contains an account of John Lancaster being captured by Indians. They nicknamed him *Kioha*, or *Running Buck*, because of his speed and agility. Eventually, he escaped from the camp, landing at the mouth of Beargrass Creek, the site of the present-day Louisville. Webb gives a lengthy account of the perils endured by Lancaster when he came to Kentucky, p. 48-50. The story of Thomas Hill and his companions being attacked by Indians is found in Webb, p. 68. A slave with Hill was killed; Hill himself was severely wounded. These episodes occurred in the late 1780s and the accounts were passed down through generations in the families.

15. According to European tradition, the dwellings for male religious were called convents while those for females were called monasteries. In the United States, it is often the opposite, or the word monastery is used for cloistered nuns.

16. In a petition to Archishop John Carroll dated 1803, residents of Cartwright Creek asked for a pastor. The petition was signed by the grandfather of Sr. Ann Hill and the fathers of Srs. Magdalen Edelen, Helen Whelan and Margaret Carrico. It read: "We, the subscribers, inhabitants of the County of Washington and State of Kentucky, and principally of the Roman Catholic Congregation of Cartwright's Creek, humbly sheweth that we are extremely distressed, wanting spiritual assistance. Therefore to you, as our chief spiritual guide, with due submission to the provision which your fatherly care and protection may make, we humbly petition to be supplied with a pastor. We presume, long before this, you have been too well informed of our situation, and the immense labors and fatigues of the Reverend Mr. Badin has to struggle through for us, to undertake at this time to give you a description of them. We will only observe that it is impossible for Mr. Badin to attend to all the Catholics in this county. Such as live at a great distance from the several chapels and have larges families, cannot get the whole of

them to attend to their duty. Consequently we are of the opinion that great numbers will be entirely lost from the Church if we are not supplied with more priests." (photocopy of letter from Archives of St. Mary of the Springs, Columbus, Ohio.)

17. *Encyclopedic Dictionary of Religion*, p. 640. Also Theodore Maynard, *Great Catholics in American History*, p. 67.
18. Unpublished manuscript of Nona McGreal, OP, who is doing research for the OPUS (Order of Preachers in the United States) project.
19. Jay P. Dolan, *The American Catholic Experience*, p. 114. One of the strongest forces for evangelization was the influence of women in the era.

Chapter Three

AN OLD ORDER IN A NEW COUNTRY

SOME PEOPLE are destined from birth to pursue a course which affects history within the confines of their own social circle or even a wider sphere embracing Church and Society. Such was the destiny of St. Dominic de Guzman. Born in the small town of Calaruega, Spain, Dominic's birth was presaged by portents of what was to come. His mother, Jane D'Aza, before his conception had a dream in which she thought she bore in her womb a dog carrying a burning torch in its mouth. The dog broke away from her and set the world on fire. It is said that at his baptism his godmother told of her own dream, in which the child appeared with his forehead lit by a shining star which illumined the whole world. Symbols of these visions are often used in the iconography of the saint. Stories such as these were commonly used by early hagiographers because such images pleased the people of that time, who liked visible signs of grace surrounding the early years of their saint.[1]

Dominic founded his Order of Friars Preacher in 1216[2] in response to a need of the times. The Albigensian heresy raging in western Europe was not only anticlerical and antisacramental, but also anti-Christian and antisocial.[3] Adherents of the heresy converted people by their inflammatory preaching, their simple lifestyle and their total dedication. In contrast, the Church allowed only bishops to preach. Some of these bishops possessed neither the rudimentary skills nor the basic knowledge needed for effective preaching. Worse still, because of their ostensible wealth and materialistic lifestyle, some became a source of scandal.

Dominic obtained permission for a remarkable innovation: to found an Order whose sole purpose was to preach truth. As a countercultural movement, Dominic insisted that his Friars Preachers practice poverty, study intensely and sustain a strong community life. Thus, there are three constraints which embody the essence of the Dominican Order: *monastic observance, study* and *the apostolate.*[4] To balance these essentials is not always easy: not in Dominic's time, not today.

From the beginning, Dominicans were both democratic and mobile. Dominican government has used a flexible approach to legislation, dispensation and adaptation so that the Constitutions are as efficient today as they were in Dominic's time.

Regarding mobility, the friars were sent to the far corners of the then-known world -- Spain, France, Italy, Poland, Scandinavia, Germany, Greece and England. They always chose university cities to pursue their studies and be more effective in their preaching mission.[5]

The Second General Chapter of the Order in 1221 sent a group of friars to England, with Oxford as their destination. Oxford, the intellectual center of England, was the third university of Europe.[6] The English Province grew from this and almost 600 years later a shoot from this ancient Anglo tree was planted in the United States by an Anglo-Marylander son of Dominic, Edward Dominic Fenwick.

Edward Dominic Fenwick, OP

Edward Dominic Fenwick, son of Colonel Ignatius Fenwick of Wallington and Sarah Taney, came from wealthy Marylanders accustomed to the English manorial way of life.[7] Because Catholic education was forbidden in England and her colonies, it was the custom for males in the family to study in Europe. Edward's uncle, John Fenwick, who studied at Holy Cross College in Bornhem, Belgium, was ordained as a Dominican for the English Province in 1785.[8] Edward was to follow in his uncle's footsteps.

When Edward was 16 years old, Colonel Fenwick sent him to Bornhem to study. After graduation he joined the Dominicans and was ordained in 1793 for the English Province, even though it was small and suffering drastically from oppression under the English government. Edward (known in religion as Dominic) had a dream of returning to the States to extend the English Dominican Province in his own country. The dream included establishing a college and seminary patterned after Bornhem, as well as setting up a group of women religious to educate youth.

Before he could implement his idea, affairs in Europe precipitated a crisis. As the French revolutionists began their advance on Belgium, the community at Bornhem fled to England. It is interesting to note the collaboration that existed between the friars and the nuns in this time of crisis. Wilson, Rector at Bornhem, was delayed in his flight to England because he took time to escort to safety 16 Dominican nuns, some of whom were elderly and sick.[9]

His friend Fr. Fenwick was left behind at Bornhem. Because he was an American, it was felt he would not be harmed, and possibly he could protect the property. This was wishful thinking. Despite his American citizenship, he was imprisoned. When finally released, he went to England to join Wilson and the others who had fled there ahead of him.

Prospects of a flourishing Dominican community were bleak in both Belgium and England. This only served to strengthen Fenwick's resolve to found a Dominican house in America. While still on the continent, he persuaded some of his Dominican brethren, Fathers Samuel Wilson, Robert Angier, and William Tuite, to join him in the endeavor. Naturally, the English Province was not happy about this raid on its membership.

Of the three recruits, Fenwick felt that his former professor, Samuel T. Wilson, was most necessary for the project. If there were to be a Dominican college and seminary, there would have to be competent teachers. Wilson had a reputation as an out-standing teacher: "His learning made him known far and wide."[10] A brief look at Fenwick's companions reveals the spirit of the first American Dominicans.

Samuel T. Wilson, OP

Samuel Thomas Wilson was born in 1761 in England, possibly London.[11] Little is known of his childhood beyond the fact that he was sent to the Dominican school at Bornhem when only nine years old. He was an avid scholar and was well-versed in languages. He spoke French and Flemish fluently, and because Spanish was often used in that region, he probably had a working knowledge of it.[12]

He received the habit in 1777, but due to the interference of the sacristan emperor Joseph II, he had to wait until 1785 when he was 25 years old to take solemn vows. Ordination followed the very next year.[13] After ordination he became a professor and Rector at Holy Cross College. Among his students were Edward D. Fenwick, Robert A. Angier and William R. Tuite, destined like himself to become founders of St. Rose and of the Dominican Order in the United States.[14]

Robert Antonius Angier, OP

Accompanying Fenwick to America was Robert Antoninus Angier, OP. Fr. Angier, who taught 25 years at Bornhem, was noted as a scholar, "learned and capable." Although he reached this country in 1804, at the request of Bishop Carroll he remained in Charles County, Maryland, to serve the people there. It was not until October 1807 that he arrived at St. Rose. Again his career had an unexpected change when Bishop Carroll asked him to go to Scott County, Kentucky, as a peacemaker in a parish having many problems.[15] Because his health failed, he returned for a short time to St. Rose. Wilson assigned him to Maryland in May, 1816 but he returned to England in 1825 and died there.

William Raymond Tuite, OP

Fenwick's third recruit was William Raymond Tuite, OP, who accompanied Wilson to Kentucky. On their journey from Maryland, their wagon overturned. Both men sustained injuries which delayed their arrival to the new mission. Since there was no place ready when they finally reached Kentucky, Wilson resided with Henry Boone near the future site of St. Rose. Tuite took charge of missions in and around Bardstown and stayed with Thomas Gwynne in that area. While something of an administrator, Tuite was a bit of an agitator and a thorn in the side of Bishop Flaget of Bardstown, who later wrote that Tuite "has returned to my diocese to the great sorrow of my soul."[16]

The Cradle of American Dominicans

These four friars were no strangers to adversity. They had experienced oppression in England and Belgium. They were survivors accustomed to adjusting to difficult circumstances. There was Fenwick, leader and missionary; Wilson, scholar and teacher; Angier, peacemaker and pastor; and Tuite, teacher and challenger.

Originally, Fenwick had hoped to initiate a branch of the English Province in Maryland. But the Master General, Fr. Pius Gaddi, insisted on establishing an independent American Province, one in tune with the Americanization of the Church. In addition, Bishop Carroll felt that two colleges already in Maryland were sufficient. Besides, he had been promising priests to the Catholics in Kentucky.[17] Thus, though disappointed, Fenwick began his foundation near Springfield, Kentucky, and named the first Dominican province in the States in honor of St. Joseph.

At the time, the country, only 17 years old, was expanding by leaps and bounds. President Jefferson doubled the size of the United States by the Louisiana Purchase in 1803 and then sent Lewis and Clark off on an expedition through the newly-acquired territory as far as the Pacific. With Sacajewea, a Shoshone Indian woman, to lead them over the Rockies, Lewis and Clark opened vast new expanses in the West.[18] Kentucky would soon change its title from the "First West" to the "Gateway to the West."

The Church was expanding in synchronization with the country. In 1808 four new dioceses were erected: Bardstown, Boston, New York and Philadelphia. It was a time of growth, a time of transition when both Church and State were concerned about freedom and equality. In time, both institutions would be confronted about the application of these very principles. The Archbishop of Baltimore was striving to develop an American Catholic Church. It was written of him:

> John Carroll, for example, while never waffling on matters of faith, felt that the manner of presenting Catholicism in the United States had to be adapted to a land which had been founded on the principles of religious liberty and democracy.[19]

America and the Church were ready for the Dominicans, a democratic, mobile Order.

Carroll and Flaget were supportive of the idea of a Dominican foundation. Once all permissions were obtained from the Order and ecclesiastical jurisdictions, Fenwick began to implement the plan.

Using his patrimony, he purchased land from John Waller, a Protestant preacher.[20] The property had one of the few brick dwellings in the area, along with a grist mill and a saw mill.[21] Fenwick lost no time in having the building blessed and dedicated to St. Rose of Lima, a Dominican tertiary who was the first canonized saint of the New World.

Although Fenwick was the first superior at St. Rose, he was more at home doing missionary work among the scattered settlers in the state. His plea to be relieved of office[22] was granted by the Master General who then appointed Wilson Prior and Provincial.

Frontier people had little or no cash and Fenwick had used his inheritance to purchase the property for the new foundation. Lack of money did not deter the community from beginning to build St. Rose Church, a convent for the brethren[23] and larger accommodations for students of St. Thomas College. With the death of his close friend Bishop Luke Concanen, OP, Fenwick and the community received an unexpected windfall of $2,000 and a valuable library.[24]

Once the building program for college and novitiate was well underway, Wilson turned his attention to the needs of the children in the Cartwright Creek settlement. Who would teach the faith? Who would educate the children for the future? Did this brand new country have educational models?

During the long period in Kentucky when there were no priests, the continuity of the faith was largely dependent upon the women who nurtured the spiritual lives of their families. Stephen T. Badin used female catechists to teach the faith to slaves and children.[25] He prepared buildings for a community of teaching sisters but abandoned the project when fire destroyed the structures.

In 1809 Elizabeth Ann Seton had founded the Sisters of Charity of Emmitsburg, Maryland. She worked with parishes and through her efforts the parochial school system developed.[26]

In 1812, two foundations of women religious were initiated: one at Loretto, Kentucky and one at Nazareth, Kentucky. Both communities taught young girls, Catholic and Protestant.

Female catechists and new foundations of women religious were forerunners of what Wilson had in mind. Over and above the models prevalent in the states, Wilson remembered the history of the Order — St. Dominic's first foundation of nuns at Prouille, and the role the women had in the mission.[27] There was some similarity in the status of women in the times of Dominic and of Wilson.

In the twelfth and thirteenth centuries the crusades claimed the lives of so many men that the number of females far outstripped their male counterparts. Consequently, it was hard for a woman to find a suitable marriage partner. During the twelfth century part of the solution was the foundation of new monasteries. When the Albigensian heresy erupted, the women became an important arm for the spread of the cult. They were formed into communities that "became hot-beds for the propagation of heresy."[28] Dominic's genius was that he adapted the methods of his enemies to solve the immediate pastoral needs of the Church and to enable women to participate in solving the social problems of the time.

Six centuries later, once again women outnumbered men. One missionary wrote that founding a congregation of women would take care of some of the old maids. Be that as it may, before ever crossing the Atlantic, Fenwick and Wilson regarded women as necessary for the apostolate. An invaluable factor was that Bishop Carroll and Bishop Flaget shared this opinion.

Chapter Three Notes

1. Bede Jarret, OP, *Life of St. Dominic,* p. 5.

   Also M.H. Vicaire, *St. Dominic and His Times,* p. 21.

   Cf. Francis C. Lehner, OP, *St. Dominic Biographical Documents,* pp. 7, 11.

2. Bull of Approval: Dec. 22, 1216; Bull of Confirmation of Order: Dec. 23, 1216; About Preaching Order: Jan. 21, 1217. Listed in Bede Jarrett, OP, *Life of St. Dominic,* p. xx.

3. *Encyclopedic Dictionary of Religion,* Vol. A/E pp. 660, 96. Cathari was one of several neo-Manichean sects professing some form of dualism, i.e., a spiritual principle and a material principle. Albigenses were the Cathari in S. France named after the city of Albi. They became so strong they threatened the very existence of the Church in S. France.

4. Reginald M. Coffey, OP, *The American Dominicans,* p. 8.

5. William A. Hinnebusch, OP, *The History of the Dominican Order,* p. 93.

6. Ibid., p. 94.

7. Victor O'Daniel, OP, *The First Two Dominican Priories in the United States,* p. 4. (Hereafter referred to as The First Two Dominican Priories.)

   Also Jay P. Dolan, *The American Catholic Experience,* p. 79.

8. O'Daniel, *A Light,* p. 30 passim. The United States was at peace with France. Fenwick's father had been a prominent leader in Maryland during the American Revolution. However, the French revolutionists were not intimidated by the fact of Fenwick's American citizenship or paternal influence. The Fenwicks were outstanding members of the Church. Fr. John Fenwick, OP, son of Colonel Ignatius of Cherryfields and Mary Cole, was the first English-speaking American to become a Dominican. After his ordination he taught for several years at Bornhem. When he came to the United States he served as a missionary apostolic. It was a disappointment to his nephew, Edward Fenwick, that he did not offer assistance in founding the Order in the United States (Cf. Coffey, *The American Dominicans,* p. 13). Another Fenwick outstanding in the Church at that time was Edward's cousin, Benedict Joseph Fenwick, SJ, who became the second Bishop of Boston.

9. O'Daniel, *A Light,* pp. 25-27.

10. Ibid., pp. 20, 21, 58.

11. Ibid., p. 1 and SCA, original letter from London.

12. Ibid., p. 4.

13. Ibid., p. 10. Also, quoted from a copy of the address given by O'Daniel on the occasion of the centenary of the death of Very Rev. Samuel Thomas Wilson, SCA.

14. O'Daniel, *A Light,* p. 15.

15. Coffey, *The American Dominicans,* p. 53.

16. SJPA. Copy of a letter from Flaget to Propaganda Fide - May 12, 1829.

17. *The First Two Dominican Priories,* p. 7.

18. *The Concise Columbia Encyclopedia,* pp. 478, 740. Waldo, Sacajawea.

19. *Origins,* p. 387, Nov 16, 1989: Vol. 19, No. 24.

20. Webb, *Centenary,* p. 201.

21. Coffey, *The American Dominicans,* pp. 37-38.

22. Webb, *Centenary,* p. 203.

23. At that time the houses of the Friars were called convents and those for women religious were called monasteries. For more detail, see Endnote 15, Chapter One.

24. Luke Concanen, OP, was a personal friend of Fenwick. So close was the relationship that some say he could be regarded as a co-founder of the first American Dominican Province. Concanen as English-speaking sociusto the Master General was helpful to Fenwick in cutting through the red tape to establish the new Province. Concanen was appointed the first Bishop of New York, but died before he could set sail for his new Diocese. See Webb, p. 202; also O'Daniel, *A Light,* p. 298; and Coffey, *The American Dominicans,* p. 14.

25. Webb, *Centenary,* pp. 165, 177.

26. Barbara Misner, *A Comparative Social Study of the Members and Apostolates of the First Eight Permanent Communities,* p. 28.

27. Hinnebusch, *The History of the Dominican Order,* p. 96.

28. Ibid., p. 97.

Chapter Four

LIFE AS A RELIGIOUS ON THE KENTUCKY FRONTIER

In THE BEGINNING, the Kentucky Dominican sisters were poor and few in number. Although their genesis may not have seemed bright with promise, the new foundation had some advantages that contributed to its growth.

As an American congregation, they were spared some of the tribulations that affected groups transferring from Europe. As Americans, the language and customs of the country were their own. As American Catholics, they had already weathered the prejudices which cropped up periodically because of their religion. They were at ease with the practice of laity assuming responsibility for preserving the faith when clergy were not available. They were imbued with a spirit of freedom and independence, and even the youngest accepted austerities of frontier life.

As Dominicans, they inherited a long-standing tradition of stability and perseverance from an ancient Order founded by St. Dominic in the 13th century.

The Order of St. Dominick is divided into three Branches; the first is composed of such as are employed in the Ministry or destined for it. The second are the enclosed Nuns who make solemn vows. The third branch make only simple vows and do not observe the enclosure. This third was originally intended by our Holy Father both for maried (sic) and unmarried persons living at home; and for such it was that the printed Rule you have was made.[1]

It is difficult to pinpoint how much preliminary preparation took place before Wilson made his public appeal. Pro-Vicar General Pius Viviani, OP, authorized by the Pope, approved the undertaking on March 24, 1821, a year before the call for recruits.[2] Wilson had no problem in getting permission from Bishop Flaget of Bardstown for the project.

...the Very Rev. Father Thomas Wilson communicated the subject to the Right Rev. Benedict J. Flaget, the Bishop of Bardstown, and supplicated him to grant the permission for forming the contemplated new Religious Community. The Venerable Bishop did not hesitate in granting and encouraging so just a request, and so beneficial to Religion and Society.[3]

Flaget had previously approved two other communities of Kentucky women in 1812 whose members were close relatives or friends of the Dominican candidates. It is conceivable that the women shared among themselves ideas about service in the church and about education of children.

While still in Europe and planning to bring the Dominican Order to the United States, Fenwick and Wilson had thought about bringing Dominican sisters from England, but that did not materialize.[4] Wilson expressed his conviction about women religious in the First Profession Book.

Religious institutions are confessed of all other establishments the most useful and important, to the progress of Religion and civilization, and to the rapidity of improvements in a new country. Important individually to each member of society and equally important to the well-being of society at large.[5]

After they came to the States, hardships and poverty prevented the two friars from carrying out their plan until 1822.[6]

Meanwhile, in his capacity as pastor of St. Rose Parish, Wilson fostered the faith and devotion of children who would become foundresses.

When the time seemed right, Wilson invited the women of his parish to consider committing themselves to religious life as Dominicans. Their mission, as he saw it, would be to collaborate with the fathers in preaching the gospel in the time-honored tradition of St. Dominic, while their particular immediate ministry would be educating youth of the settlement[2] and the sanctification of fervent Christians.

Only two of the first four received, Mariah Sansbury (Sr. Angela) and Mary Carrico (Sr. Margaret), remained. In August 1822, an additional six were received, and five remained. They were young, enthusiastic and distinctly Anglo-American.

Getting Started

Once these women responded to Wilson's appeal, they lost no time in getting started. Their first home was a rude, all log cabin located on the St. Rose Farm belonging to the Fathers, quite unlike what they were accustomed to in their own family settings. It was a humble beginning, but their aspirations were lofty.

> All day they were ready to comence (sic) the religious life and to become accuented (sic) with its duties: but they had not a place to live together in community; they were destitute of means to erect any building for themselves, and therefore the Venerable Community of the Convent of St. Rose full of charity and zeal for the honour and glory of God, early in the spring of that date set about fiting (sic) up a house which belongs to the same community of St. Rose (it was one mile and a half from Springfield). As soon as this all log house was fited (sic) to dwell in, the nine chosen Christian women inhabited in it with no other provisions but what they could obtain of the liberality of their own families.[7]

To be sure, their first small home called Bethany was overcrowded, but they set about making it as attractive as possible. They could afford little of anything with beauty. Perhaps this is where the community's passion for jonquils began. Every spring the valley at Cartwright Creek abounds with bright yellow flowers, locally referred to as March lilies. Back in Maryland these same flowers were harbingers of hope after a dreary winter. Whether the flowers were part of Maryland nostalgia or whether their sheer golden beauty captured the hearts of the beholders, jonquils, from that day to this, have been a part of the sisters' cultural heritage.[8]

Before long, the sisters moved into a larger log cabin on the Sansbury Farm. The widow Sansbury had died before the end of the year 1822.[9] It was probably after her death that the community took possession of the Sansbury land and buildings. Their second home was larger and they now had a chapel, a kitchen and dining area, plus a general purpose room for work and recreation.[10] There was a loft for sleeping quarters with the usual slanted roof, a real hazard if one popped up to full height in getting out of bed!

In addition to the cabin, there was a stillhouse on the property. With remarkable ingenuity the sisters converted this building into their first school. In July 1823, fifteen students enrolled, bringing with them what was supposed to be a year's provisions. The first Dominican sisters' school in the United States, St. Magdalen Academy, was a remodeled stillhouse in what would become the heart of bourbon country!

In order to support themselves the sisters were obliged to run a farm as well as conduct a school. Widow Elizabeth Sansbury had left a bay horse and two saddles to her daughters.[11] The horse was indispensable on the farm and must have been a fine animal because it was valued at $25, a goodly sum for those days. One sister led the horse to plow the field, while another followed behind to plant the corn, and a third brought up the rear with a hoe to cover the seedlings.[12]

The Sansbury family had cows, sheep and hogs. At the distribution of the family estate, Srs. Benven and Angela probably received their share of the animals, thus providing wool, pork and milk for the community. A favorite meal for Kentucky Dominicans has always been hot biscuits and sausage gravy, the latter made from a traditional recipe. Later when the sisters raised bees, hot biscuits and honey became a favorite treat.

One of the most important crops in the area was flax, the major source of cloth fiber until the growth of the cotton indus-try.[13] Processing the flax was time-consuming and arduous work. It had to be soaked in water to loosen the fiber from the woody tissue. After washing, drying, beating and combing, the fibers were ready to be made into linen, thread and cordage.[14] The flax seeds were crushed to make linseed oil used in paint-ing and linseed cakes used as fodder for the farm animals.

The sheep on the farm were valued for their wool. Who sheared the sheep is not known, but the sisters, like other pio-neer women, carded and spun the wool. Eventually, they used the wool to make the white habit of the Dominican Order.

Initially, the sisters wore the clothes customary for the times until Wilson imported a habit from England to be used as a pat-tern.[15] When working on the farm or traveling outside the con-vent, they wore secular clothes in order not to arouse suspicion in a sometimes hostile environment.

Spiritual Formation

Wilson lost no time in caring for the spiritual and academic formation of the new community. Although he was actually with the sisters only a short time, from the foundation in 1822 until his death in 1824, his great concern was that they internal-ize Dominican ideals. His first step was to appoint Pius Miles, OP, as their chaplain and instructor. This was wise, especially when Bishop Fenwick accepted an appointment as Bishop of Cincinnati on the condition that Wilson would be his Vicar General in the new diocese. This often necessitated Wilson's presence in Ohio.[16]

Wilson translated the Rule of St. Augustine and Constitutions of the Order of St. Dominic from the Latin and gave extracts of them to Fr. Miles to use with the sisters, "as circumstances of the country could allow to be practicable."[17] When founding his Order, St. Dominic had chosen the Rule of St. Augustine for the friars. This ancient rule, attributed to St. Augustine, was a letter on the spirit of common life.[18] The St. Magdalen community read this rule aloud each week. The Rule concentrated on the observance of charity among the members, gave advice on prayer, fasting, silence, bathing, mode of dress, observance of the vows, care of the sick and settling of disputes.[19]

In giving extracts of the Constitutions of the Nuns of the Order of St. Dominic to the sisters, Wilson, like St. Dominic, prefaced them by saying that neither the Rule nor the Constitutions obliged under pain of sin, but only of performing the penance prescribed for their infraction.[20]

According to the constitutions observed by the community for the first 73 years of its existence, the sisters were supposed to recite the Divine Office, but this meant getting up at midnight for Matins and Lauds except for the last three days of Lent. Morning prayers and meditation began at 5 a.m., making for a short night! Over and above the spiritual exercises, the order of the day included personal study, farm work and teaching, not to mention preparation of lessons. Such a regimen was soon recognized as impossible.

> The following distribution of time was made by the Very Rev. Father Provincial Thomas Wilson: it was kept up till the sisters were able, for the strength being so poor, that it was prudence which compeled (sic) them to give it up, and therefore the practice of it was for a short time.[21]

It seems peculiar that Chapter X of the Constitutions in the First Profession Book is titled: Of Communion and Tonsure.[22] A curious combination! "Tonsure or cutting of the hair is seven times a year." Preceding this brief statement there is a list of 37 special days in addition to the Sundays of the year, when the sisters were allowed to receive Holy Communion. Fourteen of these days honored our Blessed Mother, testimony to the prominent place given to Mary in their Dominican life. Four days were devoted to Jesus and the rest to the saints.

Chapter VI addressed bleeding as a remedy.

> Bleeding was formerly in fashion four times a year, and such as were bled were allowed different dispensation. It is now (almost) out of use.[23]

However, when the yellow fever epidemics broke out, blistering and copious bleeding were two of the recommended remedies.

Silence as part of monastic tradition was considered an integral part of religious life, especially in chapel, refectory and dormitory.[24] While the sisters maintained verbal silence, they devised a sign language all their own to convey messages. Sign language was not considered breaking silence and speaking was allowed when necessary.

Transgressions of the rules were regarded as faults. In the pursuit of perfection, a Chapter of Faults was held every week or two for the sisters to accuse themselves or others of external faults committed against the rule, constitutions and religious deportment. The superior imposed a penance which she felt was commensurate with the infraction. It could be to recite a Psalm, to prostrate in the venia in the middle of the assembled choir, to fast on bread and water, to receive the discipline, or to sit on the ground during dinner. More serious penances were meted out for more serious infractions.[25]

Other rules dealt with enclosure, letters and training of the novices. "It is important to note that statutes for governing the community were not included, nor was mention made of apostolic ministry."[26] It did not seem to those involved that combining the contemplative and apostolic life could be a problem.

In short, the spirituality of the first Dominican community was monastic in nature with a strong emphasis on the common life. They were "never to talk anything but good of those who are absent." The Novice Mistress, moreover, was instructed to teach them (the novices) not to eat too fast, which is unbecoming religious persons.[27] The one persistent feature regarding the Rule and Constitutions, dating from the time of St. Dominic himself, was the flexibility with the allowance of dispensation as needed.

Education Ministry

How well-prepared were the sisters for a teaching ministry? No doubt they had the education afforded to females of that day. It was part of the Maryland heritage that girls would be tutored at home while the boys were sent abroad to study. To help the sisters prepare for teaching, Wilson and Miles conducted classes in English, history and mathematics.[28] Wilson, being a linguist,[29] probably also taught French to the sisters. There is a copy of a letter written in eloquent French, believed to have been written by Sr. Angela to Very Rev. Raymond Van Zeeland.[30] Another indication that the sisters knew French is that early *Catholic Almanacs* list French as part of the curriculum for the students.

The settlers placed a high value on education. Jane Coomes, a great-aunt of Sr. Angela Sansbury, was "the first schoolteacher in the commonwealth's history."[31]

In a letter addressed to Bishop Flaget by B.B. Smith, superintendent of public instruction for the Commonwealth of Kentucky, the writer expressed concern for the education of children in rural areas. Surprisingly from today's interpretation of separation of church and state, Smith offered options for Catholics to share the revenue from education taxes and concluded:

> In case no such understanding should satisfy the Roman Catholic Community and they should altogether decline any participation in the benefits of the proposed System, as one of the Board of Education, I shall be prompt to move the Legislature to relieve our Roman Catholic Fellow Citizens, from the burden of the neighborhood tax from the advantages of which they may feel themselves excluded; on condition that some security be given for the education of every child of Roman Catholic parents, between the ages of 7 and 17 years; it seeming to me reasonable that the state should insist that no portion of its population should grow up in ignorance.[32]

The foundation of three congregations of women religious in Kentucky for the education of youth attests to the interest of the church. The Dominican sisters started a school for young boys. While the friars taught boys age 12 and older at their school at St. Rose, the Dominican sisters opened a school for young boys. This willingness to teach boys was one of the reasons that

Kentucky Dominican sisters were invited to other parishes at a later date.

The sisters were always interested in music and art. A story passed on from one generation to the next involved a New Yorker, Mr. H.V. Brown, Quaker and art teacher, engaged by the sisters to teach art. He was strongly anti-Catholic, but his contact with the sisters gradually weakened his prejudices. Eventually, he took instructions from Fr. Joseph Jarboe, was baptized by Bishop Pius Miles and was ordained. Although he was disowned by his family because of his conversion, he became the "apostle of East Tennessee."[33]

According to Sr. Althaire Lancaster's Chronicles, the sisters employed other lay teachers with special competencies such as Dr. Ballonton from St. Louis to teach French and instrumental music, and Mrs. Creote from Louisville to teach voice. It made no difference whether the person was male or female, Catholic or Protestant. What mattered was their competence.

With the help of Miles, Wilson did his utmost to ensure the spiritual formation and academic preparation of the sisters. Canonically, their status in the church was ambiguous like that of many sisters' congregations. It would take many years before this confusion would be corrected. Academically, their preparation for teaching was consonant with the times.

Chapter Four Notes

1. SCA, *First Profession Book*, p. 6.
   Encyclopedic Dictionary of Religion, Vol. A/E, p. 1094.
2. O'Daniel, *A Light*, p. 246.
3. SCA, *First Profession Book*, p. 3.
4. O'Daniel, *A Light*, p. 245 passim.
5. SCA, *First Profession Book*, p. 1.
6. O'Daniel, *A Light*, p. 246.

7. SCA, *First Profession Book*, p. 4.

8. This author visited the area in Prince George County, Maryland in the spring. The jonquils, or *March lilies* grew profusely throughout the area. Residents claim these flowers are always the first harbingers of spring.

9. Will Book C, pp. 472, 473, 474, 475. Washington County Records, Kentucky. Deed Book F, p. 356. Washington County Records, Kentucky. SCA, *First Profession Book*, (unpaginated except for introduction). Under the reception of Angela Sansbury it reads: "The said Novice Angela Sansbery (sic) brought with her fifty-three Acres of land, having a joint claim with her Sister Elizabeth Sansbery (sic) Junior to that tract of land containing one hundred and sixty (lines drawn through the ty, making the measurement 106) vallued (sic) 2400 dollars; and she does hereby agree to serve the new Conv. during her stay in it, and should she leave the Convent or be sent away from it, she is not to be remunerated or paid for her services by the members of the above-named establishement, but she is to have the amount of clothing returned to her, or its value, and also the deed of her land, or the value of twelve hundred dollars." In March 1820, the widow Elizabeth Hamilton Sansbury and her daughter Mariah purchased 106 acres of land from Elisha and Henrietta McAtee for $2400 paid in cash.

10. Webb, *Centenary*, p. 262.

11. Will Book C, p. 474, Washington County Records, Kentucky.

12. Minogue, *Pages*, p. 54, 55.

13. *The Concise Columbia Encyclopedia*, p. 294.

14. Ibid.
    Minogue, *Pages*, p. 55.
    Green, p. 24.

15. SCA, *First Profession Book*, p. 4.
    "They had not as yet the habit to put on, or even the idia (sic) how to make it, therefore the Very Fath. Provincial instructed them, and procured for them the habit."

16. O'Daniel, *A Light*, pp. 243, 244, 245.

17. SCA, *First Profession Book*, p. 6.

18. M.H. Vicaire, *St. Dominic and His Times*, p. 37.

19. SCA, *First Profession Book*, pp. 8-10.

20. Ibid., pp. 17-18.

21. Ibid., p. 20 - Distribution of Time.

22. Ibid., p. 12. Tonsure, according to Webster, is a clipping or shaving of part or all of the hair of the head signifying admission to the clerical state and separation from the World. Paul VI abolished it in 1972.

23. Ibid., SCA p. 12.

24. Ibid., SCA pp. 13, 14.

25. Ibid., SCA p. 17, 18. *Venia* is a profound prostration signifying penance and obedience.

26. Green, OP, Sr. Mary Patricia, *The Third Order Dominican Sisters of the Congregation of Saint Catharine of Siena*, p. 21.

*Mother Angela Sansbury, founder of the Dominican sisterhood
in the United States*

Cross at St. Rose marking grave of
Samuel Thomas Wilson, O.P.,
co-founder of the Dominican sisterhood

Tombstone commemorating
Mother Angela Sansbury
and other sisters
buried at Somerset
and later transferred
to Columbus, Ohio

SISTER ANGELA SANSBURY
1794 ——— 1839
FOUNDRESS OF DOMINICAN SISTER
HOOD IN THE UNITED STATES
1822

SR. ANN HILL 1805 — 1840	SR. ANGELA McCORMICK 1824 — 185?
SR. FRANCES WHELAN 1815 — 1844	SR. STANISLAUS McCORMICK 16?? — 18?1
SR. MARTHA McDERMOTT ??? — 1845	SR. DOMINICA WILSON 1824 — 1852
SR. JOSEPHA LYNCH 1812 — 1847	SR. OSANNA MORRIS 1820 — 1855
SR. TERESA SMITH 1824 — 1847	SR. MARTHA BATES 1831 — 1861
SR. ANGELA LYNCH 1822 — 1847	SR. CECILIA DUNN 1838 — 1864
SR. CATHARINE BECK 1815 — 1848	SR. TERESA McCANN 1836 — ????
SR. CLARA OSMAN 1819 — 1849	SR. MONICA LYNCH 1785 — 1867

Edward Dominic Fenwick, O.P., founder of Dominican Order in the United States at St. Rose, Springfield, Kentucky

St. Rose Church and Priory (1), St. Magdalen Chapel (2), Bethany at Cartwright Creek and old well site (3)

Calaruega, Spain, birthplace of St. Dominic

House of St. Dominic in Fanjeaux on the street of Signadou

*Sr. Elaine Shaw visiting the Lands of Dominic
on a Parable Tour*

Sign before the house of St. Dominic

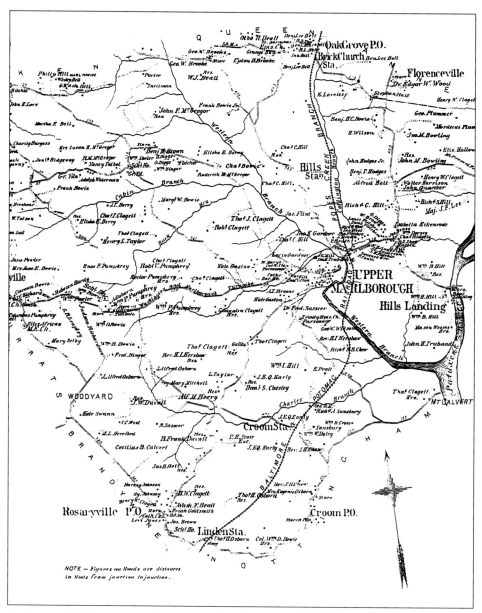

Early map of Prince George County, Maryland

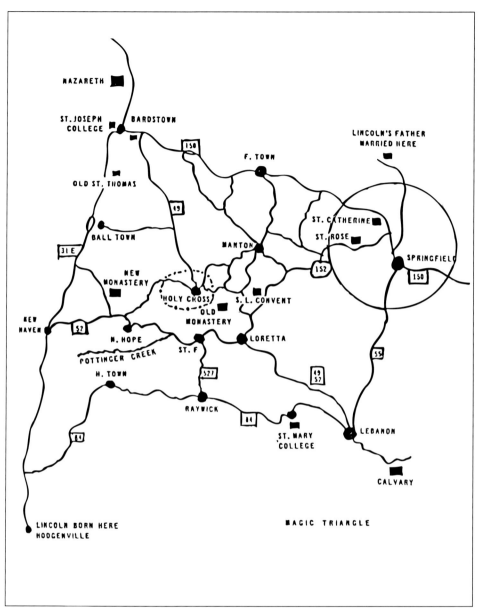

Map of area in Kentucky called the American Holy Land

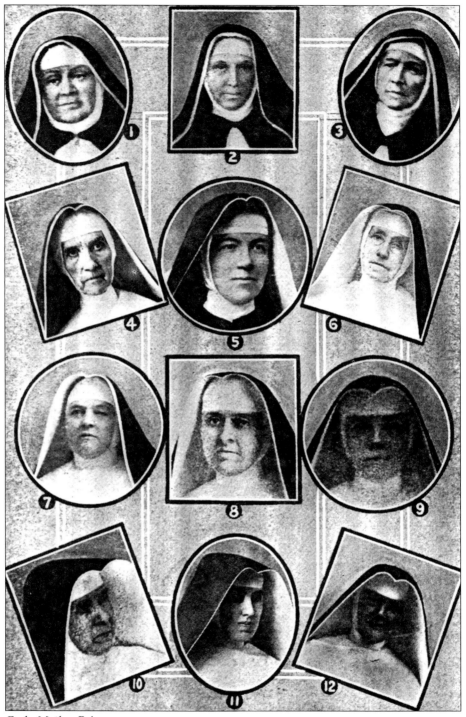

Early Mother Prioresses

1. Mother Rose Tennelly
2. Mother Columba Walsh
3. Mother Helen Whelan
4. Mother Angela Lynch
5. Mother Regina O'Meara
6. Mother Mary Benven Rumpff
7. Mother Vincent Ferrer Thompson
8. Mother Bernardine Bushue
9. Mother Agnes Hunt
10. Mother Mary Aquin Holleran
11. Mother Francesca Kearney
12. Mother Magdalen Norton

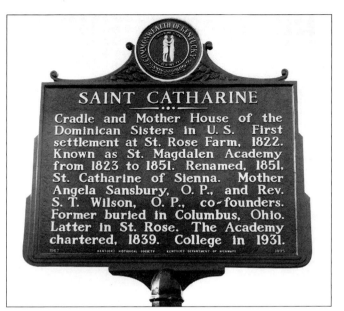

Marker at Gate to St. Catharine

SAINT CATHARINE

Cradle and Mother House of the Dominican Sisters in U. S. First settlement at St. Rose Farm, 1822. Known as St. Magdalen Academy from 1823 to 1851. Renamed, 1851, St. Catharine of Sienna. Mother Angela Sansbury, O. P., and Rev. S. T. Wilson, O. P., co-founders. Former buried in Columbus, Ohio. Latter in St. Rose. The Academy chartered, 1839. College in 1931.

Stone honoring Christopher Simmering, an early benefactor

TO OUR GREAT BENEFACTOR
CHRISTOPHER SIMMERING
1831 ——— 1853
R. I. P.

Monument to cholera victims and Louis Sansbury, African American who served valiantly during the epidemics

THIS MONUMENT IS DEDICATED TO THOSE WHO LOST THEIR LIVES DURING THE CHOLERA EPIDEMICS OF 1833 AND 1854. AND TO LOUIS SANSBURY. A BLACK MAN. WHO CARED FOR AND BURIED THE VICTIMS IN THESE APPROXIMATELY 106 UNMARKED GRAVES.

Chapel in the Valley showing grille, a carryover from European cloister influence

Academy Orchestra 1913

Graduate Alma Clements with her diploma

Junior and Senior students with Fr. Caton, O.P. — 1901 in Valley

Students of the Academy in the Heights, 1906

27. SCA, *First Profession Book*, pp. 15, 16.
28. Green, pp. 23, 24.
   Minogue, *Pages,* p. 47.
29. O'Daniel, *A Light*, p. 20, 21.
30. SMSA, copy of letter from Sr. Angela to Very Rev. Raymond Van Zeeland. The original directed to Rev. Raymond Van Zeeland at Rotterdam is not in the Archives at Nijmegen. According to Rev. P. Brink, OP, most of the records of the Netherlands Province were destroyed in World War II.
31. Crews, *Holy Land*, p. 36.
32. Filson Club, undated letters B.B. Smith to Flaget and Spalding.
33. Stritch, Thomas, *The Catholic Church in Tennessee*, p. 126. (Hereafter referred to as Stritch, *Tennessee.*)
   Also Webb, *Centenary*, p. 264.

Chapter Five

CAUGHT IN
THE CROSSFIRE

A<small>FTER</small> THE DEPARTURE of Judith McMan whom Wilson had appointed over the nunnery, the fledgling community was without a formal superior. Wilson moved toward election of a Prioress. Since all were novices, none was yet eligible. The sisters indicated that Sr. Angela was their choice as head of the congregation. Wilson appealed to the Pro-Vicar General Pius Viviani for a dispensation to permit her to make profession before the expiration of her noviceship. The dispensation was granted and Angela was professed on January 6, 1823, having spent nine months as a novice. Angela was the only one of the original nine to receive the habit in St. Rose Church. Likewise, she was the only one who made profession in the parish church "in the hands of the Very Rev. Father Thomas Wilson, Pov'l of St. Joseph Province."[1] It is believed that she was acting superior by choice of the sisters until the proper documents arrived from Rome.

First Canonical Prioress

It was at St. Rose Church that Angela's formal installation as first constitutional prioress of St. Magdalen occurred on June 6, 1823, with the reading of the official document in the presence of both communities. It read:

42

JESUS — MARY — DOMINICK

To our beloved Daughter in Christ, the virtuous Sister Angela Sansbury, Professed Religious of our College of St. Mary Magdalen, Third Order of St. Dominick: Brother Thomas Wilson, Prior Provincial of the Province of St. Joseph, Order of St. Dominick.

Greeting.

Whereas by power of a rescript from His Holiness, Pious VII, a College of Nuns, Third Order of our Holy Father, St. Dominick, has been erected in this Neighborhood and our weak endeavors blessed with some success; it becomes a duty incumbent on me to provide the said Religious College with a legitimate Constitutional head and Superior. For which reason, being well acquainted with your exemplary conduct and zeal for regular Discipline, and moreover influenced by that affection which your virtuous Sisters testified toward you on a former occasion when they petitioned to have you placed at the head of their community; I, the aforesaid Brother Wilson, Prior Provincial and as above, by authority of my office and moreover especially empowered by His Holiness to that effect, do hereby declare, establish and confirm you the said virtuous Sister Angela Sansbury, first Prioress of our said College of Saint Magdalen, in the name of the Father and of the Son and of the Holy Ghost, Amen. Giving you hereby all spiritual and temporal authority over said College and Religious Nuns, as all Prioresses of Nuns of our Holy Order possess and our Holy Constitution authorize. And though I nowise doubt of your perfect obedience and ready compliance with the will of God, thus officially intimated to you; yet for increase of merit and in conformity to the Statutes of our Holy Order, I hereby enjoin you to accept and diligently to perform the said Office of Prioress of Saint Mary Magdalen's without demur.

In virtue of holy Obedience and under a formal precept, commanding all and each of our said virtuous Sisters under the same formal precept to acknowledge and respect you as their lawful Superior before God by my authority with all constitutional impediments to the contrary and prohibiting one to reclaim against our present arrangement.

signed: Wilson, STM & Provincialis

Given at St. Rose's in presence of both Communities under our own hand and Seal, this June 1823.

To our Beloved Daughter in Christ, Sister Angela Sansbury. The enclosed patents were read and accepted June the 6th, 1823 at 8 1/2 o'clock ante meridian. Signed Wilson.[2]

The sisters had the Constitutions given them by Wilson; they had a prioress duly elected by themselves and approved by the Provincial; their school enrollment was growing, attracting both Catholic and Protestant students; and Fr. Miles, their chaplain, was their trusted friend and counsellor.

An increasing concern of the sisters was the failing health of their founder. In his foresight and wisdom, Wilson had appointed Fr. Miles as chaplain and teacher for the sisters allowing him to handle their affairs to such an extent that Miles could be considered a co-founder. When Wilson died May 23, 1824,[3] the sisters sorely grieved the loss of their friend. While they mourned Wilson's death, they now relied solely on Fr. Miles to guide them.

The Debt

It was to Fr. Miles they turned when they needed to borrow money to expand the accommodations for their students. He signed a note for $2,000. It seemed a safe risk because the sisters managed their meager finances well and had no other debts. However, affairs at St. Rose brought some surprises which affected the sisters.

After Wilson's death, Fr. Tuite took over the administration of St. Rose as senior priest. He and his friend, Fr. S.L. Montgomery, both alcoholics, indulged their habit without restraint. Fr. Miles was chaplain at St. Magdalen and Fr. Polin, the fourth priest at St. Rose, was a semi-invalid often confined to bed. Community life was conspicuous in its absence: the recitation of the office, observance of fast days, classes for the novices, all fell by the wayside. Lay men and women visited freely even to the cells of the brothers, and the novices spent most of their time working the farm. A further complication was a debt of $3,000 on St. Rose Farm.[4]

1828 marked the beginning of a tumultuous time for St. Rose and for the sisters! To remedy flagrant abuses prevalent at St. Rose, Fenwick appointed a Spanish Dominican, Francis Raphael Muños, as prior. Muños was instructed to restore regular observance at St. Rose. Not an enviable position under the circumstances!

Francis R. Muños, OP

Fr. Muños remains a controversial figure to this day: some regard him as a saint while others write him off as a harsh, insensitive foreigner. He had served as confessor to the Spanish royal family and later as Army chaplain during the campaigns of the English troops in Spain.[5] Major General Edward Capel and other distinguished officers wrote glowing letters of recommendation about Muños for his outstanding service to Irish Catholic soldiers.

When religious persecution swept through Spain in the early nineteenth century, Muños fled to England where he became confessor to the Spanish Embassy. Later, while living in Italy he met Bishop Fenwick who was visiting there in 1824. Fenwick persuaded him to become a missionary to the United States. For four years he labored on the Ohio missions, instructing children and adults ignorant of the faith. He spent weeks in the cabins of the interior teaching and preaching.[6] It was at this point in his career that Bishop Fenwick appointed him prior of St. Rose.

On arrival in Kentucky, Muños was appalled at the conditions spiritual, financial and communal existing at St. Rose. He was also dismayed beyond measure at what he saw at St. Magdalen, accustomed as he was to endowed convents of cloistered nuns in Europe.

According to mandate from the Provincial, he set about reforming religious life at the Priory. When people have had free reign with no accountability, they usually do not welcome a return to a more austere way of life. The friars at St. Rose were no exception.

Concentrating on the sisters, Muños felt they were over-worked and the matter of their debt with the note signed by Fr. Miles weighed heavily on him. This, in addition to the debt of $3,000 on St. Rose, must have seemed insuperable to him.

At a meeting with his Council dated November 18, 1828, there is a notation:

> The Council agreed that the name of Rev. Pius (Miles) should be erased out of the Deeds of St. Rose because he owes us about $2,000 on account of the Nuns and other things not belonging to the Convent of St. Rose.
>
>   signed: B. Raphael Muños Prior
>   B. Raymond Tuite
>   B. Thomas Polin Secretary[7]

Why remove Miles's name from the deeds of St. Rose? Was it to prevent the creditors of the sisters from making any claim on the finances of the friars? Was it ultimately to protect the assets of the Province? There is no doubt about it, the finances of both the friars and sisters were critical. Bishop Fenwick needed money; he needed priests; he needed sisters. He looked to Kentucky to solve his problems.

In order to pay off the sisters' debt, Fenwick wrote to the Master General seeking permission to sell the property belong-ing to the sisters as well as some of the land at St. Rose if needed. He felt a deep responsibility for the sisters because he was the one who founded them. As options for the sisters he suggested:

1. they settle temporarily on a farm near Somerset, Ohio;
2. they disperse for a while, devote themselves to various duties like the Srs. of Charity and wear a black habit.[8]

His suggested solutions were desperate attempts to help the women. Reeling from the prospects of dispersing, the sisters had further trials in store.

Threats of Dispersing

Convinced that the future of both St. Rose and St. Magdalen did not lie in Kentucky, and that Ohio held more promise,

Fenwick as Commissary General of the Dominicans in the United States, assigned Fr. Miles to the Ohio missions with Fr. Polin to follow when his health permitted.[9] The sisters were devastated when Fr. Miles was moved. Despite the heartbreaking facts, their founder dead, their chaplain transferred, their creditors nipping at their heels, their Commissary General advising them to disperse, the sisters faced the crossfire resolutely.

According to some accounts, Mother Angela wrote to the Master General stating her case:

> We will not agree to such a tragedy for we know it was God who called us to religious life. Father Wilson secured the approval of the Holy See for us, and as long as the community is faithful to the purpose for which it was organized it cannot be disbanded without the consent of the same community. Best of all, the Sisters are happy in their religious vocation and joyous in the service of their God.[10]

Muños wrote to the Master General protesting that Fenwick was acting more for his See as Bishop of Ohio than for the best interests of the Order.[11] Other letters inundated Rome. Bishop Flaget wrote his grievances not only to the Dominican Master General but also to Propaganda Fide when he felt Fenwick was about to remove both friars and sisters to Ohio.

Flaget minced no words in pointing out that he did not want this decimation of his diocese.

> It is plainly opposed to justice now to deny that aid to the faithful which they (the sisters) so holily promised, from which hope they received generous alms; and to transfer that burden to the Bishop of the Diocese. Not without Scandal to the faithful would the Monastery be sold which four years ago was erected with their money, with the certain hope of educating girls there and imbuing them with the holy principles of Religion.[12]

Flaget's protest prevailed in Rome and Fenwick gave up the idea of selling the property and transporting all personnel to Ohio.

Despite this deliverance, the sisters still had the debt of $2,000. In order to pay it, they made and sold soap, linen, garments, candles, cloth of various kinds. They even sold part of their precious little furniture. They went out two by two to beg from their neighbors and kin. They used their sewing skills; they cooked, washed, ironed for the friars. An entry in St. Rose receipts reads: To Mother Prioress for making 4 habits:

3 shirts and 2 jackets $008.70 [13]

By their own labors the sisters gradually paid off their debt.

Obviously, Fr. Muños and his Council appreciated the sisters and though so debt-ridden themselves they could not help financially, they did what they could to offer spiritual comfort.

> Sept. 3rd, 1828 — On the same day Rev. F. Prior proposed to celebrate 25 Masses for every deceased Sister of St. Magdalen's Monastery. They unanimously agree to the proposal.

> signed: B. Raphael Muños, Prior
> B. Raymond Tuite
> B. Rich. P. Miles
> B. Thomas Polin Secretary[14]

With each passing day, the health of Fr. Muños became more fragile. At great cost to himself, he had restored regular observance at St. Rose, a benefit not exactly appreciated by some! Fenwick, aware of Muños's failing health and possibly because of complaints about his austerity, called him back to Ohio. A notation in the Council Book reads:

> Rev. F. R. Muños removed from the office of Prior of the Convent of St. Rose on the 31st December 1829. Rev. F.T. Martin appointed President of the said convent of St. Rose on the said day in place of Fr. Muños.[15]

Fr. Muños died July 18, 1830 at Cincinnati. His obituary called him a friend of the poor, the widow, the orphan and one of the most useful missionaries in the diocese of Cincinnati.[16] His replacement, Fr. Martin, served only three months before the appointment of Fr. Stephen Montgomery.[17] The latter, because of personal problems, lasted only a short time when Martin returned as prior at St. Rose.

A New Friend

During this period of foment at St. Rose, the sisters quietly pursued their ministry as their numbers began to increase. One day assistance came in an unusual manner. A stranger appeared at the door asking for shelter for the evening.[18] His name was Christopher Simmering, a German tinsmith from Bardstown. The next day he told the prioress that he intended to stay at St. Magdalen's Monastery for the rest of his days because he believed God had sent him there.

He used his talent well, making pots and pans for the sisters, often loading his wagon with extra wares to sell among the settlers. On his return he would donate the proceeds from his sales to the sisters. The first piano the sisters owned was a gift from Mr. Simmering. Not much is known about Mr. Simmering beyond his kindness and generosity. He must have had some education because he witnessed some of the documents and deeds of the sisters with a firm signature in a day when many just made a mark for their names.

The sisters nursed him in his last illness and buried him in the Vale cemetery when he died. When the sisters built a new school in 1890 they dedicated a hall to their benefactor with an inscription at the entrance which read: "To the memory of Christopher Simmering."[19]

When the graves in the Vale were transferred to Siena Heights, Mr. Simmering was not moved, but a memorial stone was placed near the replica of the first chapel which stands on Locust Lane: "To Our Great Benefactor Christopher Simmering 1831-1852." He spent 21 years as a friend, associate and valued employee of the sisters.

Chapter Five Notes

1. *Profession Book I*, 1822-1919, unpaginated except for Introduction section. Making profession in the hands of the superior is a time-honored custom of the Order. While it may be reminiscent of the feudal pledge of a serf to his lord, the religious significance is that the person places his/her hands in those of the one representing the Order to indicate a living bond uniting them both to the Order and to Christ.

2. Copy of letter of appointment - Original in the Archives of St. Mary of the Springs, Columbus, Ohio.

3. O'Daniel, *A Light*, p. 262.

4. *American Dominicans*, pp. 166-170.

5. *U.S. Miscellaney* — August 14, 1830 - SJPA.

6. Ibid.

7. SJPA *Councils and Acts: St. Rose Council Book* – 1828-1869, p. 9.

8. Letter of Bishop Fenwick to the Master General, October 10, 1829 AGOP XIII, 03150,136 SCA/SJPA.

9. *American Dominicans*, p. 165.
   Also Original letter of Fenwick to Miles, October 22, 1828, SJPA.

10. Research to find this letter from Mother Angela to the Master General has proven fruitless. Monica Kiefer, OP quotes it in *Log Cabin Days*, p. 33, but she does not give a source. Joseph B. Code in *Great American Foundresses*, p. 244, gives a similar description but not a direct quote. Although a primary source is missing, it is a strong statement which epitomizes the position taken by the sisters. If the letter were written after 1828, it would have been during Mother Magdalen's term of office, so authorship for the document would also be uncertain. It would seem that such a statement would be issued by the major superior.

11. Muños to Master General Ancarani, Nov. 10, 1828 AGOP ..130 SJPA. Muños to Fenwick, Nov. 10, 1828 - AGOP 128, 129 SJPA.

12. Flaget to Cardinal Prefect, APF V9, 541rv, 542rv, K1126 SJPA Jan. 7, 1828.

13. *Councils and Acts* — *St. Rose Council Book*, 1828-1869, pp. 65, 66. Receipts 1828, 1829: one wonders if this price included the material as well as the labor.

14. Ibid., p. 7.

15. Ibid., p. 69. Some sources say that Stephen Montgomery replaced Muños on January 1, 1830. Fr. Martin succeeded Muños on that day for only three months. Montgomery replaced Martin in April, 1830. Because of some scandal involving Montgomery, Martin was appointed again in the fall of 1831. (*American Dominicans*, p. 192, footnote 10.)
    During the dispersement controversy it was said that Muños refused to say Mass for the sisters in their own chapel. After Miles went to Cincinnati, Muños was the only active priest in good standing at St. Rose. He was stretched thin with numerous sick calls requiring long rides on horseback, the operation of his flourishing parish and the instruction of his people. Contrary to some stories handed down by tradition that the sisters had to cross the icy waters of Cartwright Creek to attend Mass at St. Rose, they simply walked across the fields. Their property was adjacent to St. Rose and their monastery was on the same side of the creek as the priory.

16. *Catholic Telegraph*, May 4, 1848 - SJPA.
    US Miscellaney, August 14, 1830 - SJPA.

17. *American Dominicans*, p. 192, Footnote 10.

18. Minogue, *Pages*, p. 74.

19. Ibid.

Chapter Six

EXPANSION: MEETING THE NEEDS OF THE TIMES

THE ACQUISITION of more territory following the Indian and Mexican Wars, the improvement of transportation, plus the opening of the historic canals, Erie in 1825 and Ohio in 1830, enticed people to explore the unknown regions. Kentucky was changing from the "First West" to the "Gateway of the West." Bardstown, once considered the Catholic capital of the west, no longer was the center of activity in Kentucky. Louisville, as a rapidly thriving port city, became increasingly important. When Bishop Flaget reported to Rome on the growth of his diocese he submitted a proposal to move the site of his see to Louisville. The Pope left the decision to the American Bishops who agreed to the change at the Provincial Council in 1840. The Catholic Church was keeping pace with the expansion movement in the country. It was a Country questing, a Church searching, and a Congregation evolving.

Although other Kentucky religious communities seemed to expand faster, the Dominican sisters were making steady progress. Their debt was paid and their school was gaining a reputation for excellence. Bishop Flaget wrote in his report to Rome:

The (Dominican Fathers) have established for almost four years a monastery of young women, Tertiaries of the Third Order of St. Dominic who devote themselves to the education of girls .... And they (the friars) have established a school for boys and young men living in the country, and even though they are recent, those schools have great promise.[1]

The friars taught the older boys at St. Rose and sent the younger ones to the sisters. The fact that the Dominican sisters taught boys is notable because with many communities, teaching boys was contrary to their rules. Sr. Helen Whelan was in charge of the boys ages 7-12 in a department entirely separate from the girls. Some Protestants from the surrounding areas sent their sons to the sisters because they valued the education given the students.[2] With the increase in the enrollment of girls, the sisters closed the boys' department but throughout their history, the Kentucky Dominicans have taught male students at all levels of education.

For six years as prioress, Mother Angela had labored to bring the community into being. She had the confidence and support of her companions who for the most part were from the England-Maryland-Kentucky tradition. Young as they were, they were strong women, accustomed to working hard, to taking risks, and to making their own decisions.

Second Prioress

At the expiration of Mother Angela's second term of office in 1829, Mother Magdalen Edelen succeeded her.[3] Born in Prince George County, Maryland, to Samuel and Mary (Smith) Edelen, Teresa entered the Congregation on August 3, 1822.[4] As a novice she had the name of Eupresia (sic), but when she took vows it was changed to Magdalen.[5]

It was Mother Magdalen who endured the burden of paying the sisters' debt and who faced the crossfire between Bishop Fenwick of Cincinnati and Bishop Flaget of Bardstown. Her struggles did not go unnoticed. Webb wrote of her:

I first saw Mother Magdalen in 1837, twenty-eight years before her death. She reminded me at the time, in some respects, of the late Rev. Mother Catherine Spalding, of the Sisterhood of Charity of Nazareth. The frame was larger, the face more angular, and she was decidedly more abrupt in both manner and speech. Hard as had ever been Mother Catherine's experiences in building up, out of nothing, as it were, the great conventual and educational establishment with which her name was connected from the beginning, I judged that those of Mother Magdalen had been still more exacting and wearyful. They were alike in their gravity and in that indefinable something that makes one feel that he is in the presence of personified purity and goodness and truth.[6]

When Bishop Fenwick called on his friends at St. Magdalen to send sisters for his diocese in Ohio, it was Mother Magdalen who answered his request. About the same time, she received a request from Rev. Stephen Badin for sisters to establish a school at St. Joseph's River, Indiana.[7] With only 17 sisters in the community, to answer both requests was unfeasible. Naturally, the ties with Bishop Fenwick were stronger: he was a Dominican, he founded the Dominicans in the United States and he was their long-time friend.

Undoubtedly Mother Magdalen prayed and discussed with her sisters the idea of an independent foundation in Somerset, Ohio. It would be the first daughter of St. Magdalen.

First Daughter Foundation

On January 11, 1830, four sisters, Srs. Emily Elder, Agnes Harbin, Catherine Mudd and Benven Sansbury left St. Magdalen for Ohio. Two of them, Agnes Harbin and Catherine Mudd made their profession at St. Magdalen on the very day of their departure.[8]

Accompanied by Fr. Stephen Montgomery, the sisters set out on a rugged journey by land to Louisville. In Louisville they met Fr. Abell and Fr. Badin before proceeding to Cincinnati. They spent a week with Bishop Fenwick probably discussing plans for education in the diocese and the details of the new foundation, St. Mary of the Springs.

When they arrived in Somerset on February 20, because their

future home was not vacated, they stayed with Peter Dittoe's family for three weeks. Finally, they took possession of a small brick house on one acre of ground and the carpenter's shop which was fitted up for a school.[9]

The US Catholic Miscellany for February 20, 1830 wrote:

> Four sisters of the Order of St. Dominic, called from their monastery in Kentucky .... passed through Cincinnati on their way to Somerset, Perry Co., Ohio. They are about to establish a female school in that place, near the church of the Holy Trinity. From their qualifications and devotedness to the cause of moral and religious instruction, much good may be anticipated from their location in the large and respectable congregation of St. Joseph. The same attention will be paid by them, to the poor children, as is paid by the Sisters of Charity.[10]

Once settled, the first thing they did was to elect Sr. Emily Elder as their first prioress for one year with Sr. Benven as subprioress.[11]

Although Sr. Emily returned to St. Magdalen two years later, she did not remain there. Her bother, Fr. George Elder, first president of St. Joseph's College, Bardstown, took a dim view of Dominicans in general.[12] Wilson and some of his confreres had confronted Fr. Elder about his Jansenist tendencies. Whether this was part of the reason he advised his sister to leave the Dominicans or whether he truly believed there was no future for the small Dominican congregation is uncertain. What is certain is that he persuaded Sr. Emily to join the Sisters of Charity of Nazareth where she lived a long life as an accomplished music teacher.

When Mother Emily's term of office expired, the sisters elected Sr. Benven Sansbury.[13] Her career in and out of positions of leadership, in and out of Kentucky, Tennessee and Ohio, is a story in itself.

The ties between St. Magdalen's and St. Mary's were ever close and warm. Srs. Helen Whelan and Columba Walsh joined St. Mary's for a year until novices began to enter at Somerset, temporarily easing the crunch for help. When Sr. Benven issued another plea for assistance in 1833, two more recruits left

Kentucky for Ohio. This time, Mother Angela and Sr. Ann Hill answered the call. Picture the reunion of these three!

The year after she arrived in Ohio, the community elected Mother Angela as prioress for three years by a special dispensation. Before this, the term of office at St. Mary's was for one year. At St. Magdalen's the term was for three years from the beginning.

Mother Angela was re-elected for a second term of three years, but died before finishing it. On her tombstone at St. Mary's, this is the inscription:[14]

SISTER ANGELA SANSBURY
1794 - 1839

FOUNDRESS OF DOMINICAN SISTERHOOD IN THE UNITED STATES
1822

The mobility of the sisters during this period was due to the fact that the Dominican Provincial of St. Joseph Province assigned the sisters. He called on them to participate in the mission of the friars with the decision of assignment based on where the need was greatest.

Cholera Epidemic

Around the time Mother Angela and her cousin, Sr. Ann Hill, left for Ohio, a cholera epidemic broke out in Springfield, Kentucky. It was cherry picking time in 1833.

Dr. Michael Shuck reported the first case as that of a slave woman belonging to Mrs. Hill, Sr. Ann's mother. Judging from the report, the patient displayed the classic symptoms of the dis-

ease; violent vomiting, unbearable muscle cramps, unquench-
able thirst and excessive diarrhea. Because it is a fulminating
disease, the victim may have sudden onset and die within two
to twelve hours.[15] Sr. Ann's parents, Clement and Mary Hill,
died a short time after their faithful slave woman.

Fr. Byrne from St. Mary's College administered the last rites to
the woman but unfortunately he carried the disease back to the
college where it took a heavy toll.[16]

Bishop Flaget wrote to his friend, Monsieur Deluol:

> For around a month the cholera had made great ravages in
> two of our Counties and in localities which had always been
> regarded as the healthiest in Kentucky. Bardstown has not been
> exempt from it, although it has been much less maltreated than
> the towns of Lexington and Springfield.[17]

Tragedies usually call forth heroism. One of the heroes who
emerged during the cholera epidemic was Louis Sansbury, a
slave belonging to George Sansbury, a tavern owner in
Springfield and cousin to Mother Angela. Louis cared for the
sick and buried the dead, regardless of who they were. Others
fled, but he stayed on. Merchants left keys to their businesses
with him. When the residents returned after the danger was
over, they purchased his freedom for him and set him up in
business with a livery stable to show their gratitude.

The parish of St. Rose was hard hit. Bishop Flaget wrote about
the heroism of the Dominicans:

> It is especially in the congregation confided to the Reverend
> Dominican Fathers that this frightful scourge has made itself felt
> and has immolated more victims. Although the religious of the
> Third Order of St. Dominic (the sisters) have always been among
> the dead and the dying, not one has succumbed to those painful
> and charitable labors. The five Dominican Fathers employed in
> that parish, the most numerous in all Kentucky, have deployed a
> zeal worthy of the first ages of the church. For more than three
> weeks, night and day, they were constantly employed in fulfill-
> ing their ministry among the sick, taking rest only half-clothed,
> and I would say almost all their meals on horseback. When I

betook myself to the convent, they were so extenuated and deplorably worn out that it was almost impossible for me to keep back my tears.[18]

Flaget, impressed with the ingenuity of the Dominican sisters in devising a plan to recruit help in caring for the sick, wrote about them:

> The Sisters of the Third Order of St. Dominic deserve as much public recognition as the Sisters of Charity and the Sisters of Loretto. With only ten or eleven Sisters in the community in Kentucky, they used holy industry to multiply their resources and to render service to the sick in the district surrounding their monastery. They chose mature women of recognized virtue to be associated with them in their acts of charity. For several weeks, one saw them everywhere, night and day, in houses where there were the greatest numbers of sick and where misery had reached its peak. Not one of them nor their companions died but all were exhausted beyond what can be imagined.[19]

Bishop Fenwick himself died of cholera. While making a visitation in Indian territory he contracted the dread disease and died on September 26, 1832.

Cholera again struck Kentucky in 1854. The scenario was the same; only the characters differed. The Dominican friars and sisters worked indefatigably with the sick and the dying. Once again, Louis Sansbury was the Good Samaritan attending the sick with compassion and burying the dead with dignity.

There is an old saying, "There is nothing new under the sun." Examining the letter of Bishop Flaget quoted above, it becomes clear that the sisters engaged lay women to work side by side with them in the ministry. Both the sisters and their associates exposed themselves to danger in order to serve. This association with lay women in the ministry is evident throughout the history of the sisters but it was not until the last decades of the 20th century that St. Catharine Dominicans established a formal way for men and women to commit themselves to share in the prayer and activities of the sisters and to serve in the ministry when possible.[20]

Era of the Common Man

The election of Andrew Jackson ushered in what history called the Era of the Common Man. With the Indians pushed westward, roads being built and people moving from log cabins to frame houses, stagecoaches, inns and riverboats became part of the scene. As travel grew easier the country experienced growing pains in search of its destiny. In the Kentucky Constitutional Convention of 1849 the topics discussed were slavery, prevention of dueling and a common school system. The question of slavery was an ever burning issue — in the country, in the church and to some extent, within the Congregation of St. Magdalen.

The ramifications of the slavery question will be handled in a later chapter. Meanwhile, as the country experienced growing pains, so did the Church. While the peace of the Church was seriously disturbed by problems arising from exploitation of lay control in some parishes, the enforcement of canonical procedures and changes in civil law gradually restored a modicum of calm. However, as the number of Catholic immigrants increased to a noticeable degree, bigotry generated a great deal of violence against Catholics.[21]

During this period, the Congregation of St. Mary Magdalen was in the process of becoming a subculture within a culture. To become a truly American community while observing traditional norms of religious life as lived for centuries in Europe was a constant struggle. From the beginning, the foundresses were action-oriented. Because of their pioneer background the sisters were accustomed to do what had to be done. If the roof leaked, they patched it. If seed was to be sown and harvested, they did it. If they needed cloth for habits, they raised and sheared the sheep, carded the wool, wove the cloth and sewed the habits.

European convents were usually endowed by wealthy patrons. Not so the first Dominican foundation in the United States.[22] When they borrowed money they repaid it by their own hard labor. Their American Bishops were poor and unable to subsidize them.[23] At times, they literally lived their designation as members of a mendicant Order. They went from house to house among their relatives and friends to obtain money to build a chapel, expand a school or maintain an orphanage. Hard work, scanty food and physical exhaustion took its toll on the early members. They found it impossible to live a cloistered life while functioning in an active apostolate. In 1848 the Kentucky Dominicans and the Ohio Dominicans sent a joint petition to the Holy Father to request changes.

It is now 26 years since our first establishment in this country. During this time we have been employed in instructing young females after the manner of other literary institutions. The manifold advantages of such institutions have long been acknowledged, as well by religious government as by the Catholic population. Maxims of solid piety are impressed on the tender minds of those who have the happiness to agree with us in faith. Protestants too, gradually forget their false notions and prejudices; not infrequently, they abandon their errors, and submit to the sweet yoke of Christ. In a word, the rapid increase of these institutions and the great joy with which they are everywhere welcomed speak powerfully in their favor, so that it is needless for us to eulogise. In our profession we add a clause, to embrace the Rule of St. Augustine and Constitutions of the Order of Preachers as the Sisters of the second Order of St. Dominic do, whenever we may judge it proper to do so.

After deliberation, it has seemed to us that the present time is favorable for this end. But on account of the particular circumstances in which we are placed, it is impossible either to sustain the choir, or to be enclosed. We cannot recite the Divine Office, because the number of those who are capable of teaching being very small, it would consume more time than they could possibly devote to it. Nor can we be enclosed because our Convents are not built in a suitable manner and we have not sufficient revenues to change their present form. Again, were we enclosed, we should lose our pupils, Catholics as well as Protestants and would thus be deprived of the means of support. Wherefore, submitting these considerations to the wisdom of your Holiness, we join in one common prayer for a dispensation of being enclosed and allowing us to recite the office of the B.V. Mary, instead of the Divine Office, and to grant us the favor of making the solemn profession as the Nuns of the second Order of our Holy Father St. Dominick.[24]

One of the reasons for the request to make solemn vows was that the sisters feared that with only simple vows they would not be authentic members of the Dominican Order. In an earlier letter written by Stephen Montgomery, OP prior of St. Rose to the Vicar General, Thomas Ancarani, OP, Montgomery stated that Bishop Fenwick asked him if the sisters could be allowed to wear the black veil and say the Little Office of the Blessed Virgin.[25] One source believes this meant that the sisters wore the white veil because in Europe only nuns (Second Order) were permitted to wear black headgear. Oral tradition theorizes that in Kentucky the sisters may have worn the sunbonnet commonly worn by pioneer women in that area. This would have been particularly appropriate when they worked in the fields. Permission was granted to receive the black veil at the time of profession. The sisters did not seem fixated on what they wore. Records show that outside the monastery they wore secular clothing when traveling to avert undue suspicion among their Protestant neighbors because of their dress.

In the north, a group of sisters founded by Fr. Samuel Mazzuchelli in Sinsinawa, Wisconsin, in 1847, received a dispensation to wear a black habit because the white was too difficult to keep clean. In other words, the sisters used common sense when it came to what they wore.

More important to the sisters than any mode of dress was their status as members in the Dominican Order. At that time canon law recognized only one form of religious life for women as an authentic "state of perfection." That was the cloistered life of contemplatives who took solemn vows.

From the beginning, Archbishop Carroll felt that on the American scene it was important for women religious to be actively engaged in service to their fellow Americans and to be publicly perceived in this capacity.[26]

Not until 1900 would Rome recognize as authentic religious, sisters without solemn vows who taught, nursed and served the needs of the people outside cloister walls.[27] As for the sisters, they did what they had to do to serve the People of God, adapt-

ing to the circumstances in which they found themselves, cling-
ing resolutely to the Dominican Order while at the same time
working towards recognition of their position in the Church. It
was to be a prolonged struggle.

Chapter Six Notes

1. Propaganda Fide Archives, Sc. rif., Vol. 8, 548r - 552r - Extract of Bishop
   Flaget's Report to the Holy See, January 19, 1826. SCA (copy).
2. Minogue, *Pages,* p. 75.
3. SCA List of Major Superiors.
   Archives Copy of Minogue, *Pages* with annotations written by Sr.
   Althaire Lancaster, p. 71.
4. *Profession Book I,* 1822-1919. SCA.
5. Ibid.
6. Webb, *Centenary,* pp. 77, 78 Footnote.
7. Victor O'Daniel, *Life of Fenwick,* p. 387.
8. Sr. Catherine (Julie Ann Mudd) was first cousin to Catherine Sansbury,
   Rose Sansbury and Rose Anna Boone. Her cousin Sr. Catherine
   Sansbury died August 14, 1828. Julie Ann took the name Sr. Catherine.
   She returned from Ohio to Kentucky where she remained until her
   death June 20, 1861.
   The Mudd Family of the United States, p. 173.
   Also, New York Freeman's Journal, Vol. 22, July 13, 1861, p. 1. SJPA.
9. Sr. Benven's Brown Paper Notes, p. 1, original SMSA, Columbus, Ohio.
10. *United States Catholic Miscellaney,* February 20, 1830. SJPA.
11. *Elections: Prioresses and Superiors,* p. 3, SMS, Columbus, Ohio.
    Also *Make the Way Known,* Burton, p. 46.
12. Kiefer, *In the Greenwood,* p. 26.
13. *Elections: Prioresses and Superiors,* SMS, Columbus, Ohio, p. 3.
14. Inscription on Mother Angela's tombstone, St. Mary of the Springs,
    Columbus, Ohio.
    At St. Mary's Cemetery, Mother Angela's own sister, Sr. Benven and
    their cousin, Sr. Ann Hill, are interred near Mother Angela's grave.
    Sisters professed at St. Catharine and buried at St. Mary include Mother
    Angela Sansbury, Srs. Ann Hill, Francis Whelan, Cecilia Dunn and
    Benven Sansbury .
15. *Taber's Medical Dictionary.* Also Donnelly, *Imprints 1608-1980 Hamilton,
    Allied Families,* p. 43. Clement Hill died of cholera on 12/13/1832 and

his devoted wife followed him in death six months later of the same deadly disease. Her death occurred 6/11/1833. Both were buried on the hill of St. Rose's cemetery but through the years their tombstones have disappeared underground.

16. *Washington County, Kentucky Bicentennial History*, p. 25. SCA.

17. Extract from letter of Bishop Flaget to Deluol, July 5, 1833, Filson Club, Louisville.

18. Ibid.

19. *Annals of Propaganda Fide*, Flaget's report on cholera, p. 94. SJPA.

20. SCA. Dominican Associates Brochure.

21. Billington, *The Protestant Crusade*, Chapter VIII, pp. 193-219.

22. Dominican Congregations of Sisters as reported in IDI Bulletin, 1980.

23. Bishop Fenwick was poverty-stricken. St. Rose donated whatever vestments and other aid which could be spared. A collection was also taken up at St. Rose parish to provide money for the Bishop to settle in his new diocese.

    Also O'Daniel, *A Light*, p. 243.

24. Joint letter from St. Catharine's and St. Mary's, to Pius IX, July 4, 1848, AGOP XIII 03150, 253, p. 1.

25. Copy of letter of Rev. S.H. Montgomery to Thomas Ancarani, July 1, 1831. SCA.

26. Karen Kennelly, CSJ, *American Catholic Women*, p. 28.

27. Ibid., p. 24.

THE ERA
OF MOBILITY

A REVOLUTION in transportation began with
the advent of the railroads. In addition, improved steamships
that cut down travel time between Europe and America demon-
strated one of the triumphs of progress.

The Industrial Revolution brought about changes in the lives
of rich and poor alike. Inventions such as the telegraph, the
sewing machine, Bessemer steel, seemed to indicate that
progress was the ordinary path of earth's inhabitants.[1]

What was happening to the people during this transition? For
some, the ever-expanding West beckoned; for others, the dis-
covery of gold at Sutter's Mill lured more than 40,000 to
California. For Dominicans, to move in answer to a need was
only natural since mobility was their trademark ever since
Dominic sent out his followers two by two to preach.

A certain reciprocity existed among the Dominican women.
When St. Mary's and later St. Agnes needed more sisters, St.
Catharine's responded by sending recruits, sometimes on a tem-
porary, sometimes on a permanent basis.

Industrial and economic progress influenced advancements
in the social life in Kentucky. The natural resources of the land
available in the Commonwealth made a comfortable lifestyle
possible for the descendants of the pioneers. As part of their
Maryland heritage they believed in enjoying the gifts which
God and good fortune provided. They loved horses, cards,

dancing and a bit of whiskey now and then to warm the spirit. While the Dominican friars and sisters were more liberal in their views than some of their Jansenist-influenced neighbors or dyed-in-the-wool fundamentalists, they knew they could fulfill their mission only by offering excellence in education and soundness in doctrine. Also, they were careful to observe the legal requirements of the Commonwealth and at the same time to provide for the future of the Dominican Order.

"In the early nineteenth century, land and buildings in the United States could be protected in the civil society by an act of incorporation of the state legislature under the title of a literary or religious society, with a transferable trusteeship. Such a society was respected and acknowledged by a court of justice."[2] The foundresses felt that they should secure the community's assets by becoming civilly incorporated. By an Act of the General Assembly of the Commonwealth of Kentucky on December 19, 1839, the Academy of St. Mary Magdalen was incorporated under the title of the Literary Society of St. Mary Magdalen.

Mother Helen Whelan

Mother Helen Whelan and her Council became the officers of the new corporation, empowered to conduct schools to which pupils of every denomination were to be freely invited and admitted; to receive gifts or bequests; to make any contracts, as well as to buy or sell in their corporate capacity.[3]

Who was this astute businesswoman, Mother Helen Whelan? She and her first cousin, Sr. Rose Tennelly, entered the novitiate together and made their profession in August, 1827.[4] Mother Helen was a woman of energy and courage. Twice during her terms as major superior she steered the community through the onslaughts of cholera. She and her sisters nursed the victims, going among the families day and night. It was during the second epidemic that Sr. Theresa Lynch contracted the disease and died on July 4, 1854.

With the school expanding, Mother Helen had the foresight to purchase an additional 240 acres of land at $20 an acre running from Cartwright Creek up to the Bardstown and Springfield Road.

One of Mother Helen's objectives was to have the sisters well qualified as teachers. She promoted serious study among them with the result that during her second term of office, the Academy was chartered. She served four times as major superior, a total of twelve years, twice alternating with her cousin Rose Tennelly.

Identity Crisis

Despite their growth in numbers and the success of their ministry, the sisters struggled with an identity problem. They were saddled with constitutions which were a combination of Second and Third Order norms. This showed up even in their architecture.

One of the accomplishments of this period was the erection of a chapel. Fr. Nicholas Dominic Young obtained plans from several European Dominican chapels, namely San Sixtus and Prouille.[5] Although there was little money in the treasury, relatives and friends rallied to the appeal of the sisters for donations. Bishop Flaget laid the cornerstone in 1847; a year later his coadjutor, Bishop Martin J. Spalding, dedicated it.

Adhering to the idea that someday they would be cloistered, the sisters had an artistic grille to separate the sisters' choir from the body of the church. It was the last time in their history that this particular carryover from the cloister was maintained.

Increasingly the community became aware that European cloister was incompatible with active religious life in America. In a letter to the Master General, Fr. S.H. Montgomery, acting for Bishop Fenwick asked for mitigation of some of the customs of the sisters' horarium.[6] To date, there is no indication when or what reply was made.

In 1848 the sisters in Kentucky and Ohio wrote a joint request to Pope Pius IX asking to be released from enclosure and from the recitation of the Divine Office.[7] Again, as far as is known, no response to this communication was received. However, the sisters substituted the Little Office of the Blessed Virgin Mary and as long as they were assured they would continue to receive all the spiritual benefits and be regarded as members of the Order they forged ahead with the work at hand.

In 1858 when Rev. Joseph Kelly, OP, became provincial, he tried to remedy the situation by obtaining a copy of the Stone England Constitutions. This complicated matters. Kelly adapted the document for the sisters within St. Joseph Province, but at first, they were used only in Memphis. Although the Master General Vincent Jandel encouraged Kelly in his efforts, Jandel made it clear that it was beyond his jurisdiction to approve the Stone constitutions.

This left the sisters in an unenviable position. They needed constitutions which would provide for the canonical affiliation of mission houses with the Motherhouse; their civil charter needed an amendment not only to empower them to establish mission houses but also to acquire or sell property in other states. The fact that the Dominican provincial assigned the sisters throughout the province wherever services were needed, often without consulting them, had mixed effects. The positive side was that moving the sisters back and forth through Kentucky, Ohio and Tennessee created a strong bond among them and collaboration flourished. The downside was that some of the transfers diminished one mission while strengthening another and the sisters had no voice in the matter.

One consistent factor was that the fathers regarded the services of the sisters as a necessary component of the Dominican mission. In Tennessee, the former chaplain of St. Magdalen, Pius Miles, OP, who had become first Bishop of Nashville, sent out an urgent plea for sisters. Six Sisters of Charity of Nazareth journeyed from Bardstown, Kentucky, to Nashville to open a day and boarding school on August 25, 1842. Another Dominican, Rev. Thomas Grace, pastor of St. Peter's Memphis, begged for assistance to teach children.[8] Mother Angela Lynch responded to the call. Memphis became a joint foundation of three sisters from the Kentucky motherhouse and three from the Ohio daughterhouse. For this mission the name St. Agnes was chosen.

Fr. Grace had devotion to St. Agnes, martyr, but also as a Dominican, he honored St. Agnes of Montepulciano, one of the outstanding Dominican saints.

Mother Angela Lynch

Mother Angela Lynch was serving her first term of office when this second daughter foundation was made. She came from an interesting family of ten children born to Patrick and Christina (Ledwedge) Lynch.[9] Two children died shortly after birth. Four of her sisters joined the convent of St. Mary of the Springs. Margaret (Sr. Angela) and Mary (Sr. Josepha) both died early of tuberculosis and are buried in Ohio. Betty (Sr. Teresa), professed at St. Mary's, was sent to St. Catharine where she served one term as major superior. Later, she died of cholera contracted while caring for cholera patients in Springfield, Kentucky. Jane (Sr. Rose), professed at St. Mary's, traveled from Ohio to Texas where she was one of the foundresses of the Houston Dominicans. John, the youngest, became a friar when his mother as Sr. Monica, joined her daughters at St. Mary's.

When Ann expressed a desire to enter the convent, it was felt that she was too young or perhaps was unduly influenced by her sisters. As a compromise, she was allowed to visit St. Catharine, but she persisted so strongly in her desire to consecrate herself to God that her parents finally consented. She was professed at St. Catharine on October 2, 1836, assuming the name of Angela. This caused some confusion at times because her sister Margaret at St. Mary's was also Sr. Angela Lynch.[10]

Her leadership abilities propelled her into responsible positions within the Order as Council member and twice as major superior.[11] When Mother Angela assumed office[12], she did everything she could to ensure that the sisters were qualified for their teaching apostolate. Because of increased faculty and student enrollment, she saw to it that convent and school were remodeled and enlarged. It was during her first term of office that the foundation in Memphis took place. The story of St. Agnes can best be told in an excerpt from the early annals.

ANNALS OF ST. AGNES ACADEMY

COMMENCING WITH THE FOUNDATION OF THE HOUSE

JAN. 10TH, 51

The foundation of the St. Agnes female Academy was commenced Jan. 10th, 1851 by order of the Very Rev. Anthony O'Brien then Prov. of the Order of St. Dominic, and under the auspices of the present Bp. of St. Paul the Rt. Rev. Dr. Grace then resident pastor of St. Peters Church,Memphis, Tenn. St. Agnes owes all its past prosperity and present prestige to the fostering care of this illustrious prelate, and distinguished divine of the Order.

The first colony of Sisters were six in number. Three of them were from St. Mary's Somerset, Pery (sic) Co. Ohio. They were Sisters Emily Thorp (sic,), Magdalen Clark, Catharine (sic) McCormick. The latter was a young sister in the last stages of consumption who died the eight (sic) of August on the same year.

Those from St. Catherines (sic) Springfield, Ky were Sisters Ann Simpson, Lucy Harper and Vincentia Fitzpatrick. The Sisters from St. Mary's together with their Confessor F. Cubero and the Very R.A. O'Brien reached Louisville Dec. 21st. Whilst waiting the arrival of those from St. Catharine, put up at the Convent of the Sisters of the Good Shepherd, who received them with Sisterly Affection, and entertained them with the utmost Cordiality and courtesy. The Sisters of the Order of St. Dominic are under many obligations to this Convent and its inmates who have ever shown themselves ready and willing to offer us the hospitality of their house when passing through Louisville. The three Sisters from St. Catharine left there on the 27 of Dec. reached Louisville the same evening and set out from the City on the 28 in company with those there in waiting for Memphis which place they reached just as the year 50 was expiring. Tuesday morning Jan. 1st, 51, the little colony were conducted by Rev. T.L. Grace to the spacious residence of Mr. William McKeon there they were received with all the warmth and cordiality so characteristic of the Irish heart whether at home in their own sea-girt Isle or in this their adopted country. In the spacious and elegant mansion of this hospitable family the Sisters were entertained with the utmost courtesy and kindness till the 10th of Jan when they took possession of their new home at St. Agnes. The community of St. Catharine's gave the Sisters 800 dollars out of which their traveling expenses were to be deducted. In Louisville they purchased some few pieces of furniture and some school books which left them with a balance of 50 dollars to meet all the expenses of opening and furnishing a new convent and boarding school.

St. Agnes is pleasantly situated in the subburbs (sic) of Memphis about a mile and a quarter from Court Square, the center of the city. The buildings constituting the Convent and Academy stand in the center of a beautiful grove of native forest trees. The original purchase contained about five acres a portion of which had been cleared and cultivated for a fine kitchen garden. The grounds in front of the Academy are still studded with the majestic oak, lofty poplar, elm and other fine forest trees, which at once furnish the Academy with ornaments of natures own werkmanship (sic) and the pupils a most delightful shade, during the hours of recreation. The grounds are laid out in circular, straight and winding walks, and their borders are adorned with roses, syringa, evergreens and other flowering shrubs. Vases, statues, busts and a fountain further diversify and embellish the grounds. The "tout ensemble" forming one of the prettiest combinations of the rural and classic beauty in the city or environs. The old frame, now the center building was formerly the residence of Gen. Levi Coe from whose heirs it was purchased by Very Rev. T. L. Grace at a cost of 7,000. As the new community was without means, the 4,000 necessary to meet the first payment Michael Mageveny kindly came forward and offered to loan them the money at 6 percent and their own time to pay it. In the meantime he sent three of his daughters to the new Academy the first day it was opened for the admission of scholars. They remained at St. Agnes till 55. The Sisters opened their school the 4th of Feb. 51 with 20 boarders and about 15, or 20, day scholars.

Among their first pupils were the three daughters of M. Mageveny, Miss Mary McKeon, only daughter of William McKeon and the 4 eldest daughters of Gen. Coe, deceased, the last mentioned young ladies remained at the Academy, till they completed their scholastic course, whilst the younger ones are still numbered among those in daily attendance at St. Agnes.

Many others among the best and most respectable citizens of Memphis sent their daughters and wards to the new Academy. The school increasing beyond the most sanguine expectations of the Sisters and their friends, the expediency of enlarging the present building soon suggested itself. Accordingly a two story brick addition 40 by 80 and forming a right angle with the original frame was commenced in May and completed and used for the first time for the Exhibition July 7th, 51, when the first session closed with about 50 scholars.[13]

Foundress of St. Agnes

The six women who founded St. Agnes were strong, independent, industrious and considerate of the less fortunate. They took risks and ran institutions at a time when women seldom worked outside their homes. "Besides their school work, the Sisters paid regular Sunday visits to the city hospital and the city jail where they gave instructions and consolation to the inmates."[14]

SR. ANN SIMPSON, one of the three from Kentucky, was born in Maryland.[15] Evidently, her family migrated to Kentucky where she entered St. Catharine Convent. As one of the foundresses of St. Agnes, she served as superior but then moved to Gracewood to run a farm and an orphanage. Deprivations were daily fare. Food was scarce but even more depressing was the lack of spiritual sustenance, no Mass, no chapel. A poignant note in the annals of St. Agnes records: "Sr. Ann Simpson who had remained at Gracewood for three years without either companions or assistance returned to St. Agnes." With the outbreak of the Civil War her courage and tact were put to the test but she was equal to the task.

SR. VINCENTIA FITZPATRICK, Kentucky-born and truly an itinerant Dominican, helped with the foundation of St. Agnes but then moved on to found the Immaculate Conception day and boarding school in Jackson, Tennessee in 1869. As if that were not enough she journeyed to Pensacola, Florida in 1871, to found a school there. Three Fitzpatricks were involved in this project, Srs. Vincentia and Dominica, family sisters, and Pius, their cousin. Neither school in Jackson nor Pensacola survived. Sr. Dominica died in Florida but her body was brought back for burial at Memphis.[16] Sr. Pius appears in later pages about St. Catharine's. After the failure of the Florida foundation, Sr. Vincentia transferred to become a part of the foundation of Nashville's St. Cecilia.[17]

SR. LUCY HARPER, third member of the Kentucky contingent, moved from place to place to place, always leaving her mark of leadership wherever she served. Hers is an extraordinary story closely knit with that of a slave named Susie.

Susie was born a slave belonging to St. Catharine's. For whatever reason, the Congregation gave her to Mrs. Harper who took her to Ohio to live with the Harper family. Mrs. Harper taught Susie the niceties of gracious living and encouraged her development in music, for Susie had a beautiful singing voice and was adept at the piano.[18]

Sr. Lucy served at St. Catharine's until the foundation of St. Agnes where she became superior. "At the end of her superiorship at St. Agnes she transferred to Ohio's St. Mary's.[19] Because the slave question was causing bitterness and violence at the time, Mrs. Harper asked her daughter to take Susie to St. Mary's for safety's sake. At. St. Mary's Susie was a favorite. A born musician, she filled the music rooms with her singing and playing. In the Council minutes is an entry:

> March 3, 1857. It was agreed by the Council that we should keep black Susan as long as she continued to do well and render some service to the community and furnish her with clothes and treat her kindly. (signed: Sr. Columba Dittoe)[20]

Evidently Susie kept up her end of the bargain by waiting on tables in the school and doing other tasks about the convent.

As for Sr. Lucy, after serving on the General Council at St. Mary's she went as one of the foundresses at Nashville in 1860. Susie went with her. Before long the Civil War disrupted their lives. When Fort Donelson fell into Union hands, panic-stricken people, believing that Nashville would be next, fled in all directions. Sr. Lucy and Susie squeezed into a departing train.

Where did they go? Because of the pandemonium that prevailed, few records exist of the exodus. Apparently, Lucy left religious life, returning to Ohio where she died in 1903.[21] In religious life she had served well, as foundress in two instances, as Council member, as directress of studies and as a faithful friend. Her protege Susie eventually married "a youth of her own race and religion in New Orleans."[22]

The three foundresses from St. Mary's shared the common life and a common task with their Kentucky counterparts.

SR. MAGDALEN CLARK epitomizes the mobility of sisters during this era. Although she began as a Sister of Charity of Nazareth[23] she was professed at St. Mary's, Ohio, in 1843. She was sent as one of the founding members to St. Agnes, but much of her ministry was with orphans at St. Peter's Orphanage, Memphis. From St. Peter's she went to St. Mary's Orphanage, Nashville. Fundraising for the orphans was second nature to her. She dispatched sisters to Chicago and even to Cuba to raise money.[24] Later in her career she became Prioress of St. Cecilia's, Nashville.

SR. EMILY THORPE, the second member from Ohio, professed at St. Catharine's, was sent to St. Mary's for several years. The Provincial, Rev. M. O'Brien, assigned her to the new Memphis foundation. In later years, she lost her eyesight but her sunny disposition did not change. She spent the last ten years of her life at St. Catharine's where she died and is buried.

SR. CATHARINE McCORMACK was already in the last stages of consumption when she left Somerset for Memphis. Her superiors hoped that the climate would improve her health, but she died within eight months.

Four of the Memphis foundresses were professed at St. Catharine's and two were professed at St. Mary's. The moving about to answer the needs of the Church and the people is but another example of Dominican collaboration. Mobility for mission was the order of the day. Bishop Fenwick, personally and through designated representatives, made voyages to Europe for additional priests and sisters. When Joseph S. Alemany, OP, became Bishop of Monterey, California, he sailed to France to bring back two novices and one professed sister to help with a foundation in the far West.[25] Being poor as were most missionary bishops, he wrote to the Society for the Propagation of the Faith to beg for money for the passage of the sisters. It cost $480 each, a prohibitive sum in those days!

The French Connection

Before setting sail from Liverpool, Bishop Alemany wrote to the Mother Superior in Toulouse to allay any fears she might have had about her sisters; after all, they were leaving France without hope of ever returning.

> Reverend Mother Superior:
>
> Sister Rose, Sister Catharine and Sister Mary of the Cross, Father Vilarrasa and I with two others are in the ship Columbus, and will begin our voyage to New York tomorrow morning. The Sisters are very well, and very content; they are finishing chanting several religious hymns and are happy to find themselves on a ship as good as ours. The Captain is very good, and has told us he will do everything possible to please us. He has his children with the Sisters of New York, and his wife is Catholic. The Sisters have their English syllabi, grammars and dictionaries and we have begun the first lesson. Sister Rose and Sister Catharine send you word that they remember "God alone."[26]

Sr. Mary Goemare went to California but Fr. Sadoc Vilarrasa accompanied Sr. Rose Corbattieu and Sr. Catharine Frances Coppe to St. Mary's, Somerset, Ohio. Because they were not yet professed,

> He (Bishop Alemany) did not judge it well to assign them to California, first because they are only novices, second because his Lordship did not know whether there would be at San Francisco a conventual house to receive them.[27]

The bishop "exchanged" them for two professed sisters from St. Mary's who went to his new diocese.

After profession at St. Mary's Sr. Rose moved to Zanesville,

Ohio, and then to Nashville, Tennessee. Finally, she went to Memphis where she taught French at La Salette. Since there was already a Sr. Rose, her name was changed to Rosalie, but she was fondly called "Sister Rosie" or "French Rose."[28] During the yellow fever epidemic in 1873 she nursed the sick and the dying. Her French charm and vivacious manner won the hearts of those who knew her. She died at St. Agnes on July 26, 1876, and is buried there.

Sr. Frances Coppe was also sent to St. Catharine's after being professed at St. Mary's. She became superior at Holy Rosary, Louisville. She died rather suddenly in 1878 and was buried at St. Catharine's.

Over one hundred years later Mother Marie Pie Quocci, OP, wrote from Rome:

> Our Congregation was born in Albi (France). Our foundress is Mother Gerine Fabre. The Congregation was canonically erected in the diocese in 1852, but two years before,...a bishop from California, M. Alemany asked Mother Gerine for a foundation in his diocese. His warm appeal was listened to and two young sisters, Sr. Catharine and Sr. Rose, left Albi and went to California as missionaries. Nobody in France and in Italy, knows the development of this foundation in California....We are studying the history of our Congregation and we would like to discover something more about the link between Albi and the foundation in California. Maybe you can help us.[29]

It was in Albi that the Albigensian heresy threatened the life of the Church in St. Dominic's time. Centuries later two of Dominic's daughters left Albi to teach and preach in a country unknown to Dominic. It is only now that we are unraveling the story of these intrepid French women and their connection with the Church in America.

Chapter Seven Notes

1. *World Almanac 1988*, pp. 489-491.

2. Green, pp. 26, 27.

3. Twelve years later the sisters decided to change the name from St. Mary Magdalen to St. Catharine of Siena in honor of this renowned daughter of St. Dominic and a Doctor of the Church. As a Third Order Dominican, Catharine carried out her ministry in remarkably wide circles for a woman of 14th century Italy. See Suzanne Noffke, OP, *Catharine of Siena*, Paulist Press, NY 1980. The Kentucky General Assembly approved the name change on March 11, 1851. Initially Siena was spelled with two *n's* but another amendment to the Articles of Incorporation authorized the spelling of Siena. SCA. Henceforth, St. Catharine will be used in speaking of the Kentucky foundation.

4. Sr. Rose Tennelly, first cousin of Mother Helen Whelan, succeeded the latter in office in 1835 and again in 1841.

5. SCA, Minogue, *Pages*, p. 81.

6. San Clemente Archives, Rome, letter dated July 1, 1831.

   Also, Hinnebusch, *History of the Dominican Order*, Vol. 1, pp. 402, 403. This letter is sometimes used to prove that the sisters wore the white veil in keeping with European regulations of the Third Order members. Given the common sense attitude of the sisters about clothing, it is likely they wore Kentucky sunbonnets especially when working in the fields.

7. Copy of letter obtained at SMSA, original at Santa Sabina AGOP XII, 03151,253, p. 1.

8. Rev. Thomas Grace became Bishop of the diocese of St. Paul, MN in 1859.

   Also see Stritch, *The Catholic Church in Tennessee*, p. 106.

9. Dominican Sisters , Houston Archives, a family register compiled by J.H. Lynch, OP, Feb. 17, 1893, photostat.

10. Letter from Sr. Mary McCaffrey, archivist SMSA, dated Sept. 10, 1992.

11. SCA, handwritten memoirs of Sr. Hyacintha Peters of St. Agnes, Memphis.

12. Traditionally, the list of Prioresses General at St. Catharine's reads:

Name	Term
Mother Teresa Lynch	Jan. 6, 1847 - Jan. 6, 1850
Mother Angela Lynch	Jan 6, 1850 - Jan. 6, 1853

However, in the register of the Provincial of St. Joseph Province there is a notation: "1848. Die 6 Decem. Soror Lucia Harper electa fuit Priorissa Conv. S. Magdalenae et in talem confirmatur. [signed] J. Alemany, Prov. Traditionally, the Kentucky Dominicans have never listed Sr. Lucy as a major superior. To add to the confusion, in a joint letter to the Holy Father from the sisters in Kentucky and Ohio, dated July 4, 1848, Sr. Angela Lynch signed herself "Prioress," Photostat AGOP XIII 03150, 253, p. 1. No further documentation has been found to prove who was prioress in 1848 — Teresa, her sister Angela, or Lucy Harper.

13. *Annals of St. Agnes Academy, Commencing with the Foundation of the House,* Jan. 10, 1851. SJP. In this quotation for convenience, the author has kept the current spelling of Catharine. Also SCA, handwritten memoirs of Sr. Hyacintha Peters of St. Agnes.

14. SCA. Undated newspaper article about La Salette,

15. SCA. Profile card on Sr. Ann Simpson.
    Also see Sr. Aloysius Mackin, OP, To Others, p. 55.

16. Minogue, *Pages,* pp. 84, 230.

17. Mackin *To Others,* p. 19. Also correspondence of Sr. Aloysius Mackin to author.

18. Ibid.

19. Quoted in a letter dated Dec. 13, 1993 from Sr. Mary Agnes McMahon, archivist SMPA.

20. Ibid.

21. Excerpt from writings of Mother Frances Walsh, Nashville Dominicans Archives.

22. Sr. Rose Marie Masserano, OP, *The Nashville Dominicans,* p. 14.

23. Ibid.

24. *To Others,* p. 40.

25. Original SRA. Sr. Maria Pie Quocci, OP, to Mother Superior dated Rome, October 4, 1992.

26. Ibid. Translation from the French.

27. Ibid.

28. SMSA.

29. SRA.

— *Part Two* —

A Community Action-oriented, Parish based

CRISES, CONFLICTS, CHOICES

PREJUDICE BORN OF IGNORANCE rears its ugly head in every age. When Fr. O'Brien as Provincial asked the sisters to start a school in Memphis at the request of Fr. Grace, the proposal was met with some reservations. An old faded Chronicle gives this explanation.

> The Very Rev. Provincial told the Sisters of his desire to acquiesce to this request but Mother and her Council demurred because of the troubles then known as "Know-Nothingism." Hence when the Sisters were permitted to leave home they were disguised as seculars — a frilled grandmother's cap was worn tight around the chin under a poke bonnet to hide the bare head. Bustles, bell skirts, shawls and poke bonnets were the garb of the day. Sisters wearing a habit would have been denied transportation in stagecoaches and lodging in taverns.[1]

Know-Nothingism

Know-nothingism was an anti-Catholic, anti-immigration movement which grew out of Nativism. It was a reaction to the influx of immigrants after the Irish potato famine and German economic distress.[2]

The publication of Maria Monk's *Awful Disclosures of the Hotel Dieu Nunnery of Montreal* played a large part in the No-Popery Crusade. Matters were at fever pitch, but when the Ursuline Convent in Charlestown was burned to the ground, Boston was in an uproar. Fortunately, the sisters and children escaped. Homes occupied by Irish laborers were burned as part of the No-Popery movement. This attitude prevalent in staid Boston indicated the strength of sentiments against Catholics.[3]

In other cities the story was repeated. In New Orleans four men were killed because they were "foreigners." In the Irish section of Lawrence, Massachusetts, homes and churches were destroyed. In Louisville, the Louisville Journal carried on a No-Popery campaign. The result was "Bloody Monday," August 5, 1855, when native factions rampaged through the central part of the city killing more than 20 Irish and German Catholics.[4] German families began to migrate to Kansas and many Irish left Kentucky for Ohio looking for safe haven.

In the 1855 election, Maryland and Kentucky went solidly Know-Nothing[5] but the price of victory was a perceptible setback for Louisville. While the city's prosperity was one thing, what was of greater concern to Bishop Martin J. Spalding was religious freedom and the provision of educational facilities for Catholics in his diocese. The educational issue was intertwined with Know-Nothingism.

Public School Education

It was about this time that the Commonwealth established education under state sponsorship and control with a Presbyterian minister as state superintendent of education.[6] Religious institutions were far ahead of the state in promoting education in Kentucky, particularly Catholics, Presbyterians, Methodists and Baptists. The very first teacher in Kentucky was Mrs. William Coomes (a great-aunt of Angela Sansbury) who taught pioneer children in Harrodsburg as early as 1775.[7]

Bishop Spalding wanted public taxes to be allotted on an equal basis to any approved schools, regardless of public or private sponsorship. Of course, this was not acceptable to Nativists who feared that the young women in Catholic institutions were being brainwashed by the sisters to become Catholics, perhaps even being coerced to join the sisterhood.

B.B. Smith, Superintendent of Public Schools, wrote to Bishop Flaget assuring him that the public school system respected the private religious opinions of all classes. Because Bishop Spalding expressed his objections to the compulsory use of the Protestant Bible for Catholic students in the state system, some sharp exchanges took place. In one letter, Smith demanded assurance from Bishop Spalding that every child of Roman Catholic parents, between the ages of 7 and 17 years receive an education so that no portion of the state's population should grow up in ignorance.[8] In another letter the same author wrote:

> I am further, exceedingly anxious to anticipate, and by antici-
> pating to prevent, the imputation to which our Roman Catholic
> Fellow Citizens will, in such case, certainly expose themselves;
> that after all their zeal for Education, they are not friends of uni-
> versal popular education, that they are content that thousands of
> children of the plain farming interest should remain uneducated;
> that they, in fact, sustain their Colleges and large Female Schools
> for the sake of the funds which they derive from Protestant
> patronage; and of the insensible influence over the plastic minds
> of Protestant children in favor of their own peculiarities.[9]

From the beginning St. Magdalen's warmly welcomed Protestant children but they were not mandated to attend Catholic religious services although some did of their own volition. The fact that some became Catholics did not please some Protestants; however, as the antagonism over slavery between North and South reached fever pitch, the discord between Nativists and Catholics over education waned.

The Peculiar Institution

Slavery, which was the overriding issue of the 19th century affected the nation's economy, politics and society to such an extent that it led to the Civil War. It is difficult for the modern mind to conceive of human bondage with human beings treated as chattel, but in viewing this peculiar institution one must place it in the context of the times in which it existed.

The North was inundated with immigrants who worked in the mills; the South relied on slaves to work in the cotton, tobacco and rice fields. The conflict between the manufacturing North and the agrarian South increased every time a new state was admitted: would it be slave or free? There was a widespread early sentiment in the South for gradual emancipation but abolitionists declared that the evil of slavery should be abolished without concern for consequences.

The Catholic Church had an underlying feeling of responsibility for slaves, and Bishops exhorted slave owners to keep families together, to educate them in the faith and to treat them humanely. Protestant denominations split into regional churches on the same issues. All the Quakers held that it was morally wrong and inconsistent for church members to own slaves. Archbishop Carroll had slaves, as did the Jesuits to run their large Maryland plantations.

The Maryland pioneers who settled in Kentucky brought their slaves with them. Elizabeth Hamilton Sansbury herself had inherited slaves from her father James Hamilton.

> Item. I give unto my Daughter Elizabeth Hamilton after my wife's death my Negro man Joe, also my Negro girl Bess, also my Negro girl Gracie, also one horse and sadle (sic).[10]

When Alexius Sansbury died intestate his wife had an appraisal and division made of his estate. Sixteen slaves are listed with a cash value placed on each, ranging from "1 Negro man Len age 24 yrs @ $600 to 1 Negro child Caroline age 2 yrs. @ 80¢.[11]

Given the background of the Hamiltons, Sansburys and their neighbors and kin, it is not surprising that the Kentucky Dominicans had slaves, euphemistically referred to as servants. Some may have been brought as dowry; some may have been gifts. There is a will of Susannah Boone bequeathing to Mariah Sansbury a Negro woman named Nelly with her son George.[12]

In the distribution of Elizabeth Hamilton Sansbury's estate, there is no mention of slaves being given to either Mariah or

Elizabeth, Jr. but their sibling, Sophia, who joined the sisters of Loretto as Sr. Maxima, received two slaves. The rest of the Sansbury slaves were divided among the other siblings.[13]

In the Washington County census for 1850, St. Rose had eight slaves while St. Catharine had sixteen. This brings up another matter, that of lay sisters and lay brothers. In that 1850 census St. Rose had eight lay brothers mostly from Ireland.

St. Catharine's did not have lay sisters, but St. Mary's did.[14] When a critic observed, "St. Catharine's did not admit lay sisters," the rejoinder was, "No, they didn't; they had slaves instead."

St. Agnes as a joint foundation of St. Catharine and St. Mary adopted customs from each of their predecessors. Although St. Agnes admitted lay sisters, the vow formula did not specify "lay sister," merely omitted it, whereas the formula did specify "choir sister" for those so privileged.[15] When St. Agnes affiliated with St. Catharine in 1888, the lay sisters who transferred were admitted as choir sisters; the black scapular was no longer a part of their habit and they had voting privileges.[16]

Admission of lay sisters, a mark of religious life in European foundations, was largely abandoned by active American communities. However, it took the 13th Amendment to discontinue the use of slaves. The relationship of the Kentucky Dominicans with them was a close one. When the sisters were struggling to get started they were almost overcome by the demands of the task of studying, teaching school, working in the fields, in addition to performing their spiritual and domestic duties. When the slaves took over the chores of field and house, they freed the sisters to concentrate on religious life and school. Without the help of these faithful blacks, who is to say what might have happened?

Again, in the 1840's when the chapel was being built, "the colored people were so anxious to have a church that they gave their year's earning and help to assist in the work which God blessed."[17] An analysis of the sisters' slave list shows that many of them were children. The sisters instructed them not only in the tenets of the faith, but also in reading and writing. At times, there were non-traditional students at the Academy — black children in need, brought to live and work at St. Catharine by the sisters.[18] And in Memphis when the sisters founded an orphanage in 1852, black children were cared for, but because of the prevailing customs, the children were separated into four categories: black boys, white boys, black girls, white girls. One wonders how strictly this segregation was kept, given the space limitations of the orphanage and the small staff to run it.

Civil War

By the beginning of the Civil War, the Kentucky Dominicans had 20 slaves. They remained faithful during the conflict, thus freeing the sisters to respond to another need which arose at that time when teachers became nurses.

The secession of the Confederate States and the battles following the attack on Fort Sumter in April 1861 revealed that neither side had prepared for the medical care of casualties. Rev. Wm. Greenleaf Eliot, founder of the Western Sanitary Commission, was appalled at the deplorable conditions: no beds, no stoves, no food, few medications and fewer nurses. Although casualties were high, more troops succumbed to measles, typhoid, malaria, infection, dysentery, camp fever and smallpox than to shrapnel.[19]

Throughout the War there was a tremendous shortage of personnel to offer medical assistance. Most of those who did help had no formal training. Religious communities responded to the need, sending 640 sisters to nurse the sick and wounded. Regardless of where their sympathies lay, the sisters nursed both the Blue and the Gray, Protestant or Catholic, without distinction.[20] This unbiased and efficient service won for them the respect of the troops themselves as well as that of the commanding officers and government officials.

In Memphis

Following the battle of Belmont, Missouri, the sick and wounded were loaded on boats which docked at Memphis. Bishop James Whelan of Nashville called upon the Kentucky

Dominicans to take over the City Hospital which was to be used for Confederate soldiers.[21] After the battle of Shiloh with losses of over 23,000,[22] trainloads of casualties were brought to Memphis to the Hospital of Southern Mothers or to the City Hospital. Sixteen sisters from St. Agnes were pressed into service.[23]

Name	*Place of Birth*
Sr. M. Louise Cain	Springfield, Kentucky
Sr. M. Magdalen Clark	New York
Sr. Mr. Francis Conlon	Kentucky
Sr. M. Pius Fitzpatrick	Ireland
Sr. Rosalie Corbattieu	Paris, France
Sr. M. Ann Hanlon	Ireland
Sr. M. Bernard Madigan	Kentucky
Sr. M. Joseph McKernan	Indianapolis, Indiana
Sr. M. Magdalen McKernan	Indianapolis, Indiana
Sr. M. Vincent Nicholas	France
Sr. M. Thomas O'Meara	Ireland
Sr. M. Veronica Ray	Ohio
Sr. M. Alberta Rumpff	Washington, DC
Sr. M. Ann Simpson	Kentucky
Sr. M. Imelda Spangler	Germany
Sr. M. Josephine Whalen	Kentucky

Imagine the feelings of Sr. Alberta Rumpff when she found her own brother among the wounded! As the numbers of patients increased hotels were converted into makeshift hospitals. The Dominicans helped at the Overton Hotel, but without sufficient medicine or even basic supplies, the task was not easy.

When the Union forces took over Memphis, General W.T. Sherman was in charge. It has been said that he set up headquarters on the grounds of St. Agnes. Military records show no proof of this, but it is possible that some of his forces camped at La Salette, the orphanage run by sisters from St. Agnes. Most of the military activity in Memphis was down by the river. St. Agnes was not near the river, but La Salette was.[24]

Regardless of where his camp was, Sherman did have contact with the sisters at St. Agnes. His wife Ellen was no stranger to

Dominicans having attended St. Mary of the Springs, Ohio. Knowing this, Sherman wrote to her about the Dominicans at St. Agnes.

> August 10, 1862. Among the callers yesterday were the Sisters from St. Agnes Academy, the elder of whom Sister Ann, is well acquainted with you and your mother and asked many questions among which of course did I say my prayers. To that I answered that Bishop Alemany had specially exempted me because you were pious enough .... for ordinary families. They were delighted .... that I enabled them to get their supplies at a cheaper rate than they had hitherto done. I promised to call and see them, but I doubt if I can find the time.[25]

In a letter dated Oct. 4, 1862, he told Ellen that he had been to Church three times and added:

> I have also done many favors for the Sisters who claim me and are doing an immense amount of praying for me. I visited the School yesterday and one of them gave me a medal and tried hard to extract the promise of repeating the prayer. I told her you had that matter in charge for me.[26]

In the midst of all the pain and suffering surrounding them in the Overton Hospital the sisters took time to answer needs of mind and spirit as well as body. A letter from Sr. Mary Augusta to the mother of one of the victims reveals her compassion for the bereft woman.

> 6/27/1863
> Dear Madam,
> Yours of the 20th just came to hand. I do indeed sympathize with you with all my heart and would give you my deep consolation, but the Sanctuary of a desolate Mother's grief is too sacred for living mortal to intrude .... I only wish I could doubt for a moment, and believe that it was a mistake about his identity — but I cannot: and even if I could, he was some poor mother's pretty boy. I saw him frequently the few days he was here. He told me you had nine children that you had to support, and he would not tell you he was sick as he knew how much you would grieve and he was in hopes he could get well.

Sister then went on to explain about his death and how his last thoughts centered on his family at home.[27]

In Kentucky

In Kentucky the horrors of war were much the same. Kentucky herself was neutral, but friends, neighbors and even members of the same family had divided loyalties. Long after the war, Sr. Laurentia Filiatreau remembered how her brothers argued at table about which side was right until her parents would intervene.

Kentucky became a highway for both armies and for the guerilla attacks of John Hunt Morgan. In one episode Morgan's men tried to seize the horses of the sisters but some of the students who were neighbors of the leading perpetrator shamed him into returning the animals.

The Battle of Perryville, October 8, 1862, brought panic and bloodshed to the state as never before nor since with a total of 7600 casualties.[28] Amidst this carnage, wounded of both sides were brought from the battlefield in farm wagons or any conveyance available to makeshift hospitals or "house" hospitals. The Dominican sisters rode on some of these wagons to bring back soldiers to Siena Vale where they turned their convent and school into a military hospital. The weather on the day of the battle was so cold that the clothes of some of the soldiers were frozen into their bloody wounds. The sisters gave up their own beds, snatching sleep when possible on the floor with bags of leaves for a pillow. Since the war was brought into their very home, all the sisters helped in some way, cleaning wounds, giving drink to the thirsty, providing food, comforting the dying. Those who died at the convent were buried in Lebanon, Kentucky. Twenty-four sisters are listed as giving care to the troops.[29]

Name	Place of Birth
Sr. M. Teresa Caho	Kentucky
Sr. M. Cecilia Carey	Wisconsin
Sr. M. Clement	Kentucky
Sr. M. Rachel Conway	Canada

Sr. M. François Coppe	France
Sr. M. Magdalen Edelen	Kentucky
Sr. M. Rose Tennelly	Kentucky
Sr. M. Francis Kennedy	New York
Sr. M. Catharine Kidwell	Kentucky
Sr. M. Angela Lynch	Ohio
Sr. M. Agnes Maguire	Ireland
Sr. M. Josephine Meagher	Ireland
Sr. M. Aquin Montgomery	Kentucky
Sr. M. Imelda Montgomery	Kentucky
Sr. M. Vallina Montgomery	Kentucky
Sr. M. Ann O'Brien	Tennessee
Sr. M. Regina O'Meara	Ireland
Sr. M. Margaret Queen	Kentucky
Sr. M. Benven Rumpff	Washington, DC
Sr. M. Augusta Thomas	Kentucky
Sr. M. Columba Walsh	Ireland
Sr. M. Helen Whelan	Kentucky
Sr. M. Thomas Wight	Kentucky
Sr. M. Catharine Young	Kentucky

It was a time of destruction as well as bloodshed. Fences were burned for firewood by the troops; fruits and vegetables were stolen; horses were commandeered. Sr. Angela Lynch and Sr. Columba Walsh traveled to Frankfort to get assurance of safety for the property at Siena Vale. On their return trip, they stopped in Lexington to do some shopping but were arrested as spies. Fortunately, when word spread abroad, faithful friends expressed outrage at the action and obtained the release of the sisters.[30]

Tradition is replete with stories of the valor of the sisters during the war, but space does not permit recounting them all. Ellen Ryan Jolly, in a letter to Sr. Margaret Hamilton, wrote:[31]

> Dear Sister Margaret,
> Am stealing a few minutes in which to thank you for a great many courtesies, which favors include the precious letter which contains the few fragments that remains of the dear Sisters' war story .... The Dominicans of Kentucky and Tennessee need never

blush for the part they played during the darkest days of our great nation. ...In my story Mother Josephine Meagher comes into her own. Devotedly and gratefully,
[signed] Ellen Ryan Jolly

The mobility of the sisters has been observed before but an interesting note is that some traveled with the army throughout the war caring for the wounded. Sr. Dolores O'Neale, a woman of strong determination, was one of the itinerant teacher-turned-nurse during the Civil War. Professed at St. Catharine's in 1856, she was sent to St. Agnes. Although a teacher, she had a propensity for caring for the sick. At. St. Agnes, she tried to start a public infirmary, but it did not last because of the financial drain. She was one of the first to volunteer to nurse the troops when war broke out.

Whether she followed the army from Memphis to Wilmington, Delaware, is not certain but according to David Toll, she was in Delaware when Lee surrendered in 1865.[32] It is related that she served in field hospitals and at least once, was at risk from a storm of bullets when one grazed her.[33]

After the war she wrote to Bishop Alemany asking to join the Dominican sisters in California. Although the permission was granted, she was dissatisfied with the arrangements assigning her and her companions subject to the authority of the Superior at Benicia. She wanted an independent establishment. She left California intending to return to Kentucky but when one of her companions became violently ill on the train they were forced to get off at Reno, Nevada, to seek help. She settled in Reno where she established St. Mary's Academy, but sank heavily into debt. When Bishop Patrick Manogue delivered an ultimatum not to her liking, once again she headed for Kentucky. At the Motherhouse they received her as a "visitor" because they could not assume her debts. In due time, she requested full membership with voting privileges and died at St. Catharine's in 1915 having come full circle.[34] Today the San Rafael Dominican sisters operate St. Mary's Hospital, Reno, Nevada, a flourishing institution with 367 licensed beds.

It took the passage of many years before the services of the sisters during the Civil War came to national attention. Through

the efforts of Ellen Jolly and the Auxiliary of the Ancient Order
of Hibernians a monument was erected to their memory in
Washington, DC in 1918. Later during the centennial commem-
oration of the Civil War, the Catholic Hospital Association
awarded plaques to fourteen communities whose members
served on the battlefields and in the hospitals. Mother Mary
Julia Polin and Sr. Paschala Noonan attended a banquet at the
Catholic Hospital Association Convention in Detroit, Michigan,
June 14, 1961, to accept a plaque in honor of the Kentucky
Dominican sisters who served as nurses in the Civil War.[35]

Chapter Eight Notes

1. SMSA.
2. *The Reader's Companion to American History,* p. 622, Know-Nothing Party.
   Also Samuel B. Morse, p. 752 and Lyman Beecher, pp. 125-127. *Columbia
   Encyclopedia,* p. 76. Billington, *The Protestant Crusade,* Chapters 3 and 4.
   One of the most vehement anti-Catholics was Samuel B. Morse, inventor
   of the telegraph, who grew up in Charlestown, Massachusetts. Because
   of an unfortunate incident which happened to him in Italy, he deter-
   mined to discredit the Pope and all Catholics. Under the pen name of
   "Brutus," he wrote a series of vitriolic articles denouncing the plot of
   Catholics to take over the United States. Rev. Lyman Beecher, an
   American Presbyterian minister preached such fiery sermons against
   Popery that his church was called "Brimstone Corner." In Charlestown,
   selectmen refused to permit burial of Roman Catholics in the cemetery on
   Bunker Hill purchased by Bishop B. Fenwick of Boston, declaring that it
   was against health regulations. Yet, they allowed Protestant burials.
   Bishop Fenwick buried two children there despite the prohibition. The
   selectmen brought suit against him, but the furor over the burning of the
   Ursuline convent overshadowed the cemetery litigation which was
   dropped.
3. Billington, *The Protestant Crusade,* pp. 76, 125, 127. *Columbia Encyclopedia,*
   p. 76.
4. McGann, *Nativism in Kentucky,* p. 112. Spillane, *Kentucky Spring,* Chapter
   23. Crews, *Holy Land,* p. 144.
5. McGann, *Nativism in Kentucky,* p. 86.
6. Filson Club History Quarterly: Vol. 33, p. 14.
7. Ibid., p. 15.
8. Ibid.

9. Filson Club: Copy of two letters addressed to Bishop Flaget by B.B. Smith/no dates given.

10. Hall of Records, Dept. of General Services, State of Maryland — Will of James Hamilton, 1785, Box 15, Folder 20.

11. Prince George Records, Liber T, pages 168-174.

12. Washington County, Kentucky, Will Book D 21, Will dated August 12, 1826.

13. Washington County, Kentucky, Will Book C, p. 472, dated October 25, 1822.

14. Burton, *Make the Way Known*, pp. 102-104. Also SMSA.

15. SCA.

16. Ibid.

17. SCA. Chronicles of Sr. Angela Lynch, Book 1, p. 76. Also Minogue, *Pages*, p. 82.

18. SCA. Sr. Margaret Hamilton's Chronicles and Personal Interview with Paul Walker of High St., Springfield, Kentucky.

19. *The New York Times*, December 1861: Civil War History, Vol. 36, Mar. 1990, pp. 17-35; William E. Parrish, *The Western Sanitary Commission*; Ed. Stepsis & Liptak, *Pioneer Healers*, pp. 40-42. Minogue, *Pages*, Chapter IX.

20. SCA. St. Agnes Annals, microfilm, Reel 4, p. 3.

21. Ellen Jolly, *Nuns of the Battlefield*, pp. 97, 98: also Memphis Daily Appeal May 6, 1862 reports the staff at the Overton Hotel was expanded and among the nurses added were several Dominican sisters, no names given. In the same paper on Nov. 10, 1861, it states that the St. Agnes Dominicans served at Overton. Other sources include: Minogue, *Pages*; Sr. Margaret Hamilton's *Chronicles*; Maher, *To Bind Up The Wounds*, pp. 70, 80; and oral history reports SCA.

22. *Columbia Encyclopedia*, p. 770.

23. Burton, *Make the Way Known*, pp. 102-104.

24. "The main Union camp was at Fort Pickering on the Chicksaw Bluff, right at Memphis. However, there were a number of outlying posts and camps of Federal Troops stationed at various places outside the city. These served as outposts so that the main fort could not be attacked without some forewarning." Original letter from Judge John B. Getz, General Sessions Court, Memphis, TN, June 2, 1994, and original letter of Shelby Foote, Feb. 1, 1991 to the writer.

25. W.T. Sherman Family Papers, Microfilm Roll 3, UNDA. The letters quoted were to his wife Ellen. Some of his words were illegible.

26. Ibid.

27. Copy of letter written to Mrs. Mary P. Talmadge, a widow of the farm community of Delhi, Iowa, by Sr. Augusta then serving in the Overton Hospital. Original preserved by great niece of the soldier, Collinsville, Illinois. Apparently, the nineteen year old soldier had fallen ill from diarrhea and infection and died a few days after arriving in Memphis. Sr. Augusta returned a ring he had been wearing to his widowed mother and advised her how to collect his pay and bounty to help her with her other children.

28. Kenneth Hafendorfer, *The Battle of Perryville*, p. 383; Maher, *To Bind Up the Wounds*, pp. 76, 80.

29. SCA, Memoirs of Sr. Margaret Hamilton.

30. Ibid.

31. SCA. Original letter dated August 4, 1926. Jolly to Sr. Margaret Hamilton.

32. David W. Toll, *Commitment to Caring*, p. 1.

33. Ibid.

    See also thesis of Sr. M. Gerald VaVoy, OP, *The Foundation and Early Growth of Saint Mary's Hospital, Reno, Nevada*, pp. 7, 8.

34. SCA, File of Sr. Dolores O'Neale.

35. The plaque now hangs in Sansbury Infirmary. It bears the inscription; "For outstanding service during the Civil War. Presented to your Order by the Catholic Hospital Association, June 14, 1961. They comforted the dying, nursed the wounded, carried hope to the imprisoned, gave in His name a drink of water to the thirsty."

YELLOW FEVER EPIDEMICS

ABOUT A YEAR after the foundation of St. Agnes Academy Fr. Thomas L. Grace, OP, approached the sisters about the plight of orphans, boys and girls, throughout the city. The sisters converted the attic of the Academy into living quarters for the children who were supported for the most part by the sisters.[1] Generosity of neighbors and parents of the boarding students helped to sustain the project.[2]

In 1855 Grace moved the orphans to land he purchased on Old Raleigh Road located outside the city limits called Gracewood Farm. This was ideal for the children, with plenty of space to romp and play, plenty of fresh air and sunshine, but it was a difficult assignment for the sisters. Due to the scarcity of priests, Mass was seldom celebrated at the orphanage and the Blessed Sacrament was not reserved.

The sisters took turns on Sundays riding to the city to attend Mass while one or two remained at home with the children. Wretched muddy roads and the possibility of being stopped and searched because of civil strife added to the hazards of the trip. Whenever the sisters went to the city for Mass or to purchase supplies they wore secular clothing because prejudice against Catholics had not yet disappeared.[3]

During the War the number of orphans increased, making it necessary to find larger quarters. This time the move was to a house on Second and Poplar streets.[4] In 1864 further expansion was needed. Union soldiers helped build a small home for the children and sisters on the present site of John Gaston Hospital.[5]

Even during the War daily life was carried on as normally as possible. Young ladies needed clothes and ribbons, corsets and gloves. One bill of items bought by the sisters for Miss Clara Conway at the request of her guardian reads:[6]

gingham	$2.75
calico	4.00
shoes	1.50
thimbles	.20
corsett (sic)	1.25
hoop skirt	1.25
hair oil	.75
mitts	.40
ribbon	.15
gaiters	2.50

St. Mary's Orphanage, Nashville

Collaboration of Dominican communities was again demon-strated when three sisters from St. Mary's and four sisters from St. Catharine's responded to the plea of J. A. Kelly, OP, to take charge of an orphanage in Nashville. It opened in 1864 with eighty boys and girls.[7] Since St. Peter's was successful in fundraising with picnics and bazaars, St. Mary's adopted the same plan. One time Rev. Abram Ryan was invited as a guest lecturer at the picnic. His eloquence on behalf of the orphans touched the hearts of his audience to such an extent that they donated $10,000.

One midnight towards the end of the War Frs. Kelly and Ryan appeared at the orphanage to warn the sisters that a battle was about to begin. The two priests and some friends conveyed the sisters and children in ambulances to the basement of the Cathedral for safety. When the danger had passed all moved to a place on Franklin Pike near Fort Negley where Federal troops protected them until they could move back to the orphanage. When Kelly complained to Washington that the building had been partially destroyed, Gen. Thomas was ordered to repair the damage before the children returned.[8]

Change of Status for the Sisters

Although the War brought unexpected changes in the lives of the sisters, they coped well until 1864 when a letter from Master General Jandel caused great consternation. The letter informed the sisters that they no longer were under the jurisdiction of the Order but rather under the local bishop. Erroneously, the sisters thought this deprived them of being real members of the Dominican Order. No wonder they were concerned. However, worries about their status gave way in the face of savage epidemics which ravaged the South.

Early Epidemics

In his 1855 City Directory, Rainey praised Memphis for "its admirable situation on a beautiful, healthy bluff," the Chickasaw Bluffs. To call it a "healthy" site was grossly inaccurate.

At that time, sanitation in Memphis was non-existent. Sporadic efforts were made to improve the streets by grading and pouring in gravel. Each time the gravel sank below the level of the mud. Not until 1860 was $300,000 allocated to lay cobblestones.[9]

Although the newspapers sponsored a health campaign in the early 1850s and doctors advocated a sewage system, water works and education in hygienic practices, only talk resulted. The passage of a sanitary ordinance authorizing the purchase of some property on an island in the river to serve as a quarantine station received little support. One of the aldermen voiced the opinion, "I never knew of any good to come from quarantine. If Providence intended fever to come here, it will come in spite of all we can do."[10] With a prevailing attitude like this, little was done to eradicate disease.

It was not uncommon for two, even three virulent diseases to be raging simultaneously. For example, in 1853, a cholera epidemic gripped the city while cases of smallpox and yellow fever added to the suffering.[11] Records of that year list about 50 patients with yellow fever in Memphis but the Dominican sisters were not involved with nursing the victims at that time. They were busy establishing schools as well as an orphanage.

1867 Epidemic

After the War, Yellow Jack invaded Memphis again with more vehemence. Sr. Mary Joseph McKernan, superioress, appeared in the novitiate at St. Agnes to ask for volunteers to nurse those stricken with the fever. Sr. Agnes Ray, the oldest novice, nearing the time of her religious profession, volunteered to go to the infected area, a place like none other she had ever known.

Irish laborers who came to build railroads, to lay bricks, to cut stones, to do the heavy work required in construction, had settled in crowded districts near the river called "Pinch" and "Happy Hollow."[12] Here in inadequate housing located in a steamy, rat-infested area at the foot of the bluff, families lived "with sanitation methods borrowed from medieval slums."[13]

It was to this disease-ridden area that Sr. Agnes went but she did not last long in such an environment. A few days after nursing the sick, she became ill. Fr. Michael Lilly, OP, administered the Last Sacraments and received her profession on her death bed. Devastated at the loss of her sibling, Sr. Veronica Ray cried out, "Why? Why was she taken and I left?" Who knows the mind of God? Fortunately, other members of the community escaped the disease with the coming of the first frost as Yellow Jack stole out of town, leaving a trail of death and mourning.[14]

What the people, including the medical profession, did *not* know was what caused the recurrence of yellow fever in 1853, '54, '55, `67, '73, '78 and '79. Because the first cases usually broke out near the river, the people associated the disease with water and the "miasma" rising from the waters.

What they did *not* know was that the key factor was a small, silvery mosquito (aedes aegypti) that laid its eggs and hatched its larvae in clear, standing water. The river and marshy swamps were prime breeding places for the vector.

What the people *did* know was the kind of death caused by

yellow fever. It began with chills, constipation, nausea, severe pains in head and back and burning fever. It could be fulminating with death ensuing in a matter of hours.[15] Internal hemorrhages caused dreaded, vile black vomiting; the skin and whites of the eyes became jaundiced; stench from the sweat and vomit was overpowering. No cure was known, but remedies of the day included quinine, wine, mercury, blistering and copious bleeding which only weakened the patient.[16]

1873 Epidemic

Six years passed before the dreaded scourge struck again. In 1873 the alarming cry, "Yellow fever an epidemic in Memphis" struck terror in most hearts. At St. Agnes, the prioress, Sr. Louise Cain, had daily Rosary processions around the grounds. No deaths occurred at St. Agnes, but LaSalette Academy was not so fortunate.

LaSalette began as an annex of St. Agnes for day students in 1864. Sr. Ann Hanlon was in charge of the school until she was transferred to St. Cecilia's, Nashville. For a while, LaSalette was the home of the postulants and novices as well as of the sisters who taught at Memphis parochial schools.[17] When the epidemic broke out, school was closed and the place was converted to a hospital. Memphis was still reeling from four other disasters which occurred within a span of seven months: an epidemic affecting horses and paralyzing transportation; an unusual freeze halting river and land traffic for about a month; a devastating smallpox epidemic; and a recurrence of cholera.[18]

Since St. Peter's was in the process of erection, friars stricken with the disease were brought to LaSalette for care. Four Dominican priests died during the 1873 onslaught: Frs. R. Daily, B.V. Carey, D.A. O'Brien and T. D. Sheehy.[19]

Memphis became a ghost town overnight as a mass exodus left only 15,000 out of 40,000 in the city. The sisters not only nursed those who came to LaSalette, but they went out to the homes to attend the sick and dying.

Sr. M. Joseph McKernan from St. Agnes had been transferred to St. Cecilia's, Nashville, but when she heard of the raging epidemic she begged to return to Memphis. She had previous experience nursing yellow fever patients in the 1867 epidemic. This time she became a victim, dying October 8, 1873 at LaSalette.[20]

Death claimed Sr. Martha Quarry on October 13. A day later Sr. Magdalen McKernan, sister of Sr. M. Joseph, died. These two latest victims were buried on the same day with Frs. Kelly and Veale officiating at the sad ceremonies and burial in St. Agnes cemetery.[21]

Sr. Martha had been advisor to the Howard Association, a group of business men dedicated to aiding victims of the epidemics. The Howards who had quasi-headquarters at LaSalette donated three metal coffins for the sisters who died in the 1873 epidemic.[22]

The first frost brought welcome relief; schools re-opened; the LaSalette faculty returned to teaching.

1878 Epidemic

Spring of 1878 ushered in a series of calamities for the sisters. Early on the morning of May 16, they were startled by the clang of fire bells. "St. Agnes Academy on fire!" The flames destroyed the building despite the efforts of valiant firefighters. What escaped the flames was ruined by water. The school at LaSalette became the home for the sisters and students. Sr. Alphonsa Yakel, the superior determined to rebuild St. Agnes, and with three sisters went to other dioceses to raise funds. In July the new building was under construction but that summer was one of the hottest on record. Yellow fever returned to Memphis in the worst epidemic of its history. Construction of the new building halted abruptly. Sr. Alphonsa was in Illinois when the news of the fever reached her. Immediately she set out to return to Memphis but because of quarantine she had to go via Nashville. She sent a wire to have the novices moved, but it was too late. The Bishop tried to dissuade her from leaving Nashville but she convinced him that it was her duty as superior to be with the community. She was not prepared for what she met.

Sr. Veronica Gloss was stricken in early August. Her face was crimson, she was vomiting violently and her mind was wandering.... All were exceedingly ill and the screams of Sr. Veronica were at times heartrending.... Her body was almost entirely mortified before she died. It was therefore necessary to order her coffin immediately.[23]

After her death the hearse drove up, took off with the body for the cemetery with the sisters hurrying behind trying to catch up. Since no grave was ready, the driver placed the coffin under a tree and rushed back to town.[24]

Just as Sr. Veronica was carried out for burial, Srs. Ann Simpson and Imelda Spangler left for Kentucky at the insistence of Fr. Kelly. Sr. Josepha McGary was too sick to go with them. In their haste they boarded the train without paying the fare. When the conductor came around he was displeased because they had neither ticket nor money. After they promised to send the fare he agreed to take them as far as Bowling Green. Here the mendicants sought hospitality from the Sisters of Charity of Nazareth who loaned them money to get to Springfield. Sr. Imelda died a few days after reaching St. Catharine's where she is buried.[25]

The situation worsened. Srs. Veronica and Dolores Gloss, nieces of Sr. Alphonsa Yakel, made profession on their deathbeds. Sr. Bernadine Dalton, the tireless infirmarian, died September 1, 1878. She was placed on a mattress in a room across from the chapel with candles placed around her. Burial services were performed as she lay upon the mattress. "Under the circumstances nothing more could be done, for the living demanded all that the poor sisters had strength to do."[26]

Srs. Rose Callahan and Josepha McGary followed soon after, thus depleting the community still more. Sr. Alphonsa lost not only her nieces, but also her sister, Sr. Laurentia. In the end she gave her own life, a victim of the fever from attending the sick.

Death is no respecter of persons. When Tom and Annie Rice who worked for the sisters died, their bodies were so ravaged that Sr. Thomas O'Meara did not think it safe to carry them through the house so they were taken down the back stairs. Kelly sent some of the sisters to Nashville until such time as the plague would be over, while some remained at LaSalette to care for the sick.

How Sr. Thomas coped with all this is beyond comprehension

— three or four bodies at a time laid out on mattresses before the altar; evening burials, sisters slowly recovering in one room totally unaware of what was going on around them. The annals put it this way: "True, some sisters were there but she (Sr. Thomas) could not go to them for consolation for as they were only beginning to recover, they knew not what had taken place, nor would it be safe to tell them. In her grief she turned into the parlor where her feelings overcame her and she wept long and violently."[27]

Not only was she losing sisters in death or exile, but thirty of the children died of the fever. She and Kelly worked around the clock doing what they could to alleviate suffering, to visit the sick and to bury the dead.

Kelly, often called the Father of the Orphans, served through three epidemics of yellow fever. In one onslaught he himself was stricken but recovered even though his life had been despaired of.[28] Day and night he could be seen trudging the empty streets bringing the Sacraments, comforting the ill, conducting burial services but nowhere was he as solicitous as he was for the children. He gathered up those whose parents died, carrying them back to the orphanage.

On September 27, 1878, he placed an appeal in the papers "To the Catholics of America:"

> For the first time during the present epidemic it is deemed proper to appeal directly to you, in behalf of St. Peter's Orphan Asylum and the Dominican and other Catholic Sisters of Charity, who have already seen sixteen of their number fall as willing sacrifice to duty and suffering humanity. ...The end of the plague is not yet and our wants multiply daily, admonishing us that the actual necessities of the orphans and Sisters, even in the near future cannot be met without your further assistance. This appeal has been deferred in the hope that it might be avoided. We now ask such donations of money, clothes for children, bedding, quinine and provisions, as the charitable among you may see fit to give. Please ship to (me) designated on outside of each package whether for orphans or sisters.[29]

The response was prompt and extensive. From St. Vincent

Ferrer's, New York, Fr. Slinger sent $400 "for the orphans" promising Masses for Frs. Scannell, McGarvey and Bokel. From Cincinnati Peter Tracy wired: "More clothing for orphans to be sent this week. Telegraph me what's needed." In a message to C.G. Fisher, Esq. or Col. J. Prestidge of Memphis, Tracy wired: "Fr. Kelly telegraphs me the orphans need clothes and shoes. See him and managers of the other asylums and request our relief committee to cover all wants. It is well able. Money pouring in fast."

In a follow-up message to Fr. Kelly, Tracy said: "Call on C. G. Fisher or Col. Prestidge for supplies for orphans and sisters. May God protect you."

While it is impossible to note all donations, a sampling shows that hearts went out to the orphans and sisters. Peter McDevitt of Illinois sent $5 promising more if the plague continued; Patrick Egan of Somerset, Ohio, sent $5. Two ladies of St. Columba's Church, New York, sent $44; Al Zitterl of Madison, Wisconsin sent $75 for the sisters.[30]

Fr. Kelly, devastated by the number of children dying, contacted Bishop A.F. Feehan of Nashville to ask if the Memphis orphans could find refuge at St. Mary's Asylum, Nashville, until the epidemic subsided. The Bishop replied:

> I have delayed answering your telegram trying to make arrangements to provide for your orphans. Our asylum is over-crowded. We have 81 children there. I have spent two days trying to rent a place and offered to pay anything required but nobody here will rent a house. They are so much afraid of contagion. The only thing I could do is to build a temporary house on our asylum grounds which could be done in a few days. Could be ready by Monday or Tuesday next and with some room in this way I will most willingly provide for your orphans. Dispatch to say if this will do and in the dispatch do not mention the orphans. People are so easily alarmed. ... Praying that you may hold out.[31]

At last the welcome message came from Bishop Feehan:

> Send them on Monday. Let them bring no luggage or clothing but what they wear. We will provide everything.[32]

Sr. Thomas O'Meara accompanied 55 orphans ranging from infancy to 13 years to Nashville by train. Because people had an inexpressible terror of the disease few came near the children. People pressed against the train windows to look at them but wanted no contact. One good Samaritan pressed $10 into Sr. Thomas' hand and another brought her a pail of coffee with a tin cup. Even upon arrival at the Nashville depot the children were not allowed to get off. Instead the train backed up as close as possible to the asylum and the children walked across the fields to the house. Some men, having pity on the littlest ones, carried them. The refugees were not allowed to mingle with the St. Mary's children. Their clothes were burned; they had nothing to remind them of Memphis.[33]

Once her charges were safely settled, Sr. Thomas returned to Memphis to resume here work with fever victims. She and her companions found no relief as the scourge raged on. "Often when they returned home they could hardly get upstairs to bed." Before long from City Hospital, Market Street Infirmary and private homes, Kelly found 32 children bereft of parents. Each day the number of children increased. Once again he pleaded for clothes and necessities for them and the sisters.[34]

Towards the end of November Sr. M. Thomas was so worn out she told Kelly she couldn't stand being alone any longer and begged him to have the sisters who had gone to Kentucky and Nashville return.[35] The weather helped with a hard frost and Kelly wrote: "At length the end has come. The Brd. of Health now declares it is safe for absentees to return, so you may come home once more."[36]

Fr. Cubero had written to Kelly to tell him the sisters who had been sent to St. Catharine's "are happy and contented in their new home but they long for the day when you shall give orders to them to come back to their own home." Kelly's letter was the news they wanted.

Jubilant that the plague was subsiding Sr. Angela Lynch wrote to Kelly thanking him for all his services for the sisters and orphans and inviting him to the Motherhouse for a well-deserved rest. What a happy reunion took place when the exiled sisters and orphans joyfully returned, but life in Memphis had changed drastically. Five thousand had died within two months; Memphis would never be the same again. Undaunted the sisters and their charges "set to work full of hope for the coming years."

1879 Epidemic

One of the first things Sr. Thomas did was to arrange for the completion of the new St. Agnes Academy. In July, Kelly blessed the new buildings and said Mass in the convent chapel for the first time.[37] The respite was short-lived for the plague returned in 1879. Although it was not as virulent as that of the preceding year, nevertheless it engendered panic.

City officials urged people to leave the city if they possibly could. For those who could not leave, camps were erected on high ground outside the city. Despite the warnings, the sisters decided to enter their annual retreat with D.E. Reville, OP, as retreat master. At the close of retreat, sisters were evacuated to St. Catharine's, St. Mary's and St. Cecilia's but some remained to care for the sick at LaSalette and St. Peter's.

Fr. Reville wrote of them: "The sisters at LaSalette are well and zealously making the rounds, visiting the sick and picking up the orphans."[38] The orphanage was burgeoning but the Howard Association arranged for the sisters to take charge of all convalescent children left in the hands of the Howards at the close of the epidemic.[39] In November a welcome frost brought an end to the plague. The exiled sisters returned and school resumed even though enrollment was low.

When Kelly died August 7, 1885 the sisters and orphans were inconsolable at the loss of their best friend. With Kelly gone and the ranks of the sisters decimated, the Bishop decided to transfer the administration of the orphanage to the Sisters of Charity of Nazareth. St. Agnes sisters sent their carriage to convey their successors to the home.[40]

One more note is of interest before closing the story of the orphanage. Grace who had become Bishop of St. Paul, visited St. Agnes 37 years after leaving Memphis. He wanted to settle some business, namely a debt of $12,000 which he claimed the sisters owed for the foundation of the orphanage. The sisters made a statement regarding their 33 years of service:

> Our statement was of four sisters a year -- in reality there were often six -- estimate their remuneration at the miserable pittance of seventy-five dollars a year, added to which was five hundred dollars which in one of the epidemics was sent to us but which we in mistake sent to the Asylum and never asked for its return. The amount of our statement was ten thousand, five hundred dollars, with which he was fully satisfied that we owed nothing whatsoever.[41]

After Effects

As the enrollment at St. Agnes increased, sisters were withdrawn from local parochial schools to staff the Academy. They struggled to maintain a school for blacks begun in 1888 but closed in 1895.[42] In addition to St. Peter's Orphanage, the Sisters of Charity of Nazareth also took over St. Patrick's, while the Sisters of Charity of Cincinnati assumed responsibility for St. Brigid and the Franciscan Sisters of Lafayette, Indiana took charge of St. Mary's.[43] Even this did not alleviate the situation. Severely decimated by the yellow fever epidemics, depleted from scarcity of vocations and exhausted by their trials, the sisters examined their options. Since St. Catharine continuously sent reinforcements there was a strong bond with the Motherhouse. In the end the sisters, after prayerful consideration decided to affiliate with St. Catharine. The official date when Bishop Rademacher and Bishop McClosky approved of the affiliation was February 1888.[44]

Two novices who were transferred from St. Agnes to the Kentucky novitiate, Srs. Mary Oskamp and Imelda Brady, were later professed at St. Catharine.

After the merger when the first election of a superior took place at St. Catharine, difficulties arose. The St. Agnes sisters addressed their grievances to Msgr. Francisco Satolli, the first Apostolic Delegate to the United States.

> We the undersigned members of St. Agnes Community, Memphis, Tenn. branch of St. Catharine of Sienna Convent,

Unveiling of Memorial to Nuns of the Battlefields who nursed soldiers from both sides during the Civil War — on the right two Dominican sisters who attended the unveiling in Washington, D.C.

Cross in Memphis honoring the sisters who died in the yellow fever

Rev. James A. Kelly, O.P., often called "Father of the Orphans" because of his concern for them particularly during the yellow fever

THE WESTERN UNION TELEGRAPH COMPANY.

Dated *Cincinnati O* 21 187 8

Received at *Mem Sept. 21*

To *C G Fisher Esq*

or Col Jas S Prestidge

Father Kelly telegraphs me
the Orphans need clothes
& shoes see him
and managers of other
asylums & request our
relief Committee to Cover
all wants It is
well able, money pouring
in fast.

Peter Tracy

34 DH.

READ THE NOTICE AT THE TOP.

Telegrams of concern during the epidemic of yellow fever

HALF RATE MESSAGES.
297.

THE WESTERN UNION TELEGRAPH COMPANY.

Dated *Cincinnati O* 5 1878

Received at *Mem Sep 5 11 P*

To *Rev Father Kelly*

& Peters

Call on C G Fisher or Col
Prestidge for Supplies for
Orphans and the Sisters, May
God protect you

Peter Tracy

19 Daidy

297

READ THE NOTICE AT THE TOP.

ARCHIVES O. P.

Sr. Agnita Kavanaugh with her class at St. Michael's, Lowell in 1894

Students at Holy Rosary, Rosary Heights (Briartown), with Fr. Bernard, O.P and Srs. Celsa Nee and Francis Edward Sheehan

Sr. Winifred Miller with a class at Holy Rosary, Rosary Heights near Springfield, Kentucky

St. Joseph School, Mattoon, Illinois — the first mission house outside Kentucky, 1882

Early convent, St. Patrick's, Watertown, Massachusetts — the first mission in the East, 1888

Dismissal at St. Francis deSales School, Charlestown, Massachusetts

St. Catharine of Sienna in the Valley

After the fire in 1904

The so-called "paper house" in which the sisters lived temporarily

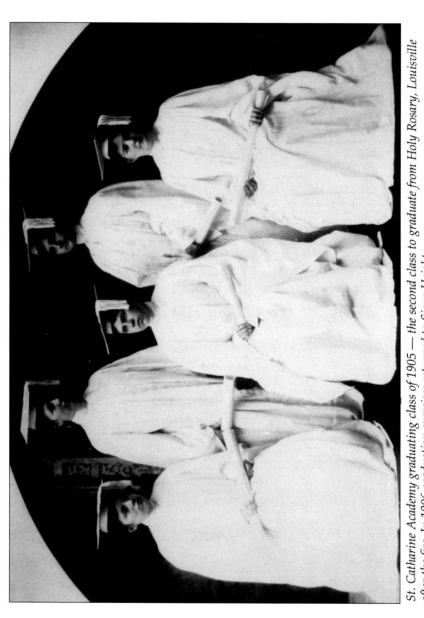

St. Catharine Academy graduating class of 1905 — the second class to graduate from Holy Rosary, Louisville after the fire. In 1906 graduation exercises returned to Siena Heights

*St. Catharine rebuilt on
the Heights 1904*

*A view of St. Catharine
from the cemetery*

Gateway to St. Catharine

St. Catharine's Academy,

SPRINGFIELD, KY.

REPORT OF DEPORTMENT AND SCHOLARSHIP.

Miss Lena Cissell. Academic Course

For Quarter ending Nov. 15. 1901.

Attendance	95	Geometry	95			Piano	
Deportment	97	Book-keeping	90			Violin	
Politeness	100	Stenography		Music		Harp	
Neatness	95	Typewriting				M'nd'ln	
Penmanship	80	Elocution	85			Guitar	
Composition	80	Drawing				Vocal	
Epistolary Essays	95	Painting				Latin	90
Arithmetic		Needlework		Languages		French	
Algebra	95	Plain Sewing	100			Germ'n	

PREPARATORY A.		PREPARATORY B.		PREPARATORY C.	
Christian Doctrine	94	Christian Doctrine	94	Christian Doctrine	
Orthography	97	Orthography	91	Orthography	
Reading	93	Reading	93	Reading	
Grammar	90	Grammar	90	Grammar	
Geography	95	Geography	97	Geography (No. 2.)	
Physiology		Bible History	84	Bible History	
Ancient History	98	U. S. History	90	U. S. History	
Mythology	100	Physiology		Arithmetic	
Mathematics A.B.	96	Arithmetic	94		

In above Report 100 per cent. is the highest attainable record in any branch, and all figures above 80 per cent. are satisfactory.

Sr. Raphael

You should be very proud of the nice reports. Mrs Cissell.

Report card of Lena Cissell, 1901

Academy transportation to Springfield, Kentucky

St. Catharine Post Office

Sr. Virginia Thomas Hamilton, Postmaster and Sr. Francine Eaton, Assistant

Springfield, Ky. do by these presents most respectfully and solemnly protest against an election for Mother Prioress to take place the 25inst. at St. Catharine Convent, Springfield, Ky. Because of the irregularity of certain proceedings antecedent to said election. The irregular proceedings are as follows. 1st The exclusion of rightful votes. There are two ex-prioresses here present who have not been given the opportunity of expressing a voice in the Chapter, Sr. Josephine Beck and Sr. Mary Thomas O'Meara. The following is taken from the Rule "The Prioress shall be elected by the Ex-Prioresses, the Sub-Prioress, the Mistress of Novices. All Sisters of the Council and all other Sisters six years professed living at the Motherhouse. Together with these another shall be elected from each Mission House that has six sisters who have also the rights to vote for the Prioress. 2nd Lay Sisters have been allowed a voice in the election of Socius.

Permit me to say here by way of parenthesis that we are encumbered at present with two Rules — one of long standing which has received the confirmation of Rome April 1822. The other of recent construction the author being the Rt. Rev. Bishop McCloskey, not yet as far as we can learn confirmed at Rome. The first objection mentioned above is based with equal force on either Rule. The Second objection finds force only on the supposition of the second Rule still existing. We maintain the election should be carried on as formerly, viz. that every Sister belonging to St. Catherine's Community except the four lay Sisters should have a voice.

We appeal to you that justice be done us. Another Act we would place before you as we have been told we must observe the Rule given by the Bishop till Rome will decide another. The Sisters here asked the Bishop for permission to elect our local Superioress but he refused. One has been appointed by what authority we know not.... [45]

A reply from Sr. Vincent Ferrer Thompson, Prioress at St. Catharine, informed the St. Agnes community, "As St. Agnes has not been a Priory since the affiliation it is my duty to appoint a Vicaress until higher authority decides otherwise."[46] She appointed Sr. M. Joseph Howard to the position and added, "Sisters Bertrand, Rose, Stanislaus and Mary Vincent will take their place and rank according to age in choir." These four lay sisters replaced their black scapular with a white one, were given voting rights and were henceforth choir sisters. These changes were probably received with mixed feeling on both sides but St. Agnes sisters had weathered war, epidemics, fire; for the sake of the mission they bowed to the inevitable.

Chapter Nine Notes

1. Copy of SCNA material transferred to Memphis Diocesan office on Sept. 13, 1979.
2. Ibid.
3. SCA, Peters, Chronicles (hereafter referred to as Peters).
4. Copy of SCNA material in Memphis Diocesan office.
5. Ibid. This indicates that the troops were in contact with the Dominican sisters. It is possible that they had a small encampment on the grounds.
6. SJPA, Memo of Receipts and Disbursements.
7. SJPA, *Freeman's Journal*, Sept. 17, 1864.
8. SJPA, Copy of letter from Mother Ursula Wiedman to Rev. J. Larkin. Original in Nashville Diocesan archives, not dated.
9. Capers, Gerald, *Biography of a River Town*, pp. 127, 128.
10. J.M. Keating, *History of Yellow Fever*, Memphis, Vol. 1, p. 441.
11. S.R. Bruesch, MD, *Journal of Tennessee Medical Association*, Dec. 1978, Vol. 71 No. 12, p. 889.
12. Edwards, Richard, *In Memoriam of the Lamented Dead Who Fell In the Epidemic of 1873*, p. 27.
13. *The Commercial Appeal*, Memphis, Oct. 31, 1978.
14. SCA, Peters, *Shadowed*, unpublished manuscript, p. 1.
15. *American Heritage*, Vol. 35, No. 6, 1984, p. 57 "Epidemic."
16. Ibid.
17. SCA, Peters, *Shadowed*, p. 2.
18. Capers, *Biography of a River Town*, p. 192.
19. Ibid., p. 188.
20. SCA, Peters, *Shadowed*, p. 3.
21. Ibid.

22. Leo Kalmer, *Stronger Than Death,* pp. 19, 20. This account mentions two metal coffins. Cf. with account of Sr. Roberta Ross (SCA) on exhumation of these bodies. Three metal caskets were found.

23. SCA, St. Agnes Annals, p. 51.

24. Ibid.

25. Ibid., pp. 55, 56.

26. Ibid.

27. Ibid., p. 71.

28. SJPA, Copy of letter of Sr. Josephine Beck, OSD, June 4, 1918, to Brother Joseph Dutton.

29. SJPA, Kelly file.

30. SJPA. All correspondence and telegrams are from the file on yellow fever at Providence College.

31. Ibid.

32. Ibid.

33. SCA, St. Agnes Annals, p. 71 ff.

34. SJPA, letter of Fr. Kelly to Col. J.S. Prestidge dated Sept. 23, 1878.

35. SCA, St. Agnes Annals, p. 80.

36. Ibid., p. 81.

37. Minogue, *Pages:* p. 137; Kalmer, *Stronger Than Death,* p. 21.

38. Reville died of the disease September 16, 1879.

39. SJPA, *Freeman's Journal,* August 30, 1879.

40. SCNA, copy of document in Memphis Diocesan Archives.

41. SCA, Annals of St. Agnes, Bk. 1, Oct. 11, 1896.

42. SCA, Peters. Daily attendance numbered about 167 children. The St. Agnes sisters taught there 11 years under difficult circumstances, but the seed they planted grew to fruition later when the Josephite Fathers started St. Anthony, an exclusively black parish with its own school.

43. SCA, original letter from Sr. Fides Gough, OP, Memphis file, undated.

44. SCA, St. Agnes Profession Book. St. Agnes Profession Book also records some Council decisions. The sisters themselves rejected a merger with St. Cecilia (p. 212) and approved affiliation with St. Catharine in October 1887.

45. SCA, copy of letter dated July 12, 1894. Signed by: Hyacinth Cooper, Vilana Young, Veronica Livers, Catharine Hoar, Evangelist Nunan, Gertrude Rapp, Teresa Webb, Thomas O'Meara, M. Bernard Spalding.

46. SCA, letter from Sr. Vincent Ferrer Thompson to St. Agnes community dated August 11, 1894.

Chapter Ten

CLOUDS OF
UNKNOWING

SOMETIMES AN ASSET may also be a liability. Such was the case with the freedom of movement of the early Dominican sisters. Their mobility left them free to answer the needs of the times, but this same freedom created obscure lines of governance. In the first Constitutions of the Kentucky Dominican sisters there were no statutes for governing the community, nor was mention made of apostolic ministry.[1] The sisters lived under this constitutions for seventy-three years.

Members of the Kentucky, Ohio and Tennessee foundations frequently were missioned together, their bond being the mission of the Order. Their experience as they grew — Kentucky, 1822; Ohio, 1830; Tennessee, 1851— was of a family helping each other out, always feeling welcome in a Dominican house. When Sinsinawa was founded in 1847 three sisters from Ohio went to Wisconsin to help them get started.[2]

Jandel's letter of 1864 introduced a new dimension. He pointed out that individual institutions were under the Ordinary of the diocese in which they were located and the Dominican Provincial no longer would assign the sisters to various houses.

The question of property ownership presented further complications. St. Catharine had two schools in Louisville, Holy Rosary Academy and St. Louis Bertrand. Since there was no convent for the teachers at St. Louis Bertrand, the sisters lived at

Holy Rosary, a community-owned institution. These loose arrangements added to the confusion which developed with a new foundation in Illinois.

Fr. P.J. Macken, pastor of Our Savior, Jacksonville, Illinois, had spoken to his bishop about recruiting sisters to teach in his school. He wanted sisters who would teach boys as well as girls. His cousin, J.A. McShane, OP, suggested that he contact the sisters at St. Catharine. Bishop Baltes wrote to Mother Regina O'Meara requesting six sisters. On April 15, 1873, she answered his letter.

> Dear Bishop,
>
> Owing to my absence from home, your esteemed favor has not had the prompt attention it should have had. And in reply, I would state that Our Rule is that of St. Augustin (sic) and the Constitutions were taken from the Great Order and from those of the Second Order.
>
> ...All the houses outside the diocese of Louisville are independent as we expect the proposed house in Jacksonville to be likewise independent. We would however, prefer their (sic) not opening a Novitiate, say for four or five years. All we would expect of the Sisters who go there is that they maintain themselves. If they contract debts they must be responsible for them. For further information I refer you to the Fathers of the Order, St. Rose Convent, Springfield, Ky. Trusting this will prove satisfactory. I am, Rt. Rev. Bishop, in our Lord and St. Dominic, Sister Regina, O.S.D. Prioress.[4]

For some unknown reason, the Bishop did not answer the letter. Since there was no response, Mother Regina and the Council decided to assign the sisters originally intended for Jacksonville to other missions. Imagine her consternation when Fr. Macken appeared in Kentucky in August begging for the sisters whom he thought had been promised!

Fr. Cubero, chaplain at St. Catharine, convoked a meeting of the Council to organize a colony for Jacksonville. Each sister was to nominate five members to go to the new mission. The results were: Sr. Rachel six, Sr. Josephine five, Sr. Cecilia five, Sr. Mary Agnes eight, Sr. Alberta four, Sr. Frances four. The tie between the last two was decided in favor of Sr. Alberta since she was older. The Council then decided to send a sixth sister choosing Sr. Osanna Powell.[5]

Sr. Josephine and Sr. Rachel each received four votes to be superior. Fr. Cubero broke the tie with a casting vote in favor of Sr. Josephine.[6]

Within forty-eight hours Mother Regina had six sisters ready to leave for Illinois which at that time seemed like the other end of the world. Because of their hasty departure there was no time for good-byes or departure ceremony. The little group left St. Catharine, August 18, 1873.

As they were leaving Sr. Rachel asked, "Mother, how soon may we return to St. Catharine?" "Sisters, you may all return at the close of the second scholastic year," was the reply. Little did they know what lay ahead.[7] They were missionaries in the truest sense of the word.

The Foundresses

SR. JOSEPHINE MEAGHER, born in Ireland, journeyed to America at age 15. Her widowed mother who became ill on the long voyage, died shortly after arriving in New Orleans. T.T. Ryan, OP, uncle of the orphaned children, enrolled the two girls at St. Catharine Academy and their brother at St. Rose, in Kentucky.[8] Later both girls entered the novitiate. Josephine kept her baptismal name while her sister became Sr. Raymunda. The latter taught at Holy Rosary, Louisville and Sacred Heart, Effingham, Illinois.[9] She died in 1903.

Sr. Josephine served as prefect of discipline at St. Catharine Academy until she was sent to Holy Rosary, Louisville. During the Civil War she assisted with the care of sick and wounded soldiers of both sides. She served 15 years as major superior in Illinois.

SR. RACHEL CONWAY, a Canadian by birth, was originally a member of the Sinsinawa Dominicans but later transferred to St. Catharine. An accomplished musician, she taught piano, harp and violin besides conducting a children's choir and playing the organ for liturgical services.

SR. CECILIA CAREY, who was from Wisconsin, probably entered St. Catharine because her brother had joined the friars at St. Rose. She succeeded Sr. Josephine as second prioress in 1888. Her term was extremely difficult because of illness among the sisters, heavy financial debts and the gnawing uncertainty about the status of the Illinois sisters with their old Kentucky home.

SR. M. AGNES MAGUIRE, born in New York, had an older sister, Sr. Vincentia, at St. Catharine. Before going to Illinois she taught for five years in Louisville. When Srs. Rachel and Alberta were struck down with spinal meningitis in 1874, Sr. M. Agnes was in charge of the school. To assist with teaching, she hired Ms. Mary Healey, another example of collaboration with laity for the sake of the mission.[10]

SR. ALBERTA RUMPFF had experience teaching at St. Agnes, Memphis, before joining the missionaries to Illinois. During the Civil War she served in the Memphis City Hospital among Confederate troops. Her own brother was one of the patients. After laboring in Illinois for seven years she returned to St. Catharine because of ill health.[11]

SR. OSANNA POWELL was sick with tuberculosis when she was sent to Jacksonville. In Kentucky she had been noted for her cooking and baking but the rigors of life in the new foundation proved too much for her. She returned to St. Catharine late in 1873 and died there the following year.[12]

The Dilemma

The sisters labored wholeheartedly in Illinois to establish their new school. Although they were poor and their quarters were cramped, they felt they could stand it for two years after which they would all return to their "old home" in Kentucky. They had a cruel awakening.

In 1875, as the sisters started to pack, the pastor, P.J. Macken, informed them that they were no longer affiliated with St. Catharine, that in fact, they had been sent out by Mother Regina to start an independent foundation with its own motherhouse and novitiate. Who were they to believe? The pastor who recruited them? Or Mother Regina, their prioress who had assured them they could return in two years?

The answer may lie in the explanation of the word "independent." Since the Motherhouse was poor it was unlikely that it could subsidize an institution outside the state of Kentucky. Regina's letter stipulated, ..."all we expect of the Sisters who go there is that they maintain themselves. If they contract debts they must be responsible for them." In other words, such establishments had to be *financially* independent. This in no way extended to the charism, service and cooperation among the sisters.

Sisters were assigned by the Provincial of the Order to where the need seemed the greatest. A prime example of the interchange of personnel was Sr. Benven Sansbury. Professed at St. Catharine, she became a foundress at St. Mary of the Springs, was assigned to St. Agnes, then to St. Mary, Nashville before returning to Ohio. To the sisters this freedom of movement did not seem unusual since they all belonged to the Dominican Order.

When Sr. Osanna became ill in late 1873, Mother Regina welcomed her back to Kentucky and sent Sr. Thomas Wight as a replacement. In 1874 when spinal meningitis struck down three sisters, Mother Regina sent Srs. M. Catherine Young and Thomasina Simpson to the relief of the neophyte community. How could a person this compassionate be so insensitive as to send them off without telling them it was to establish a new foundation cut off from the Motherhouse? Was the lapse in communication due to the haste with which the transaction took place? Or was it that Mother Regina did not anticipate the local ordinary to be involved with assignments of the sisters?

What about Fr. Cubero? He voted at the meeting of the Kentucky Council when it was deciding who should be sent to Illinois. He cast the deciding vote for Sr. Josephine as superior. As chaplain, friend and advisor, how could he later claim he did not understand what was happening? Or did he, too, think that the sisters could move freely from one place to another since they were all a part of the Dominican family? He, himself, was an example of the freedom of movement among the friars.

To add to the dilemma, when three became severely ill, Fr. Macken felt sorry for them and obtained permission from Bishop Baltes for them to travel elsewhere to recuperate, "but not to the old home." Sr. Rachel spent the summer at Sinsinawa, Wisconsin; Sr. Thomasina stayed at her father's home in Springfield, Kentucky; Srs. Josephine and Alberta went to the latter's home, Washington, D.C. While there, they enjoyed visiting the sisters from St. Catharine missioned in Washington.

Macken, blaming himself because of their "meager space and unsanitary environment,"[13] hoped to improve their situation by having them move into the spacious rectory built by his predecessor, Fr. Joseph DeCosta. The building, originally intended as a retreat house,[14] would be ideal for the sisters except for complications regarding ownership of property. Macken wanted them to buy the building but the sisters felt that decision was reserved to Kentucky. He tried to convince them that the decision was theirs. Not only that, but Bishop Baltes approved.[15]

While urging a speedy conclusion to the sale Macken realized the sisters were totally unaware that they were supposed to be a separate foundation. When he mentioned the letter Mother Regina had written to Bishop Baltes, their dismay and disbelief were such that to convince them he obtained the letter from the chancery, asking them to copy it and return the original to him. (Letter is given earlier in this chapter.) The letter seemed clear to the pastor and bishop. To them independent meant separate and self-governing.

With great sadness, the sisters halted their packing for the long-awaited return trip to Kentucky. Later, Sr. Josephine expressed her feelings in a poem.

> The bitter scenes of "seventy-four and five,"
> When fever's fetid breath prostrated four,
> And scarcely left a gleam of hope alive
> In brave, courageous soul - we must pass o'er
> The severing from old Kentucky home,
> For, from eternity God had decreed
> Far from the Valley they were doomed to roam
> To sow on distant soil His precious seed.

With nigh broke hearts whose ev'ry fibre twined
Around the dear old home and Sisters true,
But, good Dominicans, they were resigned
 To leave the Valley where the lilies grew;
And tho' their hearts seemed doomed to break and bleed,
Had they not bowed in resignation there,
The loving Spouse might ne'er have come to feed
And gather in lilies in our garden fair.16

Sr. Josephine added a note to her personal copy of Mother Regina's letter.

> N.B. This letter was sent us by B. Baltes from the Cathedral Chancery Office, Alton, Ill. May 15, 1873, requesting that it be returned to him after we viz; Sisters Osanna, Rachel, Alberta, Cecilia, M. Agnes and Josephine took a copy of it and see for ourselves the condition on which we were sent to the Diocese of Alton. This was in Sr. M. Benven's writing. I could tell you more but enough now. Sr. Cecilia and I took a copy like this to Fr. Cubero in 1877 which seemed like a revelation to him and he was kind to us. God rest the dear souls of all.[17]

The two bishops concerned (Baltes and McCloskey) agreed to arrangements for the independent foundation. The sisters, though at first bitter, felt that all had acted in good faith, there was a misunderstanding which no one could properly place, but "Bishop Baltes had the might of justice in his favor and there was nothing for the rest to do but to bow to the inevitable and accept the situation as gracefully as possible."[18] In 1891 the motherhouse was moved to Springfield, Illinois, and the community became known as Our Lady of the Sacred Heart. Despite the pain over the misunderstanding, love for their Kentucky roots never wavered among the Illinois pioneers. An entry in the annals reads,

> A well-remembered anniversary. The Nineteenth return of the day which brought the Dominican sisters to Jacksonville. It was always celebrated by a little entertainment on the evening of the day commemorative of the event and a memorial of the "Old Kentucky Home."[19]

They never forgot "down in the Valley where the lilies grew." The "March lilies," the jonquils, were always a symbol of hope despite a winter of hardships.

Before moving on from the story of the Illinois foundation there is an event involving two of the foundresses which deserves mention. In their second year at Jacksonville, Srs. Josephine and Rachel shared honors unexpectedly at the dedication of a monument in Springfield, Illinois to the assassinated Abraham Lincoln. President Ulysses Grant, mindful of the heroic services of women religious during the Civil War, wanted the Lincoln memorial unveiled by some sisters. The Ursuline sisters who were located in the city declined the invitation because of their cloister regulations. General Sherman who was in attendance to the president observed, "If I had my sisters of St. Dominic here they would not disappoint me."[20] Fr. Macken on hearing this said, "I have Dominican sisters at Jacksonville." Without delay, permission was obtained from Bishop Baltes and the president's train was dispatched to bring the sisters to Springfield. Srs. Josephine and Rachel represented all the sisters who had served during the Civil War.

> "In the procession which began moving at ten o'clock, and which preceded the ceremonies, the President, with the attendant generals dressed in full regalia, occupied the first carriage, while the second bore the unveilers whose humble, though peerless, black and white garb formed a contrast to those about them. So great and so dense was the mass of people that it was necessary for the military to clear a space through the crowd to enable them to reach the monument, where upon its concourse the two Sisters occupied seats of honor near President Grant, at the base of the obelisk against which stood the Statue of Lincoln.[21]

After the unveiling the sisters slipped quietly away to return to Jacksonville. They were not forgotten. The Illinois State Historical Society has a figurine on display honoring Mother Josephine for her contribution to education. She is identified as "A lady who found happiness in a useful life."[22] She died January 12, 1925, a victim of influenza.

Sr. Rachel died February 12, 1911, during a commemoration

of Lincoln's birthday. The committee in charge of the celebration ascertained the time of her funeral. When the funeral cortege passed the monument of Lincoln which she had helped to unveil, hymns were played and a squad of honor stood at attention in honor of Sr. Rachel and all the sisters who had served on the battlefield.[23]

Fall River Dominicans

The foundation of Jacksonville, Illinois, was a problem for Mother Regina, for the sisters involved and for the Bishop of the diocese. It is often difficult to piece together retrospectively what actually happened. In a somewhat similar vein, the freedom of movement among sisters at that time, reveals how this itineracy caused complications. To persevere in circumstances surrounding establishment of some schools. sisters had to be women of indomitable faith and unflagging courage. Such is the story of Mother Bertrand Sheridan and the Fall River Dominicans.

In 1869 the Dominican fathers appealed to Kentucky for sisters to join a contingent from St. Mary, Somerset, who had founded a school in Washington, D.C. the previous year.[24] Srs. Louise Hayden, Aloysia Sheridan and Aquin Montgomery left Kentucky for the capital city to join the Ohio group comprising Srs. Philomena McDonough, Aloysia Crossen, Columba and Cecilia Dittoe. To avoid confusion, Sr. Aloysia Sheridan changed her name to Bertrand.[25]

Soon, Srs. Teresa Kivlahan, Philomena and Sibylina Sheridan (the three Sheridans were siblings) all of whom had been professed at St. Catharine and missioned to Nashville, arrived to complete the membership. The intention of this ten was to form an independent unit of Third Order Dominican Sisters.[26]

In 1870 they were incorporated as the Academy of the Sacred Heart of Mary with Sr. Bertrand as Mother. According to their Charter, they had the right to receive and care for all acceptable novices who presented themselves for admission,[27] but few women presented themselves and death took a steady toll. One of the deaths which determined the fate of the community was that of Teresa Kivlahan.

She had so impressed her companions with her holiness and heroic virtue that when she died they began to pray to her to intercede for them in heaven. Lay people who had known her, kept her grave covered with white flowers. There were stories of miracles. Articles appeared in local papers about pilgrimages to her grave in Mt. Olivet cemetery.

Fearful of the cult which was developing before the Church had examined or approved of the sanctity of Teresa, Archbishop Gibbons (later Cardinal), appointed a commission to investigate the alleged miracles and prophecies. The result was that public demonstrations and private devotions were prohibited and the sisters were told to cease veneration of Teresa. Although they agreed to obey the injunction, further trouble erupted alienating the sisters from the friars and the Archbishop when Mother Bertrand refused to allow two professed sisters to make final vows.[28] Gibbons, siding with the friars, asked that these sisters be given a further trial but Mother Bertrand refused, saying they already had five years. Outraged by what he considered insubordination by Mother Bertrand, he asked her to leave.

Furthermore, concerned because of the few members to carry on the work in his diocese, he decided the sisters should be suppressed or affiliated with a larger, growing community. He appealed to Mother Emily Power to accept the faltering foundation as an affiliate of Sinsinawa.[29] Before agreeing to this, Mother Emily and Sr. Alberta Duffy visited the Washington house. Mother Bertrand and Sr. Gertrude Roney had already gone to New York to visit some cloistered Dominicans.

Mother Emily accepted the affiliation under certain terms, namely, that the friars not interfere with the governing of the sisters who would have an ecclesiastical advisor from Sinsinawa, and secondly, that the house be subject to the rules and regulations of Sinsinawa. Eight of the Washington sisters were accepted while Sr. Aquin Montgomery transferred to the Dominicans in Springfield, Illinois. When Srs. Bertrand and Gertrude returned, they asked Mother Emily for acceptance but were refused. Then began the wanderings of Sr. Bertrand.

Rejected by Sinsinawa, Srs. Bertrand and Gertrude went to St.

Cecilia's, Nashville, Tennessee, in 1882.[30] As experienced teachers, both were eagerly welcomed and invited to stay as long as they wished. Sr. Bertrand became novice mistress. In 1886, Sr. Gertrude was accepted for membership in the Nashville community but Sr. Bertrand was not for reasons now obscure. Her brother, James Sheridan, OP, invited her to begin a foundation in his parish, Holy Name, Kansas City, Missouri. She and Sr. Gertrude traveled there accompanied by Sr. M. Anna Scoales, one of Bertrand's novices who had been professed at St. Cecilia in December, 1884. Their hopes were dashed when Fr. Sheridan was replaced by Fr. Devereaux who did not want them. After they floundered for seven weeks in Kansas City, Bishop John J. Hogan directed them to Carrollton, Missouri. Extreme poverty and constant fevers weakened them beyond human endurance. When the Dominican fathers of Lewiston, Maine, asked for English-speaking sisters to teach in their bilingual school, the invitation was accepted.[31]

Fr. Mothon, Vicar for the Canadian Dominican Province, arranged for Srs. Gertrude and M. Anna to meet a superior of a French community who was visiting in New York. "The rendezvous failed." Undaunted, the sisters proceeded to Lewiston to meet Fr. Mothon in person, only to find he had left for France to recruit French sisters. The friars in Lewiston suggested that the two sisters stop in Fall River. Although they were warmly received, nothing was said about a foundation. Later the sisters received a letter from Fr. Estava, the Superior, asking them to return to Fall River. With alacrity, Bertrand, M. Anna and Catherine set out on August 30, 1891, the feast of St. Rose of Lima. They reached their destination five days later. Srs. Philomena Sheridan and Gertrude Roney remained in Carrollton only long enough to settle affairs and close the house.[32] At last, Mother Bertrand and her companions had come to the place where God intended them to found the Fall River Dominicans. In July, 1922, they were formally erected as a Congregation by Bishop Daniel F. Feehan.[33] The Fall River Dominicans wrote in one of their brochures: "our Mission is thus one of the many ramifications of the first shrub planted and watered by the toil of Mother Angela and her first daughters."[34]

Chapter Ten Notes

1. Green, p. 21.
2. SHDA, also Winterbauer, p. 13.
3. Green, p. 23.
   Copy of Jandel's letter SCA
4. SCA copy of letter written by Prioress Regina O'Meara to Bishop P.J. Baltes dated April 15, 1873. Original in Springfield, Illinois diocesan archives.
5. SCA, August 18, 1873. Profession Book (End Section) p. 1.
6. Ibid.
7. Winterbauer, p. 16.
8. SHDA
9. Minogue, *Pages,* pp. 122, 177.
10. Winterbauer, p. 16.
    Springfield Dominican, March 1991, p. 5
    SHDA annals, p. 6.
11. Winterbauer, p. 14.
12. Ibid.
13. Winterbauer, p. 64.
14. SHDA September 26, 1875.
15. Winterbauer, p. 63-64. "It was decided that Sr. Josephine should notify Mother (Regina) that they had presumed permission to negotiate with Fr. Macken on his own terms. And so it came to pass that a Founding Sisters of the Springfield Dominicans purchased a convent for their foundation blindly."
16. Graham, *Dominicans in Illinois.* In an unpaginated section in the back of the book is a poem titled *Our Pioneer's Story* written by Sr. Josephine, dated August 15, 1908. "The valley where the lilies grew" brings to mind the profusion of March lilies (jonquils) every spring in Siena Vale and so dear to Kentucky Dominicans.
17. SCA copy of letter, also papers of Sr. Josephine, SHDA.
    Underlines on her copy.
18. SHDA Sr. Josephine's papers.
    Cf. Winterbauer for poignant account, pp. 72-73.
19. SHDA Sr. Josephine's papers.
    Also, Carberry, Historical Sketches.
20. *Illinois State Journal,* January 13, 1925.
21. Graham, pp. 85-95.
    Jolly, p. 106.
    Winterbauer, pp. 49-53.
22. Illinois State Historical Library, *12 Women in a Pioneer World* by Janette C. Powell, pp. 22, 23.
23. *Springfield Dominican,* December 1990, p. 4. Through the efforts of Ellen

Ryan Jolly, author of *Nuns of the Battlefield*, a monument was erected in Washington, D.C. to the memory and in honor of the sisters who served the troops during the Civil War. The generosity of the Ancient Order of Hibernians and Ladies Auxiliary in America made this monument possible.

24. Minogue, *Pages*, p. 125.

25. Srs. Philomena McDonough and Columba Dittoe were foundresses of St. Cecilia, Nashville, Tennessee in 1860.

26. O'Connor, *Five Decades*, p. 265.

27. Ibid.

28. Coffey, *The American Dominicans*, p. 478 passim and O'Connor, *Five Decades*, p. 268 passim.

29. AAB, Archdiocesan Archives, Baltimore.

30. Masserano, *The Nashville Dominicans*, p. 20.

31. AFRD. As children, the Sheridans had attended school in Canada and hence were bilingual.

32. Ibid.

33. Ibid.

34. Copy, *Beginnings*, April 30, 1979, brochure relating a brief history of the Dominican Sisters, Congregation of St. Catherine of Siena, Fall River, Massachusetts.

MOVING INTO A NEW CENTURY

WHILE THE UNITED STATES was still re-
garded as missionary territory, Ireland sent some of her most
gifted sons and daughters here who helped form the American
Catholic church. Among them from County Tipperary were the
three young O'Meara women who became Kentucky Domini-
cans. Sr. M. Thomas was the courageous, compassionate heroine
of the yellow fever epidemics in Memphis.[1] From there in May
1864, J.A. Kelly, OP, brought her to Nashville to take over the
orphanage.[2] She developed typhoid fever and died just a short
time later at age 28. She was buried July 8, 1864, at St. Cecilia's,
the "first of our sisters to die in Nashville."[3]

Regina O'Meara, OP

The youngest of the three sisters, Mother Regina, served six
terms as major superior. She began her teaching career at St.
Catharine Academy and later went to Holy Rosary, Louisville.
When at age 30 she was elected for the first time as leader of the
community she could hardly believe her ears. With reluctance
she assumed office.[4] That she was a kind and well-loved leader
is attested by the number of times she was re-elected. She was a
beautiful woman with clear blue eyes, a firm jaw but a mouth
ready to break into a smile. During her various terms three mis-

sions were opened in Kentucky: 1882, St. Dominic, Springfield; 1886, St. Bridget, Louisville and Holy Trinity, Fredericktown.

An innovation she began was sending sisters to teach in the Washington County schools, Kentucky: St. Agnes, 1880; Cecil- ville and Smith schools, 1881. In effect, the sisters were teaching in public schools drawing a salary from the state. These were two room buildings with a pot-bellied, woodburning stove for heating in the winter. Usually two sisters divided the classes, one teaching the first four grades and the other teaching fifth through eighth. School began one half hour early so that religion could be taught. A member of the school board visited once a month but there were no complaints for they were pleased with the quality of education.[5] However, the sisters were disap- pointed that the children were pulled out of school many times to help with the farm, particularly the boys. In later years, these three schools merged into St. Rose school, Springfield.

The opening of the separate foundation in Jacksonville (later moved to Springfield, Illinois) was reported in the preceding chapter. It took eighteen years before that hurt and misunder- standing were healed. Undoubtedly, Mother Regina must have been distressed by this turn of events, but to date no records have been discovered where she discusses what happened. She continued to send sisters to Illinois: St. Joseph, Mattoon, 1882; St. Charles, Marshal, 1884; St. Mary, Paris, 1885. It was clear that these were branch houses dependent on the Motherhouse, yet each has its own important story. Each is connected with the his- tory of the church, the establishment of parochial education and the growth of the Congregation.

The sisters always responded to the needs of the times. When a tornado smashed through Mattoon killing 50 and leaving hun- dreds homeless, the sisters opened their home to the victims, did what they could to alleviate pain and loss, and offered their services to assist nurses at Memorial Hospital.[6] The people cher- ished the relationship with the sisters and said that their pres- ence inspired hope reminding all that "life is more than materi- alism and competition."[7]

Sandwiched in between Regina's second and third terms was a three year period during which Angela Lynch was major superior from 1876 to 1879. As an experienced and dedicated educator she was concerned about the children of the freed blacks. C.L. Egan, OP, prior of St. Rose, shared her anxiety about these children and asked her to help establish a school for them in what was than called Briartown, now known as Rosary Heights.

The sisters appealed to relatives and friends for contributions for a school. Fr. Cubero responded generously as did Frances and Rose Howe. Others offered services to help with the building. Because the school was not ready for opening session, a black woman, Mary Spalding, offered the use of two rooms in her own home. Enrollment was excellent and the school flourished until 1914. It was reopened in 1930, but like many other schools, was forced to close in 1966.

Moving Eastward to the Sea

During Mother Regina's fourth term in office, Archbishop (later Cardinal) James Gibbons called the third plenary council of Baltimore which lasted from November 9 to December 7, 1884.[8] Among the results of the council was the preparation of the Baltimore catechisms and legislation requiring the building of elementary schools in all parishes. With the opening of these schools, pastors began seeking sisters to teach in them.

Since the labors of Kentucky Dominicans were confined to inland states for sixty-six years, it was a big step when Mother Regina decided to open a branch house in Massachusetts. Once again, it was the recommendation of a Dominican priest which brought about the contact. When the first request for sisters in Illinois was made, it was J.A. McShane, OP, who suggested Kentucky Dominicans to his cousin, Fr. P.J. Macken. When Fr. Robert P. Stack wanted to start an elementary school at St. Patrick, Watertown, his friend, Louis O'Neil, OP, suggested Kentucky Dominicans.

St. Patrick, Watertown, Massachusetts

Mother Regina arranged for seven sisters from the Bluegrass to make the long journey to Yankeedom in 1888. The first group included: Srs. Vincentia Maguire, Vincent Ferrer Thompson, Agnes Hunt, Bertrand Sheehan, Cecilia Kennedy, Bridget Connelly and Margaret Hamilton. Because of a large enrollment, two more sisters joined them, Srs. Mary Oskamp and Imelda Brady.[9]

The convent was not ready when they arrived but Fr. Stack offered them his own dwelling temporarily. Popular sentiment against Catholics still prevailed in Massachusetts. Although the sisters endured persecution and bigotry when they opened St. Patrick School in 1888, before long they had won the hearts of the people.[10] Opening enrollment numbered 400 children. In three years a high school for girls was opened and a year later it became coeducational.[11]

Obviously, Fr. Stack was pleased with arrangements which included an annual salary of $175 for each teaching sister, plus house, coal, wood, water, bed, bedding and house furniture. In his enthusiasm he wrote to Mother Regina:

> Not only will the sisters of St. Dominic open a house in Watertown; but I have already the promise of another Clergyman, that he intends to build a school and place it under their charge. Provided an opportunity presented itself immediately could you supply a certain Pastor of this Archdiocese with twelve teaching sisters? The place is all that you or any community could desire.[12]

It is interesting that the pastor set aside two rooms for music. In later years and on other missions, teaching private music pupils became an important means of providing additional income to supplement the meager salaries and to make it possible to carry on the mission.

For southern women the transition must have been monumental. Their ears had to attune to a nasal New England twang from the sound of a laid-back southern drawl. Food was different and the pace of life was unlike what they had known, for New England was leading the way in the industrial revolution and the feminist movement. For some, seeing the Atlantic Ocean for the first time was an exciting event.

St. Michael, Lowell, Massachusetts

Leading the industrial revolution was the city of Lowell with its canals and mills. The mills lured women out of their homes into the work force. When hundreds of immigrants, mostly Irish women, began to work in the mills, pastors became concerned about the children. At St. Michael, Lowell, Fr. William O'Brien felt it was more important to build a school than to complete the construction of the church, just a basement at that time. Influenced by what had been accomplished at St. Patrick's in one short year, he appealed to Mother Regina for teachers. In August 1889 Srs. Raymond Bird, Alexia O'Sullivan, Sybillina Clements and Clara Simms founded the second mission of Dominican sisters in Massachusetts. Sr. M. Laurence Blandford joined them a month later.

In her memoirs Sr. Alexia wrote, "We did not expect luxuries nor did we find them." What they did find was a parish of faith-filled people whose ties with the church were lasting and deep.

In the first year only girls were enrolled but in 1890 boys were welcomed and there were 475 students. Enrollment grew steadily through the years with a peak of 1,697 boys and girls in 1954.

In the annals of the early years there is an entry, "To our surprise and regret parents withdraw their children at the age of twelve and thirteen to go to work in the mills."[13] As regrettable as this was, it was a survival mechanism for the impoverished Irish families living in the squalid settlement known variously as "Paddy's Camp Land," "New Dublin," or "The Acre."[14]

During its one hundred years of existence St. Michael's school (like St. Patrick's) was a rich source of vocations to religious life and priesthood. Today St. Michael's is one of the largest parishes in the Boston Archdiocese. Although the Kentucky Dominican sisters no longer teach in the school, two sisters, identical twins, Rose Frances and Charles Francis McOsker serve the parish as pastoral associates.

During Mother Regina's fifth term of office she arranged the affiliation of St. Agnes with St. Catharine in 1887. Her sister,

Sr. M. Thomas, was superior in Memphis. Due to the loss of sisters during the yellow fever epidemics and the lack of new vocations, it was apparent that some action had to be taken if the community were to survive. The sisters opted to merge with St. Catharine.[15]

Among other notable events during Mother Regina's administration was the visit of Master General Joseph M. Larocca with J.J. Carberry, OP, socius and interpreter, on June 22, 1881.[16] The sisters felt privileged to have the representative of St. Dominic in their midst for the first time. Not only did he celebrate Mass and Office with them, but he toured the buildings, met the students and shared recreation with the sisters even though it was through an interpreter.

Fr. Cubero was especially pleased by the visit because he was able to get news about the companions of his novitiate days. This was one of the highlights of his last years. He spent 12 years as chaplain at St. Catharine and although he was somewhat strict, he was always kind and generous to the community. One time he paid a convent debt of $8,000. He provided the library with an abundant supply of good books. When he died July 15, 1883[17], he lay in state in the beautiful Gothic chapel he had lately adorned with an exquisite Cavalry group and statues of Saints Dominic and Catharine. The last two arrived from France just a few days before his death when he was too ill to look at them.

He was buried in the sisters' cemetery. He is remembered as a friend and benefactor of the community.[18]

During the last years of her administration Mother Regina had the old convent torn down, replacing it with an aesthetic building of Gothic design. The high arches and stained glass windows emphasized a beauty reminiscent of medieval times.

When her sixth term as mother superior ended, Mother Regina spent the last years of her life at St. Agnes where her sister, Sr. Thomas O'Meara, was assigned. She died March 19, 1900. Although she may be considered one of the great builders of the Congregation, she was more than that. Frank Lily, OP, expressed it well in writing her obituary:

The death of a nun seldom evokes more than a mere passing announcement. But the death of Mother Regina should not be treated according to ordinary standards, for she was no ordinary woman. ... Once in authority, she was found equal to its most exacting requirements and entirely proof against its slightest abuse. She was an ideal superior as she had been a model subject. Again and again she was re-elected. Under her wise and prudent administration, St. Catharine of Siena came to the forefront among the educational establishments of the southwest. ... But perhaps her most distinguishing trait was loyalty to the Order. She was Dominican to the heart's core. ... The name given to Sister Regina proved prophetic for she was indeed a "queen among women."[19]

Vincent Ferrer Thompson, OP

Mother Regina's successor, Sr. Vincent Ferrer Thompson, assumed office August 4, 1891 at age 53. She had taught at Holy Rosary, Louisville, and was one of the pioneers who opened St. Patrick, Watertown. From the outset she was plagued with governance problems.

Before St. Agnes affiliated officially with St. Catharine in 1888, the Memphis sisters had been following a Constitutions adapted from the Stone Rule.[20] In Kentucky, the sisters were living according to the manuscript rule given them by Fr. Wilson in 1822.

In the summer of 1891 the sisters were stunned when Bishop William G. McCloskey of Louisville imposed on the St. Catharine community the Constitutions used in Memphis before the affiliation. Immediately the sisters voiced their objections which Mother Vincent Ferrer relayed to the Ordinary.[21]

Notwithstanding their objections to the imposition of the rule, McCloskey ordered Mother Vincent Ferrer to have copies made and sent to each house.

Dear Rev. Mother, As the Manuscript Regulations which the sisters of St. Catharine's Convent have hitherto followed, are utterly insufficient for the proper guidance of the Community, We hereby direct that the printed Rule in use among the Sisters of the Third Order of St. Dominic at Memphis and entitled "The Rule of St. Augustine and the Constitutions of the Sisters of Penance of the Third Order of St. Dominic, be in the future the Rule of the Third Order of St. Dominic at St. Catharine's Convent, near Springfield, and of which you are the Rev. Prioress; and in all the houses, schools and communities depending on the Prioress of St. Catharine's. ... You will send a copy of this letter and the rule also to all the Sister Superiors of the various schools and Communities attached to St. Catharine's. August 23, 1891.[22]

Mother Vincent did as instructed. Repercussions followed.

The chaplain, J.F. Colbert, OP, wrote to Procurator General M. Cicognani, OP, about the matter. The reply stated emphatically that the Bishop (McCloskey) "has acted neither properly, nor justly, nor lawfully.[23] Cicognani explained that as a Papal institute St. Catharine depended on The Sacred Congregation of Propaganda Fide.

It makes no difference that the old rule is small, that the rule is scanty and not suited under the present conditions to the exigencies of the Institute and for procuring its increase. Nevertheless, nothing is to be changed without the consent of Propaganda. ... Hence, I propose to you this solution, viz. that our sisters in the present state of things ought not and can not remain quiet. But, lest they should seem rebellious, let them humbly present themselves to the Bishop and explain their reasons, which they can also do in writing.[24]

Colbert's interpretation of Cicognani's letter led him to an unwelcome conclusion. Mother Vincent wrote:

Mar. 7, 1892. God help me! Still further trouble and annoyance await me. ... Fr. Colbert has just sent for me saying he understands the "Bishop's rule" has been given to the sisters and proclaims we are no longer Dominicans and that he cannot in conscience give the Dominican habit to the Postulants. After considerable argument I told him if his conscience stood in the way of his performing the ceremony, I had only one alternate; viz. to dispatch to the Bishop to appoint, or to come and officiate himself. He then yielded, saying he acted so at the entreaties of certain sisters. In this case conscience suddenly proved elastic.[25]

In the Fall of 1894 Sr. Benven Rumpff, Regina O'Meara, M. Joseph Clark and Benedicta Meany wrote their objections to Archbishop Elder and Mother Vincent. They were willing to compromise if certain revisions were made confirming their membership in the Dominican Order with the approbation of Propaganda. Elder ordered a visitation of all the houses.

On January 4, 1895, the "Mothers of Council" petitioned Elder for "home government." When Mother Vincent Ferrer submitted the letter to McCloskey he strongly objected with the result that Mother Vincent Ferrer, along with Srs. Angela Lynch, Raymonda Meagher and Vincentia Maguire asked that their names be withdrawn.[26] Only Regina and Benven Rumpff had the courage to challenge McCloskey's arbitrary imposition of a rule.

Eventually the dilemma was settled but not before the intervention of the Apostolic Delegate, Archbishop Francis Satolli. On April 3, 1895, Monsignor Sabretti and Fr. Gambon read to the sisters assembled at St. Catharine the official decree on the matter, namely that the constitutions given by Bishop McCloskey were to be observed until the Sacred Congregation of Propaganda Fide approved a permanent constitutions [27]

Although much of her energy was focused on the dispute over the constitutions and the division among the sisters caused by it, Mother Vincent had some happier moments during her two terms of office.

One was the opening of St. Francis DeSales school, Charlestown, Massachusetts in 1891, in response to an appeal from Rev. James N. Supple. Seven sisters opened the new mission at the top of Bunker Hill but enrollment was so high that two more sisters soon joined them.[28] This school became one of the largest operated by Kentucky Dominicans and flourished for one hundred years. The Church was blessed with many priestly and religious vocations from St. Francis DeSales. As social and educational needs changed, it became necessary for St. Francis to merge with St. Catherine of Siena parish in order to continue

Catholic education in Charlestown. Today St. Catherine is the site of the merged schools, now called Charlestown Catholic Elementary. Few knew that the sisters living at St. Francis had trudged back and forth to St. Catherine at the foot of Bunker Hill to teach the children before there were any accommodations other than the church. When a convent and school were built at St. Catherine, the sisters of St. Joseph were invited to take charge of the complex in 1911.[29]

Another joy to Mother Vincent Ferrer was the school for blacks in Memphis, Tennessee. The school opened in September 1888 in the Sodality hall of St. Peter Church with Sr. Agnes Brown in charge. Later it was moved to St. Peter Orphanage but as segregation was the rule of the day, it was maintained separately from the white orphaned children. Daily attendance averaged about 167 boys and girls. Mother Vincent Ferrer sent sisters there to carry on the work despite hardships and inconvenience. Although the school closed in 1895 the seed for education of black boys and girls had been sown. When the Josephite fathers came to Memphis they opened St. Anthony parish with a school under the auspices of the Sisters of Charity of Cincinnati, Ohio, thus continuing the education of black children.[30]

Diamond Jubilee — 1897

Perhaps the most joyful event for Mother Vincent Ferrer was the Diamond Jubilee celebration in 1897. A train was chartered to bring home all the sisters from the East. It was truly a "Coming Home" event.

Again the constitutions cast a brief shadow over the festival. Since it was time for election of a major superior, permission was sought to permit all the sisters who came to the Motherhouse to vote. According to the letter of the law, sisters were supposed to reside at the Motherhouse to have voting rights. Mother Vincent Ferrer wrote to the Apostolic Delegate, Sebastiano Martinelli, OSA, pointing out that "sisters of our mission houses coming home for the occasion are in no light considered visitors. They are entirely subject to the Motherhouse and *this* is the *home* of all our professed."[31] Permission for the

"visitors" to vote was denied. Martinelli advised her to observe
the constitutions strictly, adding "it is not wise to interfere with
those provisions (of the constitutions) for reasons of senti-
ment."[32] Maximum participation in voting privileges has been a
long-sought desire which would surface many times.

The sisters did not allow Martinelli's dictum to dampen their
enthusiasm for the celebration. Visitors came from far and wide
but none were more beloved than the two from Springfield,
Illinois.

> Srs. Josephine and M. Catherine attended, bearing the good
> wish of the Community voiced in an acrostic — Our Lady of the
> Sacred Heart to Saint Catherine of Sienna greeting. The poem
> contained six stanzas, each written inside a diamond figure bear-
> ing the Dominican emblems above and the picture of St.
> Dominic's dog below. It was not intentional but by some coinci-
> dence there was one dog for each Sister who left St. Catherine's a
> quarter century ago. The whole was enclosed in a painted cellu-
> loid cover in the back of which was inserted a picture of our
> Convent, the Youngest scion of Sienna's soil.[33]

As soon as the Jubilee was over, the sisters returned to Illinois
with glowing accounts of the festivities and the warm welcome
they had received at their old home. Relations between the two
communities were once more happy as if no misunderstanding
ever occurred.[34]

The second constitutions imposed in 1895 remained in effect
for twenty-three years even though not completely satisfactory.[35]
The controversy had pitted Mother Vincent Ferrer against the
sisters because she had championed McCloskey. After 1897, cor-
respondence exchanged between the two reveals their high
regard for each other. In 1906 she was elected again but declined
because of health. Before her death January 19, 1918,[36] after
sixty-four years as a Dominican she had the joy of knowing that
Hyacinthus M. Cormier, master general, in 1905 had enrolled all
members of the congregation in the Third Order of Penance,
thus granting each one every privilege, grace and indulgence
which conventual Third Order women enjoyed.[37] This decree
was an important milestone for all the sisters; it was their assur-

ance, their signadou (sign from God) that they were indeed full members of the Dominican Order.

By 1897 as a new century approached, 207 sisters had been professed, 31 institutions and parish missions had been started and two independent daughter foundations, Ohio and Illinois, had been successfully launched.

Chapter Eleven Notes

1. Minogue, *Pages,* p. 141.
2. J.A. Kelly diary, Vol. IV p. 87; also Minogue, *Pages,* p. 141.
3. J.A. Kelly diary, Vol. IV, p. 87.
4. SCA, photostat, *The Springfield Sun,* n.d.; also photostat, The Record, St. Mary's Church, New Haven, Conn., April 1900 (article attributed to Frank Lilly, OP).
5. Personal interview with Sr. Jean Marie Callahan, OP, March 20, 1995.
6. Mattoon Journal Gazette, Friday, August 17, 1990.
7. Ibid.
8. *1992 Catholic Almanac,* Councils of Baltimore p. 392; *Encyclopedic Dictionary of Religion,* Vol. A/E, p. 352.
9. Photostat, *The Pilot,* August 25, 1888, p. 5; also Minogue, *Pages,* p. 159.
10. Minogue, *Pages,* p. 163.
11. Ibid. Also *The Watertown Sun,* Wednesday, June 12, 1991.
12. SCA letter written by Fr. Stack to Mother Regina dated May 30, 1888.
13. Annals, St. Michael School, 1892.
14. Eno, Arthur L., *Cotton Was King,* p. 99.
15. St. Agnes Profession Book, notation gives primary source data re: affiliation with St. Catharine of Siena community, Kentucky in October 1887. However, the official date used is February 1888 when the Bishop of Nashville and the Bishop of Louisville exchanged jurisdiction.
16. Minogue, *Pages,* pp. 145, 146, 147.
17. O'Daniel, *The First Two Dominican Priories in the United States,* pp. 176, 177.
18. Minogue, *Pages,* p. 144. Fr. Cubero's headstone may be seen in the sisters' cemetery on the Heights. He had been buried in the Valley but his remains were transferred when the graves of the sisters were moved to the Heights.
19. Copy from *The Record,* St. Mary's Church, New Haven, Conn., April 1900. Similar sentiments were written in a letter by L.F. Kearney, OP, March 22, 1900.

20. See O'Connor, *Five Decades*, pp. 84, 85 for explanation of the Stone Rule.

21. Green, p. 36.

22. SCA letter of McCloskey to Mother Vincent Ferrer, August 23, 1891.

23. SCA letter of Cicognani to Colbert, from Rome, June 11, 1892.

24. Ibid.

25. SCA Mother Vincent Ferrer's notes.

26. SCA copy of letter to Bishop Elder from Mothers of Council, January 4, 1895, from Springfield, Kentucky.

27. For a detailed and accurate account of the constitutions see Mary Patricia Green, OP, The Third Order Dominican Sisters of the Congregation of St. Catharine of Siena, St. Catharine, Kentucky, Their Life and Their Constitutions, 1822-1969.

28. Minogue, *Pages*, p. 166.

29. Letter of Sr. Blaithin, archivist of Sisters of St. Joseph, Brighton, Massachusetts, April 18, 1990 to author.

30. SCA Writings of Sr. Hyacintha Peters.

31. SCA copy of letter of Sr. Vincent Ferrer to Sebastiano Martinelli, Apostolic Delegate, June 15, 1897. Underlining is in original letter.

32. SCA letter to Mother Vincent Ferrer from Martinelli, June 27, 1897. It was a foreshadowing of what would happen almost a century later when sisters would ask for maximum participation in election of superiors.

33. SHDA annals April 3, 1897.

34. SHDA Original papers of Sr. Josephine, p. 53.

35. Green, p. 52.

36. Minogue, *Pages*, pp. 222, 223.

37. SCA Original decree from Hyacinthus Cormier, OP, January 19, 1905. Also see Green, pp. 51, 52, 75.

THE PHOENIX

IN 1897 as the end of the century approached, the sisters elected Sr. Bernardine Bushue as prioress. Born in Somerset, Ohio, she was baptized by Albert Bokel, OP, on March 20, 1859. When she was 20 years old she received the habit in Kentucky with Fr. Cubero presiding. She taught for ten years at St. Patrick, Watertown.

When Miss Kate Kelley bequeathed her homestead in Waverly, Massachusetts, to Fr. Stack, pastor of St. Patrick, with the stipulation that it be used for religious purposes, his first thought was of the Kentucky Dominicans. He contacted Mother Bernardine who obtained permission to open a boarding school called Infant of Prague. However, Fr. Stack died before the sisters could occupy the house, but his successor, Fr. John S. Cullen, supported the project and classes opened September 1898, with 15 boarders enrolled.[1]

Like most beginnings it was a struggle. The sisters had a horse and buggy but it required several trips to convey themselves and the students to Mass at St. Patrick. Gradually conditions improved. Mass was offered daily in their school chapel, enrollment increased but in 1912 Sacred Heart Academy opened in Watertown.[2] This affected the Waverly school because pupils transferred to the new facility.

Another problem surfaced when a dispute arose over the Kelley property. These two events forced the closure of Infant of Prague; the keys were given to Sr. DeSales, the superior at St. Patrick. For a while part of the house was rented to a family and attempts were made to conduct summer classes there for the sisters. The facility remained in limbo until 1914 when it was re-opened as St. Dominic School for Boys. More about this institution will appear later.

When Mother Bernardine left office she went to St. Agnes, Memphis. She died December 4, 1903. Her successor, Sr. Agnes Hunt assumed office July 25, 1900.[3]

Mother Agnes Hunt

Mother Agnes Hunt (Katherine) born in New York in 1850, was the youngest of four children. She received her First Holy Communion at St. Patrick Cathedral and was confirmed by Archbishop John H. Hughes in 1863. At the age of 22 she traveled to Kentucky by rail and stage coach to enter the community. Traveling by stage was a new experience for her, one she never forgot. Fr. Cubero officiated at her profession. She was a dedicated teacher, having taught in Kentucky, Illinois, Tennessee and Massachusetts, being one of the founders of St. Patrick, Watertown, before being elected Prioress in 1900.[4]

As major superior, one of the first acts of her administration was the establishment of a post office at St. Catharine. John Alexander Waters, grandfather of Sr. M. Jude Waters, was post-master in Springfield at the time. He helped Mother Agnes apply for permission for a post office with Josie Holleran as first postmaster in 1900.[5] Since then, sisters who have passed the Civil Service examination have filled the position:

Josie Holleran

Sr. Francis O'Malley

Sr. Margaret Elizabeth Walsh

Sr. Virginia Thomas Hamilton

Sr. Virginia Thomas was appointed postmaster by President Harry Truman in 1952. At first, it was a Fourth Class office, the rating determined by the volume of revenue units. In 1959 it became Third Class and in 1973 Second Class.[6] Sr. Virginia, who traces her ancestry to Elizabeth Hamilton Sansbury, mother of Angela and Benven, handles 4,000 to 5,000 pieces of mail a day.

She and Sr. Francine Eaton, postal clerk, receive all the benefits available to every US postal employee. Sr. Virginia Thomas has received many awards for her 50 years of postal service, among them, that of Honorary Kentucky Colonel. Sr. M. Lawrence Curran is an assistant clerk, also employed by US Postal Service. Sr. Ann Thomas Hines is a dedicated volunteer, as was Sr. Maureen Nuttall until her death. The St. Catharine Post Office, begun by Mother Agnes, has served sisters, faculty, high school and college students for 97 years.

Spalding Academy, Spalding, Nebraska

An important act of Mother Agnes' administration was the acceptance of an invitation to staff a school in Spalding, Nebraska. The pastor of St. Michael parish, Rev. Julius E. DeVos, complained to his friend Henry S. Spalding, SJ. of Creighton University that he could not get sisters to take charge of his school. Fr. Spalding, whose three sisters were members of the Kentucky Dominicans, advised him to appeal to Mother Agnes, promising to use his personal influence to convince her the move would benefit the Order and the Church. F.J. Twohig, OP, was giving missions in Nebraska at the time. He persuaded DeVos to present his case in person. In the early Fall of 1900 DeVos visited Kentucky. Mother Agnes promised to send some sisters in August 1901. DeVos went to his native Belgium for a visit, intending to return before the arrival of the sisters.[7]

In August 1901 Srs. Raphael Huber and Margaret Hamilton left Kentucky after retreat. It was a long trip by train to Cedar Rapids. From there the last lap of the trip was by wagon.[8]

Since the town was not expecting the sisters so soon, no arrangements had been made for them. Some of the women of the parish rushed to open the convent which had been closed for two years, ever since the sisters of Mercy had withdrawn. Neither had anything been done to prepare the school Determined to start classes in September, Raphael and Margaret improvised seats for students by hauling pews from the church which had to be returned for Sunday services. In a couple of weeks, Srs. Borgia McCann and Dolores Spalding, one of Fr.

Spalding's sisters, arrived as part of the faculty. School began September 2, 1901, with only seven children present. Enrollment grew so rapidly that by November, two more sisters joined the group, Srs. Rosalia O'Daniel and Francis O'Mahoney. The school, dedicated to Our Lady of Lourdes, but generally known as Spalding Academy, has had a long history as a rich source of vocations and as an excellent educational facility down to the present day.[9] Srs. Mary Faith O'Malley, and Charlene Vogel still maintain the presence of Kentucky Dominicans in Spalding.

Unrest

In April 1902, Mother Agnes wrote to Archbishop John J. Williams for permission to open a novitiate in Waverly, Massachusetts. Her reasons were "that nearly all our candidates come from this state...vocations are not numerous in Ky. and we need members to carry on our work in the schools."[10] On the original letter in the Boston Archdiocesan archives, there is an unsigned notation: "not independent — but subject to Kentucky. See Rev. Fr. Cullen, Watertown." Another notation reads, "Cullen says, no hurry."[11] Nothing happened, but this matter would crop up later.

Trial By Fire

Fire seemed to plague Mother Agnes' regime. In April 1901 fire broke out in a dormitory at St. Agnes, Memphis. Most of the damage was from smoke and water; fortunately, nobody was injured. While a new building was being erected, students lived in rented housing. By June 1902 graduation took place in the new edifice.[12]

In November 1901, a building at St. Catharine erupted in flames. Because Sr. Angela Lynch was terminally ill, her brother John H. Lynch, OP, accompanied by an elderly gentleman, Mr. McGarvey, had journeyed to be with her. Both men stayed at St. Rose but Mr. McGarvey's horse was stabled at St. Catharine. In the early evening fire broke out in the barn. Word was sent to St. Rose and Springfield to summon help. The sisters started a water brigade passing buckets of water, assembly-line fashion, to quench the blaze. As the wind was blowing in the direction of convent and school, fear clutched the hearts of the sisters at the threat to their beautiful home. With terrified hearts they redoubled their efforts while Mother Agnes called upon the Sacred Heart to whom she had great devotion. Suddenly the wind shifted; the men extinguished the fire; the buildings were saved. The only casualty was Mr. McGarvey's horse.[13]

A much worse fiery trial occurred in 1904 during Mother Agnes' second term in office. Sr. Hildegarde Hart, a postulant, and her companions who were to receive the habit on January 6 had begun retreat on Saturday, January 2.[14] That very night Miss May Curry, a senior student from Springfield heard a muffled explosion between 10:30 and 11:00 P.M. Grabbing her crutches, for she had been crippled from infancy, she went to investigate the noise. When she reached the corridor, billowing smoke nearly suffocated her. She immediately wakened Sr. Borgia McCann, the Academy prefect.[15] Borgia instructed the girls to hasten to the children's infirmary located in the old convent wing.

Meanwhile Sr. Raymond Bird, novice mistress, had a novice ring the bell ordinarily used to summon the community to prayers and meals. The harsh clanging sounded the alarm as Raymond told the novices, "Sisters, dress quickly and go to the chapel. The Academy is on fire." Nobody could believe what was happening. Scantily clad, huddled in the chapel, they were praying the rosary when the chaplain, J.C. O'Mahoney, OP, warned, "It is impossible to save the building. Save what you can and take it out."[16] Sisters flung out the windows whatever was at hand, but the flames advanced rapidly, making it imperative for them to evacuate. When they were certain that no pupils remained in the building they escaped as best they could. Some grabbed mantles from chapel stalls as they fled into the piercing winter cold. Sr. Bernard Fogarty, the last to leave, was trapped by flames and smoke. In desperation she broke a window, climbed to the roof, inched her way across to the new building, broke another window and thus escaped.

As Sr. M. Edward Prendergast was leaving the novitiate, she noticed on the desk of the novice mistress the profession book in which the names of those to receive the habit were always recorded. Placing the book inside the desk, she proceeded to push the desk to the stairway. A man came along and carried the desk out. The profession book was saved!

The Dominican friars were the first to offer refuge to the sisters and their charges. Citizens of Springfield, sisters of Loretto and Nazareth offered hospitality so that 75 girls and 56 sisters were safely sheltered.[17]

When word of the disaster reached Louisville on Sunday morning, the response was immediate. The friars at St. Louis Bertrand organized parishioners to send relief — food, clothing, shelter. The Louisville and Nashville Railway placed a special train, free of charge, at the disposal of the relief committee.

R.F. Larpenteur, OP, prior at St. Rose, gathered some of the garments belonging to the friars to clothe sisters and students who had fled wearing only night clothes. Later, in refusing to accept a check for customary chaplain services he wrote:

> We esteem it our privilege to accept nothing for services while you are under your present circumstances. What we have done to help you has been very little indeed, but we will try to continue that little. May it encourage you under the hardships you bear and the weighty tasks which you have to perform. Please let us know when our assistance may be of benefit to you and give us a share in your prayers.[18]

Donations, messages and assistance poured in from the sisters on the missions and from other communities, relatives and friends. Fr. James N. Supple, Charlestown, Massachusetts, offered the convent of St. Francis DeSales for use as a novitiate. The sisters at Holy Rosary, Louisville, moved to other quarters leaving their rooms for the Motherhouse sisters and making room in the classrooms for some of the St. Catharine students.

A public meeting was held at Leiderkrantz Hall, Louisville, to raise funds for the sisters. B.F. Keith's Theatrical Enterprises held a concert in New York to help. Mother Thomasina of Springfield, Illinois, Mother Emily of Sinsinawa, Mother Praxedes of Loretto, Mother Perpetua of the Sisters of the Holy Cross, Sr. Vincentia of St. Mary of the Springs were among those who sent donations. Sr. Frances wrote from New York:

> We send you by today's express a box — an evidence of our heartfelt sympathy in this your hour of great trial. I trust it will reach you in safety and without delay as I am sure the contents will be found convenient at this particular time. We confined our little offering to habits, caps and capes - as we thought they would be most acceptable, and what, perhaps, you most need.[19]

The Alumnae arranged for St. Catharine seniors to graduate from the Women's Club, Louisville, but Archbishop McCloskey disapproved of having commencement exercises at a "non-Catholic Women's Club." Alumna Theresa K. McDonald informed him that not all of the graduates were Catholic, but also that the Club was the "property of ladies from the most intellectual families of Louisville who were interested in the development of women's culture and refinement." Despite this earnest plea, McCloskey remained adamant.[20] The St. Catharine students graduated at Holy Rosary.[21]

The chaplain's cottage and the laundry were the only buildings intact. On the morning after the fire the novices and postulants returned to St. Catharine.[22] The charred skeleton of their once beautiful home was heartbreaking, but the friars fixed up the chaplain's house as living quarters. The laundry became kitchen and dining room as well as laundry. They built a wooden framework house covered with tarpaulin. It became known as the "paper house."[23]

After expressing his sympathy at the tragedy the Bishop advised that the postulants be sent home until suitable quarters were erected. Mother Agnes was distressed at the thought but the chaplain, Fr. O'Mahoney, told her, "Clothe them with the habit. Then there will be no postulants to send home." She followed this advice and ten postulants received the habit on January 14. It was a simple ceremony with few visitors. Those who had been novices before the fire were professed March 8 and immediately assigned to missions.[24]

Although no lives were lost in the fire, there were some casualties afterwards. Dominic Wethers, a young black man, was killed while tearing down the walls of the chapel. After the fire Sr. Josephine Beck who had been ill for some time was hospitalized with the Sisters of Nazareth. The trauma may have hastened her death on February 2, 1904.[25]

January left St. Catharine a mass of blackened ruins. With the sisters scattered, the students dispersed and residents living in cramped, unsuitable conditions, the future seemed bleak. But in March the jonquils, the March lilies, raised their golden heads all over the desolate valley. Jonquils are hardy, not hothouse plants requiring delicate care like orchids. They persevere and spread out. Wild and survivors, they were a symbol of hope, a *signadou*, to the Kentucky Dominicans who themselves are a bit wild and definitely survivors. Once again the sisters set about rebuilding convent and school. But where?

Choosing a Site

On January 23, 1904, the members of the Council assembled to discuss three sites which the citizens of Springfield generously offered. All were closer to the RR, water works and electric light. The offers were tempting but R.H. Edelen of Mattingly and Moore Distillery Company wrote that it would be a grave mistake to locate the school in or very near town. He and his friend John I. McElroy felt there was no place more suitable than "on your own land near the pike."[26]

Bishop McCloskey met with the Council on January 31. He advised rebuilding in Louisville as being more conducive to future growth.[27] But the sisters had other ideas.

> Of course we took notes, no one saying a word, but we could not agree to such a proposition since an Acad. in a country place is preferable to that of a city. A paper was submitted to the sisters of each mission house for their consideration which the sisters signed and returned. They do not want to leave Washington Co. nor rebuild the Acad. on the old place.[28]

The question was resolved May 9, 1904, when the Council voted to build on our own ground on the hill near the Bardstown road with" reluctant permission" from McCloskey.[29] Some bricks were salvaged from the wreckage and work began.

Once again the Dominican friars demonstrated their concern by drawing up a resolution dated January 1, 1905:

> WHEREAS, there has always been, is now, and please God, always will be a truly fraternal tie between the communities of St. Catharine's Convent and St. Rose Convent, and

> WHEREAS, actions prove the existence of ties and virtues, as they do of essential natural powers; therefore,

> BE IT RESOLVED, that the Council of St. Rose Convent...do hereby declare that all indebtedness of St. Catherine's Convent to St. Rose Convent for brick, stone, lumber, sand, water and other materials....is totally and entirely cancelled....not only as a token of brotherly interest, but also as an earnest of the Fathers to help the Sisters in the work of building for themselves a new home.[30]

Mother Agnes did not focus on bricks and mortar alone. In the Fall after the fire, she and her Council agreed to purchase a harp "not to exceed in price $750 and to employ a Professor to give lessons thereon to Sr. Imelda Brady that she may be ready to impart the same to the pupils of the new Academy." It was also agreed to send Sr. Perpetua Richardson to Boston to complete her course in vocal music.[31] Audacious moves at a time when the community was scrimping and sacrificing to finance a new Motherhouse complex, but it shows the value placed on fine arts.

Shortly after the fire sisters were sent to start new schools at St. Joseph, E. St. Louis, Illinois and St. Rose of Lima, Dennison, Iowa, but neither of them remained open very long

Mother Agnes lived to see the new St. Catharine erected on Siena Heights but she contracted tuberculosis.[32] She bore her suffering patiently, always praying to the Sacred Heart for strength. She died December 4, 1908.

The first election in the new Motherhouse took place July 25, 1906. Sr. Vincent Ferrer Thompson was chosen but declined. Bishop McCloskey presided at the election. After some deliberation he acceded to her wishes and *appointed* Sr. Magdalene Norton for three years.

Chapter Twelve Notes

1. SCA Annals of St. Dominic School for Boys, Waverly, Massachusetts.
2. Ibid.
3. Ibid.
4. SCA Hunt file, undated clipping, source not noted.
5. St. Catharine Post Office official documents. According to U.S. Government postal service a person in charge of a post office, whether male or female is officially "master of the post," hence postmaster.
6. Information about the post office is based on personal interviews with Sr. Virginia Thomas Hamilton, postmaster and Sr. Francine Eaton, postal clerk, May 1995.
7. Eaton, Sr. Francine, *History of the Development of Spalding Academy, Spalding Nebraska, 1901-1951.* Master's thesis, DePaul University, Chicago, Illinois, 1951.
   Also, Esch, C., Langer, H., Glesinger, L. *St. Michael's Centennial, History of St. Michael's, 1986* and Esch. C. et al *Early Days of Spalding*, Bicentennial Book Committee, 1976.
8. Sr. Raphael Huber as a child boarded at Holy Rosary Academy, Louisville, and later at St. Catharine's along with her sisters Alice and Julia. Alice became an artist, taught art at St. Catharine and was co-founder with Rose Hawthorne Lathrop of the Servants of Relief for Incurable Cancer. Alice left two huge paintings at St. Catharine — Dominic and Catharine. In 1957 when the Dominican Mothers General met in Kentucky the paintings were donated to the Hawthorne community. Sr. Margaret Hamilton served in various leadership positions in the community. One of her greatest contributions was gathering the history of the Kentucky Dominicans to fill the gaps left by the destruction of records in the fire of 1904. She sought the help of Victor O'Daniel, OP, and had to rely at times on oral history because there was nothing else. Although her research has some errors, she deserves credit for her efforts to harvest our history. Sr. Paschala Noonan was assigned to assist her in research at the Washington County records office when her eyesight was failing. She would then transmit her findings into Braille.
9. Benjamen, Sr. Clare. Unpublished report: *A Brief History of the Western Region of St. Catharine of Siena Congregation of St. Catharine, Kentucky.* Distributed at Western Regional Conference, Waverly, Nebraska, April 1969.
10. BAA Original letter to Archbishop Williams, Boston, from Sr. Agnes Hunt, St. Catharine, Kentucky, April 5, 1902.
11. Ibid.
12. SCA, Chronology of the History of St. Agnes, Memphis — unsigned document.
13. SCA, notebook marked "Obituary," pp. 6, 7.
14. SCA. Accounts of the fire are also taken from taped interviews of Srs. Hildegarde Hart, Edward Prendergast, Wilhelmina Fogle, Alberta Johnson who were in the fire. These tapes were part of an oral history

project recorded by Sr. Dorothy Nuttall in 1974-1975. There were ten postulants in the class: Srs. Anastasia Gorney, M. John Clifford, Gervase Donovan, Germain Donovan, M. Sadoc Wimsett, Monica Woods, Rita Dellamana, Hildegarde Hart, Sabina Filiatreau, Callista Kavanaugh.

15. *The Courier Journal*, Louisville. Monday morning, January 4, 1904.
16. See note 14 above.
17. SCA *Unpublished Recollections of the Destruction By Fire of St. Catharine's Motherhouse on January 2, 1904,* by Sr. M. Edward Prendergast.
18. SCA Original letter from R.F. Larpenteur, OP, to Mother Agnes with uncashed check dated January 20, 1904.
19. SCA Original letter to Mother Agnes from Sr. Frances, OP. 152 E. 66th Street, New York, dated January 11, 1904.
20. SCA Copy of two letters to Bishop McCloskey, Louisville, from Theresa K. MacDonald, undated. Also, original letter to Mother Agnes from Bishop McCloskey dated May 14, 1904, Louisville.
21. SCA Graduation program in St. Catharine Academy files.
22. SCA. Also see note 14 above.
23. Minogue, *Pages,* p. 196.
24. SCA, Reflections on fire, 1904. On tape by Sr. Hildegarde Harte.
25. Ibid.
26. SCA Original letter from R.H. Edelen, Bardstown, to Mother Agnes dated January 16, 1904.
27. SCA Council minutes, January 31, 1904.
28. Ibid.
29. Ibid.
30. SCA copy of resolution drawn up January 1, 1905 by Frs. Larpenteur, Roach and O'Sullivan.
31. SCA Council minutes, November 13, 1904.
32. SCA Obituary Sr. Agnes Hunt.

Chapter Thirteen

MORE SCHOOLS

THE WORLD was in a period of unrest. In England, suffragettes were storming Parliament for the right to vote, while in Finland their counterparts were being sworn into their first Parliamentary seats. Ships from all over Europe were disgorging immigrants in New York with as many as 5,335 passing through Ellis Island in a single day.[1]

In the Church, Pope Pius X decried the evils of modernism and urged frequent reception of Holy Communion for both children and adults. Louisville's Bishop McCloskey wrote to the superiors of Religious Institutes in his diocese:

> Once daily Communion becomes an institution among the Religious in this diocese, it would be a gratifying assurance to our heart that the faithful at large will follow this example, and receive more universally this daily pledge of eternal life.[2]

Constitutions of some religious communities specified the days on which Holy Communion could be received, but McCloskey explained that this was merely a minimum to be expected of the piety of religious.[3]

It was during these changing times that the new Motherhouse was completed at Siena Heights. It was then, and is now an imposing structure with three wings emanating from a long façade. Upon entering the front door beyond parlors to the left and right are broad stairways on each side. Novices christened these "golden stairs" not so much because they led to chapel but because they had metal treads which had to be polished to a shining gold.

Despite the beauty and spaciousness of their new home, the sisters who had lived in the valley mourned that nothing could compare with what had been. Being too practical to waste time and energy in futile grief, they resumed the chores of community living, prepared to welcome back the students and rejoiced in the phoenix which rose from the ashes.

Mother Magdalene Norton

Mother Magdalene, the newly-appointed prioress, was born Hannah Norton (sometimes spelled Naughton), in Nashville, Tennessee. She entered St. Agnes Community, Memphis, at the age of 17 during the 1873 yellow fever epidemic. As a young sister, she was tireless in caring for fever patients during the onslaughts of Yellow Jack. She went from house to house, caring for the sick, gathering the orphans and keeping vigil with the dying. The people called her the "White Angel." When the Memphis orphans were sent temporarily to Nashville to get them out of the disease-ridden city, Magdalene was missioned with them there. As a member of the St. Agnes Community, she was one of the signers of the document of affiliation in 1887.[4]

As major superior she accepted parish schools, St. Patrick, West Lynn, Massachusetts and St. Patrick, North Platte, Nebraska both in 1906.[5] A year later she missioned sisters to St. Bavo School, Mishawaka, Indiana and to St. Stephen, Exeter, Nebraska. The latter place is poignantly connected with one of our sisters born in New York and baptized in St. Vincent Ferrer parish there.

In New York, immigration, disease, malnutrition and poverty resulted in infants being left parentless or abandoned. Mother Elizabeth Seton's community opened the New York Foundling Home in 1869 but so great was the influx of children that the Sisters of Charity devised an innovative plan to provide good homes for them. It was called the Orphan Trains or Mercy Trains. The sisters contacted bishops and pastors in the midwest to ask them to seek homes among their parishioners for the children.

In Exeter, Fr. Walter McDonald arranged for the Barkmeier family to adopt three-year-old Victoria Geyger. Victoria had a label sewn inside the hem of her dress on which was written her name, the date of her birth and the name of her prospective parents. The Barkmeiers received duplicate labels from the Foundling Home so they could identify their child.

When the train arrived at Exeter, Victoria clung to the sister who had brought her from New York and wept bitterly when the train pulled out with the sister aboard. However, it did not take long for her to fit into the Barkmeier family of seven boys and one girl. She became the darling of the older boys.

The Foundling Home always followed the development of the children to ensure that they were treated well. In 1907 Fr. McDonald received a notice from the administrator in New York that Victoria was not enrolled in a Catholic school and unless this was changed, she would have to return to the orphanage! That spring, Victoria was enrolled in St. Stephen's school. She spent part of her high school years in Exeter and completed them at Spalding Academy, Spalding, Nebraska. After her adoptive parents died, she entered the novitiate at St. Catharine, was professed in 1937 and served in many missions in the community usually among the poor. She was one of the pioneers in Louisiana to teach blacks and mulattoes.[6]

As parishes multiplied in response to the arrival of immigrants, requests for sisters became common. When a colony of Belgian people in Chicago, Illinois pleaded for a parish to serve their spiritual needs, Archbishop James E. Quigley requested the Jesuits to loan John DeSchryver, SJ, to organize the parish which was named St. John Berchmans. During the one year he spent there, DeSchryer contacted Fr. Julius DeVos, a Belgian priest who had been instrumental in bringing Kentucky Dominicans to Spalding, Nebraska. Quigley asked DeVos to leave Nebraska to become pastor at St. John Berchmans in 1906 when DeSchryver was recalled by the Jesuits.

Upon arrival in Chicago, DeVos surveyed the scene and immediately said, "The future of this parish is in the school."[7] Because of his previous contact with Kentucky Dominicans, he appealed to Mother Magdalene for help. She sent Srs. Fabian

Allen, Madeline Ferriell, Marcella Dunnigan, Cecilia Kennedy with Sr. Antoninus Nealy as superior.

In 1907 the sisters held classes on the first floor of the wooden frame convent but when the upper church was completed, the lower church became the school.[8] To the chagrin of the teachers this militated against the students when accreditation to admit St. John Berchmans' graduates to public high school was limited to one year - "due to physical conditions, ... classes being held in the basement."[9]

This fueled the incentive to build a new school. When Fr. DeVos celebrated his Golden Jubilee on the Feast of Corpus Christi in 1923, erecting a new school was uppermost in his mind. Former parishioners from his assignments in Nebraska were most generous but the delegation from Spalding made a most touching tribute. Eighteen years after he had left them, they came to their old pastor with a gift of $500 in $20 gold pieces in a satin purse.[10] He used the funds towards a new school.

Lay leadership has been a characteristic of this parish with families carrying on the tradition from one generation to the next. Walter J. DeVriendt, the only Belgian undertaker in Chicago, was a mainstay of the parish in the `30s.[11] Now his daughter Jeanne, a Dominican Associate,[12] serves in the parish and teaches in the school. No longer mainly Belgian, the parish now serves the new immigrants from Asia, Central America and Europe. Kentucky Dominican presence is still maintained at St. John Berchmans by Joan Monica McGuire, Director of Ecumenism and Interreligious Office of Archdiocese, Margaret Rose Curry, community service; and M. Pius Worland, secretary to the Chicago Director of Evangelization and Christian Life.

When Mother Magdalene's term of office expired, she returned to teaching. She never lost her Southern charm. One of her students remarked how she fascinated her eighth grade class in Chicago when she talked about her mammy taking her to church. She could go up front but she felt sad because her mammy had to stay in the back. Frequently, she used the contraction "Hon," which made the children feel close to her and her to them.[13]

She told them about the time she attended the funeral of a Union soldier who had been a prisoner in the infamous Andersonville Prison. As she stood at his casket she asked herself, "I wonder what he would say if he knew the daughter of a Confederate Officer was here praying for him?"[14]

Her pupils thrilled to her exciting tales about Joseph Dutton, who worked in the Molokai leper colony with Fr. Damien de Veuster. It was Magdalene who sensed the goodness in Dutton before his conversion and despite his lapse into alcohol and gambling after a failed marriage.[15] It was she who arranged for this former Union Army officer to meet with J.A. Kelly, OP, who later received him into the Church. It was she, along with Sr. M. Pius Fitzpatrick, who stood by his side when he was baptized.[16] Imagine their joy when Dutton decided to join Damien for service in the leper colony as Br. Joseph!

Magdalene's last assignment was St. Mark School, Gary, Indiana. She died there on the feast of St. Catharine of Siena, April 30, 1929.[17]

Mother Aquin Holleran

In the election of Mother Prioress in 1909, the community chose Aquin Holleran who had served as first postmaster at St. Catharine. Born in Louisville of Daniel and Bridget (O'Connors) Holleran, she was professed September 1, 1885. Under her leadership as major superior for two consecutive terms, new schools were opened in Nebraska and Massachusetts while existing ones were expanded.

In the spring of 1909, Mother Magdalene had visited Hastings, Nebraska to investigate opening an academy in a school once staffed by Visitation nuns. Years of drought, crop failures and bank closings caused financial strain on farmers with a consequent drop in enrollment because of tuition. The Visitation sisters, unable to meet their mortgage payments, were forced to close the school in 1895 and return to Chicago.

The abandoned building had been empty for 12 years. Caretakers housed horses and other farm animals on the ground floor while rats made themselves at home. However, Mother

Magdalene saw the potential in the dilapidated structure. She completed the business arrangements with Rev. William MacDonald of Hastings.[18] With $5,000 raised by the Commercial Club of Hastings and $3,000 donated by Catholics of the community, the creditors were paid and the Dominican sisters acquired the property for $1. The remodeling of the building fell to her successor.

Mother Aquin engaged laborers to repair the damage wrought by years of neglect on walls, floors and roof. Modern heating, lighting and plumbing were installed. A complete chemistry laboratory and an auditorium/gymnasium were added. Once the physical plant was remodeled, attention was directed toward the curriculum.

Sr. Mary Louis Logsdon was the first superior of Immaculate Conception Academy which opened August 9, 1909 with ten grades. By 1912, the Academy boasted twelve grades and became state accredited.[19] Nebraska required teachers to have normal training in college, university or normal school in order to obtain a teaching certificate.[20] To meet the needs of those who wished to become teachers, the sisters broadened the curriculum to include junior college and normal school.

Later, in May 1930, a disastrous tornado raged through Hastings, tearing off the roof and damaging the entire third story of the Academy. Two cows and a horse were killed, but students and sisters escaped unharmed. They made efforts to rebuild, but dust storms and the declining economy thwarted their plans. In 1932, the sisters sold buildings and grounds to the Crosier Fathers. What once served as an Academy, Junior College and Normal School is now the Crosier Monastery and Renewal Center.[21]

Constitutions Again

In 1913, Mother Aquin wrote to Francis G. Horn, OP, at the Angelicum in Rome to inquire about the procedure for revising the institute's second constitutions. It was a long, drawn-out process. Fr. Horn answered her:

> Such things are handled very slowly over here....We are in the throes of a European war which is dreadful to contemplate. The

mails either do not come or come with great delays. Communications are almost completely cut off. I don't know when you will receive this or whether you will receive it at all.[22]

Another Dominican, Thomas Esser, Secretary of the Index at the Sacred Congregation, who was working closely with Horn, wrote to Mother Aquin:

Just one little other delay has turned up, namely, a new regulation has been made at the Congregation that Rules and Constitutions must be presented either in Latin or Italian or French. Up to a short time ago, English was also admitted, but now they have returned to the old regulation that existed at the Congregation of Propaganda, i.e., one of the 3 above mentioned languages....I am now having your Rule and Constitutions translated into French.[23]

Horn and Esser wrote dozens of letters to Kentucky explaining delays and encouraging the sisters to keep hoping and praying. Esser described the ills of war; all U.S. mail was subject to censorship, unpleasant restrictions and lack of necessities. He had three nephews killed, three wounded, two imprisoned and a priest nephew in Ceylon imprisoned by the English.[24] He wrote all this heartbreak to Mother Aquin. At last, on July 10, 1915, Benedict XV granted the decretum laudis.[25] Esser rejoiced with the sisters at the laudatory decree which meant they were a papal institute. He offered to make the changes suggested by Rome in order to obtain final approbation which did not come until 1918.[26]

Continuing Outreach

The sisters felt that God had blessed their efforts in their early foundations in the east, and although they taught only one year at St. Catharine, Charlestown, they opened other schools in Massachusetts, namely, Sacred Heart Academy,[27] Watertown; Sacred Heart, East Boston and St. John, North Cambridge. Expansion continued in Nebraska with sisters missioned to St. Cecilia, Hastings; St. Anthony, Cedar Rapids; St. Mary, Dawson; St. Patrick, Fremont; St. Mary, Omaha and St. James, Kearney.[28]

While "preferential option for the poor" did not appear in the constitutions until a much later date, the sisters shared their resources as much as they could with those less fortunate than themselves. When Alice, a faithful black employee at St. Catharine, became blind and incapacitated, she was given a room in the Academy and was cared for by the sisters. In the Council minutes (August 8, 1906) there is a notation, "It was proposed to receive as many as four poor children to educate them free in order to bring a blessing on our community."

Response to need reached across the sea. A Council entry of September 24, 1907, reads: "Agreed to send $100 to Pere Cormier toward erection of Dominican House of Studies in Rome to continue the work of St. Thomas Aquinas."[29] Another entry dated March 4, 1909, records: "Agreed to send $50 to earthquake victims in Italy." Also noted: "Agreed to send $50 to the starving people of Russia."[30] While the sums seem insignificant in the light of today's economy, they meant sacrifice on the part of the sisters who were constantly struggling to remain solvent.

Financial resources were only a part of what they shared. When the fledgling community at Great Bend sought spiritual and professional help for their sisters, Mother Aquin and Council unanimously agreed to take two novices and a professed sister belonging to the Dominican Convent in Great Bend, Kansas, and train them for religious life and teaching.[31] Srs. Annunciata Schreiner, Inviolata Beran and Augustine Haefele left the plains of Kansas for the Kentucky hills. Sr. Augustine concentrated her studies on music.[32] The sisters attended all the exercises and studied the ideals and customs of the Kentucky Dominicans. The latter rejoiced when they learned that later at Great Bend, Sr. Inviolata became major superior; Sr. Annunciata, superior of St. Rose Hospital and Sr. Augustine, novice mistress.

Collaboration did not end there. In 1921 the Kentucky Dominicans accepted their first hospital. Since teaching had been their primary mission, they knew that if they were to branch into the health field, they needed to prepare sisters for health professions. This time, Kentucky asked Great Bend for help because the latter had St. Rose School of Nursing. Over the years, eight Kentucky Dominicans were accepted into that nursing program: Srs. Ann Michael Burke, Rachel Cooney, Catherine Imelda Corr, Joan Miriam Glaser, Lucinda Hayes, Paschala Noonan, Agnes Regina Staud and Adeline Trautwein.[33]

An interesting incident occurred when the Kansas Dominicans were celebrating the Golden Anniversary of their founding in 1952. Some Kentucky Dominicans were attending the festivities when Mother Aloysia Rachbauer intimated to Sr. Paschala that the Community was going to take a foreign mission in gratitude to God for graces and blessings received during those fifty years. Sr. Paschala knew that Apostolic Delegate Edward T. Lawton, OP (later the first Bishop of Sokoto, Nigeria) was seeking sisters for his African mission. She wrote to tell him that Mother Aloysia's community was going to take a foreign mission as a Jubilee gift to God. Immediately Msgr. Lawton contacted Edward Hughes, OP, Provincial of St. Albert Province. When Hughes in turn called Mother Aloysia about the "foreign mission," she said, "But Father, we're diocesan. When I said `foreign mission,' I meant we are going to Oklahoma."[34] Her sisters did go to Oklahoma but with persuasion from Fr. Hughes and Msgr. Lawton, her Council deliberated about the matter and Mother Aloysia and Sr. Benigna Albers went to Nigeria to examine the situation. On July 24, 1956, three sisters sailed for Nigeria on the African Patriot: Srs. Raphael Husman, Frances Joseph Biernacki and Charlotte Unrein. Sr. Bernadette Beckermann stayed in the states to complete a course in midwifery before joining the others. Approximately 20 Great Bend sisters have worked in Nigerian government hospitals, in the bush, in dispensaries and in schools. As a result of their work and example, there is now a flourishing native community of Dominicans in Nigeria.[35] The relationship begun during Mother Aquin's regime with the Great Bend Dominicans is but one example of collaboration characteristic of the Dominican family.

Mother Aquin died on July 25, 1917 two years ater the expiration of her term. She was succeeded by Sr. Francesca Kearney who was the last Prioress and the first Mother General of the Kentucky Dominicans.

Chapter Thirteen Notes

1. *Chronicle of the 20th Century*, pp. 85, 97, 100.
2. Decree of Pius X, Dec. 20, 1905.
3. Copy of letter, McCloskey to Superiors to Relgious Institutes in his diocese, Aug. 20, 1905.
4. SCA Copy of original document

   Signers of the document of affiliation:

S. Thomas O. Meara, President	S. Alberta Mosher
S. M. Josephine Beck, Treasurer	S. Francis Mahoney
S. Louise Cain, Secretary	S. Aloysia O'Connor
S. Catharine Kintz	S. M. Austin Tobin
S. Hyacinth Peters	S. Clare Glass
S. Gertrude Rapp	S. Cecilia Kennedy
S. M. Joseph Howard	S. M. Bernard Fogarty
S. Magdalen Norton	S. Genevieve Peeling
S. Rose Farrell	S. Reginald Murphy
S. M. Agnes Shannahan	

5. See Minogue, *Pages*, p. 206 for details on this mission.
6. SCA. This material is based on an unpublished autobiography written by Sr. Raphael Geyger as part of our oral history program, presented to Archives on March 3, 1984.
7. Bulletin Vol. 11, No. 25, April 12, 1964, file on St. John Berchmans.
8. SCA, Annals of St. John Berchmans.
9. SCA, Copy of letter from Peter A. Mortenson to Fr. DeVos.
10. Pamphlet titled *Carnival and Bazaar*, 1923, St. John Berchmans file.
11. Notes from interviews of Chicago pastors conducted by Sr. Helen Ann Marshall and Sr. Joann Mascari as part of a project on the history of Chicago community.
12. Dominican Associates are men and women who want to share the Dominican Spirit and mission with the sisters of St. Catharine Congregation.
13. Original letter of Rev. Lambert V. Studzinski to Sr. Ann Miriam Hickey, Archivist, Feb. 2, 1994.
14. Ibid.
15. *A Saint for St. Peter's: The Story of Brother Joseph Dutton*, William L. Huettel (1989).
16. Original correspondence between Brother Joseph Dutton and Sr. M. Pius Fitzpatrick is preserved at SCA.
17. SCA personal record of Sr. Magdalene, obituary.
18. *Historical News*, Adams County Historical Society, Vol. 22, No. 4, 1989. *The History of the Crosier Monastery and Renewal Center: Beginnings*, researched and compiled by Jerome W. Rausch, OSC, edited by Kermit Holl, OSC.
19. Ibid.
20. Eaton, Sr. Francine, *History of the Development of Spalding Academy*, Spalding, Nebraska, p. 25, Master's thesis.

21. SCA Crosier History pamphlet in Immaculate Conception Academy file.
22. SCA Original letter, F.G. Horn, OP to Mother Aquin, Aug. 6, 1914.
23. SCA Original letter, Esser, OP to Mother Aquin, Dec. 30, 1914.
24. SCA Original correspondence on Revised Constitutions, Record Group II, Sub-group A, Box 2.
25. SCA *Decretum laudis.*
26. SCA Original letter, Esser to Mother Aquin, July 12, 1915.
27. Because there was another institute in the Archdiocese named Sacred Heart, the Dominican sisters changed the name of their school to Rosary Academy.
28. See Minogue, *Pages,* Chapter XVIII, New Missions.
29. This refers to the Angelicum, see Encyclopedic Dictionary of Religion, p 3161.
30. SCA Council Minutes, Mother Aquin, 1911.
31. Ibid, June 17, 1911.
32. Original letter, Sr. Damian Schreiner, OP, Archivist, Great Bend, Kansas, May 9, 1990 to author.
33. Ibid.
34. The Great Bend Dominicans became a Papal Congregation in 1954.
35. Original letter, Sr. Damian Schreiner, OP, Archivist, Great Bend, Kansas, May 11, 1990 to author.

— *Part Three* —

From Prioress to Mother General to President

A TURNING POINT 1918-1924

SHOCK WAVES reverberated all over Europe when a Serbian student assassinated Austrian Archduke Ferdinand and his wife, Duchess Sophie von Hohenberg, on June 28, 1914. War flared over the continent, igniting a powder keg among countries spoiling for a fight. President Woodrow Wilson issued a proclamation of neutrality but when the German high command declared unrestrictive warfare against all shipping, neutral or belligerent, it became difficult to maintain neutrality. On Good Friday, April 16, 1917, the U.S. Congress voted to enter the war.[1]

In the Church, Pope Benedict XV had been elected to the papacy on September 3, 1914.[2] His position on the war was absolute impartiality but not uninterested neutrality. During his pontificate he wrote three encyclicals about peace, emphasizing cessation of hostilities, concern about child war victims and relief of those affected by the conflict.

Mother Francesca Kearney

At this point in history, Kentucky-born Alice Kearney was elected as the last Prioress General of the Kentucky Dominicans on July 25, 1915. Born November 4, 1868, she entered the community at age 20 and was professed March 7, 1889. Her brother, Lawrence Francis Kearney, OP, chose the name Francesca for her. All during her life she had a close relationship with this brother who was one of the most influential Dominicans in the St. Joseph Province and who served three terms as Provincial.[3]

Mother Francesca had the same piercing brown eyes, the same leadership qualities and the same passion for education as her brother. She seized every opportunity she could to send the sisters on to get degrees in preparation for the mission.

Some places, like Nebraska, required teacher certification. Mother Francesca provided for courses on Saturdays and summers so that the sisters would be qualified. In Nebraska, sisters attended Creighton University, Kearney State Teachers College and the University of Nebraska. Attending secular colleges/universities was considered a bold move. These affiliations generated loyal Cornhusker fans, and to this day, whenever the Big Red team plays, the sisters follow the scores and root for the Huskers.

In other parts of the country, Mother Francesca sent the sisters to Notre Dame, Loyola, Boston College and the University of Louisville. Dominican priests held summer courses at Rosary, Watertown, and also at the Motherhouse. Professor Fitzgerald of Loyola (Chicago) did the same at Hastings, Nebraska. Teaching and studying were simultaneous and though it took longer to earn a degree than full-time students took, the end was accomplished.

Missions in Nebraska

Early in her administration, pastors in Nebraska were clamoring for sisters to teach in their newly-founded schools. Nebraska was already familiar with Kentucky Dominicans in Spalding, North Platte, Exeter, Hastings, Cedar Rapids, Dawson and Fremont. Sisters, originally from the south and northeast, appreciated the rugged individualism characteristic of the people from the midwest, whereas, Nebraska-born sisters took it for granted, regarding it as a way of life.

Often farmers watched their winter wheat and later, their spring plantings, literally blown from the ground as their fields were parched by drought which lasted until late Fall. Undaunted, they would start all over again the next season. Impressed by the courage and perseverance of the people, Mother Francesca, unhesitatingly missioned her sisters to the Nebraska plains because souls hungered for God.

St. Mary, Omaha

Rev. C. Mugan requested sisters for St. Mary, South Omaha. Srs. Mary Oskamp, Inviolata Christian, Bernice Doucette and Corona Houghnon formed the first faculty. In a short time, increased enrollment called for additional teachers and a new building.[4]

Most of the employment in the area centered in the stockyards noted for their pungent odor. When parishioners complained of the smell the pastor would say, "If you didn't have that smell, you wouldn't have bread on the table."[5] These hardworking people sacrificed to send their children to the parochial school because they wanted them to have a good education as well as a strong foundation in faith. Many vocations resulted from the seeds sown in their homes and nurtured in the school.

In recent years, the Dominican sisters, affected by decreasing vocations, aging of members, reduced student enrollment and diminishing finances have withdrawn from some schools. Parishes have been forced to close convents because of exorbitant costs of upkeep for buildings inadequately used.

The stockyards are practically gone, the air is sanitized, condos have replaced modest homes and lay teachers staff the school. Two sisters still live in the convent: Sr. Caroline Miller, librarian and reading tutor and Sr. Patricius Henderson, retired x-ray technician now engaged in community service.[6]

Other Openings

In 1915, the sisters opened St. James, Kearney, and a year later, St. Patrick School, Havelock.[7] In 1916, they went to St. Patrick, Missouri Valley, Iowa. For 52 years sisters served St. James,

Kearney, 18 at Havelock and 53 in Missouri Valley.

With the changes following Vatican II, presence of sisters in schools and parishes diminished but in the Western Region, Kentucky Dominicans still serve in Nebraska in David City, Grand Island, Kearney, Omaha, Spalding, St. Paul, and also, Powers Lake, North Dakota.

Third Constitutions

The year 1918 was a very special one for the Congregation. Benedict XV approved and confirmed the Kentucky Dominicans as a "religious Congregation of simple vows under the rule of a Mother General." Furthermore, he "approved and confirmed the Constitutions as an experiment for seven years."[8] This was the third Constitutions approved for the Congregation.

A letter from John T. McNicholas, OP, to Mother Francesca conveyed the good news.

> Rev. Dear Mother Francis (sic)
> I hope my cable reached you for the feast of St. Catherine's. I was anxious that it should reach you for April 30th. His Eminence — our ex-Master General who is such a friend of Fr. Kearney's, left nothing undone. Mons. Esser was most insistent on Approval. Now that it is all over, we see the great advantage of the delay. Had your Constitution been approved of two years ago or even a few months ago, you would be obliged to introduce many changes owing to the new Code of Canon Law. Now your Constitutions has all the new provisions of the Code... Surely every sister of the Congregation should say some prayers of Thanksgiving for the approval of the Constitutions and every house should have a Mass of Thanksgiving. The great importance of your approved Constitution and the solid organization which is sure to come to you will only be appreciated with years. The 26 April will be a memorable day for your Congregation.
> I am taking the liberty of asking many Dominican Sisters to write to you for a copy of your Constitution. It will be a great charity — to print some extra copies for those requests — St. Mary's, the Mound — in fact all the Sisters even with approved

Constitutions from Rome will have to be guided by your Constitution until they can have their own remodeled and printed — All Constitutions even ours which have contrary provisions to the Code are abrogated on those contrary points next Sunday May 19th — St. Catherine's — the oldest Congregation in America will now indeed seem to be a mother to all the other Congregations of America because all will now have to turn to you for the remodeling of their Constitutions. Indeed all our Dominican Congregations in U.S. both Diocesan and those of Roman approval will and must take St. Catherine's as their pattern — It is likely that *Normae Dominicanae* shall be issued. When these come they will be practically your Constitution.... With these best wishes asking your prayers, I am Faithfully in S. Dom. (signed) John T. McNicholas, OP.   15 May 1918.[9]

When the Kentucky sisters received word of the approval of Rome, one of the first things they did was to arrange for a General Chapter. Thirty-one electors met for three days. Bishop Denis O'Donahue presided at the Mass and the election.

According to the Constitutions, instead of a Prioress General, the sisters were to elect a MOTHER GENERAL with a six year term renewable for a second six years. On July 25, 1918, Mother Francesca was elected the first Mother General of the Kentucky Dominicans. Her elected Councilors were: Srs. Mary Leo Quirk, Margaret Hamilton, Mary Louis Logsdon and Alexia O'Sullivan. In case of death, resignation or deposition, the first Councilor would take the place of the Mother General. Sr. Baptista Riley, Bursar General, though not a Councilor, presented her reports to the Council.[10]

The General Chapter was designed to be the voice of the grass roots sisters but it took many years before they realized the full extent of this. At the first General Chapter, 13 propositions were submitted. Of these, two especially stand out. "*Proposition 6:* The Chapter is asked to have modified the article relating to the term of Mother General. Why not make the term three years with the privilege of one re-election, or six years without it."[11] It failed to pass. The length of terms became a recurring question during the ensuing years.

"*Proposition 12:* One article of the Constitution requires that the Religious of the Congregation be addressed and referred to with the title `Sister.' The Chapter is asked to see that this obligation be enforced — that the word `rebel' and all its synonyms, as title, be subjected to the severe penalties which vulgarisms of this kind merit. Ordinary good breeding, even, scorns titles of this description. How do they sound on the lips of religious?"[12] There was a unanimous vote of support.

A World at War

With Mother Francesca, the Congregation entered a new era. That the first Mother General was keenly aware of her role to govern and direct "the whole Congregation entrusted to her care, according to the Rule and Constitutions" is evident from directives she sent to the community periodically. Uniformity was stressed, particularly regarding the common life. Attendance of the sisters in choir, in common for daily Mass and the recitation of the Little Office of the Blessed Virgin, was considered of utmost importance.[13]

The sisters observed the ancient custom of the Order calling for abstinence from meat on Wednesdays and Fridays of each week. Because of the War, the Food Administration under Herbert Hoover, exhorted housewives to have "meatless Mondays" and "wheatless Wednesdays." This combination of Dominican custom and patriotic conservation made for slim meals in the convent.

Countless rosaries were offered for the troops fighting overseas. Sisters and students made bandages, socks and sweaters. At every assembly the flag was raised. On Mother Francesca's feast day, October 4, 1918, the students presented a patriotic program in her honor. The orchestra opened the celebration with "Let's Keep the Glow in Old Glory." One of the young ladies, M. Spalding, played a cornet solo, "God Be With Our Boys Tonight." Then followed a flag drill, a resounding chorus sang "America" and Miss E. Harris presented a reading "To Our Union,"[14] On October 5, Rosary Sunday, a constant rosary vigil was maintained that "peace and victory might be granted to our distracted country."[15]

That same year brought other significant developments. Rev. A.H. Kunz, OMI, petitioned Kentucky for sisters to teach at St. Patrick, McCook, Nebraska. Work started on a convent and school but because of the War, construction workers were in short supply.

When Srs. Fabian Allen, Agnes Shanahan, Adelaide Jamrog, Alvarez Herlihy and Aquinas Hines arrived by train in September 1918, Julian and Anna Endres met them to tell them neither convent nor school was completed. The Endres took them to the home of Mrs. Mary Harr who gave them hospitality until the convent was ready for occupancy.[16]

The McCook School Board offered the use of two classrooms in the annex to the East Ward School. A third classroom was improvised in the basement of St. Patrick rectory. School opened immediately with an enrollment of 60 boys and girls.[17]

Influenza Epidemic

School had no sooner started than the Spanish influenza struck. In McCook, as elsewhere, schools, churches, places of public entertainment were closed.[18] Two of the sisters were stricken but the others went to the homes of those incapacitated by the disease. In an area predominantly Protestant, people grew accustomed to seeing the sisters ministering to all, regardless of religion. Because of their dedication and kindness, antiCatholic prejudice gradually lessened.

The disease raged across America and assumed pandemic proportions as it blitzed through Europe and Asia. So virulent was the epidemic that death was not uncommon. It was estimated that the mortality rate exceeded the casualties of the War. Twenty million died worldwide, 548,000 in the United States.[19]

Once again the sisters left the classroom to care for the sick. In Spalding, Nebraska, 14 of the Academy resident students became ill but under the constant care of Sr. M. Paul Philbin they were nursed back to health.[20]

In Kentucky, Fr. Regis Barrett, chaplain at Camp Zachary Taylor, pleaded for sisters to help at the camp where over 25% of 50,000 soldiers were sick.[21] Twelve Dominican sisters from Holy Rosary, Louisville, and from the Motherhouse joined sisters of various communities to assume nursing duties.[22]

One of the Knights of Columbus buildings was converted into a dormitory for the sisters. They divided the work into day and night shifts, often working more than 12 hours because each had a patient load of 100 or more, desperately ill with fever, dysentery and vomiting. Some of the men, back from overseas, had been gassed or wounded.[23] When any of the sisters became ill, they were sent back to their own convents.

At St. Catharine, Fr. Barrett spoke to the students and faculty paying "high tribute to the zeal of the Dominican sisters in their labors among the influenza victims at the camp and in the mountain districts of Eastern Kentucky.[24] Srs. Vallina Young, Vincentia Maguire, Louis Bertrand Lancaster, Laetitia Keene and Marietta Kilgannon went to Wheelwright, Van Lear, Wayland and Auxier.[25] They went from house to house nursing the sick, irrespective of creed or nationality. The mountaineers had never before had any contact with Catholics, much less with Catholic sisters. Having heard only anti-Catholic stories from their preachers, they were amazed that Roman Catholic sisters were not the embodiment of evil or the anti-Christ. The quiet labors of the sisters brought a change of vision in the plague-stricken Big Sandy and Elkhorn camps in Eastern Kentucky.[26]

In Massachusetts, when the flu broke out at Camp Devens, the sisters from St. Michael, Lowell, nursed the victims at the camp as well as their own parishioners.

> September was a short month in school as the epidemic broke out. All the schools of the city were obliged to close so dreadful was the sickness....Pitiful sights were witnessed by every sister here as each one joyfully went day after day to care for the sick and in some cases the dying....In all, the homes we visited were about four hundred and sixty, sometimes making two or three trips a day wherever we thought we could give a little helping hand or speak encouraging words to helpless victims of the flu.[27]

As the epidemic abated, the sisters resumed teaching in good health and ready to return to the sick at any time if needed.[28]

Peace and Progress

On November 11, 1918, the bells of St. Catharine pealed joyously to announce the end of war.[29] Pupils and teachers assembled in chapel for a Mass of Thanksgiving. After Mass, Mother Francesca granted a holiday from classes to celebrate, but first, all had to join in a Te Deum and recitation of the rosary to thank God for peace. In the afternoon, cars draped in red, white and blue took students to Springfield to join in the festivities.[30] Once again, life slipped into a calmer routine.

Expansion continued with the opening of St. Brendan School, Elkins, West Virginia in 1918, followed a year later by St. Mary, Red Oak, Iowa.[31]

Music was always a priority from the foundation of the community. In the first catalogues, courses were offered in piano, voice, guitar and violin. After the disastrous fire in 1904, one of the first purchases was a harp for $750 at a time when money was scarce. A notation in the annals stated that a teacher was hired to teach Sr. Imelda Brady to play the harp so that she would be ready to teach the students when they returned to St. Catharine. It is not surprising then that in Memphis a conservatory of music was opened under the direction of Sr. Teresa Webb, grandniece of Benjamen F. Webb, noted Kentucky historian.

In July 1917, Sr. Magdalene Norton had written to Mother Francesca:

> Mr. Anderson (Hon. Milton Anderson), Mr. J.K. Porter's son-in-law, our neighbor on the right side of St. Agnes, called to see me, regarding the purchase of the entire Porter block cor. Vance Ave. and Orleans St. to our alley, including Buildings — all on the property with whatever household furniture they will leave in the Porter home should we purchase it — and let him know before January 10, 1918, as that is the date of tax collection in Shelby County.[32]

The letter explained that the heirs found it a financial drain to maintain the palatial home and preferred to sell it to St. Agnes rather than to any other buyer. Sr. Magdalene pleaded with the Council to buy the Porter estate for a school for "small boys" since there was no facility for them in Memphis.[33]

The Porter property was purchased for $40,000 but not for a boys' school. Instead, it became the Memphis Conservatory of Music.

> The period from 1911 through 1924 was one of intensive academic and physical expansion. Two notable occurrences in this development program were the establishment of the St. Agnes Conservatory in 1918 and the opening of St. Agnes College in 1922. The former became incorporated under the title of Memphis Conservatory of Music and subsequently formed the department of music in St. Agnes College, a natural development since the conservatory from its inception had provided instruction for advanced students intent on professional careers as well as beginners.[34]

Another innovation was the acceptance of the administration of a general hospital in McCook, Nebraska. In a later chapter there will be more on the Conservatory, the College and the Hospital.

In the second decade of the 1900s, Mother Francesca missioned sisters to Sacred Heart, South Bend, Indiana (1921); St. Bartholomew (1921) and Our Lady of Peace (1923), Chicago, Illinois; St. Augustine, Reed, (1922) and St. Mary of the Woods (1922), McQuady, Kentucky.[35]

Archives and Annals

Archives and annals were initiated formally with the new Constitutions. Mother Francesca appointed Sr. Margaret Hamilton to organize the Annals.[36] Because many records were destroyed by fire in 1904, Sr. Margaret wrote far and wide, to Prouille, France; Stone, England; N. Adelaide, Australia to obtain missing information.[37] It was she who gathered data for the book written by Anna C. Minogue for the centennial in 1922,

Pages from a Hundred Years of Dominican History. While there are some inaccuracies in the book, Sr. Margaret did a yeoman's task in researching in an era before modern technology. There were no faxes, computers, or Internet. Travel was chiefly by train. She recorded oral histories, wrote queries to convents at home and abroad, and recorded her own memoirs, albeit with a flourish. So dedicated was she to preserving the history of the Kentucky Dominicans that when her sight began to fail, she learned Braille and used a Braille typewriter to record her research.

An important adjunct to Congregational history was the work of Sr. Althaire Lancaster who strove to correct inaccuracies in the Minogue book. In addition, she wrote a draft index to that volume which is helpful to anyone doing research. She also compiled a carefully researched necrology up to the mid-1960s.

At times, the preservation of the Archives became the responsibility of the Secretary General. Srs. Mary Ellen McTeague and Mary Patricia Green served in this capacity. Srs. Aquinata Martin and M. Esther Moore did some work in archives until Sr. Theodore Kline was officially appointed as archivist. She held that position until succeeded by Sr. Ann Miriam Hickey who was appointed in 1984.

Sr. Mary Patricia Green wrote a definitive history of *The Life and Constitutions from 1822 to 1969.* Essentially, history depends on the records kept by the sisters at the grass roots. If they fail to submit annals, the archives are found wanting when weighed in the balance.

Reverberations in Boston

Mother Francesca was a capable administrator able to cope with any situation. Once when William Cardinal O'Connell asked the superiors of academies in Watertown and Waverly to submit full financial reports of their institutions, Mother Francesca reminded him that according to Canon Law, the Congregation reported such matters to Rome. "We only wish to live in accordance with the guide given us by the Church."[38] The Cardinal informed her that he knew the law. Nothing further was made of it.

Whenever the Cardinal contacted local superiors, they informed Mother Francesca. At times, this resulted in a directive from her to the sisters:

> I have another message from the Cardinal about the "free and easy manner of the Dominican Sisters on the streets," and I wish to call your attention to the matter again....I know some of the Sisters are careless in this respect, go along the street laughing and talking, with mantles flying.[39]

The white habit drew attention to the wearers. A regulation was issued that front pieces be added to the mantles so that they could be buttoned from neck to toe. Black stockings were to be worn with low shoes when going out in public so no white ankles would show. But still, complaints continued.

> Again His Eminence has complained of the sisters being on the streets so much - he says he rarely goes out that he does not see some Dominicans on the streets. Now I know there is much necessary going out to the Cathedral lectures, to classes at the houses, etc. and I do not believe our sisters do more of it than others do, but our habit is conspicuous and some are very careless on the street about their manner and deportment. I beg of you again, sisters, stay at home as much as possible, not to ask unnecessary permissions to go out, and when you do go out, keep your mantle around you in such a way as to cover the habit. ...He has complained that the sisters go too much to St. Elizabeth's hospital. Please keep away from there unless it is necessary that you go. His Eminence seems to be under the impression that sisters get permission to go out to confession or for lessons and then go visiting. I do not know where he got this idea.[40]

One letter written by the Chancellor was anything but complimentary.

> Dear Sister Superior,
> His Eminence, the Cardinal, directs me to say that he wishes you to make a strict investigation to ascertain if any Sister in the Sacred Heart Academy drove an automobile along the North

Shore with three or four others about three weeks ago and write your findings to him at once.

His Eminence further directs me to inform you that once again he feels obliged to say he is not at all satisfied with the work of the Dominican sisters here.   signed: Rev. J. Haberlin[41]

The answer to His Eminence said it could not possibly have been Dominicans since none of them knew how to drive, and then, "It is a source of great regret and anxiety to know that you feel we are not serving the Diocese satisfactorily."[42]

Called to be Holy

Directives to the sisters were always interesting and usually indicative of what was happening within the Congregation. Special devotions increased as litanies to Our Lady, St. Dominic, St. Joseph and the Sacred Heart were added to daily prayers. Processions were held each Sunday: Holy Name, Our Lady, Blessed Sacrament and St. Dominic. Each week, suffrages for the dead included Office of the Dead and Libera procession.

One of the Council Orders read: "The three Our Fathers and Hail Marys said at noon are for benefactors, living and dead, not sinners."

Uniformity was stressed even to the width of hems on scapulars, sleeves and habits. Attention to office rubrics were emphasized with careful explanation of inclinations.

Mother Francesca exhorted the sisters to be mindful of poverty. She was known for her habit of turning off lights throughout the convent. When it came to railroad travel, she was positively frugal. Sisters about to depart for missions were summoned to her office for briefing: "Now sisters, there will be two in each upper berth. Sleep head to toe and maintain solemn silence." It was a challenge for two sisters in full habit with starched veils to fit two into an upper berth. As for solemn silence, laughter was good for the soul!

One of Mother Francesca's favorite sayings was, "Sisters, in doing the works of God, do not forget the God of good works."

When her term of office expired, she went to St. Agnes, Memphis, as bursar. She was happy to be relieved of the burden of office, but she continued to serve the community for many years. One of the interesting roles she had was with an innovative plan for formation of young sisters, which will be discussed in a later chapter. She died January 9, 1953. [43] Mother Francesca was a prayerful woman who is remembered as an outstanding leader in a time of transition.

Chapter Fourteen Notes

1. *The Reader's Companion to American History,* p. 1170 et seq.
2. Catholic Almanac 1992, pp. 131, 140.
3. Coffey, *The American Dominicans,* p. 547 et seq.
4. SCA Encactments of Prioress General, Sept. 1915, Council Minutes, July 26, 1915; Annals of St. Mary School, S. Omaha.
5. Personal interview with Sr. Fredricka Horvath, OP.
6. SCA Annals, St. Mary School, S. Omaha, 1995.
7. SCA Chronology of Institutions; Mission files of Havelock and Missouri Valley.
8. SCA, Decree, August 15, 1918.
   See also Green, Appendix IV.
9. SCA Original letter from John T. McNicholas, OP, to Mother Francesca, May 15, 1918.
10. SCA, *Report of Chapter Proceedings,* 1918.
11. Ibid. An added comment tells how the Chapter handled it. "In deciding this, a quotation from a letter from Rome was read and members of the Chapter agreed orally that the question admitted of no further appeal, so no vote was taken."
12. SCA *Report of Chapter Proceedings,* 1918. The tone of this proposition hints of sectionalism which Mother Francesca abhorred and often inveighed against.
13. SCA Administrative file of Mother Francesca Kearney, Constitutions Part I, Chapter IV. See also Green, p. 62 for details.
14. *The Record,* October 17, 1918.
15. Ibid.
16. Archives of Oblates of Mary Immaculate, Washington, D.C. Also, original letter of J. Barry Richard, OMI to writer, December 20, 1990.

17. Ibid.
18. Ibid.
19. *World Almanac 1988*, p. 448.
20. Eaton, Thesis on Spalding, Nebraska, p. 36.
21. Crews, p. 236.
22. Sisters of Charity (Nazareth), Loretto, Ursuline, Mercy and St. Francis also served at Camp Zachary Taylor. See *The Record*, October 24, 1918; November 7, 21, 1918.
23. *The Record*, October 24, 1918. Also, taped interview with Sr. Theophane Rittelmeyer, one of the volunteers.
24. *The Record*, November 21, 1918.
25. SCA Annals, 1918-1922; also, file of Sr. Vallina Young.
26. *The Record*, January 2, 1919.
27. SCA Annals of St. Michael, Lowell, Massachusetts.
28. *The Record*, November 7, 1918.
29. *The Record*, November 21, 1918.
30. Ibid.
31. SCA Enactments p. 16; Mission files, St. Patrick School, McCook, Nebraska 1918-1983, p. 16.
32. SCA Original letter, Sr. Magdalene Norton to Mother Francesca, July 17, 1917.
33. Ibid.
34. *See Siena College, Self-study Report*, History, p. 2 St. Agnes College changed its name to Siena College on January 1, 1939. The formal opening of the Conservatory occurred on October 5, 1918 under the auspices of the sisters of St. Agnes Academy and the St. Agnes Alumnae.
35. SCA Chronology of Institutions; Enactments pp. 23, 27; Mission files of these parish missions.
36. SCA Administrative file of Mother Francesca; Council Book 1904-1945, p. 136.
37. SCA original letters to St. Margaret Hamilton from various sources.
38. BAA Correspondence, Mother Francesca Kearney to Cardinal O'Connell, March 31, 1920; SCA Enactments 1904-1945, p. 20.
39. Letter from Mother Francesca to the Congregation, dated November 1, 1920.
40. Undated letter to the sisters from Mother Francesca.
41. Copy of original letter from Rev. J. Haberlin to Sister Superior.
42. BAA Original letter from Sr. Victorine to Cardinal O'Connell, September 6, 1937.
43. SCA Personal file, Mother Francesca.

THE ROARING TWENTIES AND DEPRESSING THIRTIES

IT WAS THE AGE of the Roaring Twenties with nine million cars registered in America, one for every six Americans. Women bobbed their hair, smoked, danced the Charleston and exercised their right to vote. Nellie Taylor Ross was elected Governor of Wyoming and Miriam (Ma) Ferguson, Governor of Texas. John Scopes, a biology teacher, was found guilty of teaching evolution and fined $100.[1]

Rome, alarmed at trends in America and the new emerging Catholic thought, warned against materialism and demanded an oath against modernism from its clerics. Bishops were concerned about the role of American women, especially women religious. Emphasis from the pulpit specified that women's place was in the home and women religious should definitely separate themselves from the world. As a result, lives of women religious became more restricted. Whereas, sisters had moved about freely wherever there was a need, had taken orphans or widows to live in their convent homes, had lived in the homes of lay persons when no convent was available, new regulations prohibited such activities.

A sister could not visit her own parental home; could not ride alone in a car with her own father or brother; could not go out unless accompanied by another sister. They were forbidden to have pets, such as dogs, cats or birds, because it might cause disedification.[2] Tea aprons were not to be worn; winter and summer underwear had to be obtained from the Motherhouse for uniformity; only plain black kimonos were allowed for night wear.

Newspapers, magazines, books, radios were curtailed or forbidden. Asceticism and cloister were virtues of the day. Not until Vatican II were these accretions lifted. As society touted a new freedom and the cloister retreated within itself, the Kentucky Dominicans met at the Motherhouse in 1924 in Chapter.

Mother Bernadette Clements

To succeed Mother Francesca, 47 delegates of the Second General Chapter elected a native Kentuckian, Sr. Bernadette Clements. Born in Washington County in 1873, of Robert and Eliza (Hite) Clements, Catherine attended the county public school in Clements district, a school initiated through the efforts of her father and his friends, L.A. Hamilton and Billy Smith.[3]

After completing high school at St. Catharine Academy, she entered the novitiate at age 19. She was professed in 1893 as Sr. Bernadette. Her younger sister entered the community six year later, becoming Sr. Dolorita.

Teaching assignments of Bernadette included Holy Rosary, Louisville, Kentucky; St. Francis de Sales, Charlestown, Massachusetts; and St. Dominic, Springfield, Kentucky. At Catholic University she majored in Spanish and Library Science, subjects she later taught in teacher training courses.[4]

When she assumed office in 1924 as second Mother General, her elected council consisted of Srs. Sienna Byrnes, Alexia O'Sullivan, Louise Robertson and Johanna Rowan. Sr. Mary Oskamp was bursar.[5] One of the first acts of the new Council was to implement the plan begun by Mother Francesca to open Sacred Heart School, Greeley, Nebraska.

Introduction to the new school was eventful. A tornado had seriously damaged the school under construction, and wash-outs along the way delayed the train on which Srs. Clara Simms and Ernestine Clark were traveling. At Central City they were met by James Fitzpatrick and E. Curran who drove them to Greeley.

The first classes were held in the Knights of Columbus Hall with 193 pupils enrolled. A month later on October 22, 1924,[6] the new school, Sacred Heart, was ready for occupancy. Sr. Clara Simms was principal with Srs. Gabriel Clark, Theophelia Punch, Mary Martin Langan, Ignatia Philbin and Ernestine Sullivan as faculty.[7] From Sacred Heart, in all kinds of weather, the sisters traveled to O'Connor, a nearby town, to teach at Visitation School and to conduct religion classes for three years.

Additional schools to which Mother Bernadette sent sisters for the first time were Resurrection and Sts. Simon and Jude, Brooklyn, New York; in Indiana, St. Augustine, Jeffersonville and St. Mark, Gary; and St. James, McMechen, West Virginia. Because of the large enrollment at Sts. Simon and Jude, the school schedule was divided into two sessions; from eight to twelve-thirty in the forenoon, and from one to four-thirty in the afternoon. It made for long days.

Since the seven year period of experimentation of the Constitutions was drawing to a close, Mother Bernadette deter-mined to seek final approbation from Rome. Once again, Fr. Horn worked on necessary revisions and advised the Council how to proceed.[8] They had to get approval of the ordinaries in the dioceses where the sisters served. Even though all docu-ments were in Rome by August 1925, the process dragged on endlessly.[9] It took three years before Pius XI issued the decree of approval on December 10, 1928.[10]

Financial Stress

Construction of the new chapel was begun at the Mother-house, but rising costs and lack of funds called a halt, leaving an uncompleted, empty shell. Academy students took advantage of the huge space to play basketball there.

In other action the Council decided to ask the people of Spalding, Nebraska, to buy the Academy property for $50,000. The sisters would continue teaching there, but they would be relieved of the responsibility of a parochial residence and the money would ease some of the financial burden.[11] However, it was only when Fr. James McMahon became pastor that the school was sold to the parish for $25,000, according to the deed filed August 10, 1943.

In Louisville, St. Vincent's Orphanage was overcrowded. To help remedy the situation, Bishop Floersh asked the sisters at St. Catharine, "to teach, train, clothe and feed" three children. Lucille Marcum, Henrietta Howard and Nellie Weatherington were welcomed to the Academy and were cared for by the sisters.[12]

On October 24, 1929, the stock market crash ended postwar prosperity. Black Thursday ushered in a period of worldwide financial panic and unemployment. In the United States, 12 million were jobless.[13]

Rural areas fared somewhat better than large cities; at least, they grew food. In Nebraska, farmers paid tuition for their children with eggs, tomatoes or a side of beef. At St. Catharine Hospital, McCook, bills were paid in kind. Pregnant women brought eggs or chickens in advance of their confinement. In one instance, after delivering a beautiful baby boy, the mother learned that the hospital owed her for extra produce she had brought in ahead of time. At the same hospital, nurses were happy to receive free room and board plus a small stipend.

The unemployed who rode boxcars from one place to another in the hope of finding work, often detrained in McCook, a railroad town. They gravitated to the hospital knowing that the sisters would give them a meal for mowing the grass or doing some small job, and then there would always be a sandwich "for the road."

Added to the financial stress of the time, the midwest suffered from an extended drought. Prairie fires and sandstorms swept across the plains, leaving bare fields and heartbreak. Winds whipped rounded bundles of tumbleweeds across the dried earth, becoming a prairie pest. In an effort to keep out dust, the

sisters stuffed wet rags around window frames. Among them-
selves they said, "When the dirt is red, it comes from Oklahoma;
when it is black, it is from Kansas." A task they dreaded was
returning to a convent which had been closed while they went
to summer school. It would take days to get rid of the dust.

Continuing Education

Convinced that the sisters needed to be well-educated in
order to be effective teachers, but at the same time, devoid of
funds to pay for education, the "Council decided to let Sisters
who can defray their own expenses attend Summer Schools."[14]

This brings home the fact that religious orders or congrega-
tions, as independent entities, are totally responsible for their
own living expenses, including education, health insurance,
retirement and pension. Parochial schools paid stipends for each
sister teacher, but as late as the 1940s the average annual stipend
per teaching sister was $350.[15]

What did the Council mean by "Sisters who can defray their
own expenses?" Where would the sisters, vowed to poverty, get
the money?

Appeals were made to pastors to increase stipends, but it was
Depression time and parishes were struggling. Some sisters
received money from their families to pay tuition. Others had
patrimony which they could use if proper permission were
obtained. It was not an ideal situation with the danger of divid-
ing members into "haves" and "have nots." The Congregation
realized that general education funds had to be set aside for all
members.

As in the previous administration, summer schools were set
up in the large missions by engaging professors, usually,
Dominican friars. Mother Bernadette sent a directive to the
membership regarding summer school.

> For the coming vacation the Sisters...will have studies and
> class five mornings in the week, and at least, one or two hours in
> the afternoon....It is advisable that all, unless prevented by sick-
> ness, do either advanced study or review some class work which
> will be to advantage the coming year. Study is one of the prin-

cipal duties of Dominican life and all are asked to apply themselves to it with energy and zeal to make themselves fit instruments for honor of God and good of souls.[16]

In an effort to ensure concentration on study, the sisters were not allowed visitors, even relatives, during summer school sessions.

At times, outside agents dictated regulations. In Chicago, the Board of Delegates for Religious Communities of Women wrote that superiors should not allow sisters to attend secular universities and colleges for special courses in education without the express approval of the Board. The same Board reported that sisters had been seen at public movies, much to the surprise and disedification of lay people.[17]

Mother Bernadette strove to steer a middle course between complainants and sisters, but informed that the sisters were influenced by mores of the times, she stated the case directly to the members: "Scandal has been given by the Sisters using powder, perfume, and some have gone so far as to use the lipstick." Even perfumed soap was banned.

In 1928 Mother Bernadette received a message from Cardinal O'Connell which she sent out in a directive to the Boston sisters: "His Eminence does not wish the sisters to take part in the November election."[18] It was the year Al Smith was running for president.

Once when she was in Boston, she visited the Cardinal. She described him as "very pleasant and kind," and quoted him as saying, "Some, some, not all are too free. He also told me our Sisters are doing good work in his diocese."[19] To some extent, this assuaged his earlier uncomplimentary criticism.

Promoting education was one of Mother Bernadette's strong points. Besides sending sisters to study, she expected accountability from teachers. She appointed some sisters as supervisors of the schools where Kentucky Dominicans taught.

After her term of office expired, she spent her last years teaching and preparing young sisters for the classroom until she was forced to retire because of ill health. One of the highlights of her life had been a trip with Sr. Louise Robertson to Rome where they had an audience with the Holy Father. She died March 10, 1947.[20]

Mother Mary Louis Logsdon

When the Third General Chapter assembled in 1930, 52 dele-gates met for two days, August 2-3. Bishop J.A. Floersh presided at the election of Sr. Mary Louis Logsdon as third Mother General. On her Council there were two former Mothers General, Francesca Kearney and Bernadette Clements. Srs. Victorine Donovan and Ceslaus McIntyre completed the Council with Sr. M. Michael Welsh as bursar.[21]

Born in Marion County on October 5, 1868, Mary Logsdon was the daughter of Thomas H. and Ann Elizabeth (McAtee) Logsdon. After attending St. Dominic School, Springfield, she completed her studies, entered the novitiate and was professed March 7, 1889. Two of her sisters joined the Ohio Dominicans, Srs. Gertrude and Athanasius.[22] The three visited back and forth between Ohio and Kentucky on special occasions.

Mother Mary Louis knew the farm. Underneath her bed she had a pair of "farm shoes" which she wore when walking the grounds to see what was happening in the dairy, or the apple orchard, or the vegetable gardens.[23] She had beehives, a row of square white boxes mounted on stands, from which she ex-tracted honey to go with fresh biscuits or to pour over home-made ice cream, a favorite of the young sisters. She never wore protective covering when working with the bees, but one could see her with her long white apron going from hive to hive The bees were her hobby and probably afforded her time to think in solitude because nobody else wanted to go near the bees.

She was a pragmatist, a woman of action. It bothered her to see the chapel, begun in 1924, standing incomplete. She appealed to the sisters to make sacrifices to save money for the completion of the project. She asked them to donate their Christmas gift money to the chapel fund. The Congregation and its friends responded. The dream was realized when the chapel was blessed June 8, 1931.[24]

With the influx of increasingly large classes of postulants, a more spacious novitiate was a necessity. It became part of the new chapel wing and included an extensive, sunlit recreation room, several smaller classrooms, offices for the novice mistress and some administrative offices and conference room for the Council. On the ground floor there were science classrooms, however, dormitories with curtained cubicles were on the third floor in an older wing.

As the novitiate increased, so did the requests for sisters to staff new schools. In 1932, Fr. Bernard J. Reilly asked for sisters to open a school at Our Lady of Lourdes, Queens Village, New York. It opened with only grades one to five. By 1936, all eight grades were completed and the first graduation was held. It became one of the largest schools staffed by Kentucky Dominicans. At its peak in the 1970s, when Sr. Deirdre Cotter was principal, enrollment was over 1500. This necessitated four classes for each grade.[25]

Today the school is staffed by a lay faculty with a sister of St. Joseph as principal. Sr. Marian Jude Johnson was the last Dominican principal to serve there. She and Sr. Rebecca O'Brien left Our Lady of Lourdes in 1993.

Another New York school the sisters opened in 1932 was St. Vincent Ferrer, Brooklyn. Named after a charismatic medieval Dominican preacher, the parish welcomed the sisters to a well-established neighborhood. For 53 years, Kentucky Dominicans taught there until forced to withdraw because of personnel shortages.[26]

House of Studies

With two colleges, St. Catharine Junior College at the Motherhouse and Siena College, Memphis, and the new junior college, the demand for qualified instructors was greater than ever. To facilitate advanced study for the sisters, Mother Mary Louis and Council purchased a small residence, 1236 Monroe Street, NE, Washington, DC as a house of studies.[27] Srs. Mary Michael Welsh, superioress, Sadoc Deppen, housekeeper, and Aquinata Martin opened St. Catharine House of Studies in January 1936.

The following June, Srs. Catharine Frances Galvin, Julia Polin and Albertus Magnus Garvey joined them as students at Catholic University. Sisters from other communities also lived with them, foreshadowing intercommunity living.

After Srs. Mary Michael and Aquinata received their doctorates in 1937, Sr. Jamesetta Kelly was appointed superior and studied for her doctorate in classical languages. Srs. Consuela Wilhelm, Leo Marie Preher, Anne Mary Tamme and Sheila Buckley joined the group to study at Catholic University.

Before long, the Monroe Street facility proved inadequate. Mother Mary Louis borrowed money to build a larger house on Otis Street in DC. This dwelling flourished until 1950 when serious threats of taxation caused the sisters to sell it.[28] Although they regretted the loss of the Washington House of Studies, as federal funding and private grants for education became available, the sisters took advantage of the opportunities and were able to attend colleges and universities across the country and abroad.

Conference of Dominican Mothers General

In the 1930s, letters had been coming from Santa Sabina[29] urging the Third Order Dominican sisters to consider some kind of collaboration. Mother Bernadette had liked the idea, and with Mother Samuel of Sinsinawa was ready to promote a meeting of Dominican Major Superiors, but nothing happened until 1935. The Dominican sisters of San Rafael, California, hosted the first Conference of Dominican Major Superiors.

Mother Mary Louis did not share her predecessor's enthusiasm for the movement because she feared it was an attempt at amalgamation. In no way would she agree to give up the particular identity of St. Catharine Kentucky Dominicans. She did not attend the meeting and sent no representative.

However, the 12 Congregations attending the conference proclaimed: "Resolved that the object and purpose and mind of these conferences of Dominican sisters are in no way concerned with amalgamation, federation, union or any other thing that would interfere with the autonomy of the several congregations represented."[30]

The first conference appointed six commissions to discuss matters of common interest: uniformity of Constitutions, uniformity of ceremonial, uniformity of religious habit, recitation of Divine Office, training of young sisters, and establishing a house in Rome.[31] Over the years, attendance of representatives of Dominican congregations increased. In 1957, when the conference was hosted in Kentucky, Mother Mary Julia was elected president.

A Second Term

When the Fourth General Chapter convened in 1936, 62 delegates met for two days. Mother Mary Louis was re-elected for another six years, as were Mothers Francesca and Bernadette to the Council. New Council members were Srs. Cecilia Hill and Bridget Connelly and Sr. Clara Simms was bursar.

Of the four propositions introduced at the Chapter, three dealt with changes in the habit. The face veil[32] was eliminated, the cape was changed from starched linen to one made of the same goods as the habit, and superiors were allowed to purchase habit material commercially rather than only from the Motherhouse. The fourth proposition was a detailed outline for establishing a Community Educational Plan.[33]

Because of the growth in membership, the effort to keep newly professed sisters at the Motherhouse for a year of study, and the increased number of retired and sick sisters, the Council petitioned Rome for permission to borrow money to build a dormitory to meet these needs. In the spring, Apostolic Delegate Archbishop Amleto Cicognani, sent the authorization to borrow $50,000 for the dormitory.[34] With an additional $25,000 on hand, the construction of Bertrand Hall proceeded with 55 bedrooms on five floors and a recreational, all-purpose area on the ground floor. When Mother Mary Louis had her Golden Jubilee in 1939, she donated her Jubilee gift money to the dormitory building fund, but money ran out before the installation of an elevator. To this day, one end of Bertrand Hall has a sealed, empty elevator shaft.

It was a long walk from the chapel or refectory to Bertrand Hall. With no elevator, it was too exhausting for the infirm to climb to upper floors. This did not go unnoticed.

Because the Academy was flourishing and the college was growing, bedroom space for students was at a premium. Sr. M. Paul Philbin, as college prefect, asked if the college could use the fifth floor. Students moved into the top floor. Like the nose of the camel in the tent, gradually more and more students moved into Bertrand Hall until the original purpose of the building was practically forgotten.

Two new schools were opened in 1938, St. Francis, Forest City, Arkansas, and St. Philip Neri, Omaha, Nebraska. After much deliberation, a nine-bed hospital was begun in 1942 in Spalding, Nebraska.[35]

Towards the end of her life when her eyesight became impaired, a novice was assigned to read aloud to Mother Mary Louis for her daily spiritual reading. Like an investigative reporter, she always quizzed the novice to find out what was happening around the Motherhouse. She died at the age of 81. Mother Mary Louis' accomplishments were many, but she is remembered most for her kindness and integrity.

Chapter Fifteen Notes

1. *Chronicle of the 20th Century*, pp. 320, 322, 326, 327, 330.
2. SCA Council Minutes, June 15, 1928, p. 202.
3. SCA personal file of Mother Bernadette Clements. Minogue, *Pages,* p. 151.
4. SCA Personal file of Mother Bernadette Clements.
5. SCA Proceedings, General Chapter, 1924, pp. 14-16.
6. SCA Annals, Sacred Heart School, Greeley, Nebraska.
7. Ibid.
8. SJPA letter written by Mother Bernadette to Rev. Raymond Meagher, Nov. 20, 1928.
9. See Green, Chapter IV for details.

10. SCA Decretum. Also, see Green, pp. 53, 59, 85.

11. Annals, March 13, 1926. Also, Eaton thesis, p. 45.

12. SCA letters from Assistant Chancellor of Diocese of Louisville, Francis C. Cotton, July 28, 1926; August 10, 1926; August 13, 1926.

13. *Chronicle of the 20th Century*, p. 375, passim.

14. SCA Council Minutes, March, 1925.

15. Wittberg, *The Rise and Fall of Catholic Religious Orders*, p. 52.

16. SCA Administrative File of Mother Bernadette. See *U.S. Catholic Historian* Vol. 5, Nos. 3 and 4, 1986, pp. 357-364 re: Cardinal's campaign against women's suffrage.

17. SCA Administrative file of Mother Bernadette.

18. SCA Directive of Mother Bernadette to the Congregation.

19. SJPA letter from Mother Bernadette to Raymond Meagher, OP, December 12, 1926.

20. SCA Personal file, Mother Bernadette.

21. SCA Chapter proceedings, 1930.

22. SCA Administrative file, Mother Mary Louis Logsdon, also, copy of obituary, *The Springfield Sun*, Obituary, December, 1949.

23. Personal interview, Sr. Francine Eaton, OP.

24. SCA Administrative file, Mother M. Louis Logsdon.

25. Personal interview with Sr. Deirdre Cotter, former principal of Our Lady of Lourdes, Queens, NY.

26. SCA Chronology of Institutions, also, mission file St. Vincent Ferrer School, N.Y.

27. SCA Record Group XX, House of Studies.

28. Ibid.

29. Santa Sabina is the Dominican headquarters, Rome.

30. SCA - Administrative file, Mother Mary Louis Logsdon.

31. Ibid.

32. A face veil was an extra long veil used when receiving Holy Communion or when going out. It came down over the forehead, covering part of the face.

33. SCA Report of Chapter Proceedings, 1936.

34. SCA Original letter from Apostolic Delegate, Archbishop Amleto Cicognani to Mother Mary Louis Logsdon.

35. SCA, Chronology of Institutions.

WORLD WAR II AND THE AFTERMATH

SUNDAYS WERE ALWAYS QUIET at the Mother-house but Sunday, June 28, 1942, seemed unusually so. It was mid-morning and 63 delegates were assembled in chapel to elect a new Mother General and Council. Bishop J.A. Floersh presided as the secret ballots were read and tallied. Sr. Margaret Elizabeth Walsh was elected on the first ballot.[1] When the Bishop asked her to come forward to the sanctuary he had to wait. She was not a delegate.

There was a pause as two sister delegates went to seek her. Soon, they brought the newly-elected sister to the chapel, one on either side of her, as if they feared she might run away. All the way down the aisle, she kept shaking her head in disbelief. She was postmaster, music director, Latin teacher. For 25 years her only assignment had been the Motherhouse. How could she have been chosen? She was dumbfounded!

Election of her Council included Srs. Marie Leonard, Rose of Lima Lohmeier, Paschal Mullaney and Christina Goggins. Sr. Eugene Sheehan was chosen as bursar general. Since two members of the new Council were not delegates, the inclusion of them and the new Mother General brought the number of voters to 66.[2]

The Chapter was brief with only four proposals to consider. Three, related to the persistent Dominican theme of study, called for graduate education of the sisters, establishment of a Board of Education to plan for the needs of the schools, and supervision of the teachers in order to implement the highest standards of education. One proposal called for the extension of home visits with permission to partake of a meal at home.[3]

Mother Margaret Elizabeth Walsh

Who was this woman elected by the Fifth General Chapter? Lucy Walsh, born in 1882 in Stoneham, Massachusetts, often told a story about her vocation. After graduating from Salem Normal School, she taught in the Salem public schools and was organist and soloist in her home parish. Her brother, Fr. William Walsh, at one time curate at St. Francis de Sales, Charlestown, Massachusetts, was known for counselling young women who felt they had a vocation.

One day, Lucy planned to tell her mother that she wanted to become a sister. She began, "Mother, I want to —" but she was interrupted. "Not now, Lucy," said her mother, "I want to talk to your brother." "But, Mother —" "Not now, Lucy," and turning to the young priest, she said, "And you — you stop sending all these girls to the convent. We need good women at home." Lucy decided her message would wait for a more appropriate time![4] A more appropriate time did come and Lucy entered St. Catharine Novitiate on March 4, 1916.

Professed as Sr. Margaret Elizabeth on August 4, 1917,[5] an experienced and talented musician with a beautiful contralto voice, she was put in charge of the music and choir at St. Catharine. Those were the golden days of music. Postulants and novices who never sang before learned the meaning of arsis and thesis, spent hours rehearsing Gregorian chant, and mastered three and four-part hymns from the old St. Basil Hymnal.

In addition to her music, she taught Latin and ran the post office. Sr. Virginia Thomas Hamilton remembers being taught Latin privately when she transferred to St. Catharine from another school. She needed Latin to graduate.[6] Later, she served an apprenticeship in the post office under her Latin tutor and finally became postmaster herself.

Mother Margaret Elizabeth began her administration as World War II raged, a war which reshaped the future of the world. Over 16 million troops were serving.[7] Because many men were overseas, women entered the work force, particularly to produce needed supplies. Rosie the Riveter did her share to end the debacle. What happened to the children, the first latchkey kids, whose fathers in service and whose mothers worked in factories? In Chicago, at Our Lady of Peace and St. Bartholemew, as in other schools, kindergartens were opened and filled to capacity.

Rationing of gas, fruit, meat and butter was in effect. As a butter substitute, oleo, resembling Crisco, was sold with coloring packets. If the mixing of color was not thorough, the result was a marbleized white and yellow substance. Air raid drills were the order of the day and any vacant plot was converted to a victory garden to raise vegetables.

Pupils conducted huge paper drives, saved grease and learned to observe restrictions of "blackouts." Shoes were rationed. Although each American was allowed three pairs per year, this did not affect the sisters who were accustomed to one new pair annually if necessary. They gave their extra shoe ration coupons to others who needed them. When candidates entered the novitiate they had to bring their ration books with them or write home for them.

Because of the draft, few men were available, especially for farm work. St. Catharine's large farm needed workers to handle crops and livestock. Each day at Holy Hour, the chaplain included in his petitions: "Now, sisters, let us pray for men." Until it was understood the prayer meant men for farm work, it caused a few smiles.

After the atom bombing of Hiroshima and Nagasaki, the announcement of Peace was made on August 14, 1945. At St. Catharine it coincided with the reception of candidates to the habit. The next day was profession day for the novices. A sudden halt was called to the visiting when the big bell rang to announce the end of the war and to summon the sisters to chapel. Novices and postulants abruptly left their company to file to chapel. Their visitors did likewise to join in singing the Te Deum.

During and after the war, demands for sisters to teach in parish school increased exponentially.[8] Not all requests were granted because of limited personnel. During Mother Margaret Elizabeth's two terms of office (1942-1948 and 1948-1954), 29 new institutions were undertaken: nine in Kentucky, seven in Massachusetts, three in Nebraska, two each in Tennessee, Louisiana and Illinois, one each in Puerto Rico, Ohio, New Jersey and Indiana.[9]

Numerous requests were from foreign missions, but not all missionary activity was on foreign soil. Bishop Francis R. Cotton referred to the work of the sisters in the diocese of Owensboro as missionary work. They staffed schools in Reed, McQuady, Fulton and Hopkinsville where salaries were low or non-exis- tent. Sr. Catherine deRicci Miller wrote that there was no fixed salary since it depended on the farmer's crops. Sr. Theophane Rittelmeyer also wrote that because drought ruined the crops, farmers were impoverished and barely subsisted. Some of the children even needed clothing. Sophomores at Holy Rosary, Louisville, sent clothes to relieve the situation. Bishop Cotton, aware of the poverty-stricken conditions under which the sisters worked, wrote in appreciation:

> The enclosed check for one hundred dollars is sent in appreci- ation for the work your sisters are doing in a missionary way in this missionary diocese.

The sisters labored in Fulton for eight years; Hopkinsville, 23; Reed, 42; and McQuady, 45. Their work was blessed with many vocations to the religious life.

In Bayou Country

A glorious page of home missionary work was the collabora- tive efforts in Louisiana of the Dominican friars and sisters.[11] Fr. Edward L. Curtis, OP, whose two sisters had been professed at St. Catharine (Srs. Emerita and M. Edna) asked Mother

Margaret Elizabeth for sisters to help in the Louisiana missions. In August, 1946, Srs. Rose Rita Murray and M. Joseph Fosskuhl, accompanied by Council member Sr. Christina Goggins, arrived in Campti, Louisiana, where Fr. Thomas Sheehan, OP, met them to drive them to Montgomery. A small convent like a doll house awaited them. Five women from the parish and Murphy Milling welcomed them with a fried chicken dinner. Ten days later, Sr. Raphael Geyger joined them, but she stayed in Montgomery for only a year. Once all were settled, Sr. Christina returned to St. Catharine to give an account of the foundation.

The first tour of St. Patrick parish, Montgomery, opened the eyes of the new missionaries to the appalling poverty of the people. Most homes were made of logs or unfinished lumber with plain boards to partition rooms. Few had enough chairs, but the sisters made themselves at home by sitting on the edge of a bed. The only telephone was in a garage in town. Accommodations for the sisters were simple. They did their laundry in the yard using a tub and an aluminum washboard. Water was heated in pans and pails on a four-burner stove. Keeping white habits clean was a chore! One day two parishioners, Ruth and Roberta Duffy, saw the sisters struggling with the wash. After that, they took the clothes once a week, washed them and returned them to the sisters to dry.

In 1947, Srs. Marion McCormick (Paulina), Dominica Meehan, Georgine Marie Crowley and Anne Regis Hartnett were missioned to Louisiana. The first three stayed at Nativity in Campti, while Sr. Anne Regis served at St. Patrick, Montgomery, a parish 22 miles south of Campti, the main mission. Usually, three friars worked out of the rectory at Campti. Since there was no rectory in Montgomery, one of the friars commuted for daily Mass.

The convent at Campti was large but totally unfurnished. Even the bathtub had been removed by the previous occupants. When Fr. Paul V. Barret arrived in Campti as a replacement for Fr. Sheehan, he asked his father to donate a bathtub for the sisters. This was followed by an electric washer from his father's department store in Texas. Mother Margaret Elizabeth saw to it that the sisters in Montgomery also had an electric washer.

When the Hartnetts visited their daughter in Montgomery they decided to improve the situation. Mrs. Hartnett bought curtains and hung them while the sisters were teaching. Not to be outdone, Sr. Raphael made curtains for Campti out of under-skirt material faced with a green border.

Mr. Hartnett worried about the terrain the sisters had to cover on their weekend trips to out-missions. They had to walk through slick, slippery, gumbo soil. He bought them shoes with cleats to ensure a safe trip through the red mud. On Saturdays, Fr. Curtis or one of his assistants dropped the sisters at a spot on the highway. From there they trudged through the woods across a railroad track to Red River, a mulatto settlement. Here a parishioner met them to row them across the river in a leaky boat. On the other side, another trek through more woods brought them to the house where families were gathered for instruction. Cleated shoes were a blessing on these journeys!

School segregation was strict. The government provided books, teachers and transportation to whites and blacks, but separately. Mulattos were not accepted in the white school and they refused to attend the black school. Because the issue was not only controversial, but potentially hazardous, Fr. Curtis asked his associate, Fr. Thomas Sheehan to teach the mulatto children. The latter spent time in the sisters' classrooms to observe their teaching techniques. He taught all eight grades at Black Lake, five days a week, until Fr. Arthur Kinsella arrived. Fr. Kinsella persuaded the school authorities to supply a teacher but the sisters prepared children for First Holy Communion.

Once when Sr. Marion prepared children for First Holy Communion, she lined them up according to size, regardless of color. Immediate protests were made to Fr. Curtis who visited the convent to ask, "Who was the bright star who mixed black kids with white kids?" Sr. Marion raised her hand.[12] He merely laughed and did the same thing at Confirmation time. The people tolerated it and said he didn't know any better. He stopped segregation of the people when receiving Eucharist at Mass. Color never mattered to Fr. Curtis or the sisters.

On Sundays, mission stations were always a challenge. Fr. Curtis heard confessions out in the yard. Mass in one place was offered on the kitchen table with chickens and pigs hovering underneath. It was not unusual for the sisters to give their own breakfast of fruit and cereal which they had brought with them to the children. This was in the days when fasting from midnight was the rule. It meant that the sisters had no food until they returned to the convent in the afternoon.

Some places, like Verda, Trichell, Clear Lake, Coushatta and King Hill were regular mission stops. Others like Clarence, Goldanna, Castor, Bayou Bourbea and Aloha were served only twice a month. Some stations were so remote that the missionaries reached them only once a year, usually at Christmas.[13]

Benefactors were generous making it possible for the sisters to carry on the work. Sr. Rosella Mattingly sent a tabernacle, candlesticks and vestments. She remembered special occasions with gifts for the children knowing the dreams of a child's heart.

Fr. Raymond Shevlen of Resurrection parish, Brooklyn, New York, sent packages of food and clothing from time to time. Our Lady of Peace parish, Chicago, Illinois, donated an altar and wax candles. Sr. Agnes Conway supplied much-needed books and other school supplies.

Household items were always welcomed as when Fr. Richard J. Desmond, OP, sent a coffee pot and a frying pan. Sr. Raphael's nephew donated a crate of coffee and whenever Fr. Roberts, OP, visited from Boyce, he brought bags of fruit and cookies.[14]

Missionary work in Louisiana was many things. Sometimes it was caring for a sick mother or baby; sometimes it meant babysitting while parents attended adult discussion groups facilitated by Sr. Rose Rita. Srs. Raphael and Anne Regis taxied children to school or church when the distance was too far for them to walk. Always it meant prayer and study. The friars took turns giving weekly spiritual conferences to the sisters. Office and the rosary were important threads in the tapestry of their lives. They prayed aloud sitting in the back of their pickup truck on the way to mission outposts; they prayed before Mass as the priest heard confessions; and they prayed with the children and parents as part of the instructions. To paraphrase what was said of St. Dominic, these missionaries on the road talked *to* God or *of* God.

Isla Del Encanto (Island of Enchantment)

Another missionary effort begun in 1948 occurred when Mother Margaret Elizabeth called for sisters to staff a mission in Puerto Rico. Fifty-six sisters responded. The pioneers chosen for this undertaking at Colegio San Carlos, Aguadilla, were Srs. Osanna McHugh, Amelia del Carmen Rivera, M. Thomas Shelvey and M. Jeanne White. The only one who spoke Spanish was Sr. Amelia, a native Puerto Rican, who had graduated from St. Catharine Junior College and then went to Siena College, Memphis, Tennessee.[15]

The group sailed on the Borinquen, arriving in San Juan on July 26, 1948. Jack O'Brien (brother of Srs. Ulicia and Rose Vincent), Sr. Amelia's family and two Redemptorist priests met them at the dock.[16] The people of San Carlos welcomed them warmly and apologized that there was as yet no convent. For seven months, the recruits lived with three native Trinitarian sisters. It was an excellent experience in interculturation and inter-community living. The Trinitarian sisters taught them "a great deal about the culture and started them on the rocky road to Spanish."[17]

Sr. Amelia was the keystone of the mission. Whenever there was a free moment, she taught her companions Spanish. When Sr. Felicitas Bassett joined the staff, her proficiency in the language was an added boon.

In school, textbooks were in English, but in the barrios the people knew only Spanish. How could the sisters teach doctrina (CCD) in a language they did not know? They began with the basics, learning the Our Father, Hail Mary and Glory Be. Once they mastered the Sign of the Cross, they felt they were on the way. However, when they went to the barrios, they took San Carlos students to act as interpreters.

Almost every year, new volunteer sisters arrived to serve at the Colegio which included grades K-12. Srs. Joseph Leo Pietrowski and Ann Dolores Shea taught religion on Saturdays at nearby Ramey Air Force Base. Some of the sisters took advantages of courses offered at the Base at the Inter-American University extension.[18]

Because the District Hospital was understaffed, Srs. Claire

McGowan and Ann Dolores Shea organized a group of students to help feed and entertain the patients in the Pediatric ward two afternoons each week. They sang, told stories and jokes, and learned first-hand the effects of malnutrition. The death of Juanito, a favorite patient, opened their eyes to the misery that lack of food can cause. The student volunteers learned to give of themselves and what they had to those less fortunate. Sr. Ann Christine Ryan introduced a program of community service which included work in the hospitals, health clinics, day centers for the elderly, also tutoring on a one-to-one basis. The purpose was to give the students a clear idea of their commitment as future Christian leaders in their own community.[19]

Sr. Amelia del Carmen, at the request of Bishop Alfredo Mendez, became director of a secular institute called Hermanas de la Sagrada Familia located in Arecibo. The Bishop exhorted her, "Give them the spirit of St. Dominic."[20]

She remained with the group for three years, instructing them in the religious life and helping them to lay a firm foundation. The institute is flourishing and carrying on the missionary work begun under Sr. Amelia in 1965.

In the 70s, Sr. Amelia undertook a different ministry in Parroquia Nuestra Senora de Fatima in Rabanal de Cidra. For 12 years she did everything except hear confessions and say Mass. At first, the pastor was reluctant to allow her to be Eucharistic minister, but the Bishop gave full consent. Because of the increase in the number of elderly no longer able to go to church, the people were happy to have Sr. Amelia make pastoral visitations. Among other things, she prepared children and adults for the sacraments, instructed altar servers, supervised parish celebrations such as Holy Week services and May processions. Always she preached the rosary.

On the side of a hill, the people themselves had built a little convent for her, rather like a hermitage. One tiny room was used as a chapel. Each evening a parishioner came to say Divine Office with her. It was a sad day in the parish when Sr. Amelia decided she had to return to her religious community on the mainland. Her ministry now is community service and the prayer apostolate.

There were vocations among San Carlos students but the

young would-be sisters were brought to the mainland for their novitiate. Some found Americanization too difficult; some were too lonesome away from Isla del Encanto (Island of Enchantment). Added to the language barrier, strange foods and different customs, was a certain amount of Puerto Rican prejudice. It was not intentional, but it was many years before ethnic consciousness and inculturation brought about a change. Few from the island remained in the Congregation. However, Sr. Narcisa Barreto-Perez worked with Hispanics in Chicago and then returned to do missionary work on the island where she is closely involved with Dominican Associates in Aguadilla and environs. Sr. Gladys Perez taught for some years in Dominican schools before transferring to a cloistered Dominican community in Spain. She has been missioned to another Dominican cloister in Africa.

For 28 years the Kentucky Dominicans taught in Aguadilla. Armed with great enthusiasm and love of God, they did what many missionaries did in pre-Vatican II days. Unwittingly ignorant of native customs and culture of their students, the sisters brought an American education to the island. Straddling two cultures was not easy but in the end both were enriched because of their collaboration. Both sisters and alumni were proud when Colegio San Carlos was accredited in 1963 by the Middle states Association of Secondary Schools and Colleges.[21]

Sisters were offered the opportunity to spend summers in Puerto Rico to gain experience in the language and culture. As a result, some of them returned to the mainland and chose to work in inner-city parishes with a predominance of Hispanics.

That the sisters had some impact on the people is undeniable. Loyalty of alumni is proof of that. As the number of religious personnel decreased, some of the graduates returned to teach at their alma mater. When Srs. Aquinette Le Fort, Appoline Simard, Ann Christine Ryan and Carmen Maldonado brought a close to the staffing of the Colegio by Kentucky Dominicans, devoted lay people took over the administration and teaching, determined to keep the school viable.[22] The principal, Nidya Ugarte de Nieves and practically all the teachers are graduates of the Colegio.[23]

Many sisters not mentioned in this brief sketch served in

Aguadilla. Other missionaries not to be overlooked are those who ministered at the University of Puerto Rico, Ponce, which will be discussed in a later chapter.

Boys' Guidance Center, Boston, Massachusetts

The long history of Kentucky Dominicans includes the teaching of boys from 1823 when St. Catharine Boys' School was opened in the valley of the Motherhouse. Although that institution closed because of lack of space as enrollments grew, the sisters continued to teach males in parochial or private grade schools, high schools and colleges. In addition, they owned and operated a boarding school, St. Dominic School for Boys, Waverly, Massachusetts.

In 1946 when Rev. Thomas McNamara (later Monsignor), director of Boys' Guidance Center, Boston, received a positive response to his request for sisters, he was overjoyed. Richard Cardinal Cushing wrote a personal thank you to Mother Margaret Elizabeth and Fr. McNamara wrote:

> Although I do not wish to seem to influence you in your choice,...a Sister Regina now stationed in Lowell has been recommended by our psychiatrist, Fr. Kelly, as a sister who would be, in his estimation excellently fitted for this type of work. It will not be an easy assignment because it will require great adaptability, patience and a sense of humor to maneuver these boys through the medium of scholastic work, closer to God.[24]

Srs. Rita Coleman, M. David Hannon and M. Andrew Sheehan were the first sisters assigned to this specialized youth ministry. Sr. Regina Sullivan joined the staff later, as did Sr. Brendan Cox. The sisters lived at Rosary Academy, Watertown, and commuted to the school.[25]

The students, ranging from 12 to 18 years, were emotionally disturbed. They were involved in school problems, brushes with the law, or stress from living in dysfunctional families. Some were referred by the Division of Youth Services but all had to be willing to enroll, to accept guidance and to stay a minimum of two months. The length of stay depended on the individual's progress.[26]

The Center housed up to 40 youngsters, but only 12 boys were permitted in a class. Each classroom had a telephone for security reasons. While the sisters never experienced any violence from the youths, there was the potential that it could erupt.[27]

Sr. M. Andrew, a musician, was a favorite because she organized a choral group and an orchestra. She brought out the best in the boys and they were proud of their musical accomplishments.

Another favorite was Sr. Rose Agnes Bray who often brought cookies, cake or candy from the convent. They frequently greeted her with the question, "Sister, did you bring any scoff?" Scoff was their jargon for a treat. [28]

Sr. Rita was noted for her sense of humor and ability to cope with any situation. Fr. McNamara wrote a special thanks to Kentucky for allowing her to remain at the Center.

> She has an especially trying group of boys as the boys in her
> room are usually a group that would find their way to special or
> ungraded class. Needless to say, they all love her.[29]

When Sr. Regina died, a busload of her former pupils attended her funeral Mass at St. Patrick, Watertown, a real tribute to their dedicated teacher.

Because Cardinal Cushing did not like the crime-ridden area where the Center was located, he advised the director, Msgr. William Roche, "Get the boys off the Fenway." The Center was moved to Scituate and named Cushing Hall. Because the distance from Rosary was too far for a daily commute, the sisters reluctantly withdrew from the Boys Guidance Center in 1966 after 20 years of service.[30]

Demand and Supply in the 50s

When the Sixth General Chapter convened in 1948, seventy-five delegates met on the last weekend in June. Re-elected with Mother Margaret Elizabeth were Srs. Paschal Mullaney and Rose of Lima Lohmeier. New Members of the Council were Srs. M. Julia Polin and Victorine Donovan. Sr. Joan Marie Madden was elected bursar.[31]

Space at the Motherhouse was at a premium because of larger classes of postulants entering each year. The Council applied to Cardinal Cushing for permission to open a postulate at Rosary Academy, Watertown.[32] With the Cardinal's approval, the postulate opened in September, 1948, with 12 candidates.[33] Sr. M. Eugene Sheehan became postulant mistress, a position she retained until 1956. In 1949 the postulate was moved to Plainville, Massachusetts.[34] Sr. Patricia Greeley succeeded Sr. M. Eugene as postulant mistress from 1956-1960.

Having a postulate in the east was convenient for families whose daughters were from that part of the country because they could visit more readily on visitation days. However, during the 11 years the postulate was at Plainville, it became apparent that when the eastern postulants went to Kentucky for their strict canonical novitiate, it was a major adjustment for all. The eastern postulants had bonded among themselves as did those who entered directly at St. Catharine. It took a while to unite both groups as one.[35] With the closing of the Plainville postulate and the formal development of a Juniorate Program in 1961, a different model for formation was initiated.[36]

When Pius XII declared 1950 a Holy Year, Mother Margaret Elizabeth and Sr. Paschal Mullaney sailed on the Queen Mary on a pilgrimage to Rome. They had a private audience with the Pope at Castel Gondolfo. His message was: "Tell the sisters to live their lives as close to the Divine Master as they can. Keep secularism out of their lives. Tell them to avoid worldliness and to pray for an increase of faith with a more intense love of God."

On November 1, the two pilgrims had tickets in the loggia where they witnessed the promulgation of the Dogma of the Assumption. On their journey home, they stopped in Dublin where they were met by Sr. Bertrand Gath's cousins who took them to the college of Dominican sisters at Muckross Park. They sailed home on the Mauritania. Mother Margaret Elizabeth brought a statue of Our Lady of Fatima to the community. For years it had a place of honor in St. Catharine chapel.

Two years later in 1952, the first International Congress of Mothers General of Pontifical Institutes was called in Rome. At this precedent-setting meeting, Pope Pius XII express concern because of the alarming drop in membership among women religious. He stressed the need for preparing sisters professionally for their ministry and advised that the habit be modified, keeping it modest and meeting the demands of hygiene.[37]

Although she did not attend the Congress, possibly because of her recent trip to Rome, Mother Margaret Elizabeth was keenly interested in the reports about the sessions. She wrote to the Master, Most Rev. Emmanuel Suarez, OP, that the Congregation was interested in the proposed pontifical university where sisters could study philosophy and theology in Rome. She requested that when it became a reality, the Dominican sisters who studied there be under the guidance and direction of the Dominican Fathers.[38]

The Pontiff's suggestion about modifying the habit caused ferment both inside and outside the Congregation. It was generally acknowledged that the starched inner veil, "the boards," acted as blinders and were a hazard once the sisters were allowed to drive cars. A concession to safety resulted in adopting a white sharkskin inner veil covered with soft black veiling, but a major brouhaha occurred before the habit itself was changed.

If Mother Margaret Elizabeth looked forward to a release for administration at the end of her second term as Mother, she was surprised when elected as first Councilor in 1954 for six years. Only after that did she return to music and choir work at the Motherhouse until her health failed. She lived to be 102 after spending her entire religious life of 69 years at St. Catharine.[39]

Chapter Sixteen Notes

1. SCA Chapter Proceeding, 1942.
2. Ibid.
3. Ibid.
4. Personal interview with Sr. Margaret Philip Shaw, OP, April 13, 1996.
5. SCA Personal file of Mother Margaret Elizabeth Walsh.
6. Personal interview with Sr. Virginia Thomas Hamilton, OP, March 13, 1996.
7. World Almanac, 1996, p. 166.
8. SCA. See voluminous correspondence of hundreds of unfulfilled requests Administrative files, Mother Margaret Elizabeth.
9. SCA Chronology of Institutions.
10. SCA Original letter, Francis R. Cotton, Bishop of Owensboro, to Mother Margaret Elizabeth Walsh, April 1, 1943.
11. SCA Material for this section is taken from unpublished memoirs of Sr. Raphael Geyger and Sr. M. Joseph Fosskuhl. Also, personal interviews with Srs. Marion McCormick, Anne Regis Hartnett, M. Joseph Fosskuhl. There were two mission stations, St. Patrick, Montgomery and Nativity, Campti.
12. Personal interview with Sr. Marion McCormick, November 20, 1995.
13. SCA Unpublished memoirs of Sr. Raphael Geyger.
14. SCA Annals of Montgomery, Louisiana.
15. SCA Unpublished memoirs of Sr. Amelia del Carmen Rivera.
16. SCA Unpublished report titled *Missionary Life in Aguadilla*.
17. Ibid.
18. SCA Unpublished report of *Task Force on Puerto Rico to Governing Board*, c. 1974. Srs. M. Thomas Shelvey, Claire McGowan and Ann Dolores Shea took courses at the Base.
19. SCA Unpublished report, *Missionary Life in Aguadilla*.
20. Personal interview with Sr. Amelia del Carmen Rivera, May 7, 1996.
21. Unpublished *Historia del Colegio San Carlos* undated, translated by Sr. Rose Marie Cummins, OP. Also, *Colegio San Carlos En Aguadilla* by Haydee E. Reichard deCancio, translated by Sr. Amelia del Carmen Rivera.
22. SCA Unpublished report, *Missionary Life in Aguadilla*.
23. Personal interview with Sr. Amelia del Carmen Rivera, May 8, 1996.
24. SCA Copy of letter from Cardinal Cushing to Mother Margaret Elizabeth Walsh, also, original letter, Rev. Thomas McNamara to Mother Margaret Elizabeth, August 20, 1946.
25. Personal interview with Sr. Margaret Ann Brady, OP, March 16, 1995.
26. SCA *Educational Contribution of the Dominican Sisters, Saint Catharine, Kentucky, 1823-1953*, master's thesis of Sr. M. Damian Carty, O.P.
27. Personal interview with Sr. Margaret Ann Brady, OP, May 8, 1996.
28. Ibid.

Major Superiors 1918-1996

Mother Francesca Kearney 1918-1924

Mother Bernadette Clements 1924-1930

Mother Mary Louis Logsdon 1930-1942

Mother Margaret Elizabeth Walsh 1942-1954

Mother Mary Julia Polin 1954-1966

*Mother M. Ulicia O'Brien 1966-1972

*President Sr. Joan Monica McGuire
1972-1980*

*Title changed in 1969 to President

President Sr. Elizabeth Miles 1988-1996

President Sr. Anne Margaret Cahill 1980-1988

President Joan Scanlon 1996 —

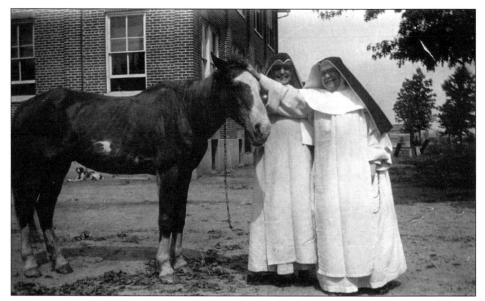

Mother Bernadette Clements and Sr. Eucharia Heaver at Reed,
Kentucky

Reed, Kentucky in Flood of 1937

Sr. Claudia Wizmann and Sr. Fides Gough made these costumes of crepe paper for a school play

Sr. Marita swinging a jump rope for her class at St. Vincent Ferrer, Brooklyn, New York

House of Studies, Washington, D.C.

The Doctors: left to right: Srs. Leo Marie Preher,
Euphrasia O'Rourke, Anne Mary Tamme,
Jamesetta Kelly — Seated Sr. Consuela Wilhelm

Colegio San Carlos, Aguadilla, Puerto Rico — students with principal
Sr. Mary Thomas Shelvey and lay teacher Mrs. Garcia

Sr. Mary Louise Hellman with her kindergarten at Our Lady of Peace, Chicago, Illinois

Sr. Rose Vincent O'Brien, hostess at the Silver Tea for the Mothers General Conference in Kentucky in 1957

Standing left to right: Mother M. Joseph, Oxford, Michigan; Mother Christina Marie, Newburgh, New York; Mother M. Edwardine, Tacoma, Washington; Sr. M. Paul, Maryknoll, New York

Sr. Mary Joachim McDonald, Bursar General for 18 years

Professor Emerson Meyers, director of Piano Department, Catholic University, shown with his former pupil, Sr. M. John Lamken, provided music for the Conference

First May Crowning in Montgomery, Louisiana, 1947

Sr. Amelia del Carmen Rivera, Puerto Rico

Postulants and novices, 1914

Postulant Class 1937

Postulants doing KP

Novices and postulants in funeral procession

Sr. Barbara Ann Fava studying in the library

Novices studying Gregorian chant with Mother Margaret Elizabeth

The Brides — 1960

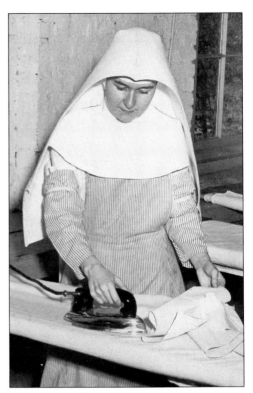

Sr. M. Clara Edelen on laundry duty

*Sr. Mary Della Quinn reading
in the refectory*

*Srs. Patricia Greeley and Ann Rita
Sullivan in charge of novitiate*

Novice Mistress Sr. Ann Rita Sullivan, with new novices on Reception Day

New Novices receiving the rosary

Students posing under the College sign

Sr. Rose of Lima Lohmeier with some of her science students

St. Catharine Chapel showing rose window

29. SCA Original letter, Rev. Thomas McNamara to Mother Margaret Elizabeth Walsh, November 27, 1950.

30. SCA Chronology of Institutions.

31. SCA Chapter Proceedings, 1948.

32. SCA Council Book, Dec. 29, 1947, p. 45.

33. SCA *Records of Postulants Admitted.*

34. SCA Dominican Postulate, Plainville, Massachusetts, Sept. 1949.

35. Personal interviews with Srs. Margaret Philip Shaw, OP and Bernadine Marie Egleston, OP, March 1996.

36. SCA Archival compilation on Postulate by Sr. Ann Miriam Hickey, OP, Archivist. Also, the Juniorate Program, St. Catharine Motherhouse, Sept. 1961.

37. SCA Personal file Mother Margaret Elizabeth, copy of clipping from *Boston Sunday Advertiser,* Sept. 21, 1952, p. 20.

38. SCA Copy of letter to Most Rev. Emmanuel Suarez, OP, from Mother Margaret Elizabeth Walsh, November 6, 1952.

39. SCA Personal file of Mother Margaret Elizabeth Walsh.

SUSTAIN
THE PITCH
AND OBSERVE
THE PAUSES

T HE NUMBER OF DELEGATES to General Chapters increased as membership grew because it was a representational system. In 1954 there were 78 delegates at the three-day Seventh General Chapter.[1] Mother M. Julia Polin was elected with her predecessor, Sr. Margaret Elizabeth Walsh, as first Councilor. Completing the Council were Srs. Mary Ellen McTeague, Leonarda Yilk and M. Charles Moranville. Sr. M. Joachim McDonald was elected bursar, a position she held for 18 years.[2]

Mother M. Julia Polin   *1894*

Shortly after Christmas, December 28, ~~1948~~, Julia Belle Polin was born to John G. and Julia (Scannell) Polin in Litsey, Washington County, Kentucky. She had two brothers, Joseph O. and John A. and a sister, Emma Rose.[3] She grew up in a family which already boasted of two Dominican religious, her aunt, Sr. Benedicta Scannell who was professed at St. Catharine and her uncle, Fr. Patrick J. Scannell, OP. Shortly after ordination at St.

Rose, Fr. Scannell, who was serving at St. Louis Bertrand, Louisville, volunteered to minister to victims of yellow fever in Memphis. He died of the disease at age 30, "a martyr to his charity."[4]

Julia Belle was professed at St. Catharine on March 7, 1918 as Sr. M. Julia. Her first mission was to St. Agnes Academy, Memphis, where she served for 27 years.[5] Like her contemporaries, study was an essential part of her life. She obtained a BA from Notre Dame and an MA from Catholic University. Her diminutive size (she was about 4 feet, 9 inches) was no indication of her powerful personality. When she said, "I prefer..." it was understood that a firm decision had been made. Her humility was surpassed only by her integrity. She never betrayed a confidence even to defend herself.

Seeds of Change

In the 50s, seeds of change were being felt throughout the country. Kentucky Dominicans reflected what was going on in the world and in the church. Instructions from their courses in Gregorian chant were applicable metaphorically to other phases of the sisters' lives: *Sustain the pitch; observe the pauses.*[6]

Schools were mushrooming; professional education of the sisters was demanded; personal autonomy was sought, particularly in participatory decision-making. To sustain the pitch of activity and yet maintain the monastic observance prescribed by the Constitutions generated constant stress. There were few pauses to refresh the spirit other than the annual retreat. Weekends, holidays and summer vacations were spent studying for certification and degrees. Classes were large. In Brooklyn, Boston, Chicago and Louisville, it was not unusual to have 60 children in a grade, sometimes even more.[7]

In a letter to her school principals, Mother Julia warned of the effects of the population explosion on Catholic schools. She predicted that religious communities would be less able to supply adequate numbers of sister teachers and advised principals to become informed on demographics in order to plan wisely for the future. This, of course, meant relying on collaboration with lay personnel. Some schools had already introduced lay teachers into the system; others were reluctant to do so. Mother M. Julia wrote:

> The role of the school principal in this history-making transition is not to be minimized. Upon her devolves not only an effectual adjustment, but also the continued efficient operation of the school for the years ahead.[8]

Although principals were concerned with local needs and their particular schools, Mother M. Julia pointed out that the situation had to be looked at from a community-wide view.

An attempt was made to establish a ratio of lay teachers to sisters. In the diocese of Louisville, the ratio was one lay teacher for every three sisters.[9] In Chicago, Cardinal Albert Meyer wanted the same ratio and advised that there be a maximum of 50 pupils per teacher.[10] Ratios varied from diocese to diocese.

Concerned about the health of her sisters, Mother M. Julia tried to alleviate some of the stress. She wrote, "In the schools, the sisters find themselves burdened by large class enrollments; while in the hospitals, the number of patients has increased by reason of prevalent insurance benefits, thereby multiplying the tasks of our nursing sisters."[11] To lessen tensions of daily life, the prayer schedule was modified to allow the sisters to fulfill their religious obligations with greater ease and to provide more time for study.

When Mother M. Julia requested permission from Bishop Francis Cotton to rent a cabin near Kentucky Lake for the hospital sisters to get away for a week or two, permission was refused because he felt it would be a source of harmful wonder and positive scandal to Non-Catholics and Catholics living in that section of the diocese.[12]

The Infirmary

As the number of sick and infirm sisters increased, it became apparent that provisions had to be made for them. Plans for an infirmary were initiated in 1948 when Sr. Joan Marie Madden, bursar general, established an infirmary fund but the need grew more rapidly than the fund.

Mother M. Julia and Council thought it would help to enlist the aid of professional fundraisers if the bishops of the various dioceses approved.[13] Personal interviews with nine ordinaries of the major archdioceses and dioceses and letters from the remaining dioceses where the sisters served, revealed that sentiment was against a professionally conducted campaign for funds. Although they "highly esteemed the sisters and valued their good work," the bishops pointed out that parishes were already heavily burdened. However, they did not object to some form of restricted fundraising for the project.[14]

Chagrined, but undaunted by the unexpected reaction of the ordinaries, Mother M. Julia called upon the sisters to submit ideas for raising funds for the much-needed infirmary. She refused to give up or postpone the plans. The sisters rallied to the cause.

At Rosary Academy, Watertown, the annual bazaar was a community-wide affair. The sisters sewed, knitted, baked, painted and crocheted to provide items for the occasion. Usually, one fourth of the proceeds went to the infirmary fund, but in 1958 the entire amount of $7,581.52 went to the infirmary.[15] Encouraged by the enthusiasm of the sisters, Mother M. Julia called for an INFIRMARY YEAR during which the sisters would pray and work toward the dream.

In 1959 the Motherhouse held a bazaar at which a turkey dinner was one of the main features. Nine hundred people feasted on turkey and all the fixin's. There were booths for aprons, baby clothes, cakes, candy, household items and other tables usually found at a bazaar, but the most popular was the Post Office booth, the novices' project. Each novice had written to relatives and friends asking for a package, about fifty cents in value, to be mailed to Kentucky from as many states as possible. The booth sold out quickly, much to the delight of the novices.

Sr. M. Joachim McDonald, general bursar, hung a long black stocking outside her office door with a sign, "Infirmary Fund." Like a limp Christmas stocking waiting for Santa to fill it, it hung as a constant reminder to all.

An unusual source of funds was *Dad's Salve*. Gabriel Heffner, father of Srs. Jean Clare and Claretta, traveled widely as a musician. On one of his tours, he bought a recipe for an ointment which was effective in relieving many ailments. After he died, Sr. Jean Clare arranged for the manufacture of *Dad's Salve* or *Do Rub* at 50 cents a jar. The profit on each jar went to the community. Mother Julia wrote to the superiors suggesting that they buy a jar for each sister for Christmas.[16]

The manufacture and sale of *Dad's Salve* or *Do Rub* continued for many years with some of the proceeds going to the infirmary fund. It is no longer manufactured commercially, but Sr. Claretta who now ministers to the elderly in her home parish, St. Louis Bertrand, Louisville, makes a batch occasionally. Her sister, Sr. Jean Clare, who lives at Sansbury Infirmary, can still sing the song she wrote years ago when trying to sell this ointment.[17]

By means of coupon drives, raffles, magazine drives, production and sale of Christmas cards, calendars and greeting cards made by community artists, the fund increased. With approximately $250,000 on hand and a loan of $350,000 from Bosworth and Sullivan, the dream became an actuality with the laying of the cornerstone on June 5, 1960. Of the many names submitted for the building, the one chosen was Sr. Althaire Lancaster's suggestion of *Sansbury Memorial Infirmary* in honor of Mother Angela Sansbury, the first Dominican sister in the United States. The chapel, officially named St. Joseph Chapel, obtained canonical status as an oratory. Dedication ceremonies took place on July 9, 1961 with the most Rev. Charles G. Malone, DD, officiating and Rev. Patrick J. Conaty, OP, as guest speaker.[18]

In his dedication address, Fr. Conaty said, "Though the hands that hold the rosary may be shaky, the eyes that read the Office may be blurred and the meditation mixed up with past events, the Dominican apostolate will be carried on at Sansbury."[19] These words truly describe Sansbury where sisters exercise the ministry of prayer and suffering.

Storm Clouds on the Horizon

While the erection of Sansbury absorbed time and energy

during Mother M. Julia's first term and into her second, an undercurrent of unrest began to surface. What was happening within the Congregation reflected what was happening in society. On May 17, 1954, the Supreme Court ordered integration of schools, setting aside the "separate but equal" doctrine handed down in 1896.[20] In Montgomery, Alabama, Rosa Parks refused to move from the "whites section only" to the back of a city bus. Thousands began boycotting bus lines even though it was against the law. Whites attacked Nat King Cole as he sang to a white audience.[21]

In the Congregation a few queries about accepting black women as postulants raised the racial issue before the General Council which had the decisive vote for admitting candidates. Nothing in the Constitutions prevented it, but Kentucky was southern in its racial attitudes. Schools were still segregated in the 50s. Restaurants, theaters, swimming pools, restrooms, depots were segregated. In 1950, the Kentucky legislature repealed the Day Law which prevented teaching blacks and whites in the same classroom,[22] but it took time before change occurred.

There is no record of a formal application for admission from an African American; consequently, it never was voted on one way or another by the Council. However, queries made by an intermediary such as a priest or sister had to be answered. How would acceptance of an African American candidate be received within the Congregation? How would white schools in the south accept an African-American teacher? Not only the south, but also the north was involved. When Cardinal Cushing asked that an African American student be admitted to Rosary Academy, Watertown, the answer was a regretful negative "because it would affect student enrollment."[23] What would be the response to a black teacher?

Trying to resolve the horns of the dilemma as to what was best for the Congregation and what was best for the individual, Mother M. Julia recommended that possible black candidates look for a black community, such as the Oblate Sisters of Providence in Baltimore. It became an unwritten policy that African American candidates be referred elsewhere. This occurred not so much as a belief in racial segregation, but to avoid faculty tension, loss of students and financial support.

Louisville, one of the oldest dioceses in the United States, was torn apart by the racial issue. In Springfield, when Fr. L. Bernard, OP, asked if St. Catharine Academy would accept "colored girls as students, it was thought best to discuss personally with him various aspects of the matter especially that of public opinion locally."[24] In the Fall of 1954, two African American girls were admitted to St. Catharine Academy where they completed their high school education.[25]

Concerned about the education of black children, Archbishop Floersch asked Mother M. Julia to send sisters to Immaculate Heart parish school in the West End of Louisville. Two African American lay women, Louella Conwell and Minnie London, had started the school but needed assistance if the school were to continue.[26] In 1955, Srs. Elizabeth Miles (Martin de Porres) and Maria Petra Cummings joined the staff. Six months later, Sr. Augustine Graninger came as superior. For 35 years Kentucky Dominicans taught there. In time, Immaculate Heart, along with St. Columba and Christ the King, became a consolidated school called All Saints. Despite heroic efforts to keep the school viable, it closed because of limited personnel and finances.[27]

The Final Fifties

As the need for personnel reached a critical point, pastors began to react. Some felt they were being discriminated against or that contracts were being broken. One wanted the principal to teach in a school with an enrollment of 1,250! Acceptance of new missions slowed to a halt. Within the ranks, sisters were torn between whether to fully staff community-owned institutions or to concentrate on parochial schools.

In April 1957, St. Catharine hosted the 12th Conference of Dominican Mothers General of America which later became known as the Dominican Leadership Conference. Sixty-four delegates from various Dominican foundations discussed commonalities — Office in vernacular, shortage of personnel, aging membership, modernization of religious garb, professional preparation for teaching sisters. Not until the 60s was much action taken.[28]

For some reason, Kentucky Dominicans found changing the habit an explosive issue. Though novice mistresses taught "the habit does not make the religious," identity was equated to some extent with the anachronistic, medieval dress. A poll was taken among the sisters in 1955 about changing the veil. Results showed 442 against the change, 250 for, and a number of abstentions from the undecided.[29]

After unfavorable publicity about a fatal accident in Connecticut which was blamed on the head-dress of the sister driver, Cardinal Cushing wrote to the sisters in the Archdiocese of Boston: "I feel it mandatory for the Superiors of the various communities in the Archdiocese of Boston to assure themselves through personal attention that those sisters who drive automobiles are not impeded in the proper operation of the machine by their habit or head-dress."[30]

Msgr. A.E. Egging of Grand Island, Nebraska, reiterated the message, advising that in case of an accident, the courts would be inclined to hold sisters guilty of "contributory negligence" because of lack of visibility occasioned by their habit.[31]

Even though Mother M. Julia had sent a letter to all convents in 1954 allowing sister drivers to wear a soft veil, some were reluctant to do so.[32] When repeated warnings about driver safety were received, Mother M. Julia used her "I prefer" — that sisters wear a soft veil when driving. Five years later, the matter was settled not only for the drivers, but for all the sisters. On August 15, 1959, the soft veil was adopted by the membership. The brouhaha over the veil was but a tip of the iceberg compared to what was to come when change was suggested about the habit itself.

As Mother M. Julia's first term drew to a close, sorrow intruded when Sr. M. Charles Moranville, 4th councillor died in office of cancer on April 25, 1959. She had been an excellent teacher and a kind administrator. A month later, the Council voted to have Sr. Rose of Lima Lohmeier fill the vacancy.[33] Previously, she had served 12 years as Council member with Mother Margaret Elizabeth. In addition to her administrative experience, as a native of Sutton, Nebraska and a science teacher, she brought to the position a love of the land. Painstakingly, she had labeled the trees on the Motherhouse campus according to species, making it easy for biology students to learn their classifications. A woman of peace and gentility, she found relief from the pressure of administration and teaching in cultivating a garden. The fruits of her labors often graced the altar.

As the 60s approached, few were prepared for the maelstrom of social revolution and dramatic upheaval which followed. At the Eighth General Chapter in 1960, Mother M. Julia was re-elected. her Council was composed of Srs. Clarita Griffin, Leonarda Yilk, Mary Ellen McTeague, and Paschala Noonan. Once again, Sr. M. Joachim McDonald was elected Bursar.[34]

In addition to their usual duties on the Council, each Councillor was responsible for a specific area of interest. Sr. Clarita, who had served as president of Siena College, as supervisor of Kentucky Dominican schools in Boston, and as teacher, became responsible for education in all its phases, that is, education of the sisters and quality of education in all Kentucky Dominican schools. As first Councillor, she was also Vicaress General, second in command to Mother M. Julia. Sr. Leonarda, teacher, superior, promoter of the Third Order lay association, was accountable for property and the Motherhouse farm. As Secretary General, Sr. M. Ellen kept statistics, legal records, official minutes, correspondence with Rome, and documents required as a civil corporation. Sr. Paschala, the first registered nurse to serve on the Council, became the Coordinator of Health for the Congregation. They entered their six-year term with high hopes, not knowing they were headed into a watershed.

Chapter Seventeen Notes

1. SCA Chapter Proceeding, 1954.
2. SCA Chapter Proceedings, 1954, 1960, 1966. In each of these chapters Sr. M. Joachim McDonald was elected for a six-year term.
3. SCA Personal file Mother M. Julia Polin.

4. SCA Personal file Mother M. Julia Polin. Also, compilation by Sr. Ann Miriam Hickey, archivist, re: Mother M. Julia. See Coffey, p. 475 Fr. P.J. Scannell, OP.
5. SCA Personal file Mother M. Julia.
6. Personal interview with Sr. Hugh Francis Carey, June 4, 1996.
7. Unpublished survey of former teachers conducted by Sr. Margaret Philip Shaw, May 1996.
8. SCA Administrative file Mother M. Julia, letter to principals, March 5, 1956.
9. SCA Ibid. Report of Mother General to the members of the general Chapter, 1960.
10. SCA Original letter, Cardinal Meyer to Mother M. Julia, May 25, 1959.
11. SCA Administrative file Mother M. Julia, Report to the members of the General Chapter, 1960.
12. SCA Original letter Bishop Francis Cotton to Mother M. Julia, 1959.
13. Religious communities were obliged to obtain permission from the local bishop before conducting any fund-raising in his diocese.
14. SCA Letter of Mother M. Julia to the sisters, Nov. 22, 1957.
15. SCA Letter of Mother M. Julia to the sisters, Sept. 16, 1958.
16. SCA Letter of Mother M. Julia to superiors, Nov. 21, 1955.
17. Interview with Sr. Claretta Heffner, May 30, 1996.
18. *SCA Dominican News*, October 1986 issue, report on Sansbury Memorial Infirmary by Sr. Paschala Noonan on the 25th anniversary.
19. SCA Copy of dedication address given by P. Conaty, OP, July 9, 1961.
20. *Chronicle of the 20th Century*, p. 753.
21. Ibid, p. 778.
22. Crews, *An American Holy Land*, p. 303.
23. BAA Correspondence between Chancellor Walter J. Furlong and Sr. M. Leonard, OP, Dec. 3, 15, 17, 20, 1948.
24. SCA Council Governing Board Minutes, July 9, 1954.
25. SCA Original letter Archbishop Floersch to Mother M. Julia Sept. 13, 1954.
26. SCA Original letter Archbishop Floersch to Mother M. Julia Sept. 13, 1954.
27. Personal interviews with Srs. Thomas Joseph Nacy, OP, Clarellen McGinley, OP, Jean Berney, OP, and Elizabeth Miles, OP, June 1996.
28. SCA Administrative file Mother M. Julia, Dominican Mothers General Conference, 1957.
29. SCA Administrative file, Mother M. Julia, Jan. 1955.
30. SCA Copy of letter of Cardinal Cushing to sisters in Boston Archdiocese, April 28, 1958.
31. SCA Original letter Msgr. Egging to Mother M. Julia, Mar. 18, 1958.
32. SCA Copy of letter of Mother M. Julia to Msgr. Egging, Apr. 3, 1958.
33. SCA Council Governing Board Minutes, Apr. 25, May 30, 1959.
34. SCA Chapter Proceedings, 1960.

THE WATERSHED

WHEN POPE JOHN XXIII was elected in 1958, surprises were in store for the Church. With the opening of the Second Vatican Council, he started a watershed with immediate and far-reaching effects. When John F. Kennedy became president of the United States in 1960, he ushered in the age of Camelot, a watershed in American politics.

Membership in the Congregation was at an all-time high, and mission houses were flourishing. One of the annual duties of the Council was to assign each of the over 800[1] sisters to their missions. This usually happened in August either by mail or in person if one were at the Motherhouse. The little white envelope contained a message: "Dear Sister, For the coming year you are assigned to _____. May God bless you and your work." These missives (called "shots" by the initiated), personally signed by the Mother General, were closely linked with the vow of obedience and were regarded as "the voice of God." The Constitutions reminded them that "obedience shall always be prompt, joyous, complete without excuses or objections, gracious and without complaint." In fulfilling a command, they were not to question in any way the conduct or the intentions of those who gave the command, but there was an escape clause. "The Sisters, however, are permitted to expose humbly their difficulties, provided they are resolved to submit to the decision of the Superioresses."[2]

Most sisters accepted their assignments without question, but if one had a strong reason for not accepting, she could make it known. Some loved the adventure of going to a new mission; others found it wrenching to leave a familiar place, but all tried to accept assignments in good grace.

In response to the 1960 Quinquennial Report[3] "the Sacred Congregation advised against opening new houses with less than a suitable number of sisters," but no definition was given as to what constituted "a suitable number." In the school year, 1963-1964, there were five houses with only two sisters in each. An additional sister was assigned to Kentucky schools of Our Lady of Perpetual Help, Campbellsville; St. Mary, McQuady; Sts. Peter and Paul, Hopkinsville; and also, to St. Francis, Forrest City, Arkansas. With sadness, Srs. M. Joseph Fosskuhl and Michael Brigid Driscoll withdrew from St. Augustine School, Reed, in June 1964. At Our Lady of the Hills, Finley, Kentucky, Srs. Jean Delaney, Josetta Barnard, M. Raymond Hines and Celine Clements closed the doors of the school in June 1965 when the Marion County School Board discontinued the educational program due to consolidation.[4]

Health Profiles

In assigning sisters to their missions, the Council tried to consider not only the qualifications of the individual, the educational requirements of the state to which she was missioned, but also, the health of the sister. As the cost of health care increased, the Generalate sought ways of meeting the expenses. In 1951, superiors were asked to send to St. Catharine "one dollar per month for each sister in her house and this amount to be used for hospital expenses."[5] It was a precursor of a self-insured health system for the Congregation.

The Constitutions had specific recommendations about health. "The Sisters shall guard against two excesses in caring for their health; the one is not to know how to suffer for the good God, complaining of the least discomfort and calling the doctor for a slight passing indisposition; the other is to say nothing of real and serious sufferings."[6] Among themselves, the sisters jokingly referred to the three D's to be avoided: the Devil, the Doctor and the Dumps. The era of wellness and preventive health care began in the spring of 1960. That year Con J. Fecher, Ph.D., professor of economics at Catholic University, and James T. Nix, M.D., of the faculty of Tulane University became interested in the health of women religious.[7] They advocated that each sister have a health profile card made out by a physician after the sister had a complete physical examination.

The Catholic Hospital Association and the Conference of Major Superiors supported the idea. Sr. Paschala Noonan, Council member and health coordinator, worked with Nix and Fecher to develop a medical file for every sister in the community. There was opposition to the idea, which called for a complete physical every two years. Some said, "If you feel all right, why bother the doctor?" Others presumably went for a medical check-up but persuaded the doctor to sign the medical profile without doing the complete physical. The purpose of the program was to anticipate the effects of aging on the medical, administrative and economic life of the sisters.

Sisters who were 65 and over were enrolled in Medicare. On October 30, 1972, the Social Security Act was amended to allow coverage of services performed by members of religious orders who had the vow of poverty.

The Governing Board employed Meidinger and Associates of Louisville to study the Social Security Amendment and its implications for the Congregation. While seriously considering the relationship of Social Security to Gospel Poverty and the Gospel value of dependence on God, on July 1, 1973, the Governing Board decided to enter the Social Security system with full twenty quarters of retroactive coverage to July 1, 1968. Election of coverage was irrevocable and applied to all current and future members of the Congregation.[8] The enormous retroactive payment had to be paid in one sum by October 31, 1973. Any available savings and assets were used for the payment, which meant there was a minimal cash flow for operational expenses. Sr. Joan Monica wrote to the sisters, "As a family which has to bear an immediate extraordinary expenditure in order to provide future benefits, each of us will have to do her part to help finance this project."

In the past, financial matters had been handled by the treasurers with little involvement on the part of the sisters, but with entrance into Medicare and Social Security, the congregational Finance Department worked intensely to educate the sisters about government regulations affecting them and to keep them informed of the financial status of the Congregation.

The Juniorate Program

In addition to health issues, a persistent theme which surfaced was the spiritual and professional preparation of the sisters. An act of the 1960 General Chapter called for the establishment of the Juniorate Program. Early in 1961, Mother M. Julia wrote to sisters and pastors:

> In September 1961, we plan to begin our Sister Formation program at the Motherhouse in accordance with the request of the Sacred Congregation of Religious ... it is in obedience to the Sacred Congregation that we shall introduce our Juniorate program this fall. Since the program will extend over a period of three additional years beyond the novitiate, we will be unable to send out any extra sisters during that period. We will be obliged, further, to consider the withdrawal of some sisters for the personnel needed to organize and staff the program.[9]

She informed pastors that the community would be unable to fill vacancies arising from sickness or other causes.

The Juniorate program began in 1961 at the Motherhouse with Sr. Patricia Greeley in charge. The space once used for the infirmary before Sansbury was built was converted into living quarters for the young professed. After one year of study at St. Catharine, the junior professed with Sr. Patricia moved to Memphis, Tennessee where the juniors were to continue two years of study at Siena College. Sr. Patricia held the position of juniorate mistress with succeeding groups at Siena from 1962-1966.

Sr. Mary Ransom Travelstead became juniorate mistress of the segment in training at St. Catharine from 1962-1965. She was followed by Srs. Agnes Richarda Blinkhorn, Rose Speckner and Mary Esther Owens[10] until the program ended. It was eventually replaced by a different Formation plan.

Juniorate mistresses were responsible for spiritual formation while Council member, Sr. Clarita Griffin, advised about their academic studies. The ideal hoped for was to have the Juniorate as full-time students who would get a sound spiritual foundation as well as professional background for nursing and teaching. The strident and overwhelming demands of the schools thwarted the plan to some extent. With fewer sisters being sent to the missions, pastors complained that without additional sisters, schools would be forced to close, yet they wanted professionally qualified teachers. If they hired lay teachers, operational expenses would increase because sisters' stipends were notably lower than a just wage for a lay person.

A compromise was reached by sending some of the juniorate sisters to teach in parochial schools close to the Motherhouse and to Siena, thus releasing older sisters to fill in some of the gaps on the missions.[11] In her report to the 1966 General Chapter, Mother M. Julia wrote:

> In the year 1965-1966, there was a total of 87 Sisters who had completed or participated in the Juniorate Program. Of these, 31 were full-time students, 50 taught school full-time, and six worked in our hospitals and infirmary.[12]

Although the ideal was not realized, the juniorate sisters received a good spiritual foundation and most were well on their way to a degree when they finished the program.

After Vatican II, when demands for social action increased, sisters wanted to branch out in other ministries involving the poor and social justice. Mother M. Julia was reluctant about this type of expansion because she feared that diversity and proliferation would undermine the impact as a Congregation. She wanted to maintain education and health care as the corporate identity, but the watershed roiled relentlessly.

Marian Manor

However, a new ministry, under the umbrella of health care, began in 1963 when Marian Manor Nursing Home opened in Lebanon, Kentucky. It was attached to Mary Immaculate Hospital, with which it shared some services. It was the first combination of nursing home and acute care hospital in the state of Kentucky.[13] Sr. Mary Agnes Wilson, R.N. was the first administrator of Marian Manor.

The facility had 38 bedrooms, cheerful dining and recreational areas, a snack room where residents could make a cup of tea or fix toast, and a physical therapy department. Sr. John Louise Wall, a licensed physical therapist, was director of the physical therapy department. Since this was a new service which had not yet come into its own, Sr. John Louise had a hard time convincing the doctors to use it. By persistence and observable results, she built up a thriving department recognized throughout the state. Nearby hospitals called on her until she became sort of a circuit rider physical therapist. She worked with in-patients and out-patients in both the hospital and nursing home. She set up a program for needy and disabled children who benefited from her service.[14]

At Marian Manor, Sr. John Louise had a second role as a musician. She played the accordion, the piano, the zither, the organ. She organized a band among the residents so they could entertain others. It was a different ministry from her teaching days at St. Catharine College, but she loved it.

The Manor developed a special affiliation with the friars at St. Rose in the person of Sr. Mary Rogan, L.P.N. Sr. Mary began her career in the health field at Mary Immaculate Hospital in 1944 and transferred to Marian Manor shortly after it opened. Brother Ignatius Perkins, OP, Director of Health Care for the Province of St. Joseph, was aware of Sr. Mary's special care and concern for the St. Rose brothers and friars when they were admitted to the hospital or nursing home. In a proposal to the Master, he wrote of her, "There are persons who in their own quiet yet deliberate way provide the Dominican Friars with the many supports necessary to carry out the work of the Order and therefore, can be called cooperators and collaborators in this work. One individual who has truly been a cooperator and collaborator is Sister Mary Rogan, OP, a Dominican Sister of St. Catharine of Siena, Springfield, Kentucky."[15] It was not unusual for Sr. Mary, after a long day on duty, to make frequent night visits to the sick and dying friars to say the rosary or to just be present with them.

> Her presence at the bedside of the dying provided the assur-
> ance that our friars would not die alone.... Her special concern
> and attention to our Friars exemplified in a unique and special
> way the long enduring relationship which has existed between
> the Friars of St. Joseph's Province and the Sisters of St.
> Catharine's — a relationship established in the early 1800s and
> rightfully called the first example of the Dominican Family in the
> New World.[16]

The Master acknowledged the proposal for recognition and in his own name and that of the Order, he commissioned Brother Ignatius to bestow on Sr. Mary the Benemerenti Medal for Distinguished Service to the Dominican Order and properly to the Dominican Friars of the Eastern Province. The ceremony took place on September 15, 1979. Nobody deserved it more and nobody was more proud than Sr. Rose Imelda Rogan, Sr. Mary's sister.[17]

Courage and Commitment

One event which occurred in 1962 with far-reaching and continuous effects was the return of Sr. Maria Rose Huong to her native Vietnam. As a young woman, she had come to the United States sponsored by Bishop Peter Chi. Since she was a candidate for religious life, he advised her to obtain her religious life formation in this country.[18] After she had obtained her B.A. from St. Mary of the Woods, Indiana, she applied for entrance to St. Catharine Novitiate in September 1959. Mother M. Julia received her religious profession in 1960 in the name of Sr. Maria Rose's Congregation in Bien Hoa, Vietnam. Following her profession, she earned an M.A. in Education at Spalding University (Nazareth College) Louisville.[19] The time had come for her to return to her native land. The Kentucky Dominicans agreed to support her repatriation in whatever way possible. It was a tearful parting when she left in 1962. Who knew what lay ahead for her?

In letters back to St. Catharine, she described appalling conditions in war-torn Vietnam. Because of chaotic circumstances, letters became more infrequent and contact with her was lost for about a decade.[20] Occasionally, Fr. Edward Gaffney, OP, stationed with the Army in Thailand relayed information about Sr. Maria Rose.

In April 1972, Fr. Gaffney was ordered to close the Army Retreat House in Cam Ron Bay because the North Vietnamese army was advancing rapidly to the area.[21] He had all the chapel equipment which had been donated by Cardinal Terence Cooke of New York, transported south to Long Binh Post where he could give it to Sr. Maria Rose. As chaplain he brought the plight of the sisters to the attention of the soldiers and American Catholics at his Post. They were magnanimous in their donations to help build a church in Da Minh and to support the orphanage and convent.[22]

Not until 1974 was actual contact made between Sr. Maria Rose and her Kentucky sisters. That year, Sr. Virginia Smith, OP, went to Bangkok at the invitation of Fr. Gaffney to teach his catechists. While she was there, Fr. Gaffney arranged for her to visit Sr. Maria Rose in Vietnam.[23] It was a risky undertaking during the last days of the war, but Sr. Virginia was a risk taker. Her experience of the primitive conditions under which the sisters lived made an indelible impression on her. When she left Sr. Maria Rose and her companions, she felt she was abandoning them to certain death. Afterwards, she could not talk about it without crying.[24]

At the Chapter of 1974, Sr. Virginia reported about Vietnam and Sr. Maria Rose. She described burned out villages, children disfigured and wounded, adults starving and maimed, and sisters forced to work in rice fields or to raise animals to support themselves and their ministry. Her report so touched the hearts of the delegates that by Chapter Act, the Kentucky Dominicans pledged to assist Sr. Maria Rose in her ministry in a tangible way for two years.[25] Sr. Virginia declared, "We are always responsible for those with whom we have shared life." Her words bore fruit. At Chapters in 1976, 1980 and 1984, commitment to Sr. Maria Rose and her people was renewed.[26]

Just prior to the fall of Saigon, April 30, 1975, the Council agreed that St. Catharine, Kentucky would assume responsibility for Sr. Maria Rose and her companions.[27] The Vietnamese sisters were scattered because they had been advised by their Bishop to return to their families until matters improved. Their schools, hospitals and orphanages were confiscated. They were forbidden to teach. Although Fr. Gaffney offered to help Sr. Maria Rose to escape to the States, she chose to remain with her people.[28]

Again, the Kentucky Dominicans tried to reach out to the refugees by contacting the Immigration Department in Washington, D.C. to offer to take care of any of the orphans from Sr. Maria Rose's orphanage.[29] Evacuation of the children was a fiasco. None of them reached St. Catharine, but, in time, some of the Vietnamese sisters found their way to Kentucky. Vietnamese Dominicans Srs. Hue Thi Le, Hoang Thi Luu, Binh Thanh Nguyen, Mary Phuc Nguyen, Rosa Thi Nguyen, Nang Thi Nguyen, Tuyet Ngoc Tran and Nang Thi Nguyen transferred to the Kentucky Dominican sisters.[30] Linkages of a Dominican Army chaplain, a Vietnamese Dominican sisterhood and Kentucky Dominicans, a continent away, attest to what it means to belong to the Dominican family.

Renewal

When Vatican II called for renewal, programs were inaugurated to encourage the sisters to understand and participate in the transition. At St. Mel's School, Gloucester, in 1964, Daniel B. Crowley, OP, conducted the first of a series of seminars. it was an intensive program in the middle of the summer with three lectures a day, six days a week, from June 28 to July 19. About 30 sisters participated. In 1965, Edward P. Doyle, OP, continued the same kind of program followed in 1966 by Edward M. Gaffney, OP.[31] An added bonus to the St. Mel's sessions was the proximity to the Atlantic Ocean and the spectacular North Shore coastline.

These spiritual and educational renewal programs were replicated in other places where the sisters worked. Sister nurses went on for nursing degrees and those in cooking received certificates in Food Service Supervising under the auspices of the Catholic Hospital Association in St. Louis. Among those to participate in the culinary program were Srs. Alverda Bonifas, Maureen Flanagan, M. Joseph Fosskuhl, Sue Keene, Loretta McManaman, Ruth Michael O'Toole and Mary Janet Riggs.

Sr. M. Joseph continued her studies and became a certified dietitian.

Liturgical changes were an important part of renewal. Most sisters were pleased when permission was obtained from Master Aniceto Fernandez, OP, to substitute English for Latin in the Little Office of the Blessed Virgin, Office of the Dead and the Penitential Psalms.[32]

The traditional Sunday processions, except the Third Sunday procession in honor of the Blessed Sacrament, were discontinued in keeping with the spirit of liturgical renewal to cut down on ceremonies accumulated through the years. The Promoter for Sisters, J. M. Donohue, OP, wrote:

> The renewed emphasis on the Paschal Mystery has made for a definite change of emphasis in the way we worship in the Mass and in private devotions to the Eucharist. I would think this might call for a review of your own Motherhouse practices; the daily afternoon Holy Hour, for example, might be more meaningful to the community if it were not held so often but was a truly Eucharistic devotion as distinct from meditation or recitation of the Little Office.[33]

The community novena book, listing 12 novenas to be said during the course of the year, was eliminated though some were retained for private devotions.

Societal Changes

As the feminist movement and the Civil Rights Act gained momentum, effects were felt within the cloister. Srs. Leo Marie Preher and Anne Mary Tamme were among those who were strong advocates against racism. When Sr. Anne Mary asked permission to join the March in Selma, she was refused, but she wrote about the experience.

> Though wedged in thickest traffic
> A man can sicken with aloneness.
> He can yearn for human brotherhood
> As he has never wanted bread.
> But let his step be pace
> By a brother's step

And he grows strong
with a spreading strength -- that reaches
to the healing of the heart.

A man can hunger for that sound
As he has never needed bread.

"I was hungry..."
And safely, safely from a distance...
You made a Holy Hour.
You lit a lovely candle.

And then you went your way.[34]

Sisters participated in protests against the Vietnam War, the Holocaust, nuclear proliferation and discrimination in the work force. The epochal transformation of sisters from quiet hand-maidens to vocal dissenters alarmed clergy, laity and sisters themselves. The clergy felt that sisters were out of control; laity were shocked that the "good sisters" were speaking out; sisters themselves were divided. While some felt changes were coming too fast, others felt they were not fast enough.

The sisters labored over collegiality, subsidiarity and consensus, outgrowths of Vatican II. By collegiality, each sister had the right and duty to share in the formation and implementation of community decisions. By subsidiarity, responsibility rested on those immediately involved in a decision. By consensus, the community sought the will of God by dialogue and prayer, agreeing to support a decision once it was articulated.[35] This was cataclysmic because for decades, superiors assumed responsibility and subjects only had to obey. After thorough study or discussion among membership, Sr. M. Jude Waters later established Policies and Procedures for those who choose acts of civil disobedience.

Because of the geographic spread of the Congregation and the notable number of its sisters, the Sacred Congregation for Institutes of Religious recommended that a study of division into Provinces be inaugurated.[36] Information was obtained and prepared for presentation at the Chapter of 1966. The sisters became increasingly aware that a General Chapter was the highest governing body of the Congregation.

Mother M. Julia's report for the Ninth General Chapter in 1966 noted construction programs at Rosary Academy, Watertown; Siena College, St. Agnes Academy, and St. Dominic School for Boys, Memphis; and St. John's Hospital, Spalding.

St. Catharine Junior College served a special need in a rural area. Students who simultaneously worked and studied could live at home and assist with the family or local farms while they pursued their dreams of education. In the 60s once again, college space became a problem. Sr. Jean Marie Callahan, president of the College at the time, asked the Council for permission to erect a new building. The debt on Sansbury infirmary was paid in full, chiefly by the sacrifices and donations of the sisters,[37] but the general treasury was depleted. Permission to build was refused until money was raised to pay for it. Sr. Jean Marie traveled to some of the cities and towns where the sisters taught to seek financial support. As a southerner, she appreciated the fact that St. Catharine was in the heart of bourbon territory. The boards of the distilleries were generous because they realized the importance of rural education. The Congregation obtained a loan of $300,000 to finance the construction.

When sufficient funds were available, a general meeting was called at the Motherhouse to discuss plans for the building. Council member Sr. Clarita arrived with an armful of catalogs. Interested sisters brought sketches and nascent ideas, while faculty members came with concepts involving their specialties. After Mother M. Julia opened the meeting with a prayer, Sr. Clarita showed pictures of Butler prefab structures, Quonset huts and packaged housing. True, they were available, affordable and functional, but they lacked architectural beauty to blend with other campus buildings.

At this point, Sr. Jean Marie said, "Unless we do it right, let's not do it at all." It took many more meetings, but finally Lourdes Hall was designed and erected. It contained a gymtorium, cafeteria, lounge, classrooms and administrative offices.[38] Dedicated in 1965, Lourdes Hall was the site used for the Ninth General Chapter the next year.

As the time for Chapter drew near, serious study focused on division into Provinces. Since this would require a revision in the Constitutions, a special Constitutions Committee was set up in addition to other committees on liturgy, government, finances, education, common life, apostolate and formation. The membership sent in 2,797 proposals for the Chapter![39] Never before had a Chapter stimulated such response. It was part of the watershed with far reaching results to follow.

Chapter Eighteen Notes

1. Official Catholic Dictionary, 1965, p. 936.
2. SCA Constitutions (193) Nos. 132, 133.
3. SCA Constitutions (1930) No. 415. A quinquennial report is a general report submitted to Rome every five years on the personal, financial and disciplinary state of the whole Congregation, signed by the Mother General, Council and the Ordinary of Louisville.
4. SCA report of Mother M. Julia to 1966 Chapter, also Annals of Our Lady of the Hills Convent, June 1965, p. 3.
5. SCA Council Governing Minutes, Sept. 25, 1951.
6. SCA Constitutions (1930) No. 304.
7. SCA Administrative file, Mother M. Julia. Original letters May 17, 1960, May 2, 1963, Dr. Con J. Fecher to Mother M. Julia. Also original letter May 1, 1964 to Conference of Major Superiors of Women's Institute from Sr. Miriam Vincent, SC, Health Commission.
8. SCA Copy of letter of Mother M. Julia to sisters and pastors, Feb. 6, 1961.
9. SCA Copy of letter of Mother M. Julia to superiors, Feb. 27, 1961. Also, BAA letter of Mother M. Julia to Rt. Rev. Msgr. Robert J. Sennott, Chancellor, Archdiocese of Boston.
10. SCA Chronology of Juniorate program compiled by Sr. Ann Miriam Hickey, archivist.
11. Personal interviews with Srs. Mary Elizabeth Thompson, Joyce Montgomery, Catherine Mary Albright, Rose Marie Cummins, Ms. Clare Tiffany and Ms. Frances Belmonte.
12. SCA Mother M. Julia's report to the Ninth General Chapter, 1966.
13. Personal interview with Sr. Joann Luttrell, former administrator of Mary Immaculate Hospital.
14. Ibid.
15. SCA Copy of proposal sent by Province of St. Joseph to Master Vincent de Cuesnongle, OP, to recognize Sr. Mary Rogan for extraordinary service to Dominican Fathers and Brothers.
16. Ibid.

17. *The Kentucky Standard,* October 4, 1979.

Copy of log kept by Sr. Mary Rogan of fathers and brothers under her care: Revs. James McKenna, James W. Owens, Charles Delivigne, James Francis Monroe, Raymond King, Adolph Frenay, Edward Clancy, Edward Cloven, George Herald, Charles Rooney, Raymond Dewdney, Aloysius Shihila, Gordon Walter, Ralph Rasher, John J. Bauer, William McLoughlin, Francis Lehner, Edmund McEinery, Robert Brennan, Michael McCaffrey, Vincent Donovan, John Joseph Madrick, James McInerney, William R. Baron, William Byrnes and Bros. Benedict Hughes, Francis Connelly.

18. SCA *Pastoral Care of Migrants and Refugees: Dominicans Reach Out to Sister Refugees* by Sr. Trinita McIsaac, OP, p. 4.

19. SCA Chronology of events re: Sr. Maria Rose, 1954-1981 compiled by Sr. Ann Miriam Hickey, archivist.

20. SCA Copy of letter of Sr. Elaine Des Rosieres to Mrs. Barbara Graybill, October 6, 1994. This letter was written to support the nomination of Sr. Maria Rose Huong, OP, for the Mother Theodore Award. The award was granted by St. Mary of the Woods College, Indiana.

21. Personal records of Edward M. Gaffney, OP, 24th EVAC HOSP, hospital chaplain, April 8, 1972, also personal memo of Fr. Gaffney to writer, July 22, 1996.

22. Copy of letter, April 2, 1972 of Parish Council Da Minh, from personal files of Fr. Gaffney.

23. Personal interview with Fr. Gaffney, July 1996.

24. Personal interviews with Srs. M. Esther Owens, Jean Berney, Maureen Flanagan, July 1996.

25. SCA Chapter Proceedings, 1974.

26. SCA Chapter Proceedings, 1976, 1980, 1984.

27. SCA Council minutes, April 25-28, 1975.

28. Personal interview with Fr. Gaffney, July 1996.

29. SCA Council minutes, October 24-27, 1975.

30. SCA Membership list, chronological sequence compiled by Sr. Ann Miriam Hickey, archivist.

31. SCA Administrative file, Mother M. Julia.

32. SCA Letter of Mother M. Julia to sisters instructing them of changes effective March 25, 1965.

33. SCA Letter of J.M. Donohue, OP, Promoter of Sisters, to Mother M. Julia, September 14, 1965.

34. SCA Day By Day, March 13, 1990. The poem was originally published in *National Catholic Reporter,* October 6, 1965.

35. SCA, *Living the Gospel Message,* pp. 40-41.

36. SCA Letter to Mother M. Julia, March 20, 1964.

37. Report of Mother M. Julia to Ninth General Chapter, 1966, p. 4.

38. Ibid., p. 5.

39. SCA Record Group II. Government — Ninth General Chapter, 1966.

Chapter Nineteen

STRIVING
FOR BALANCE

THE 95 DELEGATES to the Ninth General Chapter wasted no time in electing Sr. Ulicia O'Brien as Mother General. There were no "carry-overs" among the Council members. It was a clean sweep for a leadership which would face a radical change in religious life. The elected Councilors assumed specific tasks in addition to the usual Council responsibilities: Sr. M. Jeanne White, mission coordinator; Sr. Theodore Kline, regent of studies; Sr. Francine Eaton, aging and retirement; Sr. M. Patricia (Francis Grace) Green, director of personnel and secretary general. For the third successive time, Sr. M. Joachim McDonald was elected Bursar General.[1]

Mother Ulicia O'Brien

Catherine Louise O'Brien was born to Patrick and Katherine (Brosnan) O'Brien on June 21, 1910 in Cambridge, Massachusetts. As one of eight children (three boys, five girls) she learned the give and take in a close-knit, faith-filled Irish family. After graduating from St. John School, Cambridge, she entered St. Catharine Novitiate where she received the habit and the name Ulicia on March 6, 1928. A year later she was professed. Her sister, Mary Catherine, who became Sr. Rose Vincent was professed at St. Catharine in 1932.[2]

226

A saving grace for Mother Ulicia was her special sense of humor and the ability to perceive life's incongruities. Her six years in office were turbulent, but turbulence prevailed in church and society.

Division into Regions

The Ninth Chapter addressed the matter of dividing into Provinces as prescribed by the Sacred Congregation. The capitulars voted to divide into Regions as a testing ground for later becoming Provinces.[3] Three regions were formed: eastern, consisting of Massachusetts and New York; western with Iowa, Nebraska and Illinois; southern with Indiana, Ohio, West Virginia, Tennessee, Arkansas and Kentucky.[4] Appointed as regionals were Sr. Laetitia Anne Campbell in the east, Sr. Teresa Wolfe in the west and Sr. Ann Bell in the south. Later, other states were added or subtracted as the sisters pursued ministry. A mid-western region was formed with Illinois, Indiana and Puerto Rico in 1984 with Sr. Teresa Tuite as the first midwest regional.

Regions were a new experience and although criteria were set up for governance, implementation required education and patience at all levels. The purpose was to foster better communication among members and to link mission houses closer with central government. The Mother General delegated her authority to the regional superiors in certain matters.[5]

Polarization occurred between Central and Regional government because of uncertainty about authority and responsibility. Sometimes a local issue referred to the Generalate reverted to the Regional Superior who, unsure of her authority, hesitated to act, resulting in frustration for all involved. After attending the 1968 Conference of Dominican Major Superiors, Mother Ulicia wrote in a personal notebook: "Polarization must be faced and resolved in each community. Good of Church and dignity of the person are at stake. Work with patience and the problem can be resolved. Real bitterness is apparent in many cases."[6] Many Congregations were experiencing the same stress over polarization and other issues occurring at the time. Rome called for interior renewal stating that "even the best-contrived adaptations to the needs of our time will be of no avail unless they are animated by a spiritual renewal."[7] The reality was that it was easier to adapt external structures than to bring about a corporate interior renewal.

To deepen understanding of adaptation, each region held an Assembly with Generalate members attending. Authority, obedience and the habit generated heated discussion. Sisters worked on committees to revise the Constitutions.

Repeatedly, the sisters wanted a change in the use of active and passive voice. The young sisters in temporary vows wanted full participation in decision making, which meant being able to vote, especially at General Chapters. When the indult was requested, Rome denied the permission, limiting the privilege to those in perpetual vows.[8]

More and more sisters wanted to expand their apostolate, to move out into the world as Vatican II suggested. "Works of the community should be listed as studying, teaching, nursing and other apostolic works as they arise," wrote the Chapter.[9] What they were doing was putting their lived experience into words.

One of the most bitter struggles was over the habit. The habit, long considered a symbol of consecration and the distinctive sign of the Dominican Order, was dear to the members. Giving up the habit or any part of it tore at their hearts.

In calling religious to change the habit, Paul VI wrote, "it must be simple and modest, at once poor and becoming. In addition, it must be in keeping with the requirements of health and it must be suited to the times and place and to the needs of the apostolate."[10] To add confusion, a directive from the Master, Aniceto Fernandez, sounded an ominous note.

> It is certain, however, that Sisters could not continue to call themselves Dominicans if they make an essential change in the habit, unless they obtain the approval of the Master General and his Council for such a change.[11]

While some sisters debated the meanings of both messages,

others whipped out needle and thread to make "becoming" modified habits. In the east, a habit committee sent out specific directions: "Length of habit — at least two inches below the bend of the knee. This is important. Check your BUST SIZE (sic) when purchasing a pattern. Be sure the width at the lower edge of the skirt is sufficient to cover the knees when seated."[12]

Lay people were divided in their opinions about the habit which was actually a medieval form of dress. Some applauded the change, saying, "I feel more comfortable with sisters now." Others lamented the change as if it meant the end of "real sisters" in the church. Ultimately, the sister was free to choose traditional or modified habit, or contemporary dress, "modest and professional in style." Some pastors would not employ a sister unless she wore the habit in the classroom. The sisters wanted to be accepted for what they were, not what they wore.

A priest advisor warned the sisters not to change too much, too quickly, but it seemed no avenue of their lives went untouched. When language came under scrutiny, terms for leadership officers were called into question. Canon Law referred to the major superior as Supreme Moderator, but that did not appeal to the sisters. Mother General was changed to President; Councilors became Vice Presidents of the Governing Board; Regional Superiors became Regional Coordinators. Some felt the new terms reflected the world of capitalism, but since the Governing Board served as trustees in Civil Law, the members felt the terms would be more readily understood in civil transactions.

The sisters were eager for non-sexist language in the Psalms and liturgy. It took a while before new publications with non-sexist language came out, but some began the change in wording as they read the prayers.

The Chapter wanted the Governing Board to locate their residency in a large city where they would be more accessible and more visible. Archbishop Thomas J. McDonough recommended the empty St. George Convent, Louisville. The Governing Board checked places in other cities before deciding to rent and move into the St. George convent at 1809 Standard Avenue.

CERC

In August 1966, Paul VI issued norms for implementing the decree on the renewal of religious life.

> In each institute, in order to put renewal and adaptation into effect, a special general chapter is to be summoned within two or, at most, three years. This can be the ordinary general chapter, or an extraordinary one.[13]

Before calling for an extraordinary chapter, Mother Ulicia contacted the Catholic Education Research Center (CERC) to engage them for a study of Kentucky Dominican resources.[14] Previously, Sr. Marie Augusta Neal, SND de Namur, a Harvard-educated sociologist, had spearheaded a national survey of women religious caught up in the transition following Vatican II. A 235 page questionnaire with 649 questions was sent to over 139,000 sisters in the United States. The surprising part was that there was an 88 per cent response.[15]

While the Neal survey was a consciousness-raising and challenging experience, the Governing Board felt a study specific to Kentucky Dominicans was needed before calling the special chapter. Pastors, lay people, former members and the sisters were included in the CERC survey conducted in August 1968. The final report articulated what many knew but hesitated to say.

> It is clear... that some Sisters of the congregation do not know exactly what they are, much less what they may be in the process of becoming.[16]

CERC did not offer any solutions, but it was felt that a study of the profiles presented was important to make sound future decisions.

> It is almost jejeune to observe, in an era in which the Church, our society, and indeed all of mankind are embroiled in one crisis after another, that the Dominican Sisters of St. Catharine of Siena are most surely at a crossroad in their history.[17]

A definite turning point occurred with the Extraordinary Chapter of 1969.

Special Chapter of Affairs, 1969

MEMPHIS IN THE SUMMER! Six weeks of Memphis in the summer! No air conditioning, but plenty of fans. The forty-six delegates wilted in the humid conference rooms at Siena College, but forged ahead with the business at hand, such as decrease in professions, increase in dispensations, financial questions, governance and liturgical reform.

In the 1950s, the number of women professed was at its peak.[18] In the 1960s, 171 were professed, an almost 20% decline from the previous decade.[19] This decline was occurring in religious congregations throughout the United States. The Chapter examined possible reasons for the drop-off and wondered how to attract women to life as a Kentucky Dominican. One of the suggestions was that perhaps there was a "temporary" type of commitment instead of "for life." Although the idea was discussed as plausible, no action was taken.

Another element affecting the ministry was the exodus of professed members. From 1960-1965, there were 39 dispensations, but from 1966-1972, there were 117. Gradually, the number leaving leveled off in ensuing decades, but professions dropped to single digits or even zero.[20] This meant fewer sisters available for ministry. Sisters were aging in place, or as the CERC report put it, "steadily shrinking in number, rapidly advancing in age."[21] To the 1969 Chapter delegates the picture looked grim with the median age at 53 and a total membership of 729.[22] However, they were determined to find solutions.

Since the sisters themselves were the most valuable resource, the Chapter sought the best way to deploy the members of the apostolate and for the good of the individual. During the period of experimentation, the sisters were free to explore new paths in various phases of their lives. Mother Ulicia reminded them, "In essentials, unity; in non-essentials, liberty; and in all things, charity."[23]

It was inevitable that the Congregation had to withdraw corporate commitment from some institutions, that is, they could no longer guarantee to send a specific number of sisters to staff a place. However, sometimes, individual sisters felt so strongly about a school where Kentucky Dominicans had served for many years, that the individual stayed on even after the corporate commitment ceased.

Open Contracting

When the Chapter decided that each sister could apply and contract for her own position, open contracting was introduced. Sisters who had entered the convent right after high school and who had always been assigned to their ministry, had never had to challenge the job market. It was a new experience for them to prepare a resume, face interviews and seek a position. The Congregation offered workshops in different regions for career counseling and job searching. For some it was an exhilarating experience to assume personal responsibility, but for others it was a frightening break-down in the religious life they had known.

Srs. Sheila Marie Pendergast, Grace (Thomas Aquin) Simms, Joanne (Michael Edward) Gill were appointed as personnel directors to acquaint the members with available openings. A process was established for the members to discern about changing ministry and the sisters were free to move from region to region.

Since stipends paid to sisters in parochial schools were low, often below subsistence level, sisters were, in effect, subsidizing some of the institutions where they served. In the deployment of resources, it was decided that if the community were subsidizing, it should choose where to do so. Should personnel and money be poured into community-owned institutions? Should inner-city schools be a priority? What about the option for the poor? The decisions were difficult ones. Each region did a self-study of the schools to see which were viable and in keeping with the mission statement of the Congregation.

Residency

Closely related to ministry was the question of residency. Occupancy in convents which once housed 30-40 sisters, dropped drastically as the number of sisters decreased. In many cases, maintaining these buildings was a financial drain on the parish. When pastors or parish councils felt they had to close the convent, sisters sought rental housing near the ministry. Some pastors, even when the parish school closed, invited sisters to live in the local convent. Inter-community living became more common as members of different communities lived together. An example of this is St. Francis deSales Convent, Charlestown, Massachusetts, where women religious of five different communities have shared residency at the invitation of the pastor, Rev. Daniel Mahoney. An entry in the Council minutes stated:

> "...inter-community living is seen as a means of deepening the quality of life. Some members see it as the future for religious life. Sisters should be going to something, not escaping from community."[24]

To rent an apartment for several sisters to live together was difficult if not financially prohibitive. Sometimes when sisters sought an apartment for two or three, they were asked if they were lesbians because the owner had no conception of celibate religious life. Some sisters settled to live alone in an apartment. The great concern was what did this do to community. Local chapter groups were established so that all sisters, living alone or with others, met periodically to sustain mutual support through dialogue, prayer and sharing time as community.

Since the Chapter emphasized sharing on a deeper level among members, it was felt that in large houses, such as the Motherhouse, smaller living units were preferable to achieve this goal. At St. Catharine the sisters divided into smaller groups, each having its own community room and kitchenette.[25] Members of these units attended Mass together and usually dined in the common refectory. This pattern was initiated at St. Patrick, Watertown; St. John, Cambridge; and Rosary Convent, Watertown. Once again, some liked it; some did not.

When the extraordinary Chapter ended, the delegates returned to their missions to share the sobering facts with those who were at home. The sisters reaffirmed the purpose of the

Congregation as daughters of St. Dominic, dedicated to sharing in the mission of Christ. They felt that diversity was a thread woven into the tapestry of their lives.

When the Eleventh General Chapter opened in 1972, Sr. Ulicia O'Brien, the last mother General and the first President of the Kentucky Dominicans, bade farewell to the sisters and welcomed the new leadership team with a sesquicentennial celebration. Five hundred sisters gathered at St. Catharine to observe 150 years of service and to embrace their mission statement, come what may.

Mission Statement
In our search for truth,
our mission is to hear and proclaim God's Word,
promote the dignity of persons
and participate in the mission of the Church
through our call to teach, to heal,
to serve and to transform oppressive structures.[26]

Chapter Nineteen Notes

1. SCA Administrative file of Mother Ulicia.
2. SCA Personal file of Mother Ulicia.
3. It was generally felt that the Congregation was not large enough to set up autonomous provinces. In addition, the financial outlay for separate provinces would have been tremendous. Regions, dependent on the Motherhouse, seemed do-able.
4. SCA Administrative file of Mother Ulicia, Oct. 26, 1966.
5. SCA Regions — a document describing areas, purpose, government, duties, rank and finances of program.
6. SCA Personal notebook of Mother Ulicia.
7. Flannery, *Documents of Vatican II, Renewal of Religious Life,* p. 613, Vol. 1, 1984.

8. SCA Governance File 3, March 1966, also Letter to Mother Ulicia from Sacred Congregation, March 5, 1971.

9. SCA Governance File 2, #282.

10. Flannery, *Documents of Vatican II, Renewal of Religious Life*, p. 621. Vol. 1, 1984.

11. SCA letter to Mother Ulicia from Master Aniceto Fernandez, OP, Jan. 2, 1968.

12. Eastern Regional Archives, July 15, 1968, Watertown, Massachusetts, Regional Annals.

13. Flannery, *Documents of Vatican II, Norms for Implementing the Decree: On the Up-to-date Renewal of Religious Life*, p. 625, no. 3.

14. SCA Information in this section is from the report of the Catholic Education Research Center (CERC), the Stanwyck Corporation, Washington, D.C., 1968.

15. Kennelly, *American Catholic Women*, p. 186, also, Wittberg, *The Rise and Fall of Catholic Religious Orders*, p. 215.

16. SCA CERC report, Chapter 8, 9-3.

17. Ibid., 9-13.

18. SCA Profession list — 212 professed in 1950s.

19. Ibid.

20. SCA Profession list and dispensation list.

21. CERC 4-21.

22. SCA Newsletters, File 14.

23. SCA Message of Mother Ulicia to Western Regional Conference, 1968.

24. SCA Council minutes, Aug. 8-14, 1973.

25. SCA Residency Directory of the Kentucky Dominican Family, 1995-1996.

26. SCA Mission Statement of the Congregation.

LIVING
THE GOSPEL
MESSAGE

THE CHAPTER OF 1969 labored to bring forth something which would give direction to the lives of the sisters moving from a hierarchical authority, "the blind obedience" model, to one of individual initiative with personal responsibility and accountability. It was indicative of the paradigm shift taking place in the Congregation and in society. The mandates of the Chapter, called *Living the Gospel Message*, became interim directives but they were not fully approved until 1984 because of Item 364, which dealt with voting rights of sisters not finally professed.

> As for including among the delegates to the General Chapter, sisters in temporary commitment, this Sacred Congregation has never favored such a measure. It is somewhat imprudent and therefore inadvisable to allow those who are not yet definitively members of the Institute, and who could leave before their mandate expires, to participate in the determination of policies for the whole Institute.[1]

The General Chapter of 1972 reconsidered Article 364, but the groundswell for maximum participation kept burgeoning.

Sr. Ulicia O'Brien was the bridge from the old to the new way of religious life, but the sisters had questions about crossing the bridge. What was in store on the other side? Was the crossing of the bridge to be ongoing, a process of becoming?

To continue the journey, the Chapter of 1972 elected Sr. Joan Monica McGuire, the first Nebraskan to hold the office of major superior. The length of the term was changed from six years to four and the number of Governing Board members to assist the president was increased to six. Two members were at central — Srs. Helen Cahill (Anne Margaret) and M. Patricia Green (Francis Grace). Four, Srs. Paschala Noonan, Marina Gibbons, Helen Ann Marshall and Jean Marie Callahan, were "in the field." The purpose of having field members was to increase contact of the central government with the sisters on the missions.

One of the first issues Sr. Joan Monica addressed was community living.[2] Did community life mean living together under one roof? Did it mean participating in the same ministry? With sisters moving into apartments as more and more convents closed, and with ever-expanding ministries because of open contracting, drastic changes were taking place. No more was there a bell to summon all to common prayers, meditation, study, recreation or meals. To some it seemed that religious life was dying; to others, it seemed the opening of opportunities to penetrate the world with Christian values in a whole new way.[3]

With fewer sisters earning salaries, the increase of the median age and no new members entering, the financial picture was dismal. In 1973 when the Congregation bought into Social Security retroactive to 1968, each sister contributed $10 and the General Congregational funds were strained beyond measure. One summer the sisters were asked to find extra work during vacation so that each one could bring in an additional $100 to help out. Numerous fundraising ideas were tried, such as bake sales, bazaars, raffles, buy-a-brick and booster club. Individual efforts were faithful and unwavering, but the issue was broader and needed national attention if ministries were to be maintained.

Conference of Religious Treasurers (CORT)

The Conference of Major Superiors of Women (later the

Leadership Conference of Women Religious, (LCWR) aware of what was happening among sisterhoods, felt there was an advantage for treasurers of the various communities to work together sharing information on costs of living, formation, administration and retirement. On January 4, 1969, sisters from 18 different congregations met and formed the Conference of Religious Treasurers (CORT).[4]

The movement grew rapidly with the result that in 1972, some 150 religious treasurers met for two days in Dayton, Ohio. LCWR suggested that each regional LCWR establish a group of their treasurers and/or fiscal officers.[5]

In Kentucky, the General Chapter of 1972 stressed the necessity of an educational program on finances, not only for the sisters themselves, but also for those with whom they worked. The Chapter pointed out that the Congregation should choose where to put its resources whether that was personnel or finances. Wealthy parishes did not need to be subsidized; in fact, doing so, reduced what could be done in ministry with the poor. Sr. Marie Jeanne Surette, General Treasurer, began an educational program which called for collaboration among sisters, clergy and laity. For three months, she visited each local community, met with pastors, lay councils, bishops and boards of education. She compiled an analysis called *Resources for Ministry*, which emphasized that the Congregation had to act immediately in order to survive for ministry.

She requested bishops to cooperate on the diocesan level to raise stipends of all sisters working in their dioceses. Response was often less than enthusiastic. Moreover, not all Congregations shared the same opinion about larger stipends. Some felt they did not need an increase, thus giving bishops a double message.

Pastors, although sympathetic, felt stipends were set by the diocese and they did not want to go against the bishop. Because of the recession, some felt it was the worst possible time to ask for an increase.

For the most part, the sisters did not understand the financial situation. Local superiors and treasurers in conjunction with the Generalate Finance department had always handled money matters. High finance for the sisters in the ranks consisted in having $15 to spend *annually.*

Some sisters were strongly opposed to entering Social Security because they felt it would be taking money away from the poor. They feared that asking for an increase in stipends would cause the closing of some schools.

Lay people serving as directors on boards of some Congregational institutions were appalled at the low stipends for women religious. They advised them in strong terms to participate in Social Security and to set up a pension plan. Harold R. Romanoff, a hospital advisory member, tried to allay misgivings about depriving the poor: "Sisters, if you want to help the poor, you must have bread in your basket. As poor as you are yourselves, you will be unable to help others unless you do something about your own situation."

Many lay people were unaware that the "Church" did not provide for all the needs of the sisters. "We thought the Pope took care of you," they said. Some parishes responded immediately by taking up special collections. Leading the way was St. Patrick, Watertown, Massachusetts, followed by St. Michael, Lowell; St. John, Cambridge; St. John, Quincy; St. Francis deSales, Charlestown. In Nebraska, St. Cecilia and St. Michael, Hastings; Sacred Heart, Greeley and St. Mary, Bellevue; responded generously. In Chicago, St. Bartholomew and in Brooklyn, SS. Simon and Jude and St. Vincent Ferrer donated in gratitude for past services.[6]

When she evaluated the program, Sr. Marie Jeanne felt that the best result was the raising of consciousness to the situation. This was reinforced when *The Wall Street Journal* (5/19/1986) carried an article on the financial plight of American sisterhoods. Gradually stipends increased and through the efforts of National Association of Treasurers of Religious Institutes (NATRI), an outgrowth of CORT, combined with the efforts of LCWR, some dioceses adopted the custom of taking up an annual collection for women religious to be dispensed to Congregations within the diocese on a pro rata basis.[7] St. Catharine set up its own fund for the care of the aged, infirm and disabled sisters.

Changes in Ministry

During Sr. Joan Monica's first term in office, no new missions were accepted. The decrease in numbers precluded assigning a full staff of sisters to a parochial school or to a community-owned institution. Nevertheless, she wrote a series of booklets in which she voiced her belief in a future for religious life and ministry through educational institutions. Above all, she stressed the importance of presence as ministry. She wrote: "An important aspect of our ministry is our presence in the places where we reside. From our convents, large of small, our apartments, housing projects, or small homes, we can minister to our neighbors in many ways and be visible to them as women religious."[8] Although no new missions were accepted, new programs developed in already existing places.

Adaptations at Plainville, Massachusette

An example of adaptation occurred at Plainville, Massachusetts. In 1949, James and Mary Toner donated 85 acres of land to the Kentucky Dominicans in appreciation for the loving care given to their daughter Patricia by Sr. Bernardine Sullivan and the sisters at Rosary Academy, Watertown, Massachusetts.[9] The buildings and property at Plainville, known as Crystal Spring Farm, have been adapted to many ministerial activities over the years.

In the summer of 1950, Crystal Spring Camp for resident and day girls, ages 6 to 14, offered an exciting opportunity for children to have a hands-on experience of growing things, becoming conscious of the earth and enjoying uncluttered life in the country.

It has already been noted that the farmhouse served as a Postulate for 11 years (1949-1960). It housed the regional office when Sr. Laetitia Anne Campbell became the first Eastern regional (1960). Regional meetings were held there as well as retreats, workshops and planning sessions.

Sr. Bernadine Marie Egleston, artist and sculptor, had an art studio in the garage building where she taught art to the students from the kindergarten and Dominican Academy.

For eight years the old farmhouse served as Womancenter, a project with Sr. Christine Loughlin and Carolyn McDade as co-directors (1983-1991). Womancenter was a feminine response to spirituality, politics and the arts. It created a space for women to gather to study their own experiences and to stand in solidarity with the oppressed, to raise consciousness of the plight of women in Central and South America and to engage in non-violent protests against oppressive situations. Carolyn, an accomplished musician, composed and published music used internationally to confront systems that exclude and deny. Women from Guatemala, South Africa, Palestine, Mexico and Mozambique were some of the people who came to Womancenter to share their stories.

When Womancenter closed a new ministry began at Crystal Spring. An intentional community was formed there in 1992 composed of Srs. Rose Marie Cummins, Pauline LaMothe, Christine Loughlin and Carole Rossi. Their purpose was to live simple sustainable community, aware of the interconnectedness of all of God's creation. The renewed Crystal Spring Farm became an ecology center as these sisters sowed, harvested and shared the fruits of the land and their own endeavors to repair in part the rape of the earth. Other buildings on the Plainville property were used at various times as a school, kindergarten, spirituality center and housing for homeless mothers with infants.

Reconciliation

In 1975 when Paul VI called for a Holy Year Jubilee, *Reconciliation: The Way to Peace*, Sr. Joan Monica echoed the call inviting the sisters to reconciliation and justice with God, self and others.[10] She talked about former members and urged the sisters, "Heal wounds which may have been part of life with us." Though some members withdrew from the Order, they bore witness with courage and caring to women's share in shaping the Congregation and the Church. The work they did while in the community still bears fruit.

Five years after Bishop Carroll T. Dozier was consecrated as first bishop of Memphis, Tennessee, he invited Sr. Frances Belmonte to become his Diocesan Theologian and to open the Office of Theology. It was a first to have a resident woman theologian to a Bishop in the United States.[11]

The bishop called on her to set up a liturgical ceremony of reconciliation with alienated Catholics in his diocese. Sr. Frances, convinced that an educative process was necessary to effect reconciliation with those "outside the pews," penciled on a legal pad an outline for a year of intense study to prepare for the reconciliation event. Little did she know that Bishop Dozier would send the penciled outline to Rome via Apostolic Delegate Jean Jadot. The plan was approved.

It meant a media blitz to prepare the news, to write letters to priests, laity, parish organizations and the alienated. It meant a call to prayer, penance and outreach throughout the diocese. It meant taking risks.

There were two reconciliation ceremonies in December 1976, which centered attention on Bishop Dozier and his diocese, one in Memphis and one in Jackson. The national news focused on the use of General Absolution, overshadowing all the preparation behind the scenes.

The Coliseum in Memphis held 12,000 people. This troubled Sr. Rosalie Van Ackeren, the diocesan liturgist. She voiced her fear to the Bishop. "The place is going to be jammed. How can I direct music for such a vast throng? The place is so large, nobody will see me and the music will be a mess without direction." She solved the dilemma with a pair of white gloves. Though her face was a blur to the participants, nobody missed the rhythmic movements of her white-gloved hands waving high in the air!

A similar reconciliation event occurred at the Civic Center, Jackson, Tennessee. The results of both events continued long after the public celebrations. The second phase of continuing education, counseling and action made reconciliation a reality. In his last illness, Bishop Dozier remarked, "The Reconciliation was one of the best events of my life," and then he added, "and Sr. Rosalie wore white gloves."[12]

Although she withdrew from the Congregation, in reviewing

her role as a member, Belmonte said she felt the concerns of the sisters are larger than local concerns; that their contributions to the Church and to Catholic education have not yet been recognized. At present she is professor of theology at Loyola University, Chicago, where she continues her work of teaching and preaching. Her relationship with Kentucky Dominicans remains warm and close. She often visits St. Catharine and occasionally conducts workshops and retreats for the sisters.

Relationships with former members were not limited to the sisters. Their students long remembered their influence. At an alumni reunion of St. Catharine College, classes of 1967-69 recalled Sr. Lois Ann Pfeister. They reminisced about science classes with her and how she was advisor and friend. In appreciation they decided to plant a tree on campus in her memory.

Having received her doctorate in science, Sr. Lois became a full professor of botany at the University of Oklahoma. After she withdrew from the community she married Dee Fink. Through an exchange program between the United States and Czech Academies of Science she did research in Prague and became internationally known for her research on algae. In an interview in 1991 for Dominican News she said, "I want to say that I still consider St. Catharine's a part of my family and I gained so very, very much from my years in the community." She died at the height of her career. On her headstone her relationships are described as wife, mother, international scientist and "a member of St. Catharine Congregation." She never forgot her Dominican ties. These are only two examples of the contributions made by former members to the Congregation, the Church and the world.

The Bicentennial Chapter 1976

As the nation prepared to celebrate its 200th birthday with tall ships, unrestrained fireworks displays and countless public festivities, President Gerald Ford warned against resting on accomplishments of the past and called for an improvement of the quality of life.[13]

In Kentucky the Bicentennial Chapter of 1976 re-elected Sr.

Joan Monica McGuire for a second four years. Also re-elected were: Srs. Helen Cahill, Marina Gibbons and Jean Marie Callahan. New members on the Governing Board were: Srs. Joann Luttrell (Jane Frederic), Elaine Shaw and Catherine Galaskiewicz. In 1978, Srs. Helen and Elaine resigned. Sr. Marie Jeanne Surette was chosen to fill one of the vacancies created by the resignations.

Two significant notes of interest included relationships with Vietnamese sisters who were encouraged to live at St. Catharine, thereby giving them an opportunity to study at the College as they adjusted to life in the United States. The other item was the formation of a Constitutions Committee which worked tirelessly to draft a new Constitutions.

The hunger for justice was heard on all sides. Women called for the use of inclusive language in the liturgy but it was slow in coming. Some felt called to be priests, even though it was a closed but painful issue. Sr. Joan Monica placed strong emphasis on personal spiritual development and on religious and scriptural education. Every effort was made to implement these ideas.

The Struggle for Autonomy

The Chapter of 1980 elected Sr. Helen Cahill with a four-member Governing Board composed of Srs. Joann Luttrell (Jane Frederic), Ann Dominic Roach, Marie Jeanne Surette and Mary Jude Waters. It was a period of turmoil for the sisters. On all sides they were bombarded with articles, workshops and retreats about survival, self-identity, cultural change and their place in the Church. That some did not feel they had much of a place in the Church they loved was particularly painful.

Sr. Helen, as chairperson of the Dominican Leadership Conference (DLC), chairperson of Leadership Conference of Women Religious (LCWR) Region VI, and member of the National Board of LCWR, had her finger on the pulse of religious life. Beautiful words had been spoken and written, government structures had been revised, but still, deep revitalization seemed ephemeral. The sisters recognized that a radical commitment to Christ in faith was the only way for religious life to have any meaning. The question was, how to bring it about!

In the Eastern region an earnest effort was made to bring it about by means of a Reconciliation Process with skilled outside facilitators to help. Sr. Helen called the entire community to a Transformation Process which created a safe space where sisters could voice their fears, hopes and anger. A real healing process began.

Digging for the Past: Building for the Future

Interest in the Order's past prompted Sr. Mary Otho Ballard in 1983 to arrange for a History Week complete with an archaeology dig in the valley on the actual site of the old Motherhouse. Nancy O'Malley, an archeologist from the University of Kentucky, assisted by three experienced archeological field workers and a group of eager sisters, supervised the shovel probes. From the investigation it was possible to describe the size of the original buildings and to note the Gothic influence of European convents, especially in the massive chapel.[14] Lectures by Sr. Mary Nona McGreal, OP, a noted Dominican historian from Sinsinawa, Wisconsin, breathed life into the probe of the past. Interviews with older sisters, tours and slide presentations helped to compile information which had been lost in the 1904 fire.

Special rejoicing occurred in 1984 when Rome (The Sacred Congregation for Institutues of Religious Life) approved of the fourth Constitutions, *Journeying in Truth*. Each sister received a copy, along with the accompanying directory which fleshed out details of observation and implementation. There was in place a policy handbook with clear, concise policies which could be initiated, amended or deleted in response to issues arising from the members and the mission.

Dissent was one such issue. "Response of some of our members to the cries of the human family and to injustices in our times have taken the form of civil disobedience," wrote Sr. Helen.[15] When some sisters staged protests at nuclear test sites, participated in civil rights marches, fought for higher wages and employment benefits for garbage strikers, signed *The New York Times* ad on abortion (2/2/1986), or publicly questioned the Church's stand on the ordination of women, the news media highly publicized these items. Sisters not involved in those issues were uneasy. Did those who chose civil disobedience act as individuals or in the name of the Congregation? Even if they acted as individuals, did not the fact that they were identified as Kentucky Dominicans implicate the community? If they were imprisoned or fined, what then? Wouldn't that involve Congregational liability? Sr. Helen did not take a stand for or against civil disobedience, but she opened the question to the entire community for corporate reflection in each region.

Since the mission statement calls for transformation of oppressive structures, it was inevitable that some would take action in opposition to oppressive civil, congregational and/or ecclesiastical authority. A 1988 Chapter Act points out that inter-action between lawful authority and individual conscience may be in oppostition. It urges dissidents to engage in prayer, reflec-tion and dialogue with their local community and regional lead-ership, as well as with those with whom they stand in solidari-ty before and after taking action. In each case, they are to study and prepare for possible consequences including legal ramifica-tions for themselves and the Congregation.[16]

Those not involved are requested to pray, study and accept their sister's choice in charity and with respect for personal con-science. The Constitutions remind all: "These Constitutions are an expression of our communion with the universal church and to our fidelity to papal authority."[17]

As Dominicans, the pursuit of Truth prompted frank discus-sion on topics seldom before handled openly. Because of issues prominent in today's society, the Policy Handbook now carries procedures for responding to allegations of sexual misconduct, substance abuse and durable power of attorney for medical care. Social justice issues are considered a constitutive element of religious life.

Sr. Helen conducted workshops for religious and civic groups on Gospel values for economic justice and served as a consul-tant to the Bishops Committee on the Pastoral, *Economic Justice for All: Catholic Social Teaching and the U.S. Economy.* Social issues claiming the attention of the sisters were racism, sexism, ageism, ethnocentrism and consumerism. In response to ageism, a dynamic project was launched at Rosary Academy, Watertown.

Ecumenical Life Center, Watertown, Massachusetts

Sr. Trinita McIsaac, long a voice for the elderly, spearheaded a movement in the Archdiocese of Boston to address the needs of aging religious, but she wanted to extend this to all elders. Her dream was to establish a drop-in Ecumenical Life Center with multiple programs for senior citizens. With a subsidy of $25,000 from Congregational funds and permission to use available space at Rosary, she opened the program in November, 1974, as a hospitality center for the Watertown area. A short time later, she added the Institute of Lifetime Learning.

The first director, Sr. Lois Pineau, organized physical, educational, spiritual and recreational services for senior citizens. A volunteer nurse monitored blood pressure, delivered talks on healthy aging, and administered flu shots in season. Retired professors from nearby colleges and universities lectured on a variety of interests.

Through a grant proposal, Sr. Lois obtained a van for infirmed and disabled, the first transportation for elderly in Watertown. She negotiated with the Town Council on Aging for a bus to be shared between the Center and other seniors in the area.

Friars from Dover, local priests and ministers offered religious programs, days of recollection and Bible studies. Under the direction of James Bergin, the New Life Singers were formed to offer entertainment for nursing homes. One of their annual programs was a Christmas Concert given at the Watertown Mall. Their Christmas swan song was in 1993 with Win Regan conducting and Sr. Teresita Trelegan accompanying.

The Center had a well-rounded program designed with a holistic approach to life. For 18 years it continued to offer services and the friendships formed during those years had a value beyond measure.[15]

Changes in the 80s

In 1984, the Chapter re-elected Sr. Helen Cahill for a second term with Srs. Ann Dominic Roach, Mary Helen Thieneman, Mary Jude Waters and Pauline LaMothe as Governing Board. When Sr. Ann Dominic resigned, Sr. Rita Carr was elected as fourth Governing Board member.

In 1983, Sr. Helen appointed Sr. Trinita McIsaac to a new ministry, Promoter of Mission. Because of prior commitments, Sr. Trinita began her work a year later. For her, it meant inviting people to share in the mission of Kentucky Dominicans, thereby enriching their own baptismal calling. It was a rich source of collaboration. She became an itinerant preacher, traveling to all the places where the sisters served and beyond. In addition, she worked with other communities on retirement planning, development of community and days of recollection. Her ministry took her to the Cabra Irish Dominicans and the King Williamstown Dominicans in South Africa. She worked not only with religious but also with the poorest of poor tribal people. Her work in Ireland with Cabra Dominicans led her to Dublin, Belfast and Galway areas. For 13 years she continued as Promoter of Mission. Perhaps she is best described in the name given her by the Vietnamese sisters: Chi Minh Huom, meaning "strong and courageous woman."[19]

More Changes at Plainville

The property at Plainville, Massachusetts, proved adaptable to many ministries. In 1986, Sr. Virginia Smith was appointed director of the Spirituality Center located in a two-story red brick building. It needed some renovation before it could accommodate 12 people in residence or 20 day participants. Sr. Virginia, who came from a large family, called upon her siblings to clean, plaster, decorate and paint until the house was attractive and homey. Sr. Mary Walsh (Thomas a Kempis) assisted with secretarial work. Although it held promise of becoming a flourishing center, it came to an abrupt halt when Sr. Virginia died in a tragic car accident, August 19, 1988.

Once again, another innovative ministry developed there in

1990 under the leadership of Sr. Blaise Flynn, who established Celeste House. She prepared the people of Plainville in advance about her program which offered two-year transitional housing and supportive services to homeless mothers with children. Convinced by Sr. Blaise of the value of the project and because of the respect and trust in the Dominican sisters developed over the years, the Plainville people welcomed Celeste House. It was named after the late Celeste Walls Fitzpatrick, a co-worker of Sr. Blaise and counselor at Pine Street Inn an agency for homeless people.

For the women, it was an opportunity to be rehabilitated, family-style. Women who ordinarily would be separated from their children could live in a safe family setting and have their children with them. The rules were strict: no substance abuse, no telephone calls or visitors during the first six months, compulsory attendance at drug and alcohol meetings, random drug tests weekly. Celeste House is funded by the Massachusetts Department of Public Welfare, which still operates the program.

Sr. Blaise moved on to another ministry under the auspices of Pine Street Inn's new residence in Dorchester, Massachusetts (1995). She opened a house for formerly homeless men and women living with HIV/AIDS. One of the first things she did was to apply to the Kentucky Dominican Jonquil Fund, an Earth Education Fund established by the Governing Board in 1993. From the Jonquil Fund she obtained money to buy garden tools, tulip bulbs, and of course, jonquil bulbs, the traditional flower of Kentucky Dominicans. Sr. Rose Marie Cummins and Patricia Daley, OPA, helped plant the bulbs as residents watched and gave bits of advice here and there. Spring was late; the flowers seemed to take forever to bloom. Residents watched and waited. Norman talked to the bulbs, encouraging them to grow.[20] At last, they burst forth — purple and pink tulips, and above all, the golden jonquils, a signadou, a sign from God of hope and promise of new life.

The Mary and Elizabeth Chapter, 1988

The theme of the 1988 Chapter, *Mary Greeting Elizabeth* —

Women Greeting Women, was powerfully symbolized by a sculp-
ture designed and executed by Sr. Bernadine Marie Egleston. It
occupied a sacred space during the Chapter, reminding the
sisters of the words written by Sr. Rose Marie Cummins:

> "There is a sacred moment we experience,
> when our eyes meet, understanding registers,
> our hearts grieve in unison,
> strong bonding transpires,
> the volcano erupts,
> the truth is spoken and set free
> and silence is broken."[21]

These words presaged what occurred in the years following the
election of Sr. Elizabeth Miles as president. On the Governing
Board were: Srs. Joann Luttrell, Catherine Mahady, Margaret
Marie Hofstetter and Ann Bell. The group was a microcosm
reflecting the expansion of ministries taking place within the
Congregation. Sr. Elizabeth was a missionary in Belize; Sr.
Joann, health administrator; Sr. Catherine, college president; Sr.
Margaret Marie, teacher at Bethlehem University, Israel; Sr. Ann
Bell, school and regional administrator. Sr. Joann resigned in
1991.

For a long time, the members had called for an updated
history of the Congregation. In answer to a Chapter mandate, Sr.
Elizabeth commissioned Sr. Paschala Noonan to write it.
Because many records were lost in the 1904 fire, the task called
for extensive research in archives here and abroad. Francis
Furgang, a descendant of the Sansbury family, was most helpful
in tracing the genealogy of Angela Sansbury and obtaining
copies of records from the Maryland Hall of Records and from
Prince George County archives. Steeped in Maryland history,
Mr. Furgang was a rich source of information.

In addition to commissioning an update of the history, Sr.
Elizabeth exhorted the sisters to become more involved in the
Dominican charism of preaching. Sr. Sheila Marie Pendergast,
associate director of the Louisville Archdiocesan Spirituality
Office had been Promoter of Preaching, but her sudden death in
1989 from cancer left a void in the Archdiocese and in the

Congregation. In 1990, Sr. Elizabeth appointed Sr. Mary Louise Edwards as Promoter of Preaching.

Invitations for sisters to preach in the Roman Catholic pulpit are rare. Sometimes they are allowed to preach before or after Mass, on special feast days, jubilees or funerals. It is more common for them to be invited to preach at prayer services and ecumenical meetings. Sr. Mary Louise learned to take advantage of any available opportunity to preach.[22] With the emphasis on the Dominican charism of the *holy preaching*, sisters rely on their presence, example and ministry as valid ways of proclaiming the Truth when pulpits are not open to them.

The Catherine of Siena Award

St. Catherine of Siena always has had a special place in the hearts of Dominicans and especially Kentucky Dominicans who chose her as their patroness. When Catherine was declared a Doctor of the Church in 1970, it caused great rejoicing. Only three women, Catherine of Siena, Teresa of Avila and Therese of Lisieux, have received this title in the whole history of the Church to date. More people like Catherine are needed to face ecclesial issues honestly and courageously; to empower the poor and marginalized; to quest for peace and justice.[23] For these reasons the Catherine of Siena Award was established.

Sr. Elizabeth called a group of sisters from Kentucky and Indiana to develop a process, establish criteria and confer the award, a print of an oil painting by artist Sr. Dorothy Briggs. Recipients of the award have been: Anne Russell Mayeaux, activist in the field of feminist ethics, 1990; Honora Elizabeth Nacy, a Dominican laywoman involved in the care of the poor and oppressed, 1991; Joan Chittister, OSB, author and lecturer on contemporary issues in the Church, 1992; Gilda Victoria Larios, who works with impoverished Mexican and Central American refugees, 1993; Mary Lavinia Graves, founder/director of Love the Children, 1995. Each was selected from a group of nominees because she embodied Catharine's qualities of prophetic vision and deep compassion.

Full Participation at Chapter

A long-sought dream became reality at the 1992 Chapter. Ratification of full participation! It had taken countless requests to Rome, revisions of Constitutions, consultations with Canon lawyers, endless Congregational studies, meetings and painful dialogue. "Each member of the Congregation participates in Chapter through one or more modes: supportive member, non-voting participant; voting delegate."[24] The delegates of the 1992 Chapter elected Sr. Elizabeth Miles for a second term with Srs. Claire McGowan, Barbara Sullivan, Joan Monica McGuire and Nora Rita Mudd as Governing Board Members.

One issue causing heated Chapter discussion was Eucharist. The development of Eucharistic doctrine through the centuries has by no means remained static, fueling debates among Christians concerning the proper understanding of Eucharist. For many years, the communal nature of Eucharist tended to be obscured by concentration upon the benefits given to individuals through private and personal devotion.[25] Discussions on Eucharist often surfaced at Chapters following Vatican II. The writer, reporting on the Pastoral Plan of the 1994 Extraordinary Chapter, wrote in *Dominican News* that there is more than one reality of the Eucharist. "In the Mass, God is present

in the Word where God reveals the God who is,
in the minister where God leads in the person of the presider,
in the species where God abides and remains in the tabernacle,
and in the assembly where God is in the people gathered in
God's name."

Questions were raised about being Eucharist for each other, about services in the absence of an ordained priest, about sacrament and symbolism. Agreement was reached after long deliberation with the following Chapter Act.

The Eucharist is the center of our lives as Kentucky Dominican Family. In Eucharistic mystery, Jesus gave of himself even to death. We receive and return the gift in self-giving, thanksgiving, unity and in reverence for creation. Our on-going commitment is to respect each other as we seek and live faithful and adequate expressions of Eucharist in harmony with the actions and intentions of Jesus.[26]

The Chapter committed the sisters to disciplined study, dialogue and accountability on this and other issues.[27] The delegates at the 1992 Chapter elected Sr. Elizabeth Miles president for a second term with Srs. Claire McGowan, Barbara Sullivan, Joan Monica McGuire and Nora Rita Mudd as Governing Board members.

Extraordinary Moment: Sacred Emerging

Sr. Elizabeth called for an Extraordinary Chapter in 1994 to ratify a Pastoral Plan for the future of the Kentucky Dominican Family.[28] The theme was Extraordinary Moment: Sacred Emerging, using the life cycle of the butterfly to parallel the growth of the community into the future. The entire community had spent three years in preparation from which emerged five major topics: Relationship and Identity, Spirituality, Community, Vowed Life and Collaboration for Mission. In the life cycle of the butterfly, a complete metamorphosis is imperative for species survival. The Pastoral Plan called for a radical transformation of each member in order to reverse the downward spiral which threatened religious life.[29]

Closer Union

Dominican congregations of women have made many efforts toward collaboration. In 1995, thirty communities of Dominican women met to look at ways of being more collaborative. While this was taking place in the United States a similar movement to create a closer union of Dominican sisters throughout the world was taking place in Rome. Sr. Nora Rita Mudd represented the Kentucky Dominican Family at this meeting in May, 1995.

Kentucky Dominicans already collaborated with other Dominicans in various ways, such as Common Novitiate, Parable Conference, Promoter of Preaching, Dominican Lands

Initiative and Las Casas Project with native Americans. Membership was encouraged to study other ways of collaboration for the future of U.S. Dominican women and for the Church.[30]

When the 18th General Chapter assembled in Kentucky from December 27, 1995 to January 2, 1996, the delegates met in the newly-renovated conference room, which at one time was the main chapel. The transformation was bittersweet. There was nostalgic sadness to see the end of what once had been, but there was exhilarating pleasure at the aesthetically designed, much-needed meeting space.

Delegates elected Sr. Joan Scanlon as president with Srs. Claire McGowan, Barbara Rapp, Joye Gros and Regina McCarthy on the Governing Board. With faith and optimism they headed for the millennium when their term will expire in 2002.[31]

Chapter Twenty Notes

1. SCA letter from Sacra Congregatio Pro Religiosis to Rev. Mother Ulicia O'Brien, Mar. 5, 1971.
2. SCA, *A Message to the Sisters: Community Living*, Sr. Joan Monica McGuire, Sept. 1973.
3. SCA, *Living the Gospel Message*, p. 12.
4. Brief Historical Notes, National Association of Treasurers of Religious Institutes (NATRI), compiled by Br. Louis J. Laperle, SC, May 1990.
5. Ibid.
6. SCA Report to Governing Board by Sr. Marie Jeanne Surette.
7. A Tri-Conference group composed of members from leadership groups of women (LCWR) and men (CMSM), NATRI and the bishops worked on stipends. Later, The Consortium of Women Religious also joined.
8. SCA, *A Message to the Sisters: Ministry Through Educational Institutions*, Sr. Joan Monica McGuire, Jan. 1974.
9. SCA Community-owned Institutions, Phase I, 1972, by Sr. M. Patricia Green.

10. SCA, *A Message to the Sisters, Holy Year: Renewal and Reconciliation,* Sr. Joan Monica McGuire, 1975.
11. Personal interview, taped recollections and paper by Frances Belmonte, 1996.
12. Personal interview, Sr. Rosalie Van Ackeren, 1996.
13. Chronicle of the 20th Century, p. 1111.
14. SCA, The Archaeology of St. Catharine's Motherhouse, Washington County, Kentucky: *The First Congregation of Dominican Sisters in the New World,* June 1983, Office of State Archaelogy.
15. SCA, Letter to the Sisters, Sr. Helen Cahill, Sept. 1985.
16. SCA 1988 Chapter Act, Dissent, p. 14 and Policy Handbook, p. 5, policy 1.5, Dissent.
17. SCA Constitutions, *Journeying In Truth,* June 1984, Article 8.46, p. 33.
18. Personal interview with Sr. Lois Pineau, Dec. 1996.
19. Personal interview with Sr. Trinita McIsaac, Jan. 1997.
20. SCA *Day by Day,* June 25, 1996.
21. SCA Agenda for Chapter, 1988.
22. SCA *Dominican* News, Sept. 1990.
23. SCA Criteria for Catherine of Siena Award, 1989.
24. SCA Chapter Acts, 1992.
25. *Encyclopedic Dictionary of Religion,* Eucharist, p. 1250.
26. SCA Chapter Acts, 1992, #3.
27. Ibid. #4.
28. SCA Chapter Acts, 1994. Also, Opening Address of Sr. Elizabeth Miles, June 27, 1994.
29. SCA *Extraordinary Moment: Sacred Emerging, Our Pastoral Plan for the Future,* Sr. Paschala Noonan, July 30, 1994, *Dominican News,* pp. 1-2.
30. SCA *Closer Union,* Srs. Elizabeth Miles and Claire McGowan, 1996.
31. SCA Chapter Acts 1994, The term of office was changed from four years to six.

— *Part Four* —

La Bella Brigata

TO TEACH

PART FOUR OF THIS HISTORY differs from the three preceding sections which were mainly chronological. This part focuses on four themes mentioned in the Mission Statement: to teach, to heal, to serve, to transform oppressive structures.

When St. Catherine of Siena was recruiting followers to go on a crusade she called them "La Bella Brigata", the Beautiful Brigade or the Party of Friends. It included a broad mixture of women, men, married, single, religious, clergy — in all, a delightfully diverse crowd, drawn from all walks of life, all ages and different religious traditions.

The Kentucky Dominican Family is like Catherine's La Bella Brigata. The original base of ministry was broadened from teaching and nursing to a wide variety of services embracing the needs of the times. The family expanded from only vowed members to include associates and friends who share the Dominican charism. This chapter will focus on teaching.

When the Plenary Councils held in Baltimore during the 19th century gave impetus to the establishment of Catholic schools, the Kentucky Dominicans responded to the demand for sisters to teach in them. Hundreds of requests were received but it was impossible to accept even a fraction of them.

During the course of 175 years, the Kentucky Dominicans have staffed about 15 community-owned academies including some for boys, over 100 elementary schools, 17 high schools, three colleges and one university.[1] This represents "corporate commitments" and does not include places where sisters have served since open contracting began in 1969.[2]

St. Catharine College — 1931

Fr. Wilson as an educator realized that in addition to careful spiritual formation the sisters needed professional preparation. He and Fr. Miles instructed the pioneer sisters *daily* in English, history and mathematics.[3] In 1839 a Kentucky State Charter authorized the sisters to confer academic and college degrees. The charter was amended in 1920 to include the power to found colleges and grant collegiate degrees. When a teacher training program was initiated that year, not only the sisters but lay persons took advantage of these courses to obtain teacher certification. In 1931 St. Catharine College was entitled to grant Associate in Arts (AA) degrees. This made it possible for young professed sisters to obtain an AA before starting out on their teaching careers. The college was accredited in 1958 by the Southern Association of Colleges and Schools and has been reaccredited every ten years since.[4]

Originally, the Mother General served as college president with Mothers Mary Louis Logsdon, Margaret Elizabeth Walsh and M. Julia Polin in this capacity. The position was separated from the role of Mother General in 1955 with the appointment of Sr. Jean Marie Callahan, followed successively by Srs. Margaret Marie Hofstetter and Catherine Mahady. Next was Sr. Dolores Enderle, a Racine Dominican, who served as president until elected to a leadership position in her own community. The first lay person to head the college was former Kentucky Governor Martha Layne Collins, the eighth president. In 1997 she was succeeded by William D. Huston.

While maintaining a strong liberal arts tradition, the college has introduced programs in animal husbandry, agriculture, business and computer information systems and a bridge program for licensed practical nurses who want to become licensed registered nurses. In the late 30s students collaborated in catechetical work at Thompsonville, Kentucky with the St. Rose friars and also participated in a radio broadcast for evangelization. Today the college hosts Elder Hostel each year, has outreach programs to Appalachia and welcomes prominent speakers such as, Sr. Theresa Kane and Master of the Order, Timothy Radcliffe.

Sister Formation at St. Catharine College

As States began to demand certification of teachers, and society focused on integrated development of the individual, religious communities began to seriously study the empowering of women religious through education. Postulates and novitiates had traditionally prepared women for their role in the apostolate but no longer was that sufficient to equip them for effective leadership in the modern world.

In 1934 an effort was made to have the newly professed sisters remain at the Motherhouse to finish junior college courses before being sent out to teach. Although it was a good idea, implementation was somewhat difficult. The newly professed were not permitted to associate with the novices and postulants, nor with other professed sisters. They were in classes with lay students but were forbidden to talk to or mix with them. It was intended to be a time for contemplation and study. Because of social restrictions they felt like neither fish nor fowl. It was a time for them to become contemplatives but with a wry sense of humor they called themselves "the contemptibles." The program was changed in three years.

When the Vatican repeatedly called for renewal and adaptation, women religious responded with alacrity. Internal and external pressures created an urgency which brought about a united response among religious communities never before experienced in America.[5] Major superiors felt a serious obligation to prepare their members spiritually and professionally. The Sister Formation Conference (SFC) conducted surveys in the 50s, began publishing an SFC bulletin, created regional conferences and offered workshops for formation personnel.[6] To implement the decisions to educate sisters required sacrifice on many levels.

In a previous chapter it was pointed out that Mother M. Julia announced to pastors and superiors where Kentucky Dominicans served that a Sister Formation program would be initiated on February 27, 1961.[7] The die was cast; the program launched. Space does not permit tracing the development of the program from its beginnings to the present collaboration with a common novitiate in St. Louis for male and female members of different Dominican communities. Sr. Mary Louise Edwards who studied sister formation in Rome is co-director of the Common Novitiate.

Expansion of Formation Program

The present model for formation is called Life Development and embraces life processes from initial contact with the Congregation through retirement years for both vowed and associate members.

Sr. Teresa Tuite, promoter of On-Going Formation, has encouraged preaching and study by conducting communal days of study and prayer among sisters and associates spread out over 17 states. She initiated Advent tapes inviting sisters and associates to record their thoughts on daily Scriptural passages. For Lent she encouraged them to contribute written reflections for Lenten Reflection books. Both the tapes and the booklets were shared with other congregations as well as family and friends. Some who thought they never could preach, developed self-confidence in sharing the fruits of their contemplation.

Sometimes Sr. Joye Gros, an education associate and grief counselor, worked in tandem with Sr. Teresa in making communal presentations on the Dominican charism or communal study on the Eucharist. These two itinerant preacher-teachers continue to bring spiritual enrichment to the Dominican family and interested lay people. Formation never ceases but is a lifelong, on-going process.[8]

St. Catharine College has contributed greatly to the sisters' preparation for ministry and another resource offering them spiritual and professional development was Siena College, Memphis.

Siena College 1922-1972

St. Agnes Academy had the authority to issue academic and college degrees granted by a Tennessee State Charter issued in 1852, a year after its foundation.[9] In the early 1920s the sisters, convinced that Memphis needed a Catholic college for women, initiated plans for a college. Bishop Thomas S. Byrne of Nashville approved the plan and St. Agnes offered its first college classes in 1922 in a section of St. Agnes Academy.

An early brochure stated the purpose: St. Agnes College...has for its purpose the higher education of young women and their training toward model womanhood.[10] An ad for the college read: "St. Agnes College, a Southern College for women with all the advantages of a Northern institution."[11] What comprised those advantages was left to the imagination!

St. Agnes College was overshadowed by the older, well-established St. Agnes Academy. Within two years of its founding, it was evident that the college needed a separate location from the academy. By 1927 it had its own new structure and to complete the establishment of its own identity, St. Agnes College became Siena College in 1939.[12] It was named after the town in Italy where St. Catherine was born.

Siena College offered innovative late afternoon and Saturday classes to meet the needs of teachers in the area who were required to be certified. In 1934 the college started evening classes, the first such venture in the mid-south community. Night school was co-ed.

One of Siena's most successful programs was a TV series aired on Memphis educational station WENO. These courses offered college credit. Sr. Sheila Buckley taught elementary Spanish; Sr. Charlesetta Ryan gave a survey of English literature; and Sr. Fides Gough offered college algebra and trigonometry. This was in the 50s before the adoption of contemporary dress. Sr. Fides felt that the cameras and lights made the traditional Dominican habit look gray and washed out. She dyed hers pink! It improved the look to pristine whiteness.

Sr. Sheila received a letter asking a question which had not entered her mind. "Dear Madam, May blacks take this TV course?" The answer was, "Of course." This college without walls offered opportunities to those unable to attend regular college classes for one reason or another. It was another way of preaching and teaching.

The Catholic Church of the South (CCS) conducted a survey of Catholic teacher preparation in the South. The findings revealed objectively that undergraduate education of most Catholic elementary school teachers had been rather haphazard, disorganized and with little theological background. The CCS appealed to the Catholic University of America to open a Southeastern branch of the university's summer school at Siena College. Catholic University consented and Dr. Roy J. Deferrari, secretary of CU, established the courses and hired the teachers.

At its inception in 1942 a total of 294 students registered in the various professional courses. There was an observation school where the sisters had "hands-on" experience under supervision. One of the most important classes was religion. For the first time many of the sisters had explanations of doctrine and instructions on how to teach it to children.

The student body was composed of sisters from 11 different States and from many religious communities. There was a balanced mixture of work and play during the summer sessions. Much of the instructional materials came from Catholic University Summer School (CUSS). One of the standing jokes was, "Who will empty the CUSS buckets?" These were waste baskets painted with huge letters, CUSS, marking the ownership of Catholic University Summer School. In 1945, this program was transferred to Loyola University, New Orleans.

The sisters missioned to Siena worked under tremendous hardships. There was never enough money, expansion was always thwarted or delayed by zoning problems and enrollment remained small. Siena presidents Srs. Raymunda Cuniff, Clarita Griffin, Agatha Dutton, Albertus Magnus Garvey, and Marina Gibbons with their dedicated faculties worked valiantly to offer excellence in education but in 1972 the Congregation was forced to close the college.

This brief account of Siena does not do justice to the love and labor expended by the sisters and lay faculty who worked there. It would take a book in itself to tell the whole story.

The Catholic University of Puerto Rico 1955-1978

Seven years after the first Kentucky sisters had sailed to Puerto Rico to teach at Colegio San Carlos, Aguadilla, another group answered the invitation of Bishop James E. McManus, CSSR, to join the faculty of the Catholic University of Puerto Rico (CUPR) in Ponce.[13] The Bishop was persuasive. "Rev. Mother, the reports from Aguadilla regarding the work of your Sisters there, are very favorable and I hope you will try to extend the good work being done by sending some sisters to Ponce...you will be helping a missionary work that is most important for the island of Puerto Rico."[14] He explained that the work at Ponce reinforced what was done in elementary and high school, "most of which is lost if we cannot offer college courses to our graduates."[15]

Our University ministry was a collaborative effort with Dominicans (Amityville, Adrian and Kentucky), Sisters of St. Joseph, Immaculate Heart of Mary, Divine Providence and Carmelites from Spain. The University furnished housing for each Congregation on a street called "Convent Row". In addition to a separate furnished residence for each community, each sister received $100 per scholastic month.[16]

Srs. Consuela Wilhelm and Consilia Bohan were the first to represent the Kentucky Dominicans. When she became head of the foreign language department and professor of German, Sr. Consuela did not know she would remain at her post for 23 years. Sr. Consilia remained six years teaching in the education department.

In time, other Kentucky Dominicans served at CUPR: in administration, Srs. Felicitas Bassett, M. Edna Curtis, Mariana Dake; in the English department, Srs. Anna Blandford, Rosaria Hogan, Clementia Johnson, Magdalena Leonard, Olivia Schang; in education, St. Albertus Magnus Garvey; in business, Sr. Noreen Sullivan; and in French, Sr. Sheila Buckley. According to Sr. Sheila, "Practically everyone on the faculty taught English as a second language at one time or another."[17]

The sisters loved their adopted island but when the movement for independence created political unrest it caused some apprehension among them. When signs were posted across the street from their convent saying, "Yankee go home," they wondered about personal safety. While no incident ever occured against the sisters, some returned to the mainland to take up other ministry. Sr. Consuela was the last Kentucky Dominican to leave the University. At the Commencement Exercises, May 20, 1979, she was awarded the title of Professor Emeritus of the Interfacultative Department of English and Foreign Languages in gratitude for her 23 years of service. Francisco J. Carreras, president of the university, wrote, "An excellent professor and efficient administrator you have always been and a living example of devotion to duty and religious life."[18]

The Fine Arts

Ever since the pioneer sisters received their first piano as a gift from Christopher Simmering, music has been important in the life of the community both artistically and economically.

Early in 1918, the sisters bought the palatial home of Dr. D.T. Porter on Orleans and Vance, Memphis, Tennessee, for $40,000. It was intended for use as a boys school but Bishop Thomas S. Byrne objected on the grounds that a boys school would be injurious to the enrollment of parochial schools of the city. He wanted the community to convert it to a home for working girls.[19] However, the sisters decided to use it as a conservatory of music, art and expression for St. Agnes Academy. Under the auspices of St. Agnes Alumnae the formal opening of St Agnes Conservatory of Music, Art and Expression occurred on October 5, 1918 with Sr. Teresa Webb as first director.[20]

Memphis Conservatory of Music

The building was a magnificent structure with solid maple paneling, onyx around the fireplace, carved wood over the window frames, stained glass windows and imported decorative tile in some sections. The maple doors were so thick that it took three men to remove one for repairs. A spiral staircase became the traditional setting for picture taking of Conservatory graduates in their robes.[21] The school was honored when Mary Catherine Craig, in 1923, became the first graduate to win a scholarship to Juilliard School of Music, New York.

The Conservatory drew both those seeking serious musical careers and those wishing enrichment for personal pleasure. Courses were offered in piano, organ, violin, harp and voice. The voice teacher insisted that proper food, rest and exercise were absolutely necessary to cultivate the voice. When Sr. Dolores Spalding was director, she promoted a program in public school music taught by Sr. M. Ambrose Deppen. This offered an opportunity for public and private school music teachers to obtain certification.

One of the first musicians engaged to teach piano was Patrick O'Sullivan who received his musical training in Paris and Berlin. Joseph Cortese, a brilliant violinist from Canada, presided over the strings department and Madame Valentina Tumanskaya from Russia headed the voice department.

One of the interesting courses was in the Department of Theatre Organ Playing under the direction of Harry O. Nichols. Those were the days of silent movies when the musician accompanied the action on the screen with suitable selections. This called for a skilled musician with a repertoire adaptable to the newsreel, feature picture, comedy, cartoon and travelog. It meant playing for about two hours straight. Students in this program practiced the piano or organ in front of the movie screen!

The organ department was important in Memphis because many people came to use the three-manual Moehler pipe organ. Ernest F. Hawke, a concert organist from England, was the organ instructor.

Under the leadership of Sr. Dolores, prominent international musicians such as Silvio Scianti, were invited to give summer sessions. Mrs. Marian MacDowell, wife of American composer

Edward MacDowell, presented a lecture-recital featuring her husband's music. Sr. Consolata Callender visited the MacDowell Colony in Peterborough, New Hampshire, a colony associated with artists and authors, such as, Aaron Copeland, Roy Harris, Willa Cather and Thornton Wilder. She was invited to play on the carefully protected piano of Maestro MacDowell.

When St. Agnes Conservatory was reorganized to fill the needs of the music department of Siena College, the name was changed to Memphis Conservatory of Music. Sr. Consolata served there as dean for 18 years. In all she spent 58 years in Memphis teaching music. She saw the Conservatory acclaimed as a cultural center and one of the outstanding schools of music in the South.[22] Now retired, she sometimes plays the chapel organ in Sansbury Infirmary for Eucharist and Office.

In addition to music, the Conservatory had a strong program in Expression and Dramatic Art. Srs. Hildegard Hart, Agnes Richarda Blinkhorn, Joseph Edward Marine and Dorothy Nuttall were instructors in the department. "The course is designed to broaden the intellect...strengthen the imagination and develop personality."[23] Plays, operas and operettas were social attractions for the city and the annual Christmas cantata was the gala of the season.

Music in the Schools and Elsewhere

Memphis did not have a monopoly on music for in 1954 there were 56 Kentucky Dominicans teaching music in grade schools, high schools and colleges throughout the country.[24] They were versatile and dedicated, directing choirs, marching bands and orchestras, in addition to teaching music theory and harmony in classrooms and music lessons to private pupils. Since pastors did not require that tuition earned by teaching music lessons be turned in for school operational funds, it became a much needed source of income in the days when stipends were inadequate or non-existent. Superiors were happy to have this extra "music money" to help defray household expenses.

Sometimes music teachers acted as substitute classroom teachers. It was not unusual for the order to come from the principal's office saying, "Sister, drop whatever you are doing and take the 4th grade. That teacher is ill." It seems fitting to mention a few of these sisters in the name of all of them to pinpoint the versatility of these women.

Sr. M. Andrew Sheehan formed an orchestra wherever she was missioned. If the children were too poor to acquire an instrument, she begged from friends or borrowed a trumpet or trombone from one of her brothers. Sr. Gregoria Maguire taught voice as well as instrumental music. She participated in the Chicago Children's Theater, played the organ for church services and had rhythm bands for kindergarten children.

When Mt. Trinity Academy could not afford music books, Sr. Mary John Lamken improvised her own for the entire student body on the old purple mimeograph. She accompanied the Archdiocesan Symphony Choral group of sisters and also the Boston Archdiocesan Orchestra (BAO). In the BAO, Srs. Marian O'Donnell and Ursula Marie Kerrissey played trumpet, Sr. Agnes Mary Green (Pancratia) played the clarinet and Sr. Denise Glynn held her own on the bassoon.

In Chicago, Sr. M. Pius Worland, Secretary of the Archdiocesan Office of Evangelization and Christian Life, plays the French horn with the Glenview Concert Band as an avocation. The group goes from place to place sharing their musical talents. Sr. M. Pius acquired her love of music while in St. Joseph grade school, Mattoon, Illinois.

Sr. Joseph Edward Marine, along with having a beautiful voice, was a distinguished composer. Her four-part Masses and Propers are frequently used by the community as are her over 50 hymns for adult choirs and her many intonations.[25] Another composer was Sr. M. Oliver Vanderstock whose symphony was made into a record with the proceeds going to the Dominican Building Fund. She presented her Missa Trinita with a choir of Dominican sisters conducted by Sr. Joseph Edward at the DePaul Center, Chicago.

Sr. Judith Rose was noted for her productions of Broadway musicals with high school and college students. She published a Gregorian Chant workbook for use in the Boston archdiocese which became popular with sisters who were teaching chant in other parts of the country.[26]

The teaching of music received great emphasis in the community-owned academies. Usually, an entire corridor of music rooms was reserved for aspiring musicians or future divas. There was always a studio or two for the sister or sisters in charge with a baby grand piano at their disposal.

A litany of music teachers unmentioned here could go on and on, however, painting and sculpture are also arts with a long history in the Congregation and the Order. Some of the early sisters who were artists taught "sketching, Italian oil painting, china painting, charcoal drawing and painting in water colors."[27]

Painting and Sculpture

Akin to the music teachers were the classroom art teachers who brightened the day for students as they enjoyed a respite from math, science or language. Srs. Loyola Blake, Seraphim Bulger, Alberta Johnson, Josephine Keene and Eleanor Rooney were some of the art teachers.[28] When a young sister received her first teaching assignment one of her first tasks was to decorate her classroom. The art teachers were usually obliging mentors. Sr. Loyola Blake was noted for taking fledgling teachers under her wing to introduce them to ways of making a classroom aesthetically attractive.

The 40s and 50s were the days when the usual Christmas or birthday gift from a sister was a hand-painted spiritual bouquet with roses or lilies in delicate colors and a message printed in spidery calligraphy. So prevalent was this type of art that one novice felt that when she took vows the Holy Spirit would grant her this gift.

Artist Sr. Gerald Vincent Burke specializes in sketches of early history of the community, depicting the first buildings from the one-room log cabin to later structures on the Motherhouse campus. Her work appears in numerous community publications.

Sr. Dorothy Briggs, whose portrait of St. Catherine appears in this book, studied art in Italy. Upon her return she taught art at

Sacred Heart school, East Boston, before moving to Siena College and later Mississippi Valley State University (MVSU). At Siena she initiated the "first floating art semester abroad."[29] The students had an intensive orientation at Siena in art history, artistic techniques and the culture and customs of the places where they would be studying. They went to art centers in Paris, Rome, Florence, Venice, Siena, Delphi and Pompeii.

Because the students at MVSU were very poor Sr. Dorothy appealed to the Cardinals and Bishops, even the Pope, for donations to fund an art semester abroad for them. Their response made it possible and the Irish Dominican sisters granted free room and board for those students.

Sr. Dorothy has had art shows in Massachusetts, New Mexico, New York, Kentucky and Colorado. Although oil painting is her preferred medium, she does pen and ink profiles and sketches, especially of children.

Another artist, and also a sculptor, is Sr. Bernadine Egleston. Like Sr. Dorothy, she studied in Italy and later at Providence College under Richard Ambrose McAlister, OP.

The Magdalen Chapel at St. Catharine reflects her quiet inspiration and artistic skill. Sr. Bernadine, who works mostly with wood, handcarved the altar of thick walnut with four carvings on separate panels to represent fire, air, water and earth. She created a backdrop in the sanctuary of dark walnut portraying the hills of Kentucky and a lighter wood for the cultivated land. She chiseled nine "March lilies" on the lectern in honor of the nine women who founded the Congregation. Each of these art works has profound meaning derived from her prayer and meditation on the beauty of nature.

For most of her work, love of earth and nature have been her inspiration. She has sculptures in a New Hampshire bank; in the library of St. Agnes Academy, Memphis; at Rosary Manor and St. Joseph Hall, Watertown, Massachusetts; and at Sansbury and the Motherhouse. She uses paint and pen to create brilliant pictures of the Southwest and delicate drawings of the ocean. Some of these works are displayed at art galleries and various Dominican houses. The talents of these artists reflect the glory of God. Their work brings beauty, hope and joy to the world.

Rosary Academy Learning Center —
Watertown, Massachusetts

Education has many forms and not always in a formal class-room setting. Education means bringing the Gospel to God's people in whatever way possible, at any level. It may be with preschoolers in the early developing stages of their lives.

Rosary Academy Learning Center is a unique educational undertaking. Sr. Rosaire Hickey, director of the center from its inception in 1981 to the present, obtained her Master's from Lesley College. She and her staff provide a safe, caring environment for children ages 3-5 years. About 70 children register annually but limited space precludes accepting more despite the demand.

The program which runs from 7:30 a.m. to 5:30 p.m. affords peace of mind to parents who rely on day care for their young ones. Under Sr. Rosaire's creative leadership the program stimulates development of the whole child with plenty of play, fun and interaction. These children, completely at home with computers, are being prepared for the upcoming challenge of elementary school.

Sisters involved in the center include Srs. Hugh Francis Carey, Bernadine Egleston, Mary Keenan, Mary Martin McGreal and Teresita Trelegan. Sister Teresita who was professed in 1927, still shares her musical ability by playing the piano or organ for special events. "I love my babies," admits Sr. Teresita and they love her judging from the hugs she receives.

Vacation Schools

A little known apostolate, usually in the midwest, was the so-called "Vacation Schools", definitely an oxymoron. It began in 1924 When Sr. Carmelita Fisher was missioned to Missouri Valley, Iowa. The Pastor of St. Patrick, Fr. Luigi Ligutti, spoke with sisters about the need of religious education for children not in the parish school. On July 6, 1925 Srs. Carmelita Fisher and Georgine Ladenburg went to Magnolia, Iowa to open the first religious Vacation School.[30]

The movement grew rapidly in Nebraska with classes lasting

from one to four weeks. The sisters usually went two by two to mission stations, sometimes living in unusual circumstances. In the 30s, 40s and 50s, there were strict regulations about sisters visiting in the homes of seculars or even of their own families, but practicality for the mission prevailed in the West. Sometimes the sisters lived with Jehovah Witnesses, remarking later they did not know who was more afraid of whom.[31] They were housed with a Methodist minister or a farming family with eight or ten curious children who peeked to see if "them ladies wore all them clothes to bed."

Temperature on the prairies ranged from 90 to 106 degrees but heat was no deterrent. Classes were conducted from 9 a.m. to 3 p.m. with students ranging from 3 to 18 years. Evenings were spent with adults who wanted to socialize with the sisters. The day began with Mass, instructions, prayers, Bible stories, health talks, and first aid demonstrations. Boys learned Latin to serve Mass. Girls were taught to sew, to make linens for the altar, and to keep the church clean.[32] There was supervised recreation and instructions in politeness and table manners. The sisters used every conceivable skill to teach religion through art, music, drama and games. And this was vacation??? Usually 55 - 60 sisters participated in the summer Vacation Schools in Nebraska. A record of a similar program in the East was that of Sr. Agnes Clare Griffin teaching in Sharon, Massachusetts.

With the passage of years, with better transportation and with fewer available sisters, this ministry has changed. Now there are huge Confraternity of Christian Doctrine (CCD) classes conducted during the year to answer evangelization needs.

In the middle 60s the sisters taught at Fort Robinson, Nebraska in a program called Outward Bound. It differed from the Vacation Schools in that its purpose was to promote learning experiences which enhanced self-esteem. It was a one week resident program for junior and senior high school students with participants living in a lodge on the Fort grounds.[33]

Janice Vierk, one participant and now an instructor of English Composition and Women's Studies, said, "One of the most important things for me was...realizing I had important thoughts and that others would listen to and respect them. I credit Outward Bound with much of my outward behavior today." Janice and her sister Julie have fond memories of Srs. Joan Dunning and Jacinta Wimsatt who served at Fort Robinson. One of their most vivid memories is of sunrise Masses on the bluffs.[34]

To Teach as Jesus Did

Catholic schools have been a real gift to the Church and to the nation. They have exerted a strong influence on religious, academic and social life. "We live in a global world, thus Catholic school education must be not only global but ecumenical and Christ-centered," stated Sr. Ann Dominic Roach, OP, Superintendent of Catholic Schools in the Archdiocese of Boston, in an interview.[35]

Kentucky Dominican sisters have answered the call for teachers from 1822 to the present. Drastic changes have taken place in recent years; schools once staffed entirely by women religious are now conducted by dedicated lay people. However, although fewer in numbers, the Kentucky Dominicans teach in seminaries, elementary schools, high schools, colleges and universities. They teach adults, immigrants, inner city children, prisoners and pre-schoolers. They bring the Gospel to people in Belize, Romania, Peru, Africa, Guatemala, Mexico and Viet Nam. In short, what they have received as gift, La Bella Brigata gives to others by their teaching.

Chapter Twenty-One Notes

1. SCA *The Dominican Sisters of St. Catharine of Siena:* report prepared for Washington County Bicentennial. The three colleges were: St. Catharine College, St. Catharine, Kentucky; Siena College, Memphis, Tennessee; Immaculate Conception College, Hastings, Nebraska. See copy of letters from Herbert L. Cushing, Secretary of Instruction, Lincoln, Nebraska to Sr. Bonaventure Peake, "I am happy to make this statement, and sincerely trust that it may convey to Dean Boyd...the high

esteem in which you and the I.C. College were held and are held by the State Department of Education in Nebraska. No institution under the direction of Sr. Bonaventure could be other than high class, because she possesses to an unusual degree all of the qualifications which are characteristic of members of the order to which she belongs." March 7, 1932, Lexington, Kentucky

2. A corporate commitment refers to the assignment of a sister by a major superior in the name of the Congregation. Open contracting refers to a choice made by the individual sister to contract for service with approval of her regional coordinator.

3. Green, *The Third Order Dominican Sisters*, p.23.

4. SCA Report prepared for Washington County Bicentennial.

5. SCA Copy of paper on the Evolution and Impact of the Sister Formation Conference 1954 to 1975 excerpted from doctrinal dissertation of Dr. Marjorie L. Noterman, president of Mallinkrodt College.

6. Ibid. See also, Neale, *From Nuns to Sisters.*

7. BAA Original of Mother M. Julia to Robert J. Sennott, Chancellor.

8. SCA Sr. Elizabeth Miles to the sisters, May 8, 1990.

9. SCA Siena College file, also, charter of the Literary Society of St. Catharine Congregation.

10. SCA Siena College file.

11. Ibid.

12. SCA Siena College, Record Group XXIII.

13. Bishop James E. McManus founded Colegio San Carlos, Aguadilla, Puerto Rico, 1948. He was Bishop of Ponce 1947-1963.

14. SCA Bishop McManus to Mother General, December 7, 1950.

15. Ibid.

16. Ibid.

17. Personal interview with Sr. Sheila Buckley.

18. SCA Francisco J. Carreras, president Universidad Catolica de Puerto Rico to Sr. Consuela Wilhelm, May 16, 1979.

19. SCA Enactments of Prioress General 1906-1918, p.12.

20. SCA Memphis Conservatory of Music file

21. Personal interview with Sr. Consolata Callender.

22. Ibid.

23. SCA Brochure on St. Agnes Conservatory of Music, Art and Expression.

24. SCA Central Administration, Mother M. Julia Polin.

25. *In Memoriam,* privately published obituary, Sr. Joseph Edward Marine by Dennis Demas, 1994, also personal interview with Sr. Margaret Ann Brady.

26. SCA Administrative files, 1960-1962.

27. SCA Early academy catalogues, also Metropolitan Catholic Directories of the 1800's.

28. Some of their art work is on display at St. Catharine Motherhouse and Rosary Manor, Watertown, Massachusetts.

29. SCA Community Newsletter, December 1970.

30. SCA Annals, Missouri Valley, Iowa.

31. SCA Unpublished memoirs of Sr. Clare Benjamin, OP.

32. SCA Annals, Missouri Valley, Iowa.

33. Original letter Janice M. Vierk to Paschala Noonan, OP, February 4, 1996.

34. Ibid.

35. The Pilot, February 10, 1989.

TO HEAL

FROM THE EARLY DAYS of the United States until the beginning of the 1800s, nursing as an institutionalized profession was not needed because the population was small and widely scattered. As the pioneers moved westward and immigrants from Europe began to arrive, epidemics were common. A few hospitals existed in cities such as Philadelphia, Boston, New York and New Orleans.

In a previous chapter it is recorded that when cholera broke out in Washington County, Kentucky, the sisters left their classrooms, invited some dedicated pioneer women to assist them and together they visited the homes to care for the sick and the dying. In Memphis whenever yellow fever struck, the Dominican sisters were seen everywhere ministering to the sick and burying the dead. Children left orphans were brought to the convent and so began an orphanage.[1] When the epidemics abated, the sisters resumed their teaching duties.

During the Civil War, they nursed the sick and wounded of both Armies. Whenever natural disasters occurred, floods, famine or fire, they were ready to do what they could to relieve suffering.

Touched by the growing need for health care, they made some attempts to found hospitals. According to Memphis annals, Sr. Dolores O'Neale opened an infirmary there in 1870 but it was short-lived because of prohibitive costs. In Boston, the sisters applied to Cardinal O'Connell to open a 16-bed hospital but were refused.[2] Not until 1921 was health ministry under-taken by Kentucky Dominicans on a formal basis.

St. Catherine Hospital, McCook, Nebraska

Rev. Andrew Kunz, OMI, pastor of St. Patrick, McCook, Nebraska knew Kentucky Dominicans from the teachers in his parish school and from visiting the Motherhouse. Impressed with their dedication and service, he solicited their help to oper-ate a hospital. After repeated appeals, Mother Francesca and Council agreed to accept the invitation to manage a hospital in McCook.[3]

Backed by McCook citizens, Fr. Kunz promised to raise $40,000 for a new hospital if the sisters matched the amount. Terms were mutually agreeable and two sisters were assigned to the new undertaking.

When Srs. M. Pius Kennedy and Carmelita Fisher arrived at the McCook depot on August 13, 1921, John Endres met them to take them to their new home. Although tired and dusty from the long train ride, they were happy to have Ms. Pearl Angel, RN, tour them through the small facility which had served as a hos-pital. The sisters teaching at St. Patrick's welcomed them warm-ly and listened to news from Kentucky. Soon two more sisters joined the group. Srs. Zita Schatzel and Odilia Clifford. Both were registered nurses from St. Elizabeth Hospital, Boston, Massachusetts. Professed as Franciscans, they had transferred to Kentucky Dominicans. Three other sisters transferred from Kenosha Wisconsin Dominicans to Kentucky. Originally from Ireland, they were Srs. Bertrand Gath, nurse; Veronica Ryan, x-ray and laboratory technician; Aloysius D'Arcy, financial offi-cer. These five sisters with hospital experience were a welcome addition to the fledgling hospital.

McCook General Hospital was located in the home of Dr. D.J. Reid until his death in 1918. After his death it stood idle, forcing seriously ill patients to travel to Omaha or Denver for health care at great inconvenience and expense.[4] To relieve the situa-tion, the sisters leased Dr. Reid's building, opening their doors to accept patients on August 18, 1921.

Plans for a new hospital began at once. Frank Colfer, Frank Real, and W.W. Somerville headed fund-raising efforts; J.E. Kelley donated land; E.J. Lamb, P. Walsh, J.E. Kelley, McCook Chamber of Commerce, McCook Knights of Columbus, McCook BPOE Elks and Bell Telephone furnished rooms.[5] St. Patrick's Altar Society and St. Rose Club equipped the chapel. The Business Women's League furnished the nursery with the latest equipment, including their pride and joy, a cabinet for warming blankets for newborns.[6] The new facility, named St. Catherine of Siena, held open house September 23, 1923.

Not everyone was enthusiastic about sisters operating the hospital. McCook was predominantly a Protestant town; Roman Catholics were a minority. One night, Sr. Zita, alarmed at seeing flames leaping into the sky, stood on the hospital porch to get a better look. To her astonishment, she saw a 30-foot cross blazing nearby in the dark night. White-hooded figures surrounded the emblem as spectators milled around. Her heart pounded with fear lest violence erupt, but she stood there until the fire died out and the crowd dispersed.[7]

The Klan had made its debut in McCook on July 23, 1923. F.L. Cook, the Ku Klux Klan spokesperson, told some 700 — 800 townspeople attracted by a burning cross that the Klan had no quarrel with Roman Catholic people, but was opposed to the Roman Catholic hierarchy. He stated that prior to 1880, immigrants to this country were largely Nordic, Anglo-Saxon Protestants, but since 1880, immigrants from South and East Europe and Asia "were the scum of the whole earth and 80% Catholic."[8]

Although some prejudice existed in the city, most people were happy to have the sisters. Srs. Mary Paul McDonald, Rachel Cooney and Brendan Kelleher joined the growing staff. To ensure the best professional care possible, Sr. Zita opened a school of nursing in 1924. However, the program was short-lived because Sr. Zita was transferred and the cost of operating it was prohibitive. Nursing students went elsewhere for nursing education.[9]

In February 1924, the sisters invited G.B. Moulinier, SJ, associate of the American College of Surgeons and president of the

American Hospital Association, to visit McCook to assist in setting up quality care and standardized procedures. At meetings with the doctors, the Chamber of Commerce, the hospital staff and interested townspeople, he convinced them of the necessity of securing accreditation from national agencies.[10] The hospital earned conditional approval in 1931 with full approval in 1937. Sisters, doctors and staff spent much time and energy in maintaining accreditation through the years. This proved beneficial later when government programs like Medicare and Medicaid became available.

As technology improved, the increased patient load required more space. Hill-Burton funds, a Ford Foundation grant, a bequest from the Barnett estate and donations from Mary Brady made on-going expansion and remodeling possible. Although the hospital grew from six beds to 120 bed capacity, it was getting obsolete, unable to keep up with increasing government specifications. Sr. Ulicia and her Council appointed an Advisory Board of lay people in McCook to assist in planning future health care. A driving force on this board was secretary Charles P. Noll whose three sons, Edward, William and Steve had attended St. Patrick School. As a longtime friend of the sisters, he prepared short and long-range plans as options for the hospital, acting as liaison between the lay board and the sisters. Meantime, the state health inspectors reported that only five beds conformed to state standards; corridors were six inches too narrow; plumbing and electrical wiring were too old and hazardous.[11]

Countless meetings ensued with the people of McCook and Sr. Ulicia and Council. Professional studies, surveys, consultations with auditors, lawyers (both Canon Law and Civil) and the Catholic Hospital Association were unanimous in declaring something had to be done: remodel, build new, sell or close.

Sr. Ulicia declared that it was impossible for the sisters to finance a new facility at an estimated cost of $2,000,000. Another factor was the decrease in the number of sisters to staff the institution. Unwilling to abandon the people after 50 years of devoted services, she promised to work with the city to ensure the continuity of health care. She announced, "We think in consideration of the people of McCook area, the new facility should be theirs."[12] The sisters set up a Search Committee with Charles Noll as chairperson. The purpose of the committee was to enlist persons to function as a Management Board. Sr. Ulicia and Council interviewed 21 candidates in McCook and selected the following for the Management Board; Donald Harr, Sarah J. Cunningham, John. T. Harris, Jr., Dr. Roger Mason, Aileen Murray, Kenneth Wallace, G.E. Allen, Peter Graff, Ronald W. Hull, and Stanley Marr. In April 1970, new members added were Robert E. Ault, Angus Garey and Charles J. Wagner. In August of that year, the Community Hospital Association was incorporated. The new corporation conducted a membership drive and began raising funds. On Januury 1, 1974, the sisters entered a lease-purchase agreement with the Community Hospital Association, Inc.[13] From then on, the objective was an orderly transition of health care from the sisters to the townspeople.

Allen Strunk, owner of the *McCook Daily Gazette*, was chairperson of the fund drive with Donald Harr and Lynn Wallace assisting. Architect Leo A. Daly Company, Omaha, appointed William T. Noll as project manager for the new hospital. Noll, in addition to his professional interest, had a personal investment because McCook was the town where he had grown up and attended St. Patrick School.

The Board chose the northeast edge of the city for the new facility. The design consisted of three circular patient pods attached to a rectangular area of supportive services. The new Community Hospital was dedicated June 16, 1974.[14]

The Supreme Court decision, Roe vs. Wade (January 22, 1973), legalizing abortion nationwide, challenged the Catholic Code of Ethics which supports the right to life of the unborn fetus. Shortly after Community Hospital was opened, a doctor applied for abortion rights. Previously, the medical staff had asked Sr. Paschala Noonan to remain in her position as administrator and they had promised to continue to observe the Catholic Code as they had when they served at St. Catherine Hospital.

However, with the Roe vs. Wade decision, the climate

changed. The city owned the hospital; some doctors pressured for abortion privileges under the law. Although the sister administrator would not participate in the surgical procedure, it would be inconsistent for her to be in charge of a facility performing abortions. She withdrew.

Sr. Ruth Ann Rezak remained working in the finance department of Community Hospital for awhile. Srs. M. Lawrence Curran, Ernestine Choquette and Patricius Henderson continued to live in the convent on Fourth Street, doing pastoral work at the new hospital and in the community until the diocese purchased St. Catharine Convent as a Motherhouse for a new diocesan order of Franciscan teaching sisters.

The Kentucky Dominicans served over 50 years in the health field in McCook. When they withdrew, they had the satisfaction of knowing they left in place an uninterrupted and well-developed system of health services and pastoral care for the people of the area. They had fulfilled their mission and it was time to move on.

St. John — Sullivan Memorial Hospital

Twenty-three years after undertaking hospital work in McCook, the sisters expanded their health ministry in 1944 to Spalding, Nebraska and Lebanon, Kentucky. Spalding was predominantly a Catholic settlement and Lebanon was located in what Fr. Clyde Crews called "an American Holy Land."[15]

Among the first to come to Spalding were John and Jane Sullivan. They dreamed of having a hospital in their town and Jane was noted for assisting sick neighbors or attending the birth of a newborn. The Sullivans died before realizing their dream, but their two children, Hannah and Murt, brought it to fruition. After her parents died, Hannah donated the family home to the Dominican sisters for a hospital; Murt had obtained his medical degree from Creighton Medical School, Omaha in 1903 and returned to practice in Spalding with Dr. J.G. Giever as associate physician. Hannah wanted the hospital named Sullivan Memorial Hospital in memory of her parents, but at the dedication May 14, 1944, Bishop Stanislaus V. Bona called it "St.

John — Sullivan Memorial Hospital," thus honoring the Sullivans and Mr. Sullivan's patron saint.

The Sullivan home, while spacious for a family dwelling, was very limited for a hospital. Sr. Rachel Cooney, the first administrator, with the help of Sr. Leonilla Adamowski as fiscal officer, was undaunted by the limitations. The first floor was converted to a lobby/admission area, three patient beds, a kitchen, general purpose room and a room for two sisters. The second floor was remodeled for maternity patients, emergency cases and minor operations. Six beds were on the second floor. Because there was no elevator, the sisters sometimes enlisted the help of firefighters to carry patients up the narrow stairs.[16]

Some of the sisters assigned to the hospital in its early days were Srs. Agnes Regina Staud, Lucinda Hays, Anacleta Hickey, M. Dominc Stine and M. Peter LaJoie. The sisters gave holistic care. Over and above pastoral and nursing care they cooked, delivered the meals, washed the linens, cleaned the rooms, painted the walls and raised chickens. Sr. M. Peter said the only task she disliked was "dusting the chickens" to prevent them from having lice.

By 1947, it became necessary to enlarge the facility. The Motherhouse donated funds which were matched by area citizens and a new building was completed on the same grounds but apart from the old hospital in 1951. That year, St. John Hospital was admitted to the American Hospital Association.[17]

In Spalding, as with the nation, the population was aging. Desirous of caring for its senior citizens, the Spalding community took steps to build a nursing home. Under the supervision of Sr. Mary Ann Guthrie, Our Lady of Spalding Nursing Home was erected and dedicated on May 22, 1966.

Scarcity of sisters and physician personnel, rising costs and increasing government regulations threatened the existence of both hospital and nursing home. Forced by external circumstances, the sisters withdrew from the hospital in 1970 and from the nursing home in 1971.[18] Unable to meet hospital and nursing home state standards, the two institutions were merged to form a rest home called Friendship Villa under the management of a private corporation.

Sr. M. Faith O'Malley continues to maintain a Dominican presence in Spalding, giving pastoral care to the residents of the Villa and others in the area. With her is Sr. Charlene Vogel who teaches religion in the high school in this town noted as a remarkably rich source of vocations to Kentucky Dominicans and to the priesthood.

Rosary Hospital, Campbellsville, Kentucky

At the request of Bishop John A. Floersh, the Kentucky Dominicans opened Rosary Hospital, Campbellsville, Kentucky in July 1948.[19] The people of Taylor County first encountered Dominican sisters who taught at Our Lady of Perpetual Help, Campbellsville, a school abutting the hospital property. Some people who were patients at Mary Immaculate Hospital, Lebanon, Kentucky, had met the sisters there and were impressed with the care given by "the Lebanon ladies."

When Sr. Rosine Price, Rosary Hospital's first administrator, and Srs. Noreen Sullivan and Bertand Gath assumed responsibility for the place, they had no convent, but occupied empty patient rooms in one wing of the building. In 1954 a second floor was added, containing living quarters for the sisters.

The Catholic population in the area was small, which caused a certain amount of distrust of Catholics in general. Gradually, the work of the sisters in both school and hospital inspired confidence.

Dr. Wanless Mann, an ardent Baptist, introduced the sisters to medicine "in the hollers." He believed that all Christians had an obligation to help their neighbors. If the hill people were afraid to come to the hospital, he would go to them. Sometimes he took the sisters, loaded his car with food, packed his black medical bag, then drove up a dry river bed. A white rag tied to a bush indicated that someone was sick up in the knobs. At this sign, the doctor stopped the car, and with the sisters in tow, he climbed the hill to check on patients. Some had never seen a sister. Children were curious about the rosary worn on the sister's belt. Contact with Dr. Mann and trust in him, dispelled some of the fear of the hospital and of sisters. The informal visits to the hills gave the sisters a better understanding of those patients.

Campbellsville was rapidly becoming a leading city in west-central Kentucky with new industry and an expanding college. In a speech delivered at the annual banquet (1968) of the Campbellsville Taylor County Chamber of Commerce, Dr. Henry F. Chambers noted that the Sisters of St. Dominic bore the cost of hospital care for poor patients in Taylor, Adair and Green Counties without any help from city, county, state or federal government.[20]

He remembered an elderly woman brought to the hospital sick and paralyzed. At dismissal time, her family refused to take her home. She remained with the sisters, free of charge, until she died a natural death two years later.[21]

The sisters took a lead in racial integration of patients and employees at the hospital before the Civil Rights Act made it mandatory. They were in the vanguard providing preventive health care in the area and adopting new techniques in child health. Despite constant improvements in the building and its equipment, the Congregation reached the point where it no longer had the finances or the personnel to continue.

The sisters and the Campbellsville Chamber of Commerce engaged hospital consultants to study the situation. The recommendation was: purchase a new site; erect a new hospital twice as large as Rosary Hospital; establish a new management corporation of local people. Under the circumstances, Sr. Ulicia and her Council announced the withdrawal date of the sisters as December 1, 1968.

In a touching testimonial, Dr. Chambers praised the sisters for their more than twenty years of unselfish, compassionate service. He made special mention of Sr. Agnes Regina Staud.

Sr. Agnes Regina has been nursing supervisor on the 11:00 p.m. to 7:00 a.m. shift, or the graveyard shift, for the past 18 1/2 years, or 1 1/2 years since the hospital first opened. Since most babies seem to be born at night, Sr. Agnes Regina has assisted at the birth of the majority of people of Taylor County aged 18 1/2 and under. I wish there was some way to convince the Pope, and I did say Pope, because this St. Dominic Order is so important they don't answer to the bishop, just the Pope. I wish there was some way we convince the Pope that you (Sr. Agnes Regina) should not leave this community, but continue operating the hospital from 11 to 7.[22]

On November 30, 1968 at midnight, Sr. Joan Miriam Glaser, administrator, turned over the keys and operation of Rosary Hospital to the chairman of the hospital board. Henceforth, the hospital was known as Taylor County Hospital.[23]

Mary Immaculate Hospital, Lebanon, Kentucky

In August, 1944, Mother Margaret Elizabeth, in response to a request from Dr. B.J. Baute, brought four sisters to Lebanon, Kentucky to manage the Baute Memorial Hospital. Sr. Frieda Payne, administrator, assumed the responsibility aided by Srs. Paschal Mullaney, Aloysius D'Arcy and Mary Rogan.

Dr. Bernard J. Baute had opened the J.A. Baute Memorial Hospital in Lebanon in memory of his physician-father in 1942.[24] During the war years, it was difficult to get personnel and supplies but when Dr. Baute asked the Kentucky Dominicans to take over the hospital, they accepted the challenge, purchased the hospital and called it Mary Immaculate Infirmary. One advantage was having an additional place to which hospital sisters could be missioned.

Improvements were made on the old building but high occupancy rate demanded more space. During the administration of Sr. Bertrand Gath, a new hospital was dedicated December 8, 1951 and appropriately named Mary Immaculate Hospital.

Growth continued at a phenomenal rate, especially in obstetrics and nursery. Once again, in 1963, during the administration of Sr. Clara Edelen, the hospital was expanded to accommodate 79 patients. This time, because of growing concern for senior citizens in the area, a 39-bed nursing home also was erected. Named Marian Manor, it was the first model of its kind in Kentucky to have a nursing home attached to a hospital. However, each facility had its own administrator, Sr. Jane

Frederic Luttrell at the Manor and Sr. Clara Edelen at the Hospital.[25] A beautiful chapel served the entire complex.

In Kentucky, at Campbellsville and Lebanon, racial segregation of patients came into question. At Campbellsville, the sisters quietly integrated maternity patients and newborns. After that, it was accepted in medical/surgical wards. in Lebanon, when some doctors demanded segregation, Sr. Mary Dominc Stine, admistrator, made it clear that Mary Immaculate was an integrated hospital and an equal opportunity employer.[26] Mindful of the comfort of the patients, she installed air conditioning and later added an outside swimming pool on the grounds. Sisters from the Motherhouse often enjoyed the pool during hot, humid summer months.

Events in the 70s impacted greatly on many hospitals including Mary Immaculate. Employees clamored for union membership; some doctors wanted abortion privileges;[27] government regulations called for expensive renovations.

Rev. Adam J. Maida, (later Archbishop of Detroit) advised the sisters on legal and canonical ramifications if they sold the hospital.[28] The hospital had a Management Board composed of religious and lay people. Representing the Kentucky Dominicans were Srs. Jean Marie Callahan, Marie Jeanne Surette and Mary Agnes Wilson. Lay persons on the board were Jimmy Avritt, Carla Cox, Frederic Higdon, Dr. John W. Ratliff, Hamilton Simms, Jimmy Thomas, Albert Trosino and David Yeiser. Sr. Dorothy Peterson, SCN, and Br. Ignatius Perkins, OP, completed the membership.[29]

Marian Manor had a similar Management Board with Srs. Jean Berney and Linda Gahafer representing the Congregation. Dr. Joe Green, Charles Mattingly, Don Metzmeier and Darnell Waters were the other members.[30]

These two boards were most helpful in making decisions about both institutions. Br. Ignatius was especially knowledgeable and supportive. In May 1979, he wrote to the staff:

> It is with a great deal of pride that I congratulate each one of you as you celebrate the 35 years of operation of Mary Immaculate Hospital and approximately 15 years of the operation of Marian Manor Nursing Home. It has been through your

very special concern and good work that the Hospital and Manor has been able, through the years to provide excellence in patient care. Together with the Dominican Sisters, you have opened up your own hearts to the sick, the suffering and the dying, ministering to people of all races and creeds, in the very same spirit and concern which Christ ministered to the sick and dying of His own time.[31]

His words of commendation were treasured because with his doctorate in the health field, he fully understood the challenges and changes which were being met.

The Congregation sought a buyer for both institutions. After numerous interviews a decision was made. *The Lebanon Enterprise* announced: "The Dominican Sisters of St. Catharine last week entered into negotiations with the Hospital Corp. of America. Hospital Corp. of America will begin managing the hospital August 20."[32]

The sisters chose Hospital Corp. of America because it had a proven record of giving quality care. Even so, it was a painful wrench to withdraw from the Congregation's only remaining hospital.

In making the decision known to the sisters, Sr. Joan Monica McGuire, president, wrote:

It is with regret that we end our health care mission to the people of Marion and Washington Counties. The Hospital and Manor have allowed us to serve the Catholic, Protestant, black and white, rich and poor people of north central Kentucky. As is the case of our other three health care facilities, Spalding, Campbellsville, and McCook, we can be proud that the Dominican sisters in collaboration with the local communities established health care facilities where none existed and provided a transition which enabled them to continue after our mission was completed.[33]

One of the closure events was a reception honoring Dr. Baute for 50 years of service as a surgeon par excellence. Sr. Joan Monica presented him with a quilt made by Sr. Roberta Ross with the help of sisters in Sansbury Infirmary. In making the presentation, she said,

"Doctor, you have taken many stitches in your life to help and to heal others. Please accept this quilt made with hundreds of stitches by our Sansbury sisters and with each stitch is a prayer of gratitude and appreciation."

A Change in the Charter

An interesting fact about the health care apostolate is that the original charter of the Kentucky Dominicans specified teaching as their ministry. True, during wars and epidemics, they left classrooms to nurse those in need, but once the crisis ended they returned to teaching. When they began health ministry in 1921 and gradually assumed ownership and operation of additional hospitals, they had nothing in their charter to approve the move.

Twenty-two years after taking St. Catherine Hospital, there is a notation in the Council minutes, "A letter (was read) from the Apostolic Delegate, stating that our request to own and operate two hospitals was sent to Rome."[34] Evidently there was no response because in the minutes of the Sixth General Chapter (1948) it is recorded that by a unanimous vote, the delegates agreed to send a petition to Rome to own and operate hospitals.[35] Thus, permission was obtained after the fact and the Congregational charter was amended to grant

> ...full power and authority to establish, erect, maintain Hospitals and Hospital service, at any and all points in the state of Kentucky, state of Tennessee, state of Nebraska, state of Massachusetts, and any and all other states in the United States of America (in compliance with the laws of the State in which such hospitals may be erected.)[36]

In the Constitutions approved in 1984, ministry was not limited to teaching and nursing. The mission statement declared that the members are to hear and proclaim God's word, and to transform oppressive structures.[37] This opened up numerous new works; however, even before this broadened definition, the sisters had reached out to where there was need.

Unwed Mothers

Over and above physical care of patients, the sisters exercised a pastoral role in keeping with their mission. At McCook, Nebraska, during the 1960s, Sr. Alverda Bonifas (Alphonsine) directed a program for unwed mothers with Sr. Lucinda Hays sharing the responsibility for the young women who came. There were no grants, no government funds, no subsidies to underwrite what was done.

Usually a pastor, minister, doctor or parent requested that the sisters accept the girl. Some came very early in their pregnancy from Nebraska and neighboring states. All were welcomed. Sr. Alverda said, "They came distraught, upset, scorned by society and with many hang-ups."

The sisters furnished room and board and gave them small jobs around the hospital so they could earn some money. They assisted in food service, record room, switchboard and supply room. One, who was a seamstress, took apart the long habits and made them into the modified dress adopted by the sisters after Vatican II. Srs. Alverda and Lucinda worked closely with social workers to help the young mothers decide what was best for them and their babies. Some kept their newborns; others relinquished them to state agencies for adoption.

Rural Nebraska had few, if any, African-Americans at that time. When a pregnant black woman came from Tennessee, it caused some tension at first, but when employees observed the sisters' kindness and respect towards the young woman, they followed the example.

Religious beliefs made no difference. The women were free to follow their own religious practices. Some had no religious affiliation but Sr. Alverda, who now serves as a chaplain in St. Joseph's Hospital, Chicago, said, "The lives of these girls were transformed. They left us with a more spiritual outlook. Many kept in touch after they left because they learned to love the sisters."

Home Visiting

Need always called forth action. Sr. Joan Dunning began home visiting of patients after discharge. This was pioneering because the health care system had not yet introduced this service or any discharge planning for patients. Sr. Joan was particularly interested in following up on newborn infants, but she was also concerned about surgical patients with dressings to be changed, or families who had lost a loved one. Her love for children eventually led her to the Rosebud Indian Reservation, South Dakota, where she worked with Native American children. Some babies were born with alcohol addiction because their mothers were alcohol dependent. Sometimes mothers gave their newborns alcohol in their bottles to keep them quiet. In order to help the babies, Sr. Joan worked to overcome the hopeless desperation of the mothers by offering classes in child care and nutrition, by giving counsel and by being a friend. Results were meager due to long-standing environmental conditions.

Licensed Practical Nurse Program

Srs. Mary Peter Lajoie started a licensed practical (LPN)/ nurse course for nurse aides at St. Catherine Hospital, McCook. She felt it was one way to promote the dignity of persons by enhancing their job skills and enabling them to improve their status in the job market. The first class who took State Board exams and earned their LPN license were: Irene Teters, Hope Hunter, Lucille Hoff, Maude Plourd, Zolona Chinn, May Anthony and Mattie McBride. Unfortunately, this was another occasion where lack of sufficient funds caused a good program to close.

Continued Presence in the Health Field

Although the Congregation relinquished its community-owned hospitals, sisters maintained interest in health ministry. With the freedom afforded by open contracting, members may choose to serve in the healing arts. One avenue of health service is as a chaplain in hospital or nursing home. The National Association of Catholic Chaplains (NACC) and Clinical Pastoral Education (CPE) programs offer an opportunity to learn pastoral practice in a clinical setting under clinical supervision. Some sisters enrolled in these courses for personal enrichment in holistic health and others did so with the intention of becoming chaplains.

Sr. Mary Carmel Gerrior is director of a nationally accredited CPE program at St. Mary Hospital, Lubbock, Texas, which offers basic and supervisory CPE units. She emphasized the importance of listening to the patient, believing "that sometimes all the patient needs is a listening heart."

Ever since the Roe vs. Wade decision, the Church has been concerned about the possibility of legalization of positive euthanasia. The bishops published a statement, *Society and the Aging,* in 1974. Sisters have served and continue to serve the elderly in nursing homes, rehabilitation centers, clinics for homeless, Alzheimer units, general and psychiatric hospitals, hospice facilities and in private homes on a one-to-one basis.

An interesting development initiated in 1984 by Rev. Michael Groden, director of the Boston Archdiocesan Planning Office, was a coalition with the University of Massachusetts and Pope John XIII Seminary to instruct volunteers in practical aspects of the aging process and also, the theology of aging. Sr. Paschala Noonan was appointed Archdiocesan Director of this program. She recruited volunteers from the 410 parishes to prepare them to serve the elderly. At the University of Massachusetts, instructions centered on physical and psychological aspects of aging with an intense concentration on advocacy for elderly by monitoring legislation affecting their lives. At Pope John in a three week live-in semester, emphasis was on the value of life in all its stages and the spirituality of the older person. Guest lecturers included Msgr. Charles Fahey, professor of Aging Studies at Fordham University and Henri Nouwen, internationally renowned author and lecturer on spirituality and aging. The objective was to prepare volunteers to work with aged and infirm persons in the 410 parishes of the Archdiocese. Approximately 20 Kentucky Dominicans took one or both sections of this program.

These few examples by no means convey a complete picture of the health ministry of the sisters. It would take a lot more time and space.

Chapter Twenty-Two Notes

1. SJPA Copy of undated report on St. Peter's Orphanage SCA *Shadowed*, Sr. Hyacintha Peters, OP, p. 11. *Freeman's Journal*, Aug. 30, 1879.
2. BAA O'Connell correspondence, Mar. 26, 1917.
3. SCA, Council Book 1904-1945, June 29, 1921, p. 149.
4. *The McCook Tribune*, Aug. 18, 1921.
5. McCook Golden Anniversary Souvenir Edition of *McCook Daily Gazette*, p. 64, June 15, 1932.
6. *The McCook Tribune*, Sept. 24, 1923.
7. Personal interview with Sr. Zita Schatzel.
8. The McCook Tribune, July 23, 1923.
9. SCA Unpublished report by Sr. M. Bernard Dwyer, OP, p. 4.
10. SCA Annals of St. Catherine Hospital, McCook, Nebraska, 1924.
11. SCA Unpublished report by Sr. M. Bernard Dwyer, OP, p. 15. *McCook Daily Gazette*, June 14, 1974, p. 11.
12. Ibid. p. 16.
13. *McCook Daily Gazette*, June 14, 1974, p. 6.
14. Ibid.
15. Crews, *An American Holy Land*. p. 24.
16. Personal interview with Sr. M. Peter Lajoie, OP.
17. SCA Unpublished report by Sr. M. Bernard Dwyer, OP, p. 19.
18. SCA Chronological Listing of Institutions.
19. Personal interview with Sr. Jane Frederic Luttrell, OP.
20. SCA Copy of talk delivered by Dr. Henry F. Chambers, Friday, June 21, 1968.
21. Ibid.
22. Ibid.
23. SCA Annals, Rosary Hospital, 1968.
24. *Springfield Sun*, Mar. 11, 1992, p. 5. Before that, Dr. Baute owned and operated Baute Infirmary for 12 years.
25. Personal interview with Sr. Jane Frederic Luttrell, OP.
26. SCA Compilation of Mary Immaculate administrators by archivist Sr. Ann Miriam Hickey, OP.
27. The Catholic Code of Ethics bans abortions.
28. Archbishop Adam Maida of Detroit is both a Canon lawyer and a civil lawyer. The sisters engaged him as a consultant on hospital options. Also, SCA Governing Board correspondence from Sr. Paschala Noonan, June 28, 1979.
29. SCA Mary Immaculate Hospital file, Management Board, 1978.
30. SCA Marian Manor Nursing Home file, Management Board, 1979.
31. SCA letter to staff of Mary Immaculate Hospital and Marian Manor Nursing Home from Br. Ignatius Perkins, OP, May 1979.

32. *The Lebanon Enterprise,* Aug. 16, 1979.
33. SCA Correspondence, Sr. Joan Monica McGuire to the sisters, Aug. 9, 1979.
34. SCA Council minutes, July 23, 1943.
35. SCA Minutes Of Sixth General Chapter, 1948.
36. SCA Congregational Charter Amendment, June 27, 1950.
37. SCA The Constitutions, 1984, p. 2.

Chapter Twenty-Three

TO SERVE

IN THEIR VISION STATEMENT, the Kentucky Dominicans declare: "We will collaborate with others sharing our gifts and resources." Collaboration has been a lodestar of the Congregation since the first nine women answered Fr. Wilson's invitation to form a community for education.

Sharing implies giving and receiving. At times, the sisters gave; at times they received. Those who gave to the sisters during their 175 years of existence have made it possible for them to expand and improve the mission and ministry. The litany of benefactors is too long to list everyone, but a few are mentioned to represent all those who have helped in any way.

Ministering to the Ministers

It began with Christopher Simmering, the eccentric German tinsmith who decided that God directed him to Sienna Vale. He made pots and pans to sell to settlers in surrounding areas and then donated the money to the sisters.

In the struggle to get started, faithful black servants assisted the sisters, side by side in the fields, gradually relieving them of farm chores, enabling them to devote themselves more fully to study and teaching.

In later years, the motherhouse was gifted by those who served in kitchen, laundry, rectory, school and convent. Summer in Kentucky is often hot and humid, but summer in Kentucky in a laundry is like being in an inferno. Cheerful, faithful Dolly

Mudd worked in the laundry no matter what the season. She and Flora Hamilton started early in the morning, scrubbing the white wool habits, starching the chapel linens (with cooked starch) or the sisters' caps and capes. However, their tasks were diversified, for on weekends they killed chickens for Sunday dinner. Novices ironed the clothes and also de-feathered the chickens. Scalding hot water filled the laundry tubs where the chickens were dunked to loosen the feathers. Some novices were skilled in plucking chickens, but others were initiated into the process by Dolly.

Who could forget Hazel Spaulding, her daughter Barbara, Edwina Hamilton, Mamie Hamilton, Lucille and Bernice Linton and Lulabelle Hodgins who alternated working in laundry, Motherhouse, Academy and College? Not to be forgotten is Katie Hagan who kept the rectory spotlessly clean for many, many years.

In the kitchen, Mary Jo Reed was a legend. She prepared delicious meals — Southern style beans, hot biscuits from scratch, sausage gravy, Southern fried chicken better than Colonel Sanders.' Her three daughters, Catharine, Mary Elizabeth and Louise followed in her footsteps preparing and serving meals three times a day for sisters, chaplain, students and visitors. Mary Jo, and later her daughter Catharine, looked over the novices and postulants who served the meals and predicted almost infallibly who would stay and who would leave. Louise worked with Sr. Marietta Kilgannon, the infirmarian, serving meals to the sick. The infirmary was located on the second floor of the Motherhouse until the erection of Sansbury. Sometimes that meant carrying heavy, large trays of food from basement to second floor when the small temperamental elevator was not working. It was with delight that Louise transferred to the new modernized Sansbury to assist with the sick.[1]

Anna Lydia Tucker was only a child when she started to work at St. Catharine. After her mother died, her father, Dominic Boone, brought her sister Dolores and her brother William to St. Catharine. Her sisters, Alice and Susan, went to St. Agnes, Memphis to help there. William worked on the grounds under the tutelage of the farm manager while Anna Lydia and Dolores

Mother Mary Julia Polin laying cornerstone for Sansbury Infirmary as Srs. M. Joachim McDonald, Rose of Lima Lohmeier and Mother Margaret Elizabeth Walsh observe

Sr. Maria Rose Dai, graduate of St. Catharine College, who was professed at St. Catharine for her congregation in Vietnam

Sr. Hue Thi Le, the first Dominican sister from Vietnam to transfer to the Kentucky Dominicans, pronouncing her vows into the hands of president Sr. Helen Cahill as Sr. Joan Monica McGuire witnesses

Sr. Tuyet Ngoc Tran on her profession day with Srs. Nora Rita Mudd & Helen O'Sullivan

LIFE GIVING AND LIFE SUPPORTING LABORS BEYOND THE UNITED STATES

Belize - Missionary work with the Poor.

Mexico - Community and family help with emphasis on enabling women to recognize and claim their dignity.

Latin America - A sister psychologist travels among five nations to provide necessary pastoral psychological support services to missioners and local Church teachers. These include counseling, holistic personal and professional education, facilitation of group processes for healthy community living, ministry planning and decision making, and directed retreats.

Peru - A phone call received from the Dominican Sisters in the poor barrios of Peru makes a heart rending appeal for funds to obtain food and medicine for the people. The crisis situation in that country has imposed incredible hardships on the poor. The sisters have had to turn people away from the soup kitchen because the food ran out. Any donations sent to us for this purpose will be forwarded immediately to buy some of what is needed to alleviate suffering and starvation.

Vietnam - A number of Dominican Sisters fled their homeland in the years following the Vietnamese War and have joined their lives with the Dominican Sisters here in Kentucky.

The Vietnamese Sisters suffer the constant pain of loss and separation; and the agony of knowing the relentless suffering being endured by their religious Congregations and their own families in Vietnam. The word that is used over and over again to describe life in Vietnam is "desperate."

This agony tears at their hearts making it impossible to engage fully in their new lives in America.

One Sister got word that seventeen members of her family (one a nun) were in jail. Thirteen are now free, but four are still incarcerated. Why? Who knows! Trials and defenses are not part of the picture in Vietnam today.

Another sister learned that her own sister, whose husband had been killed in a refugee camp, tried to escape from Vietnam with her three children and was picked up by the military and jailed for months. What does it mean for little children to be in jail?

The stories go on and on. We can make a difference; you can make a difference.

The Refugee Sisters must find some relief from the burden of unparalleled suffering so that they can look to a new life of commitment and service. We need to recognize an opportunity to embrace with love people whose lives are broken by a war in which we as a nation played a major role.

Missions beyond the United States

Srs. Aquinette Le Fort and Appoline Simard in Chimbote, Peru

Sr. Aquinette with volunteers Srs. Mary Agnes Wilson and Evelyn Catherine Barrett

Sr. Joan McMaster in Central America with the Project for Children

Sr. Regina McCarthy with children in Guatemala

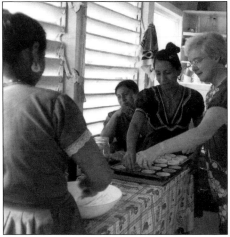

Sr. Mary Otho Ballard preparing food with some of her friends in Belize

Sr. Trinita McIsaac, promoter of mission, in Africa while giving a retreat to African Dominican sisters who have a school for deaf children

Sr. M. Jeanne White teaching the sign of the cross to children in Aguadilla, Puerto Rico

First Kentucky Dominican missionaries sailing to Puerto Rico: Sr. Amelia del Carmen Rivera, M. Jeanne White, Osanna McHugh, M. Thomas Shelvey (kneeling)

Sacred space at Chapter

Group at General Chapter studying issues

Srs. Lucinda Hays and M. Margaret Kelley reviewing Scripture

Srs. Alverda Bonifas and Mary Janet Riggs, dietary supervisors, prepare Thanksgiving dinner

When the troops came home from the Gulf War, Sr. Maureen Flanagan baked a cake to feed 20,000 people in a welcoming celebration

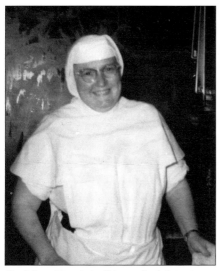

Sr. Mary Dominic Stine, administrator of St. John Hospital, Spalding, Nebraska

Sr. M. Joseph Fosskuhl, registered dietitian, serves hot biscuits for breakfast at Sansbury

Srs. Benigna Bigott, Charlene Harvey, Veronica Ryan, Mary Jane Fitzgibbons, Angela Hewitt, Barbara Arthaud, Engelbert Allewelt and Callista Kavanagh (seated) pose with cardiac equipment at St. Catharine Hospital, McCook, Nebraska

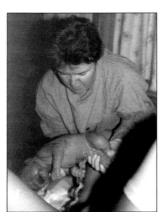

Sr. Peggy Duggan, midwife, delivers a baby in Harlingen, Texas

Memphis Conservatory of Music, Memphis, Tennessee:
back row — Srs. Dolores Spalding and Consolata Callender

Sr. Alberta Johnson, art instructor at St. Catharine Academy and College, with an art student

Sr. Sheila Buckley, Assistant/Alumni and Development, St. Catharine College

Sr. Thomas Ann Ford, Sansbury treasurer

Sr. Mary Eva Kimbel, pastoral and community service

The first group to make renewal at St. Mel's, Gloucester, Massachusetts with their director Edward Gaffney, O.P.

Sr. Rosaire Hickey, director of Rosary Learning Center, Watertown, Massachusetts, checks on some of the little ones

Golden Jubilarians 1986: Srs. Gregoria Maguire, M. John Lamken, Bertille Maurer, Eleanor McGonagle, James Vincent Mattingly and M. Aubert Parziale

Catharine Reed and
Edwina Hamilton
who faithfully
served the sisters
and students for
many years

Nobody served the Kentucky Dominicans
longer or more faithfully than Philip
McConnell, known by all as "Mr. Phil"

Lydia Tucker (90 years old) on a visit to
Magdalen chapel — as a child Lydia resided
at St. Catharine, attended some classes and
worked for the sisters

Alfred Roach, educated by Kentucky Dominicans at Resurrection School, Brooklyn, New York, an international humanitarian known for alleviating poverty, illiteracy and unemployment in Africa, Asia, Puerto Rico and the United States — long time friend and benefactor of the Kentucky Dominicans, pictured with his sister, Sr. Ellen Cecile who is engaged in community service at Rosary Manor, Watertown, Massachusetts

Mr. and Mrs. James Toner shown with their daughter Patricia, Cardinal Richard Cushing and Sr. Bernardine Sullivan — the Toners donated an estate in Plainville, Massachusetts in gratitude for the loving care Patricia received while residing at Rosary Academy

Associates in Puerto Rico after signing their covenant: left to right: Myrna Cerez, Carmen Amelia Accevedo, Sr. Narcisa Barreto Perez (promoter), Rose Julia Aviles, Maria Adelaida Acevedo-Perez (co-promoter), Alma Cordero and Clemencia Ramos

Srs. Noreen Sullivan and Matthew Marie Beirne with associate Jessica Pirreault

Associates Joan O'Connor and Elinor Hartnett

Sr. Bernadine Marie Egleston, sculptor of the wood furnishings in the Magdalen chapel

Lectern in Madalen chapel carved of walnut wood by Sr. Bernadine Marie Egleston — the nine jonquils represent the nine women who answered Fr. Wilson's call to establish a foundation of Dominican sisters in the United States

Artist Sr. Dorothy Briggs — see her painting of
St. Catharine of Siena at the end of this book.

Sr. Ann Miriam Hickey, dedicated archivist
and historian, 1984-1997

*Statue of Sr. Angela Sansbury sculptured by Sr. Jeanne Dueber, SL,
for the 175th aniversary of the Kentucky Dominicans in 1997*

helped in the kitchen. In the afternoons they had classes in reading, writing and arithmetic. On special school exhibition days, the two girls served the formal tea for the guests. In later life, Anna Lydia worked for Sr. Margaret Thomasine Kennedy at Sansbury, and later with Sr. M. Lawrence Curran.[2] Anna Lydia died September 25, 1993 at age 96, beloved but not forgotten by the Sisters.

The hundreds of farm acres[3] required constant attention. Over the years, there were many dedicated farm managers and grounds supervisors, up to the present Danny Spalding and James Young. Outstanding in this list is Phillip McConnell, who served most of his life with the sisters. At age 17 he came to work in the dairy. After two years, he transferred to Immaculate Conception Academy, Hastings, Nebraska because the sisters needed a maintenance man there. Like the sisters, he went where there was a need. After 12 years he returned to St. Catharine. No job description defined his duties. He was Mother M. Julia's chauffeur, bus driver for the college and academy, mail carrier between St. Catharine P.O. and Springfield, farmer, dairyman, electrician and plumber.

Kentucky sometimes has prolonged droughts. Mr. Phil kept a watchful eye on the water tower, lake reservoirs and filter system. Whenever a drought occurred, the sisters processed around the walkways reciting the rosary for rain while Mr. Phil attended to the mechanics of the water system and at times hauled water from Springfield.

At other times, heavy rainfall caused consternation. In 1962, when the roads around St. Catharine were under construction, heavy rainfall made transportation not only hazardous but almost impossible. Young women in the dormitory were crestfallen because there was no way to get to their prom in Springfield. "For the prom, one escort had 26 girls." recorded the May 1962 St. Catharine Newsletter. Mr. Phil was that escort. He drove the girls to town in the school bus and picked them up at 1:00 a.m. to bring them home. Graduation that year was problematic, but Rev. James T. Blandford offered St. Dominic Church for commencement exercises. Mr. Phil drove students and faculty in the school bus as far as possible. Then Mr. Marvin Wheatley met the bus, pulling it through the worst stretch of mud by tractor. Mr. Phil saved the day!

When he became a fourth degree Knight of Columbus, the sisters were among the first to congratulate him and admire his garments so different from his usual cap and work clothes. He served the sisters faithfully for over 70 years. In his last illness, the sisters visited him frequently at Marian Manor. He died August 11, 1988. He was brought back to St. Catharine one last time for his Mass of Resurrection in Sansbury Chapel dedicated to St. Joseph, a man who served humbly and faithfully.

Even in death, Mr. Phil continues to serve the sisters in their ministry. He bequeathed $135,000 to be divided equally for St. Catharine College, Sansbury Infirmary and the Congregation.[4] On the campus, beside the house where he used to live, the Knights of Columbus placed a memorial in his honor. It is the sphere which graced the top of the old water tower. The house in which he lived was named McConnell House in his honor.

Community-owned institutions were also blessed with dedicated employees. At. St. Agnes, Memphis, Michael Kelley, straight from Ireland at age 17, was caretaker for almost 50 years. At Siena College, Mattie and Clarence James served faithfully for decades. When the college closed, Mattie transferred to St. Dominic Boys School to continue in maintenance and Clarence continued to care for the Siena property. Sister Suzanne Callahan taught Mattie and Clarence to read and write. She was happy when they earned their GED.

At Holy Rosary, Louisville, Thomas Ellery, janitor and jack-of-all-trades had a variety of duties, among them to deliver lunch in a covered basket to the sisters who taught at St. Louis Bertrand but lived at Holy Rosary before they had their own convent.

At Rosary Academy (formerly Sacred Heart), Watertown, Massachusetts, Dennis Corbett managed the farm in the 1920s and 30s. He chauffeured the sisters, calmed the students when the cows invaded the playground, shoveled the snow in the days before snow blowers, and kept the heart-shaped garden at the entrance in pristine condition.

Mindful that the service of faithful employees augment their ministerial efforts, the sisters remember them daily in prayers for benefactors.

The Associate Program

Since Vatican II, a powerful movement has been quietly erupting in the Church — the Associate movement. At a time when the Church is promoting the age of the laity, this movement seems most appropriate. While the sisters discussed recruitment, the possibility of temporary commitment, and how to cope with aging and diminishing membership, the Spirit opened a new vocation idea — the vocation of a lay person, male or female, single or married, of differing faiths to share in the charism of the Congregation.

The Dominican Order traditionally has had Third Order members; St. Catharine of Siena and St. Rose of Lima are examples. While there are some similarities, associate membership differs from Third Order membership. Associates are persons who feel called to the charism of a congregation and wish to share its faith life and mission in a non-canonical way. The Third Order laity is a worldwide branch of the Dominican order with a rule approved in 1285 by the Holy See.[5] A new Rule for Dominican Laity, approved in 1987, calls them to share the Gospel with the Dominican Family.

In 1976, a Chapter Act established the Kentucky Dominican Associate Program. Sr. M. Otho Ballard researched the movement in other religious communities and sought input from the Kentucky Dominicans. In 1978, she was appointed Director of the Associate program. She designed a brochure to explain the program and in 1980 she formally invited applicants to join.

Enthusiasm among the sisters was reserved. There were many questions. Sharing prayer life and charism was acceptable, but what about sharing private information at Chapters and assemblies? What about finances? If associates attended Chapters, did they have the right to vote about issues affecting only vowed religious? Did the sisters want to let go of some of the control in their lives? The vowed members were struggling with their own identity issues. How could they add another unknown quantity to the discussions?

Acceptance grew gradually as it became clear that associates were longing for a deeper spirituality, for study, community and ministry. In a survey conducted on the associate program, associates and sisters were in overwhelming agreement that associates should not be included in decisions regarding sisters' finances. Furthermore, associates and sisters were to be financially independent of each other, but there was no agreement on how to handle the costs of the associate program.[6]

Marybeth Irvine of Louisville was the first associate accepted in May 1981. Other members followed from Massachusetts, Kansas, Kentucky, Tennessee, New York and Nebraska. With the midwest came associates from Puerto Rico. Sr. Narcisa Barreto-Perez translated associate documents into Spanish for them.

Associates from Nebraska were Third Order tertiaries who had been meeting for years with Sr. Leonarda Yilk for prayer and study. They were familiar with Dominican objectives and easily became associates.

In autumn of 1983, when Sr. Mary Otho resigned as director, there were nine women and one man as associates. Sr. Virginia Smith brought her rich background as retreat director and spiritual counselor to the position of director when she succeeded Sr. Mary Otho. A year later, Marybeth Irvine, was appointed as co-director. The Chapter of 1984 defined associates:

> Dominican Associates are women and men who in a non-canonical status share the Dominican spirit and mission with the Sisters of Saint Catharine Congregation. They have a desire for spiritual growth, accept our philosophy, share in prayer and activities and serve in the ministry when that is possible.[7]

One of the statements causing question was "Associates... may belong to other religious denominations."[8]

If the associates were Christians that was one thing, but if the persons were other than Christian, how would they preach the Word if they did not believe in Jesus Christ? This last question remains unanswered and challenges the vision statement which calls for a more inclusive community.

According to the 1996-1997 Residency Directory of the

Kentucky Dominican Family, there are 109 associates. Just what do they do? They share the Dominican charism in formal and informal ways. Elaine Riley is always present at the Motherhouse to videotape significant events such as Chapters, assemblies, special celebrations and programs. Her tapes are a way of preserving history with new technology. Patricia Daly preserves history with her zoom lens, catching the membership in candid shots on film or highlighting the beauty of the environment at places where the sisters live and serve. Some preach at Mass or prayer services and some serve on committees. Fifteen associates are on the Associate Study Committee; seven on New Dominican Life team with five serving as team co-promoters. They work side by side with the vowed members on the Issues, Multicultural and Earth committees.[9]

At the 1996 Chapter, sisters, associates and friends celebrated the 20th anniversary of the Kentucky Dominican Associate program. Sr. Elizabeth Miles, president, missioned the new Associate Co-Promoters, Sr. Rita Petrusa and Cindy Boulton. Cindy wrote a song for the occasion, *In the Heart of the Bluegrass,* a lively melody which relates the original vision to what is yet to be.[10]

If you ask an associate the reason for committing to this new arm of the Dominican Family, the answer may be, "Because I feel called — it is a special vocation to journey with Dominicans and to share God." The fact is, associates are not just an idea any more; they have been with us since the beginning when our founding sisters first enlisted pioneer women to help nurse the sick in the cholera epidemics. Now they are committed in a more formal way.

Special Services for Children

Jesus had a special love for little children. This love is an essential force in the life of Sr. Joan Dunning. Babies and toddlers have always been her special concern as a pediatric nurse in a child care center or a general hospital in Nebraska, on an Indian reservation in South Dakota, in a remote village in Belize, and more recently in Marks, Mississippi. As director of San

Martin Maternal Child Health Center in Marks, she not only supervises the physical care of children but tries to eradicate the root causes of poor nutrition, illness and neglect. When Sr. Joan went to Marks in 1990, infant mortality rate in Quitman County was the worst in the nation.[11] She initiated a rehydration and emergency day care, which helped to reduce the death rate 36% from a decade ago.[12] Her prenatal and parenting classes have a direct effect on the welfare of the littlest of God's children.

When children suffer a loss by death of a parent, sibling, relative, playmate or even a pet, or when torn by divorce, separation, remarriage or drug addiction, they are traumatized and confused. Rainbow is a program to help them through these crises. Sr. Maureen Flanagan is part of a Rainbow program at St. Angela's School, Mattapan, Massachusetts. She gathers children weekly in groups of four to six to express what is bothering them. They have a safe haven where they can talk about their hurts and fears, knowing that the utmost confidentiality is respected. The listening heart is what they need most.

In Brooklyn, New York, Sr. Veronica Colahan is director of the Little People Playschool. She opened this facility in 1990 with Sr. Ann Davette Moran in response to a need of working parents. Most of the children, ranging in age from two to four, come from single parent families and are racially diverse. The program, privately sponsored, is located in the former Resurrection convent. Usually, about 25 little ones are enrolled. Sr. Veronica has one assistant teacher and a secretary. At the end of a day with busy active children, Sr. Veronica says, "Nobody has to rock me to sleep at night."[13]

Serving by Preaching and Prayer

A complaint sometimes voiced by ministers busy serving others, is that they do not have as much time to pray as they wish. One consolation for them is that some sisters are dedicated to the ministry of preaching and prayer. At Sansbury Infirmary, although members may be retired or semi-retired from ministries they once exercised, the ministry of preaching and prayer continues.

The preaching is informal but nonetheless real. Patient acceptance of suffering is as eloquent as any word from the pulpit and prayer ministry is a powerful extension of the mission of the congregation. Each day the sisters gather for Liturgy, Office and Rosary. There are special prayers offered for priests, benefactors, vocations and the sisters on the missions. Requests for prayer flood in by phone, mail, or in person. Each request is honored and the channels of prayer are continuous. Dominic had nine ways of prayer. His daughters at Sansbury follow his example and by prayer serve their sisters and all those who ask for their help.

Chapter Twenty-Two Notes

1. Personal interview with Sr. Virginia Thomas Hamilton.
2. Personal interview with Mrs. Anna Lydia Tucker.
3. At different times additional acres were purchased and added to the original 106 Sansbury acres. At present, the farm has 640 acres.
4. Interviews with Srs. Francine Eaton, Virginia Thomas Hamilton and Catherine Siena Whitehouse. Also, taped interview with Mr. Phillip McConnell.
5. Dominican Tertiaries Manual, 1954.
6. SCA Kentucky Dominican Associate Study, Oct. 1995.
7. SCA, The Directory of the Kentucky Dominican Sisters, June 1984, Art. 1.2, p. 1.
8. Ibid., Art. 1.3.
9. SCA, See Residence directory 1996-1997 for names of associates and sisters serving on various committees, pp. 35-37.
10. SCA Videotape of 20th anniversary of Dominican Associate Program, filmed by Elaine Riley.
11. SCA Day by Day, April 29, 1997, quoting excerpt from *Extension Magazine*.
12. Ibid.
13. Personal interview with Sr. Veronica Colahan, May 10, 1997.

Chapter Twenty Four

TO TRANSFORM

WHEN THE KENTUCKY DOMINICANS pub-
lished their Mission and Vision Statements including the stated
goal "To Transform Oppressive Structures", the question arose,
"What is meant by oppressive structures?" There was a myriad
of answers: discrimination because of color, age, gender; pover-
ty, hunger, ignorance; violence in the home, in the streets, in the
world. The list was lengthy. Many sisters feel that education is
fundamentally the best way to transform structures which beget
misery and oppression. For this reason, in responding to the
needs of the times, they undertake the education of the
oppressed so that these very people can participate in processes
needed for lasting transformation.

Teaching the Intangibles

Like many schools across the nation, St. Matthew, Dorchester,
Massachusetts exemplifies the kind of institution which makes
a difference in the lives of its students. Sr. Deirdre Cotter who
was principal there for nine years, praises the sacrifices of the
parents, "many of whom hold three jobs because they want their
children in a Christian atmosphere." Sr. Lourdette Gangemi
who has taught there for twelve years says, "If you want multi-
culture we have it with Haitians, Cape Verdeans, West Indians
and African Americans." During Sr. Deirdre's leadership, the
school was visited by a team of examiners headed by William J.
Bennett, Secretary of Education. The Bennett report which re-

ceived national media attention, cited St. Matthew's for "its remarkable achievements and its ethos of excellence." The highest praise, however, may have come from one of St. Matthew's students who said, "We do wonderful things here."[1]

A remarkable transformation took place at St. Matthew at a critical time when racial violence was tearing the area apart. Many sisters of the various communities teaching in inner city schools began to meet once a week for a Holy Hour to pray for peace and reconciliation. To involve the students in the struggle for non-violence and to have them begin to meet as a community for prayer, an invitation was extended by Sr. Norah Guy to all junior high students to attend a Holy Week liturgical experience of the Passion of Jesus. Through dance and mime the eighth grade students of St. Matthew's school reenacted *His Last Days*. Cardinal Bernard Law was also invited to participate in this prayer experience. He and approximately 500 junior high students, joined by faculty and administration from across the city, were deeply touched by the obvious grace of the profound and solemn prayer of the youth.

Sr. Norah is no longer at St. Matthew[2] but each year during Lent the children continue the tradition of prayer of the Passion through dance and mime. They have taken the special service to nursing homes, hospitals, parishes and the sisters at Rosary Manor. Sr. Norah says, "The peace and reconciliation which flows from this prayer is beyond imagination. It has touched and changed many hearts. It is transformation that works."[3]

Inner City Shakespeare

How does a teacher transform Chicago college youth who have a second grade reading level into lovers of literature and Shakespearean actors? Sr. Joan McVeigh can answer that question. Her initiation began at Holy Angels, Chicago, the largest black Catholic grade school in the world.[4] "It was total immersion in black culture and history," she recalled. "When I asked them about their roots, they wanted to know about mine. I told them about my Irish heritage, about the poverty and oppression in Ireland, about fathers in prison and random killings in the streets. I told them I am active in support of the Freedom Movement for Ireland."

From Holy Angels Sr. Joan transferred to Malcolm X, a Chicago city college. There she taught remedial reading and writing. It was her introduction to the smell of alcohol in an early morning class and to a student "freaking out" on PCP during a writing period.[5] To help these students she took courses to become a drug counselor as well as a teacher.

After ten years at Malcolm X she accepted a position as assistant professor of English at Harold Washington, another Chicago city college. She decided to combine her two loves, remedial reading and Shakespeare. For the students it meant reading aloud in class; it meant preparation by reading aloud at home. At first, the students wanted no part of it but gradually they began to enjoy beating out the rhythm and acting the gamut of emotions in Shakespeare. Self-esteem was enhanced and reading scores improved. Other teachers of these "Shakespearean actors" noticed a new self-confidence as they became more vocal in class. An academic transformation had taken place in a Chicago multicultural college.[6]

Other Multicultural Ministries

According to their Vision Statement, the Kentucky Dominican Family hopes to be a more inclusive multicultural community by the year 2001. Multicultural ministries were the focus of a Multicultural Conference jointly sponsored by Sisters of Charity of Nazareth (SCN) and Kentucky Dominicans in the summer of 1995. The history of the two Congregations depicts a collaborative effort as neighbors, friends and partners in ministry in Kentucky, Tennessee, Massachusetts and Belize.[7]

Collaboration in Belize

Collaborative ministry has been a hallmark of Kentucky Dominicans. It was in response to an appeal delivered by an SCN that Sr. Joan Dunning, RN, went to Belize in 1981 to help set up small clinics in remote barrios. Her efforts in organizing these centers did not go unnoticed. Belize City Hospital requested her to set up a high risk nursery. In any area of grinding poverty and inadequate nutrition the infant mortality rate is high. To get at the root of the problem in Belize, Sr. Joan strove to improve birthing practices, postnatal and pediatric care.[8] Because of her success, she was asked by the health commission of Antigua to replicate her program there but she was called back to serve health needs at the Motherhouse.

Other Kentucky Dominicans volunteered for summer service in Belize. Some of these volunteers, like Srs. Mary Otho Ballard and Eileen Hannon, returned to Belize to do a stint at full time ministry. Their work consisted in training lay catechists and developing lay leadership. One of their goals was to help young people, mostly Maya Indians, to get a high school education. Although the usual mode of transportation to remote villages was bicycle, the sisters often walked, used a boat, or rode a mule to get to their teaching post.[9] It was in Belize that Sr. Elizabeth Miles preached and taught from 1984 until she was elected president of the Kentucky Dominicans in 1988.

Collaboration in Peru

Another collaborative multicultural ministry evolved in 1981 when Sr. Aquinette LeFort responded to a call for help from the St. Mary of the Springs community serving in Chimbote, Peru. The work revolved around food, health and education.

For five years Sr. Aquinette lived with the Columbus Dominicans. However, when Sr. Appoline Simard joined her, they moved to a hillside barrio to live among the people.

The sisters found living conditions primitive. Water was scarce, often necessitating a mile walk to get a pailfull. Diet was a monotonous repetition of rice, beans, carrots and onions. There were no prepared foods or canned goods. Poor nutrition caused disease and a high infant mortality rate. Smoke belching out of steel mills and fish factories polluted the air, causing respiratory infections.

The two sisters conducted a supplemental food program with soup made from ingredients such as, rice, flour, and oil, received from the United States and other countries. Green vegetables and sometimes meat were included in the meal prepared by the Mothers' Clubs. Much of this was made possible through the donations of friends and relatives of Kentucky Dominicans and faculty and parishioners where they served.

When the soup was cooked it was sold at below market price to the people who brought containers to carry home sustenance for their families. More than 1000 were served daily. For two cents, a breakfast of a roll and a cup of powdered milk was given daily to hundreds of children but funds ran out. Because of extremely limited finances, Sr. Aquinette asked herself, "Would it be better to spend the money for more food? Then maybe, the people would not get sick. Or should it be spent on the few medicines our resources can afford?"[10] There was no easy answer.

Grants from the Dominican Development Fund (DDF) help to support a medical station, Posta Medica. However, political unrest and inflation continually increased medical costs up to 1,000% (one thousand percent)! Nurses, Srs. Mary Agnes Wilson and Mary Anne Guthrie, assisted temporarily at the dispensary to improve health conditions. Sr. Evelyn Catherine Barrett volunteered eight summers in Chimbote to lend a helping hand in whatever way she could. Twice a year Sr. Evelyn Catherine mounted fund-raising campaigns where she taught, St. Sebastian, Needham, Massachusetts. She was called, "our home missionary." Sr. Appoline was responsible for Posta Medica, also for a special club for the elderly, and several bible study groups.

Educational efforts focused on teaching the women how to improve their lives. The sisters chose three community-minded women to educate them in the formation of a center for social services. The sisters worked with them until it seemed that the women themselves could carry on the work.

Although Srs. Aquinette and Appoline withdrew from Chimbote in 1993 the work continues, carried on by the women they instructed and members of other religious congregations.

Prayerful and financial contributions from friends, relatives and Kentucky Dominican Family members help to transform the situation.[11]

Hispanic Ministry

"Integration *not* assimilation is the answer," claims Sr. Regina McCarthy after spending thirty years in Hispanic ministry. In 1969 she joined a diocesan migrant ministry team in North Platte, Nebraska. The goal was two-fold: to be of service to Mexican Americans and to proclaim the importance of Hispanics to the Church.

Contacts with migrants were of short duration because they moved with the crops, hoeing or thinning the sugar beets or helping with the harvest. Their work fluctuated with wind, rain and storm. Sr. Regina observed the Church as a constant in their lives. Whether young or old, the Latinos spoke Spanish everywhere except in Church. She worked to change this so that Mass was in Spanish. For the liturgy she encouraged the use of their own music and their own liturgical dances.

Because they moved so frequently, education of the children was sporadic. The state set up schools but six or eight weeks in summer was the usual school term for migrant children. She helped with school programs in some of the cities of the Nebraska Panhandle.

In addition to the migrants, there were Hispanics with as many as five generations who had lived in the same place. They had come with the railroads and remained ever since. Some had lost their native language; others retained it at home and were delighted whenever it was used in Church.

While engaged in community service at the Motherhouse, 1979-1981, Sr. Regina spent three summers in Hispanic ministry in Toledo, Ohio. After that she returned to North Platte to found the Diocesan Office of Hispanic Ministry. This ministry includes Guatemalans, Hondurans, Salvadorans, Mexicans and other Latinos. Sr. Regina discovered that wherever there is a Latino community, there is a lay leader who helps the people live out their faith. She loves their joyousness, their music, their fiestas.

By integration not assimilation she feels that the meeting of two cultures brings out the best in each other while respecting differences.[12]

Hispanic Health Ministry

"Have you thought of health as a political issue?" asked Sr. Barbara Harrington when she addressed a group in Mexico City. She was there at great risk to her own life to help refugee Guatemalan women who had been violently uprooted from their own country. Some were tortured, raped, or were witness to brutal deaths of family members and friends. They suffered from poverty, disease, and most of all, from the loss of their own culture. They called it "tristeza de corazon" — sadness of the heart. "I know it means heartbreak," Sr. Barbara said. As refugees, they had to blend in with local culture.

Sr. Barbara found that in Guatemala, women traditionally carried bundles on their heads but in Mexico, for security reasons, they had to carry packages using arms and shoulders which puts strain on the spine. "They had to shift carrying the baby from the back to the front, to be in disguise," said Sr. Barbara. "In rural Guatemala, the women wear a traditional huipil each village weaving a distinctive, identifying pattern, but in Mexico, they had to adopt Western dress for safety sake," she added. The women came to realize that poverty is repression, often resulting in poor health. They came to realize that health is a political issue.

In group therapy, Sr. Barbara enabled the women to see that change lay within themselves. By becoming mental health promoters they could help other women deal with similar situations. Transformation is taking place gradually as the trained women act as leaven with other women, preparing for the day when they can return home.[13]

Midwife in Texas

In 1984, Sr. Peggy Duggan, nurse practitioner and certified midwife, joined the Su Clinica Birth Center at Harlingen, Texas near the Mexican border. About ninety percent of the clients were Hispanic. Before going to Texas, she had worked in Buckhorn, Kentucky among the poor and medically deprived mountain people. Her practice was mostly family nursing with an occasional delivery of a newborn. While there, she was convinced that her ministry demanded working against oppressive structures which prevented the poor from receiving deserved health services. She carried this idea to Texas.

When she first went to Su Clinica as a midwife, prenatal, delivery and postnatal care took place at the clinic. Sr. Peggy felt that since hospitals are geared to curing disease, the best place for a normal healthy delivery is in a place like Su Clinica where the midwife is always there for the mother, where husband and family are a welcome part of the birth process and where confidence and trust have time to develop between client and midwife.

Sister was disappointed when the clinic administration decided that actual delivery had to take place in the hospital. Hospital deliveries increase hospital income, are more expensive and more impersonal. Sr. Peggy lodged her protests with management officials to no avail. However, despite the injustice of closing a cost-effective birth center and thus denying women the choice of delivering in a family-centered environment, Sr. Peggy persevered. Her goal, along with that of her team of midwives, was to change the hospital environment and hopefully some attitudes.

The midwives insisted on continuing their holistic model of midwifery, staying with and supporting the laboring mother through the entire childbirth process. They also insisted on the option of "rooming-in" whereby a new mother and father are not separated from their baby during the hospital stay.

Sr. Peggy said, "When we are in the process of change, we cannot always see what God's plan is for us as we grope for understanding of the transition. It is difficult to see the big picture." Two years after the move to the hospital, God's plan became more visible to Sr. Peggy. The midwives continue to give pre and postnatal care at Su Clinica but now they serve more clients, especially high risk patients who were previously not eligible for delivery at the clinic. Transformations which have taken place have increased the caseload of clients and also the capability and availability of the midwives. The latter agree with Sr. Peggy, "God works in mysterious ways."[14]

Criminal Justice Ministry

To handle some of the social issues of the day, the Chapter of 1988 initiated an Issues Committee[15] to bring matters of concern to the membership for study and to ascertain and publish a corporate stance as Kentucky Dominicans. The first issue statement was: We strongly oppose the death penalty.[16]

Before considering capital punishment, the words of Jesus come to mind, "I was in prison and you visited me." The Congregation has a history of prison ministry long before a public stance was taken in 1988. It began in the 1850s in Memphis where the sisters at La Salette visited prisoners on weekends, praying with them and tutoring them. It continued during the Civil War when the St. Agnes sisters visited prisoners on both sides in the fratricidal conflict. It was much later before this corporal work of mercy was considered a formal ministry.

In 1978, Sr. Margarita Stidolph volunteered for prison ministry in a collaborative, ecumenical program in Memphis. She assisted in setting up the first Memphis diocesan office for criminal justice ministry and worked with Arthur Kirwin, OP, who oriented volunteers to serving in prisons.

At first, Sr. Margarita tutored offenders in basic reading and writing skills on a one-to-one basis. Her students were school dropouts, youths with criminal records. "Quite different from teaching in a parochial grade school," she said. Later she worked with groups in a course called Decisions Making.[17] She also participated in religious celebrations in the jails. One of her happiest moments was when a prisoner studying to be baptized, asked her "Sister, will you be my godmother?" She agreed and later followed his career after his release. "His bank robbery days to support a drug habit are past; since his release he is continuing university studies and has a job," said Sr. Margarita. He turned his life around because somebody visited him in prison.[18]

In Massachusetts, Sr. Dorothy Briggs initiated a local chapter of Citizens United for Rehabilitation of Errants (CURE). Appalled at the lack of rehabilitation programs for prisoners, Sr. Dorothy became an advocate for prison reform.[19] She found that some offenders incarcerated for a first offense, are teenagers or youths in their early twenties. To her it seemed an incredible waste when no attempts were made to help them change their lives. She admits there will be failures even with the best of rehabilitative programs, but she feels that not to offer help is a worse failure. She held a collaborative meeting at St. Catharine Motherhouse with CURE volunteers from seven states to plan ways to change injustices in the prison system, particularly, with regard to families of offenders.[20] Bit by bit, CURE hopes to transform some of the injustices of the system.

In Kentucky, Sr. Judy Morris has been a member of the Kentucky Coalition to Abolish the Death Penalty.[21] This group has worked to raise awareness to the blatant examples of racism in determining who receives the death penalty. They rejoiced when the state legislature declared it illegal to execute mentally retarded people in Kentucky.

When the Kentucky Dominicans took a stance opposing the death penalty they were well aware that it was a controversial issue, however, they felt it was consistent with their policy to choose life. In their studies on the issue, the sisters learned among other things the death penalty is not administered fairly among all economic and racial groups. The Bishops of Kentucky wrote a pastoral letter, *Choose Life*, which affirmed the stand taken by the sisters.

The evening before the execution of Harold McQueen on July 1, 1997, a vigil was held at St. Catharine Motherhouse. Prayers for reconciliation and healing were said, not only for McQueen but for death row inmates and particularly for victims of their crimes. Candles were lit in memory of the victims as their names were read.[22] The sisters deny that they are "soft" on crime. For them, perpetuation of violence is not in keeping with the Gospel message of Jesus. Sisters and associates continue to speak out against the death penalty in an effort to transform a structure which continues the spiral of violence.

Broken Promises

There is no doubt that society has suffered and does suffer at the hands of criminals, however, society has inflicted and does inflict unjust, untold suffering on the vulnerable. One of the saddest pages in American history is how this country has treated Native American Indians. Because of a long series of broken promises, ignored treaties and corrupt policies, Indian life has been dominated by grinding poverty, poor education, continual unemployment and attempted destruction of tribal culture.

Among the Arapaho and Cheyenne

When Andrew Broderick, OP, and Regis Ryan, OP, conducted a campaign, primarily among US Dominicans, to support a project for demonstrating the need of legal assistance to the Cheyenne-Arapaho tribes of Northwest Oklahoma, the response was overwhelming. The generosity of 136 Dominicans and their friends enabled the Legal Assistance Project for Cheyenne-Arapaho tribes (LEAPCAT) to hire a lawyer on September 19, 1977 to defend criminal and juvenile cases for low income tribal members in three counties. Out of this project grew the Las Casas Fund.[23]

When the Las Casas Fund was incorporated on January 7, 1978, Sr. Joan Monica McGuire was one of the 14 trustees on the first board with Sr. M. Francis McDonald (HOPE) as legal agent of the corporation. The board met with grass roots leaders, Wayne and Emma Red Hat, Viola Hatch, Floyd Black Bear, Osage and Mae Wilson to learn the needs of their people.[24]

Sr. Verona Weidig spent three years in Oklahoma working for LEAPCAT as a legal advocate, tutor, counselor and friend. Living among the Cheyenne and Arapaho, she learned the richness of Native American spirituality. Two customs which impressed her were the Sun Dance and the Purification Ritual.

The Sun Dance was the most important religious event of the year. Many Indians from other areas and different tribes came to participate, to join in the praying and to form community. During the Sun Dance a small group of Indians spent a week fasting, praying and dancing. The Purification Ritual took place in a sweat lodge where men and women sat around steaming hot rocks; it was a serious, silent, and strenuous purifying of the body. It united them to the Great Spirit.

Sr. Verona said, "Native Americans are noted for gift giving to honored and trusted friends. I knew I was trusted and accepted when a Cheyenne woman lovingly placed around my neck a beaded necklace with an unusual cross. The woman said, 'There will never be another necklace like this and I have said a prayer for you with every bead.'"[25]

Among the Sioux

In the summer of 1979, Srs. Josepha Buckley and Gertrude Mary Christoffel sought to make a difference by teaching school readiness at Watonga, Oklahoma. The sisters felt helpless because the structure anchored the Indians on the reservation, gave them welfare checks but no hope or incentive and made no reparation for decades of broken promises.

Srs. Norah Guy, Rosaire Hickey, Marie Cleary and Jean Delaney also spent a summer on an Indian reservation in Yankton, South Dakota. Their mission was to teach religion but the Benedictine Fathers had just turned over the management of the reservation and the school to the Sioux Council. The Council asked the sisters to supervise Indian youth workers so the sisters found themselves mowing grass, collecting garbage and driving a truck.

When they accompanied their students to the supermarket, they could not believe the clerk waited on all white customers before allowing the Indians to approach the register. Working closely with the Sioux caused the sisters to become part of the oppressed. When they took the children to a pool on a hot, sticky day, the whites withdrew, hurling insults at them and the children. "Here come those red savages and their red skin lovers." Prejudice was high among whites but the Sioux knew and trusted the sisters. One proof was when Indian women placed special shawls around the sisters during the Sun Dance ritual. The summer was a brief encounter; no major transformation took place in the system but there was one in the hearts of the sisters and their young charges. As a parting gift, the sisters received peace pipes, a lasting reminder of a proud nation.[26]

At Rosebud, South Dakota, Srs. Barbara Sowers and Joan Dunning worked for the US Public Health Service with babies born with alcoholic syndrome. Here, little ones were kept in the hospital for months to "dry out" and receive proper nutrition. The sisters found it frustrating to send a baby back to a hopeless environment where the cycle of alcoholism claimed the child again. "The reservation was so barren and incentives so lacking that one felt powerless," reported Sr. Joan.[27] Those sisters who worked among the Indians said they experienced the oppression and frustration of the tribes they served.

Reaching Out to the Wampanoags

On special occasions at Crystal Spring Farm, Plainville, Massachusetts, the chant of the Wampanoags and the rhythmic beating of drums draws attention to an intertribal ritual taking place. The sounds come from a sweat lodge erected on the Dominican property. How did it get there?

Once when the Kentucky Dominicans were celebrating Earth Day, Sr. Christine Loughlin invited Chief Running Deer to lead the blessing ceremonies. Later, he asked permission to build a sweat lodge in the woods on the property, explaining that the sweat lodge is the scene of intense fasting, praying and purification. Srs. Barbara Harrington, Christine Loughlin and Carole Rossi, the Crystal Spring Community, welcomed the proposal with enthusiasm because as an ecology center, Crystal Spring shares with the Indians a reverence and love of the land.[28]

Sisters who have worked with Native Americans feel there is much to be done to reconcile the injustices and the broken promises perpetuated against the tribes who were on this land first. Although they found the reservations depressing, the sisters feel that the hope is in foundations like Las Casas, helping but not imposing, and above all, reverencing the art and deeply spiritual culture of Native Americans. Sr. Elizabeth Miles wrote to the Dominican Family at Thanksgiving, 1992, "Let us challenge and support one another to be Las Casas persons, addressing today's evils courageously in word and lifestyle."[29] Respect for persons of other cultures became a growing concern.

Center for Reconciliation and Ecumenism

World attention has been focused on relationships in the mideast because of the violence on all sides. When Srs. Adrian Marie and Margaret Marie Hofstetter reflected on justice and peace in the mideast, they determined to do something about it. With foundation money from the Congregation, Sr. Adrian Marie established the Center for Reconciliation and Ecumenism (CRE) in 1973. The Center which is still in operation has a two-fold purpose: the reconciliation of Jews, Christians and Muslims and the reconciliation of men and women in ministry.

Under the auspices of the National Council of Churches, Sr. Adrian participated in a peace mission to Egypt, Syria, Jordan and Israel. The group consisting of 18 Christians and 15 Jews opened dialogue with peace activists in the troubled countries.[30] Since then Sr. Adrian has made many trips to the mideast to speak out, hold workshops and promote dialogue for peace. Through the CRE she has awarded scholarships to religious and lay people for study about the mideast and other Third World countries.

Her sister, Sr. Margaret Marie, taught for five years at the University of Bethlehem where she witnessed the sufferings of Palestinians in their struggle for a homeland and in their humiliation under cruel surveillance. She does not condone Palestinian violence against Jews but she said, "I have great sympathy for the Palestinians. I have some understanding of the Arab/Muslim culture and I believe the Palestinians love their land just as much as Native American Indians love theirs." At one time, she was a prisoner in the University with her students during an uprising against Palestinians. She encourages Arab women to pursue studies seriously if they want to bring about change. She continues her efforts by preaching about her experience in the mideast, writing about it and exhorting others to study the situation in depth.[31]

Sr. Joan Monica McGuire, long an advocate of reconciliation and ecumenism was partially sponsored by CRE to study at Tantur, the Notre Dame University ecumenical center for theology students from all over the world.[32] In 1995, she accompanied Cardinal Joseph Bernadin as one of seven Catholic delegates on a Chicago Catholic/Jewish Dialogue to the mideast. Seven Jewish delegates, including three rabbis, completed the peace mission group. They had meetings with Shimon Peres, Yitshak Rabin, Yasser Arafat, Michel Sabbah, Msgr. Andrea Cordero Lanza Di Montezemolo[33] and other political, academic and religious leaders. The purpose was to hear hopes and concerns regarding the peace process.[34]

An exchange of gifts took place between the cardinal and Yasser Arafat. The latter gave the Cardinal a beautiful creche made in Bethlehem. The Cardinal's gift to Arafat was engraved with a cross and the star of David, traditional symbols of the Catholic and Jewish faiths. When he received his gift, Arafat remarked, "Islam is not represented." Pointing to his wall he showed the delegates that all three traditions were depicted by the Ten Commandments, a Christian sculpture and verses from the Koran. The lesson was obvious. In Chicago, as director of Ecumenism and Inter-religious Affairs for the Archdiocese, Sr. Joan continues to work with many religious groups locally, nationally and internationally to promote reconciliation.[35]

Teaching Tolerance in Romania

Another part of the world torn by centuries-old ethnic animosity and strife is Romania. Despite the fall of communism, old hatreds continue. Hoping to live and teach tolerance and acceptance of differences, Sr. Martha McNulty in 1991 signed a contract to participate in Yale's Civic Education Project. She left her professorship at College of the Ozarks, Missouri, to teach ethnic and national relations at two theological institutes in

Cluj-Napoca, northwestern Romania: one for Romanian Orthodox students and one for Hungarian Protestants.

Although her students were accustomed to a system of no questions, no discussion, she quickly changed that by encouraging them to express their own thoughts. She told them, "Learning is not a spectator sport." She was an anomaly to students in this front line of newly emerging democracy for whom this was a first contact with a Westerner. They learned that it was safe to challenge and dialogue in her classes. For Sr. Martha this change was a welcome effect but an even greater accomplishment was that reconciliation began when students commenced to respect each other's differences.

Sisters' Senate

In the 70s women religious became deeply involved in social justice issues but the needs of the powerless poor were so broad that the task seemed insurmountable. In Boston, Sr. Jean Vianney Norris felt that a collaborative effort among women religious was necessary to work out solutions. She invited grassroots representatives of 35 communities to meet at Rosary Academy, Watertown, on October 31, 1970 to explore the possibility of forming an advisory council in the Archdiocese of Boston. The goal was to help women religious fulfill their role in the Church in the light of contemporary needs of the People of God.[36]

As chairperson of a twelve member steering committee, Sr. Jean called monthly meetings over a period of one year to prepare for a Sisters' Senate. She set up a meeting with Cardinal Humberto Medeiros to dialogue about the role of women in ministry. In December, 1971 the Cardinal affirmed the Constitution and approved the Sisters' Senate. He urged the sisters to become the "leaven in the midst of God's people." Sr. Jean was elected first president of the group. She addressed current social issues by forming committees on Peace and Justice, Personal and Professional Development and Public Relations.

The Sisters' Senate raised social awareness of violations against peace and justice by boycotting Gallo wines, non-union lettuce and grapes and citing injustices by J. P. Stevens Co. at that time. The Senate supported Bread for the World and organized a letter writing campaign to request World Food Reserve. It was the Sisters' Senate which initiated dialogue with the Cardinal regarding an increase in salary for women religious.[37]

In New York, Sr. M. Justin Foley was one of the founding members of the New York Sisters' Senate which had the same objectives. The movement spread to other dioceses with Sisters' Senates becoming a prophetic voice seeking justice for the poor and oppressed.

Women in Crisis

It is often difficult for the poor and oppressed to find justice. Women, victims of rape, live an agony of shame and disgust to such an extent that some will not report the crime. Often when they do report it, they are treated in a demeaning way. Former president of St. Catharine College, Sr. Catherine Mahady, works in a Rape Crisis Program which seeks to transform the situation. She serves at the Center for Women in Louisville, which has a three-pronged project to empower women. It embraces (1) creative employment; (2) counseling in cases of domestic violence with emergency shelter available for 60 women and their children; and (3) the rape crisis segment. Often Sr. Catherine is called to the hospital at night to be with a rape victim and to let her know what help is available when she wants it. Sr. Catherine prefers to call these women "survivors" rather than victims because of their courage in handling this most brutal crime.[38]

A somewhat analagous program was initiated in Rhode Island by Sr. Elaine Shaw and Rev. Patricia Liberty, a Baptist clergywoman. Together they formed Associates in Education and Prevention in Pastoral Practice (AEPPP) with seed money obtained from a grant from the Kentucky Dominicans in 1992. They believe churches have an ethical obligation towards survivors, whether child or adult, who suffer sexual abuse from clergy, nun, church worker, employer or volunteer.

Their program stresses the need for education about the problem which impacts on faith, spirituality and sexuality. The two women offer workshops for clergy on ethical behavior in ministerial relationships. They bring knowledge and healing to situations which too often are swept under the rug.

Housing

The plight of the homeless is one of the greatest needs of our times. Shelters for the homeless are needed in every area of our country. Since 1969 sisters have the option to choose their ministry. As a result, there are few areas now where large groups of sisters are engaged in the same service in one place, for instance, 35 sisters teaching in the same school or 20 sisters working in the same hospital. It is a bit unusual to find a group serving in the same ministry under the same umbrella but such is the case at Pine Street Inn (PSI) in Boston.

Pine Street Inn

Five sisters and two associates work under PSI auspices with the homeless. Sr. Blaise Flynn, supervisor and case manager for formerly homeless men and women with AIDS or HIV positive, regards her ministry as "quite wonderful." It provides permanent housing for persons who are afraid of dying alone or who do not choose to die in a hospital. Deep relationships develop quickly because life takes on new meaning when days are numbered. Associate Pat Daly is a relief worker with Sr. Blaise.

Sr. Rita Pineau provides transitional housing for homeless women while Sr. Helen O'Sullivan is case manager for homeless men. Sr. Eileen Linehan works with homeless elderly women in a special unit. Associate Eileen McGee, R.N. works in the PSI clinic for the homeless. Sr. Pauline LaMothe is Director of PSI's Paul Sullivan Housing. She supervises 15 sites, each one of which she wants to be a *home*, not just a rooftree. She attributes the success of the housing program to supportive services furnished by a caring staff. The follow-up on all these programs is what makes transformation possible.[39]

Other Programs for Homeless

Like Eileen McGee, associate Cindy Boulton, nurse practitioner, works in a clinic for homeless at St. John Health Center, Louisville. The gamut of cases she treats ranges from heart conditions, alcoholism, and mental illness to AIDS testing, drug addiction and diabetes.[40] In the same vein, Sr. Theresa McManus, as program administrator of Health Care Network at 35 clinic shelters in Washington, D.C. is responsible for coordinating medical care for the poor, homeless and low income population.[41]

Dehon House

Few shelters accept children, yet more and more are found in the ranks of the homeless. In 1981 Sr. Lois McGovern opened Dehon House in Chicago which can accommodate 35 homeless adults and children at one time. Named after the founder of the Sacred Heart Fathers and Brothers of Hales Corner, Wisconsin, the shelter is one of the few places which allows an extended period of residency. Rules are strict: no drugs or drinking, curfew for adults as well as children and shared responsibility for household chores.

The Sacred Heart Fathers and Brothers provided the building and maintenance for 15 years but they can no longer afford to subsidize it. The Chicago Department of Human Resources, a major source of Dehon House funding is facing federal funding cuts. Sr. Lois said "While at Dehon House residents improve their skills living as a family but when they leave, because of lack of jobs and affordable housing, it is difficult for them to be successful." She worries about what funding cuts will do to the program. She believes, "Only a systemic change in society will eradicate the problems of poverty and homelessness."[42]

Project Women, Inc.

Hoping to effect a systemic change for disadvantaged women, six congregations of women religious in Louisville, donated money to open Project Women/Sophia Center. The facility, dedicated in November, 1996 provides housing for three women and ten children.

Sr. Clarellen McGinley, social worker and case manager at Project Women, hopes it will expand to include a day care facility, housing for about 12 families and office space. She calls on local parishes, organizations and individuals to donate furniture and household items to equip the units. Sr. Mary Ann Budka is on the Member Board and lawyer Sr. Barbara Sullivan is on the Board of Directors.[43] Sr. Barbara, a member of the Louisville Legal Aid Society and the Appalachian Research and Defense Fund, provides legal representation for persons involved in spousal abuse, homelessness, house eviction, bankruptcy and those who need welfare and/or for unemployment benefits. She works closely with the local community and is a breath of fresh air within the legal system serving the poor and oppressed.

Ministry and Law

A new dimension was added to law, Canon Law that is, when Sr. M. Patricia Green was appointed in 1975 to the Marriage Tribunal of the Archdiocese of Louisville. She was Director, Collegiate Judge and Defender of the Bond for the Appeal Tribunal and Auditor, Defender of the Bond, Judge and Director of the Louisville Archdiocesan Tribunal. She was the first woman religious to work on that tribunal at a time when only a handful of women religious were doing this kind of ministry historically dominated by male clergy.

Often women who came before the tribunal found it easier to relate to another woman who was a good listener and had the facility to help them pick up the pieces of their broken lives. Her ministry was one of compassion and healing. At her death, Ladislaus Orsy, SJ, who directed her licentiate dissertation said, "She has done more for the diocese than will ever be recorded in histories."[44]

Immigration Law is confusing to immigrants unfamiliar with English. When Sr. Rose Marie Cummins observed their difficulties she became a paralegal advocate for Latino immigrants from Central and South America. She has learned from experience, sometimes even in danger, and often with struggle, how to help new immigrants.

Meeting Today's Needs

In 1992, Vincentian Rev. David J. Nygren and Corondolet Josephite Sr. Miriam D. Ukeritis released the results of a three-year study they conducted among 10,000 US men and women religious. One of the findings revealed that some religious communities increasingly have shifted members into individual ministries thereby losing some of their corporate identity and impact. To offset this loss, Sr. Miriam identified two elements critical to insure a dynamic religious community: fidelity to the founding purpose and responsiveness to unmet needs.[45]

The Kentucky Dominicans strive to remain true to the heritage of St. Dominic and St. Catherine in a wide variety of ministries to answer modern needs. In a concrete way, they believe what they have received as gift they should give as gift. The Congregation has several alternate investments with "organizations which use their resources to help low-income individuals, primarily minorities and women in their economic self-help efforts. These include buying homes, building businesses and strengthening community resources."[46]

In addition, there are three special funds set aside annually for grants, (1) to groups serving economically poor, (2) to earth education projects, (3) to alleviation of oppressive situations involving housing, food, clothing and medical needs.[47]

An exciting gift the Kentucky Dominican Family made to Habitat for Humanity in honor of the 175th Jubilee was a check for $30,000 to build a New Kentucky Home for Habitat for Humanity. The first permanent home for the sisters was a gift and now, 175 years later, they are giving land and a home in thanksgiving.[48] No doubt, some jonquil bulbs will accompany the gift as a reminder of those sturdy, wild flowers which were harbingers of hope along the way.

A Sign from God

According to tradition St. Dominic received a sign from God, Signadou, when he was pondering what to do with the nine women converts from the Albigensian heresy. Fr. Thomas Wilson received a sign from God in affirmation of his plan to found a group of pioneer women to teach the children of the settlers when nine women accepted his invitation. Mother Angela Sansbury received a sign from God when approval came from Rome appointing her prioress of the first foundation of Dominican sisters in the United States.

From 1822 until the present the Congregation of St. Catharine of Siena has been blessed with many signs from God. Each of the 1385 women professed during those 175 years has been a sign from God with everyone she has contacted. The story of each sister and each mission is not contained in this book but an attempt was made to portray where the sisters are in service. You will find Kentucky Dominicans addressing needs in all levels of education, housing, domestic abuse, pastoral ministry, social services and retreat work.

Sisters and associates can be found with the homeless in Boston, the jobless in Louisville, the poor in Marks, Mississippi, the sick in Omaha, the elderly in Memphis, the hungry in Chicago. They seek to embody the language of love preached by Jesus by transforming

> homeless to shelter
> pollution to ecological balance
> jobless to employed
> sickness to health
> uneducated to knowledge
> violence to justice and peace.

Kentucky Dominicans have seen the death of cherished ideas and the discontinuance of life-invested ministries, but, being an EASTER PEOPLE, they wait for the resurrection of whatever is yet to be. Mother Angela's vision lives on!

Chapter Twenty Four Notes

1. *The Pilot*, January 30, 1991.
2. Sr. Norah Guy was appointed Eastern Regional Coordinator in 1994.
3. *The Pilot*, April 5, 1991.
   Personal interview with Sr. Norah Guy.
4. SCA *The Dream Lives On*, April 7, 1822 - April 7, 1995
5. Ibid.
6. Personal interview with Sr. Joan McVeigh.
7. SCA *The Dominican News*, Special Joint Multicultural Edition, January, 1996.
8. Personal interview with Sr. Joan Dunning.
9. SCA *Going Forward,* Winter, 1992.
10. Personal interview with Sr. Aquinette LeFort.
11. SCA *The Dominican News*, January, 1990.
    The Dream Lives On, April 7, 1822 - April 7, 1994.
12. SCA *The Dream Lives On*, April 7, 1822 - April 7, 1995.
    The West Nebraska Register, May 3, 1991
    August 6, 1994
    September 23, 1994.
    The Dominican News, February 1995.
    Going Forward, Summer 1996.
    Personal interview with Sr. Regina McCarthy.
13. *A World Split Open*, information paper from Guatemala Committee on Human Rights (no date).
    Personal interview with Sr. Barbara Harrington.
14. *SCA Community Matters*, May 1982.
    Going Forward, Fall 1983, Winter 1990.
    The Dominican News, November 1989.
    Sisters Today, Vol. 56, August-September 1984.
    Personal interview with Sr. Peggy Duggan.
15. SCA *Chapter Acts*, 1988.
16. *Corporate Stances of the Kentucky Dominicans* compiled by Sr. Dorothy Briggs, OP, chair of the Issues Committee. Any sister may submit an issue to the Committee. The Committee sends pertinent educational material on the issue to the entire membership. The sisters vote on the issue. If the majority of the returned ballots indicate favoring the stand, it is promulgated as a Congregational Corporate Statement. From October 1988 to June 1996, ten statements have been published in the name of the Kentucky Dominican sisters.
17. *Ministry to the Imprisoned*, Teachers' Manual, Diocese of Memphis, this course was designed to assist offenders to take control of their lives by making value decisions.
18. SCA *Community Matters*, October 1983.
    The Dominican News, December 1995.

Inside Story, Criminal Justice Ministry Volunteer Newsletter, October 1980.

Personal interview with Sr. Margarita Stidolph.

19. CURE was founded in Washington, DC by Charles and Pauline Sullivan.

See *America,* October 5, 1996, p. 26.

20. SCA *The Dominican News,* December 1995.

21. *Sisters Today,* Vol. 63, No. 6, November 1991, Death Row Banquet by Sr. Judy Morris, OP.

St. Anthony Messenger, July 1997, Death Row Chaplain by Sr. Judy Morris, OP.

22. SCA *Day By Day,* July 8, 1997.

23. Las Casas Fund was named in honor of Bartolome de Las Casas, a one-time slave holder who was converted by the preaching of Dominicans. He joined the Order and for over 50 years he preached and wrote on emancipation of slaves. His efforts bore little fruit with gold-hungry colonists who depended on the labor of Indian slaves.

24. Chronology and Narrative on Las Casas Corporation prepared by Sr. Bette Jean Goebel, OP, (Great Bend, Kansas) for presentation to the Dominican Leadership Conference.

25. Unpublished memoirs, Sr. Verona Weidig, OP, July 24, 1997 to Sr. Paschala Noonan, OP.

26. Personal interviews with Srs. Marie Cleary, OP, and Norah Guy, OP.

27. Personal interview, Sr. Joan Dunning, OP.

28. Personal interview, Sr. Christine Laughlin, OP.

29. SCA Sr. Elizabeth Miles, OP, to the Dominican Family, November 17, 1992.

30. *The Creightonian,* April 23, 1982.

The Courier-Journal, January 20, 1976.

Sr. Adrian Marie Hofstetter, OP, and associate Laura Miller presently conduct a homesharing project in Highland, New York.

31. *The Record,* August 10, 1988.

The Springfield Sun, March 13, 1991.

Sisters Today, September 1994, Vol. 88, No. 5.

SCA *The Dominican News,* March 19, 1991.

32. Sr. Joan Monica McGuire, OP, earned her License and Doctorate of Sacred Theology in Ecumenism at the Angelicum, Rome. She is Director of Ecumenism and Interreligious Affairs for the Archdiocese of Chicago.

33. Mickel Sabbah is Latin Patriarch of Jerusalem, Msgr. Andrea Cordero Lanza di Montezemolo is Papal Nuncio to Israel and Apostolic Delegate to Jerusalem.

34. SCA *The Dominican News,* Vol. 9, No. 2.

35. Ibid.

36. Files of Sisters' Senate Archdiocese of Boston, Chronological history, September 1990.

37. Ibid.

38. SCA *The Dominican News,* May 1996.

39. SCA *The Dominican News,* February 1997.

40. SCA *The Dominican News,* May 1990.

41. SCA *The Dream Lives On,* April 7, 1822 - April 7, 1995.

42. SCA *Going Forward,* Fall 1988.

    The Dominican News, February 1997.

    Founders' Day, April 7, 1822 - April 7, 1994.

43. SCA *The Dominican News,* February 1997.

44. SCA Eulogy delivered by Sr. Susan C. Morris, OP, at Memorial Mass for Sr. M. Patricia Green, OP, June 9, 1993.

    The Record, Louisville, KY, March 11, 1993.

    The Lowell Sun, March 10, 1993.

    Sr. M. Patricia who received her Licentiate in Canon Law, wrote a masterful study on the Constitutions of the Kentucky Dominicans from 1822-1969.

45. *Origins,* Vol. 22, No. 15, September 24, 1992, Future of Religious Orders in the U.S.

46. SCA *Day By Day,* September 3, 1997.

47. SCA *The Dominican News,* May 1996.

    Day By Day, September 3, 1997.

48. SCA *The Blackberry Special,* Vol. 1, No. 1, February 28, 1996.

Sisters Professed at St. Catharine Who Are Buried at St. Mary of the Springs

Name	Professed	Died
Mother Angela Sansbury	Jan. 6, 1823	Nov. 30, 1839
Sr. Ann Hill	Aug. 30, 1823	Apr. 1, 1840
Sr. Francis Whelan	Oct. 2, 1836	Feb. 4, 1844
Sr. Cecilia Dunn	Oct. 2, 1859	June 25, 1864
Sr. Benven Sansbury	Aug. 30, 1823	May 29, 1873

Chronological Sequence of Order of Profession: 1822-1996

Member Number and Name	*Profession Date*
1 Sr. Angela Sansbury	01-06-1823
2 Sr. Magdalen Edelen	08-30-1823
3 Sr. Benvin Sansbury	08-30-1823
4 Sr. Ann Hill	08-30-1823
5 Sr. Margaret Carico	08-30-1823
6 Sr. Frances Sansbury	08-30-1823
7 Sr. Teresa Kaho	02-15-1824
8 Sr. Emily Elder	11-09-1824
9 Sr. Catharine Sansbury	11-09-1824
10 Sr. Osanna Montgomery	03-26-1826
11 Sr. Lucy Boon	08-17-1826
12 Sr. Columba Smith	07-04-1827
13 Sr. Helen Whelan	08-04-1827
14 Sr. Rose Tennelly	08-04-1827
15 Sr. Agnes Harbin	01-11-1830
16 Sr. Catherine Mudd	01-11-1830
17 Sr. Dominica Kaho	05-20-1830
18 Sr. Columba Walsh	05-20-1830
19 Sr. Villana Montgomery	05-20-1830
20 Sr. Catharine Johnson	10-01-1832
21 Sr. Joanna Simpson	12-25-1833
22 Sr. Emily Thorp	08-15-1835
23 Sr. Mary Clements	05-29-1836
24 Sr. Martha McLain	05-29-1836
25 Sr. Frances Whelan	10-02-1836
26 Sr. Angela Lynch	10-02-1836
27 Sr. Margaret Queen	01-01-1841
28 Sr. Imelda Montgomery	01-01-1841
29 Sr. Benvin Carney	08-30-1842
30 Sr. Ann Simpson	03-27-1843

31	Sr. Sybillina McLane	03-27-1843
32	Sr. Lucy Harper	08-30-1844
33	Sr. Monica Conlan	01-01-1845
34	Sr. Francis Conlan	01-01-1845
35	Sr. Benedicta Montgomery	05-18-1846
36	Sr. Vincentia Fitzpatrick	05-18-1846
37	Sr. Osanna Powell	09-03-1847
38	Sr. Benven Musgrove	09-03-1848
39	Sr. Agnes Maher	10-28-1849
40	Sr. Louise Hayden	10-28-1849
41	Sr. Josepha White	10-28-1850
42	Sr. Mary Pius Fitzpatrick	03-25 1851
43	Sr. Clare Montgomery	03-25-1851
44	Sr. M. Francis Kennedy	03-27-1853
45	Sr. Dominica Fitzpatrick	03-27-1853
46	Sr. Mary Josephine Whelan	03-27-1853
47	Sr. Hyacintha Reed	05-26-1853
48	Sr. Mary Rose Rogers	05-26-1853
49	Sr. Ann O'Brien	08-04-1854
50	Sr. Vincent Ferrer Thompson	11-25-1854
51	Sr. M. Benvin Rumph	03-07-1856
52	Sr. Dolores O'Neale	03-07-1856
53	Sr. Gertrude Roney	03-07-1856
54	Sr. Mary Stanislaus Davis	03-07-1856
55	Sr. Mary Thomas O'Meara	03-07-1856
56	Sr. Lucy Mills	03-07-1856
57	Sr. M. Catherine Madigan	03-07 1856
58	Sr. M. Felix Perrong	08-24-1856
59	Sr. Alberta Rumph	06-14-1857
60	Sr. Philomena Sheridan	09-12-1858
61	Sr. Raymunda Meagher	09-12-1858
62	Sr. Josephine Meagher	09-12-1858
63	Sr. Aloysia Sheridan	09-12-1858
64	Sr. Gertrude O'Meara	10-02-1859
65	Sr. M. Teresa Kivlahan	10-02-1859
66	Sr. Regina O'Meara	10-02-1859
67	Sr. Cecilia Dunn	10-02-1859
68	Sr. Veronica Logsdon	04-20-1860

69	Sr. Sybillina Sheridan	04-20-1860
70	Sr. Augusta Thomas	11-04-1860
71	Sr. Ursula Wildman	07-22-1862
72	Sr. Dominica Logsdon	12-25-1865
73	Sr. Benedicta Scanlon	12-25-1865
74	Sr. Cecilia Carey	04-29-1866
75	Sr. Catherine Kidwell	01-06-1867
76	Sr. Villana Young	04-29-1867
77	Sr. Catharine Kintz	03-25-1868
78	Sr. Hyacintha Peters	03-25-1868
79	Sr. M. Thomas Wight	06-28-1868
80	Sr. Vincentia Maguire	06-28-1868
81	Sr. M. Agnes Maguire	06-28-1868
82	Sr. M. Joseph Clark	06-28-1868
83	Sr. Gertrude Rapp	08-15-1868
84	Sr. Magdalen Jacquot	03-05-1869
85	Sr. M. Sienna Young	08-28-1869
86	Sr. Frances Slinger	02-26-1871
87	Sr. Thomasina Simpson	02-26-1871
88	Sr. M. Dominic Simms	02-26-1871
89	Sr. M. Joseph Howard	10-15-1871
90	Sr. Aloysia Mulligan	03-07-1872
91	Sr. Alphonsa Dubourg	02-26-1872
92	Sr. Dominica Canty	08-04-1873
93	Sr. Gertrude Hogan	03-25-1874
94	Sr. Columba Ryan	03-25-1874
95	Sr. Dominica Lanigan	03-25-1874
96	Sr. Stephana Cassidy	03-25-1874
97	Sr. Agnes Hunt	03-25-1874
98	Sr. Reginald Mulligan	06-04-1875
99	Sr. M. Alberta Mosher	07-02-1875
100	Sr. Benedicta Meany	08-30-1875
101	Sr. Magdalen Norton	02-02-1876
102	Sr. Francis Mahoney	02-02-1876
103	Sr. M. Bernard Spalding	04-30-1876
104	Sr. Antoninus Nealy	04-30-1876
105	Sr. Dolores Mattingly	04-30-1876
106	Sr. M. Lawrence Blandford	04-30-1876

107	Sr. Aloysius O'Connor	08-04-1876
108	Sr. Mary Louis Murphy	08-30-1876
109	Sr. M. Bertrand Sheehan	03-19-1877
110	Sr. M. Raymond Bird	11-01-1877
111	Sr. M. Austin Tobin	02-17-1878
112	Sr. Clare Glass	02-17-1878
113	Sr. Cecilia Kennedy	04-30-1879
114	Sr. Catherine Hoare	05-22-1879
115	Sr. Teresa Bennett	05-22-1879
116	Sr. Raphael Huber	07-22-1879
117	Sr. Martina Neely	07-22-1879
118	Sr. Gabriel Plier	07-22-1879
119	Sr. M. Austin Boyd	11-01-1879
120	Sr. M. Bernard Fogarty	03-01-1880
121	Sr. Bernardine Bushue	11-07-1880
122	Sr. Genevieve Peeling	11-21-1880
123	Sr. Rose Farrell	11-21-1880
124	Sr. Angelica McGill	11-01-1881
125	Sr. M. Thomas O'Leary	03-07-1882
126	Sr. Bridget Connelly	03-07-1882
127	Sr. Vincent Ford	04-05-1882
128	Sr. Agatha Brown	10-25-1883
129	Sr. Cecilia Hill	03-07-1884
130	Sr. Teresa Webb	03-07-1884
131	Sr. Rose McCarthy	03-07-1885
132	Sr. M. Bertrand Manning	03-07-1885
133	Sr. Alexia O'Sullivan	04-30-1885
134	Sr. Mary Pius Kennedy	04-30-1885
135	Sr. Thomasina Gilmartin	08-04-1885
136	Sr. M. Aquin Holleran	09-08-1885
137	Sr. Camilla Henneberry	11-15-1885
138	Sr. Stanislaus Tracey	11-15-1885
139	Sr. Reginald Murphy	04-30-1886
140	Sr. M. Rose Spalding	05-02-1886
141	Sr. Catherine Conniff	11-09-1886
142	Sr. Margaret Hamilton	03-07-1887
143	Sr. Osanna Haydon	07-19-1887
144	Sr. Agnes Shanahan	08-30-1887

145	Sr. M. Agnes Brown	01-23-1888
146	Sr. M. Louise Robertson	01-23-1888
147	Sr. M. Ambrose Deppen	01-23-1888
148	Sr. Sybillina Clements	03-07-1888
149	Sr. Clara Simms	03-07-1888
150	Sr. Evangelista Noonan	03-07-1888
151	Sr. Genevieve Dale	03-07-1888
152	Sr. Mary Oskamp	08-26-1888
153	Sr. Imelda Brady	08-26-1888
154	Sr. Magdalene Towle	10-07-1888
155	Sr. Veronica Livers	10-07-1888
156	Sr. M. Louis Logsdon	03-07-1889
157	Sr. Francesca Kearney	03-07-1889
158	Sr. Ceslaus McIntyre	10-10-1889
159	Sr. Sienna Byrnes	03-09-1890
160	Sr. Ursula Clark	03-09-1890
161	Sr. M. Sadoc Deppen	03-09-1890
162	Sr. Patricia Moran	05-11-1890
163	Sr. Henrietta Osbourne	05-11-1890
164	Sr. Josephine Spalding	05-11-1890
165	Sr. Pauline Burke	11-01-1890
166	Sr. M. Leo Rudd	03-10-1891
167	Sr. M. Augustine Donnelly	03-19-1891
168	Sr. Loretto Donovan	03-19-1891
169	Sr. Angela Clements	03-19-1891
170	Sr. Hyacintha Cooper	05-11-1891
171	Sr. Barbara O'Neil	08-04-1891
172	Sr. Clementine Hearn	08-04-1891
173	Sr. Thecla Brick	11-01-1891
174	Sr. Lucy Spalding	05-17-1892
175	Sr. Catherine deRicci Miller	01-06-1893
176	Sr. M. Zita Cambron	01-06-1893
177	Sr. Marcolina Craycroft	01-06-1893
178	Sr. Sebastian Conley	01-06-1893
179	Sr. Emily Trainor	01-06-1893
180	Sr. M. Dominic Elder	03-07-1893
181	Sr. Constantia Hart	03-07-1893
182	Sr. Rosalia O'Daniel	03-07-1893

183	Sr. Philomena Twohig	03-07-1893
184	Sr. Bernadette Clements	05-20-1893
185	Sr. Francis deSales Donovan	07-16-1893
186	Sr. Catherine Wheatley	08-27-1893
187	Sr. Antonia McDonald	12-08-1893
188	Sr. Moneta O'Neil	03-07-1894
189	Sr. Margaret Mary Kiley	03-07-1894
190	Sr. Agnita Kavanagh	05-10-1894
191	Sr. Mancini Higdon	05-10-1894
192	Sr. Osanna Quinn	05-10-1894
193	Sr. M. Leo Quirk	09-16-1894
194	Sr. Ignatius Connie	09-16-1894
195	Sr. Borgia McCann	11-01-1894
196	Sr. Dolores Spalding	11-01-1894
197	Sr. M. Francis McConnell	12-08-1894
198	Sr. Helena Monahan	03-17-1895
199	Sr. Sybillina Tobin	03-17-1895
200	Sr. Gonzales O'Connor	07-22-1895
201	Sr. Verecunda O'Hearn	11-01-1895
202	Sr. Emmanuel Fagan	11-01-1895
203	Sr. M. Clement Burns	04-19-1896
204	Sr. M. Ursula Greenwell	04-30-1896
205	Sr. Irene McDonald	08-04-1896
206	Sr. Fidelis Silver	02-10-1897
207	Sr. M. Agnes Kelly	02-10-1897
208	Sr. Baptista Riley	08-04-1897
209	Sr. Matilda Thome	08-04-1897
210	Sr. Isadore Larner	08-04-1897
211	Sr. Angelica Whitney	08-04-1897
212	Sr. Fabian Allen	12-29-1897
213	Sr. M. Michael Welsh	02-11-1898
214	Sr. M. Paul Gregg	02-11-1898
215	Sr. M. William Whalen	04-30-1898
216	Sr. M. Joanna Rowan	08-04-1898
217	Sr. M. Roberta Sheridan	12-29-1898
218	Sr. Winifred Schwaner	02-24-1899
219	Sr. Louis Bertrand Lancaster	04-30-1899
220	Sr. Francis O'Malley	04-30-1899

221	Sr. M. Rose Filiatreau	04-30-1899
222	Sr. Dolorita Clements	04-30-1899
223	Sr. Theresa Brennan	08-04-1899
224	Sr. Isabel Trainor	08-04-1899
225	Sr. Bernadine Medley	03-07-1900
226	Sr. Sylvester Bishop	03-07-1900
227	Sr. Felicita O'Connor	03-07-1900
228	Sr. Christina Goggin	03-07-1900
229	Sr. Justin Murphy	03-07-1900
230	Sr. Jerome Broslin	03-07-1900
231	Sr. Borromeo Brennan	08-04-1900
232	Sr. Boniface Higdon	08-04-1900
233	Sr. Innocentia Farrell	08-04-1900
234	Sr. Lucilla Croft	03-07-1901
235	Sr. Xavier Murphy	03-07-1901
236	Sr. Perpetua Richardson	03-07-1901
237	Sr. Octavia McNally	03-07-1901
238	Sr. Madeleine Ferriell	03-07-1901
239	Sr. Collette Buckley	08-04-1901
240	Sr. Leona Ferriell	08-04-1901
241	Sr. Helen Veader	03-07-1902
242	Sr. Loretto McCloskey	03-07-1902
243	Sr. Aquinas Durkin	03-07-1902
244	Sr. Adelaide Healey	03-07 1902
245	Sr. Seraphim Bulger	03-07-1902
246	Sr. Ligouri Murnane	08-04-1902
247	Sr. Dosithea Shields	03-07-1903
248	Sr. M. James Fitzpatrick	03-07-1903
249	Sr. Anthony Roddy	03-07-1903
250	Sr. Basil Hennessy	03-07-1903
251	Sr. Clotilda Nixon	03-07-1903
252	Sr. Josepha Loughran	01-10-1904
253	Sr. Elizabeth Hannon	03-07-1904
254	Sr. Alice Keyes	03-07-1904
255	Sr. Thecla Rafferty	03-07-1904
256	Sr. M. Regis Carraher	03-07-1904
257	Sr. M. Edward Prendergast	03-07-1904
258	Sr. M. Regina Sullivan	03-07-1904

259	Sr. Irene Callahan	08-26-1904
260	Sr. Angela Cullinane	08-26-1904
261	Sr. Augustine Sapp	08-26-1904
262	Sr. Anastasia Gorney	03-07-1905
263	Sr. M. John Clifford	03-07-1905
264	Sr. Gervase Donovan	03-07-1905
265	Sr. Germaine Donovan	03-07-1905
266	Sr. M. Sadoc Wimsett	03-07-1905
267	Sr. Monica Woods	03-07-1905
268	Sr. Rita Dellamana	03-07-1905
269	Sr. Hildegarde Hart	03-07-1905
270	Sr. Sabina Filiatreau	03-07-1905
271	Sr. Callista Kavanaugh	03-07-1905
272	Sr. Rosine Price	04-30-1906
273	Sr. M. Clement Tyner	04-30-1906
274	Sr. Immaculata Maroney	04-30-1906
275	Sr. Alexandrine Fleming	04-30-1906
276	Sr. Adrian Blandford	04-30-1906
277	Sr. Andrea O'Brien	04-30-1906
278	Sr. Mercedes Buckman	10-07-1906
279	Sr. M. Stephen Hartley	10-07-1906
280	Sr. Eulalia Shea	03-07-1907
281	Sr. Raymunda Cunniff	03-07-1907
282	Sr. Marcella Dunnigan	03-07-1907
283	Sr. Dolorita Lavelle	08-04-1907
284	Sr. Geraldine O'Brien	10-07-1907
285	Sr. M. Richard O'Brien	10-07-1907
286	Sr. M. Albert Hauck	01-01-1908
287	Sr. Fidelis Thompson	01-01-1908
288	Sr. DeChantal Dunnigan	01-01-1908
289	Sr. Gabriel O'Brien	07-02-1908
290	Sr. Jordan McDonald	08-04-1908
291	Sr. Theophane Rittelmeyer	10-07-1908
292	Sr. Cornelius Butler	10-07-1908
293	Sr. Constance O'Brien	01-01-1909
294	Sr. M. George McDonald	03-07-1909
295	Sr. Helen Burns	03-07-1909
296	Sr. Marie Welsh	04-30-1909

297	Sr. Justina Hooker	06-07-1909
298	Sr. Gregory Donnelly	08-04-1909
299	Sr. Victorine Donovan	10-07-1909
300	Sr. M. Philip McDonald	01-01-1910
301	Sr. Consilia Bohan	03-07-1910
302	Sr. Amadeus Coleman	03-07-1910
303	Sr. Sylveria Naughton	08-04-1910
304	Sr. Dionysius Burke	08-04-1910
305	Sr. Catherine Twomey	08-04-1910
306	Sr. Helena Manning	08-04-1910
307	Sr. Damian Hatton	08-04-1910
308	Sr. M. Matthew Desmond	08-04-1910
309	Sr. Anselma Sullivan	08-04-1910
310	Sr. M. Bernard Dwyer	10-07-1910
311	Sr. Norbert Horgan	01-01-1911
312	Sr. Rosanna Meagher	01-01-1911
313	Sr. Florence O'Connor	01-01-1911
314	Sr. Virginia Ford	01-01-1911
315	Sr. M. Raymond Hines	01-01-1911
316	Sr. Gerard Hughes	01-01-1911
317	Sr. Ann Joseph Murphy	01-22-1911
318	Sr. Carmelita Fisher	03-07-1911
319	Sr. Alphonsa Coffee	03-07-1911
320	Sr. M. Lawrence Welsh	08-04-1911
321	Sr. Marietta Kilgannon	08-04-1911
322	Sr. Alberta Johnson	08-04-1911
323	Sr. Aquinas Mullaney	08-04-1911
324	Sr. Miriam Devine	03-07-1912
325	Sr. Sylvester Sullivan	03-07-1912
326	Sr. Bernard Marie Burke	03-07-1912
327	Sr. Praxades McAleer	03-07-1912
328	Sr. Jane Marie Flynn	03-07-1912
329	Sr. M. Zachary Shore	03-07-1912
330	Sr. M. Gonzaga Edelen	08-04-1912
331	Sr. M. James Diggin	08-04-1912
332	Sr. Scholastica O'Daly	08-04-1912
333	Sr. Mildred Conway	08-04-1912
334	Sr. Alvarez Herlihy	08-04-1912

335	Sr. Berenice Doucette	03-07-1913
336	Sr. Berchmans Ennen	03-07-1913
337	Sr. Wilfred Mullen	03-07-1913
338	Sr. Eutropia Horan	03-07-1913
339	Sr. M. Charles Moranville	03-07-1913
340	Sr. Bonaventure Peake	03-07-1913
341	Sr. Casilda Brennan	03-07-1913
342	Sr. Wilhelmina Fogle	03-07-1913
343	Sr. Josephine Keene	03-07-1913
344	Sr. William Marie Torpey	03-07-1913
345	Sr. Roberta Ross	03-07-1913
346	Sr. Elizabeth Sheehan	03-07-1913
347	Sr. Mauricia Scott	03-07-1913
348	Sr. Adrian Kirby	03-07-1913
349	Sr. Theodosia Conway	03-07-1913
350	Sr. Dalmatia Connolly	03-07-1913
351	Sr. Zita Keefe	03-07-1913
352	Sr. Theresa Marie Keefe	08-04-1913
353	Sr. Domitilla Landry	08-04-1913
354	Sr. Aquinata Martin	08-04-1913
355	Sr. Edmund Harrington	08-04-1913
356	Sr. Rosaria Forgette	03-07-1914
357	Sr. Clarissa Leonard	03-07-1914
358	Sr. Laurentia Filiatreau	03-07-1914
359	Sr. Rose Marie Sullivan	03-07-1914
360	Sr. Edwina Carroll	03-07-1914
361	Sr. Gertrude Marie Hayes	03-07-1914
362	Sr. Marjorie McGonagle	03-07-1914
363	Sr. Kevin Quinn	03-07-1914
364	Sr. Eugenia Phelan	08-04-1914
365	Sr. Clarassina McCarthy	08-04-1914
366	Sr. Ernestine Wathen	08-04-1914
367	Sr. Paschal Mullaney	08-04-1914
368	Sr. Cleophas Sheehy	08-04-1914
369	Sr. Antoninus Hynes	03-07-1915
370	Sr. Martha Nally	03-07-1915
371	Sr. Amata Boyle	03-07-1915
372	Sr. Anita Hughes	03-07-1915

373	Sr. Beatrice Clarke	03-07-1915
374	Sr. Benignus McCarthy	03-07-1915
375	Sr. Leonarda Kline	03-07-1915
376	Sr. Corona Houghnon	03-07-1915
377	Sr. Evaristus Klein	03-07-1915
378	Sr. Claudia Wizmann	03-07-1915
379	Sr. Dorothea Butler	03-07-1915
380	Sr. Euphemia McCarthy	03-07-1915
381	Sr. Lutegarde Meehan	03-07-1915
382	Sr. Agnes Marie Smith	03-07-1915
383	Sr. Modesta Hanley	03-07-1915
384	Sr. Pelagia Brannigan	03-07-1915
385	Sr. Simplicia Barron	03-07-1915
386	Sr. Mario Caplinger	03-07-1915
387	Sr. Redempta Donovan	08-04-1915
388	Sr. Inviolata Christian	08-04-1915
389	Sr. Marie Leonard	08-04-1915
390	Sr. Joseph Marie Walsh	08-04-1915
391	Sr. M. Anthony Griffin	08-04-1915
392	Sr. Virginia Marie Davis	08-04-1915
393	Sr. Catherine Frances Galvin	08-04-1915
394	Sr. Frances Rosemary Bowen (Antoinette)	08-04-1915
395	Sr. Leon Ripley	08-04-1915
396	Sr. Ann Elizabeth LaForet (Mannes)	08-04-1915
397	Sr. Inez Callahan	08-04-1915
398	Sr. Helen Marie Maloney	08-04-1915
399	Sr. Stanislaus O'Brien	03-07-1916
400	Sr. Hilda Wright	03-07-1916
401	Sr. DePaul Slattery	03-07-1916
402	Sr. Charlesetta Phelan	03-07-1916
403	Sr. Adele Kirby	03-07-1916
404	Sr. Cyril Anderson	03-07-1916
405	Sr. Athanasius Fitzgerald	03-07-1916
406	Sr. M. Paul Philbin	03-07-1916
407	Sr. Clotilda Ennen	03-07-1916
408	Sr. Benedict Heffernan	03-07-1916
409	Sr. Norberta Jenks	08-04-1916
410	Sr. Loyola Blake	08-04-1916

411	Sr. Amelia Gould	08-04-1916
412	Sr. Alicia Marie McGinley	08-04-1916
413	Sr. Walburga Durkin	08-04-1916
414	Sr. Josita Mylott	08-04-1916
415	Sr. Evelyn Kirby	08-04-1916
416	Sr. Adelaide Jamrog	08-04-1916
417	Sr. Generosa Healy	08-04-1916
418	Sr. Bernardo Goff	08-26-1916
419	Sr. Perpetua Newton	03-07-1917
420	Sr. Hyacintha McFarland	03-07-1917
421	Sr. Celestine Wathen	03-07-1917
422	Sr. Jane Frances Clancy	03-07-1917
423	Sr. Paula Ruth	03-07-1917
424	Sr. M. Andrew Sheehan	03-07-1917
425	Sr. Dominic Marie Langley	03-07-1917
426	Sr. Prudentia Foster	03-07-1917
427	Sr. M. Patrick Coleman	03-07-1917
428	Sr. M. Dennis Lynch	03-07-1917
429	Sr. M. Robert Shea	03-07-1917
430	Sr. Dolorita Tansey	03-07-1917
431	Sr. Theophelia Punch	03-07-1917
432	Sr. Eleanor Rooney	03-07-1917
433	Sr. Dorothy Nuttall	03-07-1917
434	Sr. M. Eugene Sheehan	03-07-1917
435	Sr. Anne Marie Doyle	03-07-1917
436	Sr. Mary Martin Langan	08-04-1917
437	Sr. M. Esther McGough	08-04-1917
438	Sr. M. David Hannon	08-04-1917
439	Sr. Sylvia Logan	08-04-1917
440	Sr. Aurelia Cadigan	08-04-1917
441	Sr. Cletus Guynan	08-04-1917
442	Sr. Angeline Cahill	08-04-1917
443	Sr. Emeliana Morrissey	08-04-1917
444	Sr. Juliana Crowley	08-04-1917
445	Sr. Dolorosa Martin	08-04-1917
446	Sr. Augusta Davis	08-04-1917
447	Sr. Robert Hugh Barry	08-04-1917
448	Sr. Margaret Elizabeth Walsh	08-04-1917

449	Sr. M. Emma Reardon	08-04-1917
450	Sr. M. Therese Cecil	03-07-1918
451	Sr. Irenaeus Plante	03-07-1918
452	Sr. Carolyn Coyne	03-07-1918
453	Sr. Clarita Griffin	03-07-1918
454	Sr. Euphrasia O'Rourke	03-07-1918
455	Sr. M. Bertha Morrisroe	03-07-1918
456	Sr. Agnes Mary Green (Pancratia)	03-07-1918
457	Sr. Gerald Johnson	03-07-1918
458	Sr. M. Timothy Regan	03-07-1918
459	Sr. Mary Victor MacDonald	03-07-1918
460	Sr. Rose of Lima Lohmeier	03-07-1918
461	Sr. Celine Clements	03-07-1918
462	Sr. Mary Julia Polin	03-07-1918
463	Sr. Lucille McCabe	03-07-1918
464	Sr. Laetitia Keene	08-05-1918
465	Sr. M. Ruth Deloury	08-05-1918
466	Sr. Anastasia Riney	08-05-1918
467	Sr. M. Carmel Mara	08-05-1918
468	Sr. ReginaIda Jacobson	08-05-1918
469	Sr. Rita Coleman	08-05-1918
470	Sr. Richarda Grant	08-05-1918
471	Sr. Aquina Hynes	09-09-1918
472	Sr. M. Julius Waranko	01-03-1919
473	Sr. Paracleta Hastings	03-08-1919
474	Sr. Benvenuta Rooney	03-08-1919
475	Sr. Hilary Quinn	03-08-1919
476	Sr. Mary Mark Kelley	03-08-1919
477	Sr. Egedia Nevins	03-08-1919
478	Sr. Albertina Huston	03-08-1919
479	Sr. Thomas Aquinas Cahill	03-19-1919
480	Sr. M. Innocent Hayden	05-01-1919
481	Sr. Ambrosia Roberts	05-01-1919
482	Sr. Martina Blake	05-01-1919
483	Sr. Eucharia Heaver	08-05-1919
484	Sr. Vincent dePaul McDonald	08-05-1919
485	Sr. M. Alice Mooney	08-05-1919
486	Sr. Agatha Dutton	08-05-1919

487	Sr. Aimo Wiszmann	08-05-1919
488	Sr. Ignatia Filbin	08-05-1919
489	Sr. Prisca Naughton	08-05-1919
490	Sr. Jane of Aza Towey	03-07-1920
491	Sr. Mary Rachel Cooney	03-07-1920
492	Sr. Eileen Driscoll	03-07-1920
493	Sr. Gabriel Clarke	03-07-1920
494	Sr. Francis Dominic Kline	03-07-1920
495	Sr. Aurea Johnson	03-07-1920
496	Sr. Romuald Hickey	03-07-1920
497	Sr. Ethelreda Sullivan	03-07-1920
498	Sr. Theodore Kline	03-07-1920
499	Sr. DeLourdes Hyde	03-07-1920
500	Sr. Gilberta Johnson	03-07-1920
501	Sr. Bernardine Sullivan	03-07-1920
502	Sr. Urbanita Kelley	03-07-1920
503	Sr. M. Maurice Nebel	08-04-1920
504	Sr. Antonine Hanrahan	08-04-1920
505	Sr. Valeria Mara	08-04-1920
506	Sr. Gonsalva O'Connor	08-04-1920
507	Sr. Ann O'Brien (Eustace)	08-04-1920
508	Sr. M. Leonard McSorley	08-04-1920
509	Sr. Vincent Ferrer Salmon	08-04-1920
510	Sr. Romana Conway	08-04-1920
511	Sr. M. Alma Donovan	08-04-1920
512	Sr. Henrica Walsh	08-04-1920
513	Sr. Nicolina Dugas	08-04-1920
514	Sr. M. Emily Hennessey	03-07-1921
515	Sr. M. Priscilla Lyons	03-07-1921
516	Sr. Mary Clare Benjamin	03-07-1921
517	Sr. John Dominic Ferguson	03-07-1921
518	Sr. Bertranda McAleer	03-07-1921
519	Sr. Hilda McMahon	03-07-1921
520	Sr. Mary Daniel Lynch	03-07-1921
521	Sr. M. Cosma Flanagan	03-07-1921
522	Sr. Gabriella Sullivan	03-07-1921
523	Sr. Osanna McHugh	03-07-1921
524	Sr. Angelita Hewitt	03-07-1921

525	Sr. Francelle Dillon	03-07-1921
526	Sr. Felix Noon	03-07-1921
527	Sr. Isidore Donovan	03-07-1921
528	Sr. Patrice Hogan	03-07-1921
529	Sr. M. Aquin Richards	03-07-1921
530	Sr. Magdalena Thompson	03-07-1921
531	Sr. Geraldine Henry	03-07-1921
532	Sr. Catherine Dominic Burns	03-07-1921
533	Sr. Francis Gertrude Thompson	08-05-1921
534	Sr. M. Pierre Hays	01-01-1922
535	Sr. Lidwina McLean	03-07-1922
536	Sr. M. Joan Kerens	03-07-1922
537	Sr. Annette Barry	03-07-1922
538	Sr. Ernestine Sullivan	03-07-1922
539	Sr. M. Nicholas Adrian	03-07-1922
540	Sr. Lucina MacDonald	03-07-1922
541	Sr. Marianna Dake	03-07-1922
542	Sr. M. Vincent Trant	03-07-1922
543	Sr. M. Justin Foley	03-07-1922
544	Sr. M. Luke Keenan	08-04-1922
545	Sr. Charlesetta Ryan	08-04-1922
546	Sr. Victoria Hesterworth	08-04-1922
547	Sr. Jamesetta Kelly	08-04-1922
548	Sr. Genevieve DesJardins	08-04-1922
549	Sr. M. Oliver Vanderstock	08-04-1922
550	Sr. Amy McNamara	03-07-1923
551	Sr. Brendan Kelleher	03-07-1923
552	Sr. DeRicci Crosby	03-07-1923
553	Sr. Florentia Coughlan	03-07-1923
554	Sr. Rosaria Hogan	03-07-1923
555	Sr. Flavia Althaus	03-07-1923
556	Sr. Humbert Brannigan	08-04-1923
557	Sr. Alvarez Osborne	08-04-1923
558	Sr. Annunciata Keenan	08-04-1923
559	Sr. M. Urban Lyons	08-04-1923
560	Sr. Petronilla Filbin	08-04-1923
561	Sr. Zita Schatzl	01-11-1924
562	Sr. Odilia Clifford	01-11-1924

563	Sr. Francis Joseph Kilroy	03-07-1924
564	Sr. Rose Marie Martin	03-07-1924
565	Sr. Huberta Cronin	03-07-1924
566	Sr. Maureen Nuttall	03-07-1924
567	Sr. Athanasia Laux	03-07-1924
568	Sr. Austina Harrahill	03-07-1924
569	Sr. Ann Shields	03-07-1924
570	Sr. Georgine Ladenburger	03-07-1924
571	Sr. Rosalia Woods	08-04-1924
572	Sr. Anacleta Hickey	08-04-1924
573	Sr. M. Arthur Connors	08-04-1924
574	Sr. Aquinella Callahan	08-04-1924
575	Sr. Jeanette Van Buren	08-04-1924
576	Sr. Edith Laux	09-08-1924
577	Sr. Cyprian O'Connor	09-08-1924
578	Sr. Blanche Weigel	03-07-1925
579	Sr. Gonzaga Noyes	03-07-1925
580	Sr. M. Benvin Hinton	03-07-1925
581	Sr. Macaria MacNeil	03-07-1925
582	Sr. Rosella Mattingly	03-07-1925
583	Sr. Celsa Nee	03-07-1925
584	Sr. Patricia Greeley	03-07-1925
585	Sr. M. Bertrand Gath	06-15-1925
586	Sr. Aloysius D'Arcy	06-15-1925
587	Sr. Veronica Ryan	06-15-1925
588	Sr. M. Fides Gough	08-04-1925
589	Sr. Althaire Lancaster	08-04-1925
590	Sr. M. Thomas Shelvey	08-04-1925
591	Sr. Diana Thompson	08-04-1925
592	Sr. Ethelreda Corley	09-08-1925
593	Sr. Florian Barry	09-08-1925
594	Sr. Marceline Lynch	09-08-1925
595	Sr. Eutropia Horan	09-08-1925
596	Sr. Mary Hugh Kankowsky	03-07-1926
597	Sr. Asuncion Ford	03-07-1926
598	Sr. Rose Agnes Bray	03-07-1926
599	Sr. Agnes Leo Costigan	03-07-1926
600	Sr. Adele Austin	03-07-1926

601	Sr. Thomasina Murray	03-07-1926
602	Sr. Virgilia Brady	03-07-1926
603	Sr. Florita Young	03-07-1926
604	Sr. James Suzanne (Mary Walter) Burke	08-04-1926
605	Sr. Angela Ford	08-04-1926
606	Sr. Maria Gratia Brady	08-04-1926
607	Sr. Agnes Teresa Gillan	08-04-1926
608	Sr. Gertrude Kelly	03-07-1927
609	Sr. M. Jeanne White	03-07-1927
610	Sr. Edwardo Weeks	03-07-1927
611	Sr. Maura Linehan	03-07-1927
612	Sr. Noreen Sullivan	03-07-1927
613	Sr. Mary Ralph Moran	03-07-1927
614	Sr. Rose Margaret Carpenter	03-07-1927
615	Sr. Teresita Trelegan	03-07-1927
616	Sr. Clementia Johnson	03-07-1927
617	Sr. Evangelista Murphy	03-07-1927
618	Sr. Marie Concepta Nolan	03-07-1927
619	Sr. Mary Claude Grant	03-07-1927
620	Sr. Marguerite Boland	03-07-1927
621	Sr. Frances Raphael Butler	03-07-1927
622	Sr. Rosalie Van Akeren	03-07-1927
623	Sr. Fredricka Horvath	08-04-1927
624	Sr. Rosemary Lafayette	08-04-1927
625	Sr. Catherine Joseph McHugh	08-04-1927
626	Sr. Leonilia Adamowski	08-04-1927
627	Sr. M. Cornelia Leahy	08-04-1927
628	Sr. Mary Grace Brogie	08-04-1927
629	Sr. Margarita Stidolph	08-04-1927
630	Sr. Pauletta Dolan	08-04-1927
631	Sr. Mary Ellen Fulton	03-07-1928
632	Sr. Gerald Vincent Burke	03-07-1928
633	Sr. Agnes Cecilia Walker	03-07-1928
634	Sr. Anna Louise Surette	03-07-1928
635	Sr. Joseph Patrick Carey	03-07-1928
636	Sr. Consolata Callender	03-07-1928
637	Sr. Tarcisius Crossan	08-04-1928
638	Sr. Margaret Thomasine Kennedy	08-04-1928

639	Sr. Marianella Barry	08-04-1928
640	Sr. Marita Wightman	08-04-1928
641	Sr. Catherine Linehan	08-04-1928
642	Sr. M. Charlotte Harrahill	08-04-1928
643	Sr. M. Anthony Hamlin	08-04-1928
644	Sr. Claire Adrian	03-07-1929
645	Sr. Rosalita McMahon	03-07-1929
646	Sr. Natalie Lafayette	03-07-1929
647	Sr. M. Lorenz McIntire	03-07-1929
648	Sr. Mary Jane Fitzgibbons	03-07-1929
649	Sr. Frances Claire Tuttle	03-07-1929
650	Sr. Rosita Colman	03-07-1929
651	Sr. M. Edna Curtis	03-07-1929
652	Sr. Carina O'Connor	03-07-1929
653	Sr. Lucinda Hays	03-07-1929
654	Sr. M. George Scales	03-07-1929
655	Sr. M. Corrine Hunt	03-07-1929
656	Sr. Rose Irma Doyle	03-07-1929
657	Sr. M. Judith Rose	03-07-1929
658	Sr. M. Alfred Murphy	03-07-1929
659	Sr. M. Ulicia O'Brien	03-07-1929
660	Sr. Olivia Schang	03-07-1929
661	Sr. Marian O'Donnell	03-07-1929
662	Sr. Alice Marie Glaser	08-04-1929
663	Sr. Agnes Regina Staud	08-04-1929
664	Sr. Brigeda Ruane	08-04-1929
665	Sr. Anna Blandford	08-04-1929
666	Sr. Engelbert Allewelt	10-08-1929
667	Sr. Esther Marie Moore	10-08-1929
668	Sr. Mary Suso Colgan	03-07-1930
669	Sr. Kathleen McGillicuddy	03-07-1930
670	Sr. Leonarda Yilk	03-07-1930
671	Sr. Michaela Marie Phillips	03-07-1930
672	Sr. M. Columba Casey	03-07-1930
673	Sr. John Joseph Hogan	03-07-1930
674	Sr. Francis Edward Sheehan	03-07-1930
675	Sr. M. Gilbert Adams	03-07-1930
676	Sr. Margaret Frances Murphy	03-07-1930

677	Sr. Mary Jude Walsh	03-07-1930
678	Sr. Francita McKernan	03-07-1930
679	Sr. Theona Walla	03-07-1930
680	Sr. Thomas Aloysius Spalding	03-07-1930
681	Sr. Thomas James Mullins	03-07-1930
682	Sr. Moneta Vanderstock	08-04-1930
683	Sr. Thaddeus Gillan	08-04-1930
684	Sr. Stella Maris Fleming (Louise)	08-04-1930
685	Sr. Mary Henry Woodford	03-07-1931
686	Sr. Mary Walsh (Thomas a Kempis)	03-07-1931
687	Sr. Elizabeth Marie Norton	03-07-1931
688	Sr. Albertus Magnus Garvey	03-07-1931
689	Sr. Mary Emmanuel Preshong	03-07-1931
690	Sr. Magdalen Hatton	03-07-1931
691	Sr. Mary Laura Halpin	03-07-1931
692	Sr. Jean Clare Heffner	03-07-1931
693	Sr. Rose Catherine Hennigan	08-04-1931
694	Sr. Mary Augustine Graninger	08-04-1931
695	Sr. Hugh Francis Carey	08-04-1931
696	Sr. Frances Anna Cronin	04-30-1932
697	Sr. Rose Vincent O'Brien	04-30-1932
698	Sr. Mary Felicitas Bassett	04-30-1932
699	Sr. M. Alacoque McGloin	04-30-1932
700	Sr. Sybillina Halloway	04-30-1932
701	Sr. Rose Rita Murray	04-30-1932
702	Sr. Emerita Curtis	04-30-1932
703	Sr. Lucia Parker	04-30-1932
704	Sr. Agnes Gertrude O'Neil	04-30-1932
705	Sr. Veracunda Pendergast	04-30-1932
706	Sr. Frances Angela Hennessey	04-30-1932
707	Sr. M. Elise Groves	04-30-1932
708	Sr. Clarissa Garrity	04-30-1932
709	Sr. Catherine Sullivan (Henrica)	04-30-1932
710	Sr. Estelle Kilbane	04-30-1932
711	Sr. Florentine Kelleher	08-15-1932
712	Sr. Annine Connearney	08-15-1932
713	Sr. Catherine Gertrude Halligan	08-15-1932
714	Sr. Francis Borgia Kenna	08-15-1932

715	Sr. Sophia Hennegan	08-15-1932
716	Sr. M. Joachim McDonald	04-30-1933
717	Sr. Stephanie Grant	04-30-1933
718	Sr. Celeste Souza	04-30-1933
719	Sr. Barbara Arthaud	04-30-1933
720	Sr. Antonia Prudenti	04-30-1933
721	Sr. Agnes Shields	04-30-1933
722	Sr. Amata McCleary	04-30-1933
723	Sr. Catherine Elizabeth Burke	04-30-1933
724	Sr. Matthias Adams	04-30-1933
725	Sr. Eloise Ballam	04-30-1933
726	Sr. Mary Keenan (Mary Assumpta)	04-30-1933
727	Sr. Consuela Wilhelm	04-30-1933
728	Sr. Catherine Cecilia D'Arcy	04-30-1933
729	Sr. Rose Imelda Rogan	04-30-1933
730	Sr. M. Lawrence Curran	04-30-1933
731	Sr. Muriel Campbell	04-30-1933
732	Sr. Benigna Bigott	04-30-1933
733	Sr. Felice Murphy	04-30-1933
734	Sr. Agnes Richarda Blinkhorn	04-30-1933
735	Sr. Venard Murray	08-15-1933
736	Sr. Mario Gooley	08-15-1933
737	Sr. Vincent de Paul Hutton	08-15-1933
738	Sr. M. Villana Sheeran	08-15-1933
739	Sr. Cyrilla Hayden	08-15-1933
740	Sr. Ernestine Choquette	08-15-1933
741	Sr. Joan Marie Madden	04-30-1934
742	Sr. Marie Michelle Lavin	04-30-1934
743	Sr. Vincentia Coyne	04-30-1934
744	Sr. Charlene Harvey	04-30-1934
745	Sr. Kathleen Mattingly (Ludovica)	04-30-1934
746	Sr. Mercedes Duffin	04-30-1934
747	Sr. Leo Marie Preher	04-30-1934
748	Sr. Agnella Brocklebank	04-30-1934
749	Sr. Jean Marie Callahan	04-30-1934
750	Sr. M. Frederick Malfy	04-30-1934
751	Sr. Rose Alice Murphy	04-30-1934
752	Sr. Anne Mary Tamme	04-30-1934

753	Sr. Agnes Clare Griffin	04-30-1934
754	Sr. M. Cecile Wilhelm	04-30-1934
755	Sr. Dorothy Agnes Haschke	04-30-1934
756	Sr. Laurene Yancovitz	04-30-1934
757	Sr. Julita Dorsey	08-15-1934
758	Sr. Francis Bertrand Glaser	08-15-1934
759	Sr. Claudine Hanlon	08-15-1934
760	Sr. Reginalda Jeffrey	08-15-1934
761	Sr. Rosaleen Pantenburg	08-15-1934
762	Sr. Evangela Trott	08-15-1934
763	Sr. Gertrude Marie Doherty	04-30-1935
764	Sr. Ann Joseph Cronin	04-30-1935
765	Sr. M. Freida Payne	04-30-1935
766	Sr. Adelaide Donovan	04-30-1935
767	Sr. Martha Jane Edelen	04-30-1935
768	Sr. M. Anselm Walsh	04-30-1935
769	Sr. Rebecca O'Brien	04-30-1935
770	Sr. Damian Carty	04-30-1935
771	Sr. Suzanne Callahan	04-30-1935
772	Sr. Irmina Cambron	04-30-1935
773	Sr. Geneva Kelley	04-30-1935
774	Sr. Jerome Collins	04-30-1935
775	Sr. Caroline Miller	04-30-1935
776	Sr. Corita Mahoney	04-30-1935
777	Sr. Benita Bevins	04-30-1935
778	Sr. Sheila Buckley	04-30-1935
779	Sr. Eunice Mader	04-30-1935
780	Sr. Leila Neumann	04-30-1935
781	Sr. Humilia Wagner	08-15-1935
782	Sr. M. Gervase Consilvio	08-15-1935
783	Sr. Mary Louise Helmann	08-15-1935
784	Sr. Sara Dickerson	08-15-1935
785	Sr. Gertrude Ann Stanford	04-30-1936
786	Sr. M. Aubert Parziale	04-30-1936
787	Sr. M. Gregoria Maguire	04-30-1936
788	Sr. Norberta Cheetham	04-30-1936
789	Sr. M. Ferrer Fitzgerald	04-30-1936
790	Sr. Anna Clare Chuse	04-30-1936

791	Sr. Mary Joseph Sheahan	04-30-1936
792	Sr. Mary John Lamken	04-30-1936
793	Sr. James Vincent Mattingly	04-30-1936
794	Sr. M. Cyril Guthrie	04-30-1936
795	Sr. M. Bertille Maurer	04-30-1936
796	Sr. Eleanor McGonagle (Mary Austin)	04-30-1936
797	Sr. M. Vivian Murphy	04-30-1936
798	Sr. Naomi Kubat	08-15-1936
799	Sr. Clarisse Meehan	08-15-1936
800	Sr. Margaret Louise Sullivan	08-15-1936
801	Sr. Mary Ellen McTeague	04-30-1937
802	Sr. Angelica Lehr	04-30-1937
803	Sr. Loretta McManaman (M. Ivo)	04-30-1937
804	Sr. Helen Schmeits (Ceslaus)	04-30-1937
805	Sr. Honora Hooper	04-30-1937
806	Sr. Mary Alice Connelly	04-30-1937
807	Sr. M. Alphonsa Clancy	04-30-1937
808	Sr. Mary Margaret Kelly	04-30-1937
809	Sr. M. Augusta Johnson	04-30-1937
810	Sr. M. Josetta Barnard	04-30-1937
811	Sr. Verona Weidig	04-30-1937
812	Sr. Mary Eva Kimbel	04-30-1937
813	Sr. Marion McCormick (Paulina)	04-30-1937
814	Sr. Aguinette Lefort	04-30-1937
815	Sr. M. Columba Casey	04-30-1937
816	Sr. Adeline Trautwein	04-30-1937
817	Sr. Paschala Noonan	04-30-1937
818	Sr. Isadore Barbarosa	04-30-1937
819	Sr. Rosellen Davey	08-15-1937
820	Sr. Theresa Fitzpatrick (Mary Roger)	08-15-1937
821	Sr. M. Dominic Stine	08-15-1937
822	Sr. M. Raphael Geyger	08-15-1937
823	Sr. Christine Burton	04-30-1938
824	Sr. Rose Angela Burke	04-30-1938
825	Sr. Magdalena Leonard	04-30-1938
826	Sr. Giovanni Reed	04-30-1938
827	Sr. Pauline Reynolds	04-30-1938
828	Sr. Ann Rita Sullivan	04-30-1938

829	Sr. Thomas Aquinas Ross	04-30-1938
830	Sr. M. Burcharda Brinkley	04-30-1938
831	Sr. M. Brendan Cox	04-30-1938
832	Sr. Reparata Grey	04-30-1938
833	Sr. Agnes Conway	04-30-1938
834	Sr. Bernetta Kwasiborski	04-30-1938
835	Sr. M. Cajetan Winters	04-30-1938
836	Sr. Francine Eaton	08-15-1938
837	Sr. Sydney Joseph Carey	08-15-1938
838	Sr. Mary Peter LaJoie	04-30-1939
839	Sr. Elizabeth Ann Collins	04-30-1939
840	Sr. Ann Raymond Boone	04-30-1939
841	Sr. Agnes Walsh	04-30-1939
842	Sr. Patricia Marie Cunningham	04-30-1939
843	Sr. Thomasine Dolan	04-30-1939
844	Sr. M. Clara Edelen	04-30-1939
845	Sr. Patricia Ann Terry	04-30-1939
846	Sr. Anastasia Dillon	08-15-1939
847	Sr. Eleanor Ryle	08-15-1940
848	Sr. Virginia Roche	08-15-1940
849	Sr. M. Denise Glynn	08-15-1940
850	Sr. Virginia Thomas Hamilton	08-15-1940
851	Sr. Miriam Joseph Zlotow	08-15-1940
852	Sr. Ellen Cecile Roach	08-15-1940
853	Sr. Margaret Vincent	08-15-1940
854	Sr. Mary Rogan	08-15-1940
855	Sr. Marie Therese Martin	08-15-1941
856	Sr. Maurine Walsh	08-15-1941
857	Sr. Claire Walker	08-15-1941
858	Sr. Rosa Maria Mattingly	08-15-1941
859	Sr. Ann Damian Whittier	08-15-1941
860	Sr. Mary Joseph Fosskuhl	08-15-1941
861	Sr. Maria Fitzpatrick	08-15-1941
862	Sr. Olivia Lohmoeller	08-15-1942
863	Sr. Robertina Fitzpatrick	08-15-1942
864	Sr. Vincent Marie Quinn	08-15-1942
865	Sr. Ellen Joseph Riley	08-15-1942
866	Sr. Elena McNeil	08-15-1942

867	Sr. Regina Elizabeth Shelley	08-15-1942
868	Sr. Elizabeth Glynn	08-15-1942
869	Sr. Ellen Frances Hopkins	08-15-1942
870	Sr. Rita Agnes Clifford	08-15-1942
871	Sr. Catherine Roby	08-15-1942
872	Sr. Madeleine Louise McCune	08-15-1942
873	Sr. Leonita Blandford	08-15-1942
874	Sr. Mary Regis Cullen	08-15-1942
875	Sr. Amelia del Carmen Rivera	08-15-1942
876	Sr. M. Gemma McMahon	08-15-1943
877	Sr. Ellen Madeline Murphy	08-15-1943
878	Sr. Mary Martin McGreal	08-15-1943
879	Sr. Patricius Henderson	08-15-1943
880	Sr. Teresa Wolfe	08-15-1943
881	Sr. Mildred Leary	08-15-1943
882	Sr. Claretta Heffner	08-15-1943
883	Sr. Adrian Marie Hofstetter	08-15-1943
884	Sr. Dorothy Ann Cowan	12-15-1943
885	Sr. Laurita Diekemper	08-15-1944
886	Sr. Teresa Clare Condon	08-15-1944
887	Sr. Margaret Ann Brady	08-15-1944
888	Sr. Charlita Clayton	08-15-1944
889	Sr. Assumpta Marie Doherty	08-15-1944
890	Sr. Mildred Joseph Carroll	08-15-1944
891	Sr. Evelyn Catherine Barrett	08-15-1944
892	Sr. Catharine Marie Harris	08-15-1944
893	Sr. Joseph Edward Marine	08-15-1944
894	Sr. Celeste Marie Heppe	12-15-1944
895	Sr. Pauletta Kelly	08-15-1945
896	Sr. Terence McTighe	08-15-1945
897	Sr. Veronica Mary Sullivan	08-15-1945
898	Sr. Geralda Fitzpatrick	08-15-1945
899	Sr. M. Francis Callahan	08-15-1945
900	Sr. Dorothy Smith	08-15-1945
901	Sr. Frances Marie Byrne	08-15-1945
902	Sr. M. Imelda Murrin	08-15-1945
903	Sr. Catharina Kernan	08-15-1945
904	Sr. M. Loyola Campbell	08-15-1945

905	Sr. Angelica Netherland	08-15-1945
906	Sr. Elaine Marie Carey	08-15-1945
907	Sr. Mary Rose Meade	08-15-1945
908	Sr. Mary Michael Leonard	08-15-1945
909	Sr. Theresina Greenwell	08-15-1945
910	Sr. Mary Esther Owens	03-07-1946
911	Sr. Dominica Meehan	03-07-1946
912	Sr. Marina Gibbons	03-07-1946
913	Sr. Margaret Marie Hofstetter	04-30-1946
914	Sr. Eileen Marie Byrne	04-30-1946
915	Sr. Ann Thomas Hines	08-15-1946
916	Sr. M. Antonia Gallagher	08-15-1946
917	Sr. M. Rita Beausoleil	08-15-1946
918	Sr. Lola Brown (Mary Bede)	08-15-1946
919	Sr. Clare Travelstead (Mary Ransom)	08-15-1946
920	Sr. Reparata Coates	08-15-1946
921	Sr. Jean Vianney Norris	08-15-1946
922	Sr. Mary Anne Guthrie	08-15-1946
923	Sr. Scholastica Gilbride	08-15-1946
924	Sr. Catherine Lawrence Jones	03-07-1947
925	Sr. Rita Eileen Quinlan	03-07-1947
926	Sr. Marion O'Keefe	03-07-1947
927	Sr. M. Michaeleen Whalen	03-07-1947
928	Sr. Mary Agnes Sullivan	03-07-1947
929	Sr. M. Trinita McIsaac	03-07-1947
930	Sr. Anne Regis Hartnett	03-07-1947
931	Sr. Thomas Bridget Whelan	03-07-1947
932	Sr. Richard Marie Powers	03-07-1947
933	Sr. Martha Ann Corbett	03-07-1947
934	Sr. Ann Frederick Leonard	03-07-1947
935	Sr. Charles Francis McOsker	04-30-1947
936	Sr. Rose Frances McOsker	04-30-1947
937	Sr. James Ann Ross	08-15-1947
938	Sr. Ann Miriam Hickey	08-15-1947
939	Sr. Ann Dolores Lynch	08-15-1947
940	Sr. M. Deirdre Cotter	08-15-1947
941	Sr. Georgine Marie Crowley	08-15-1947
942	Sr. Agnesine Howell	08-15-1947

943	Sr. Maria del Rey Mangan	08-15-1947
944	Sr. Ann Bell (Ann Austin)	08-15-1947
945	Sr. Mildred Kelly	08-15-1947
946	Sr. Madonna Root	08-15-1947
947	Sr. M. Laura Feltman	08-15-1947
948	Sr. Marie Celine Day	03-07-1948
949	Sr. Mary Faith O'Malley	03-07-1948
950	Sr. Rosaire Curran	03-07-1948
951	Sr. Josepha Buckley	03-07-1948
952	Sr. Bernadette Marie Lynch	03-07-1948
953	Sr. Rose Ann Hanley	03-07-1948
954	Sr. Eucharia Geiger	03-07-1948
955	Sr. Verita Pendleton	03-07-1948
956	Sr. Mary Pius Worland	03-07-1948
957	Sr. Marilyn Clifford (Thomas Mary)	03-07-1948
958	Sr. Elizabeth Miles (Martin de Porres)	03-07-1948
959	Sr. Leah Morrill	03-07-1948
960	Sr. Catherine Thomas Perkins	03-07-1948
961	Sr. M. Cabrini DeBruler	03-07-1948
962	Sr. Deborah Flynn	08-15-1948
963	Sr. Marianela O'Brien	08-15-1948
964	Sr. Joan Miriam Glaser	08-15-1948
965	Sr. Ursula Marie Kerrissey	08-15-1948
966	Sr. Rosemary Kirsten (Joseph Mary)	08-15-1948
967	Sr. Rose Catharine Jones	08-15-1948
968	Sr. Louise Quinlan (Fabian)	08-15-1948
969	Sr. Therese Vincent (Philomena)	08-15-1948
970	Sr. Ignatius Marie Clifford	03-07-1949
971	Sr. Dorothy Briggs (Louis Mary)	03-07-1949
972	Sr. Anne Robert Gray	03-07-1949
973	Sr. Anita Marie Biondini	03-07-1949
974	Sr. Sheila Marie Pendergast	03-07-1949
975	Sr. Rose Speckner (Rose Dominic)	03-07-1949
976	Sr. Theresa McManus (M. Siena)	03-07-1949
977	Sr. Ann Catherine Boone	03-07-1949
978	Sr. Rose Anthony Heitzman	08-15-1949
979	Sr. Gertrude Veronica Zablotny	08-15-1949
980	Sr. Mary Michael Greaber	08-15-1949

981	Sr. Patricia Green (Francis Grace)	08-15-1949
982	Sr. Laetitia Anne Campbell	08-15-1949
983	Sr. John Marie Austin	08-15-1949
984	Sr. Helen Hogan (Maria Thomas)	08-15-1949
985	Sr. Louise Ann Crowley	08-15-1949
986	Sr. Virginia Mary Sammett (Alicene)	08-15-1949
987	Sr. Angela Marie Wickham	08-15-1949
988	Sr. Ruth Marie Smith	03-07-1950
989	Sr. Mary Bennet Neault	03-07-1950
990	Sr. Mary Brigid Gregory	03-07-1950
991	Sr. Marie Dominic Knowles	03-07-1950
992	Sr. Veronica Colohan (Thomas Catherine)	03-07-1950
993	Sr. Regina Marie Bruner	03-07-1950
994	Sr. Angela Marie Fitzgerald	03-07-1950
995	Sr. Ann Michael Burke	03-07-1950
996	Sr. Mary Elizabeth Quinan	03-07-1950
997	Sr. Marie Petra Cummings	03-07-1950
998	Sr. Elaine DesRosiers (Gregory Anne)	03-07-1950
999	Sr. Devota Maria Hanrahan	03-07-1950
1000	Sr. Patricia Reed (Rose Patrice)	03-07-1950
1001	Sr. Mary Christine Shea	03-07-1950
1002	Sr. Ann Dominic Roach	08-15-1950
1003	Sr. Mary Jacinta Wimsatt	08-15-1950
1004	Sr. Clare Marie Bell	08-15-1950
1005	Sr. James Marie O'Rourke	08-15-1950
1006	Sr. Margaret Regina Naughton	08-15-1950
1007	Sr. Joann Mascari (Agnes Joseph)	08-15-1950
1008	Sr. James Catharine Boyle	08-15-1950
1009	Sr. Mary Rosanna Hughes	08-15-1950
1010	Sr. Mary Carla Golom	08-15-1950
1011	Sr. Rita Maureen Gary	10-03-1950
1012	Sr. Dorothy Marie Sageser	10-03-1950
1013	Sr. Margaret Rose Curry	10-03-1950
1014	Sr. Georgeanne Sutherland (George Ann)	08-15-1951
1015	Sr. Frances Eda Coyle	08-15-1951
1016	Sr. Rosemary Carraher (Miriam Patricia)	08-15-1951
1017	Sr. Joseph Margaret O'Brien	08-15-1951
1018	Sr. Geraldine Flattery (Cor Marie)	08-15-1951

1019	Sr. Frances Catharine Lehan	08-15-1951
1020	Sr. Jean Delaney (John Marion)	08-15-1951
1021	Sr. Eileen Hannon (Ella Mark)	08-15-1951
1022	Sr. Margaret Philip Shaw	08-15-1951
1023	Sr. James Patrick Ryan	08-15-1951
1024	Sr. Patricia Kilbane (Ellen Patrick)	08-15-1951
1025	Sr. Thomasella Sheehey	08-15-1951
1026	Sr. Mary Lou Rhode (Ann Jeremy)	08-15-1951
1027	Sr. Helen Bernadette Stevens	08-15-1951
1028	Sr. Patrina MacDonnell	08-15-1951
1029	Sr. Thomas Marie Shelley	02-02-1952
1030	Sr. Mary Bernadette Deeney	02-02-1952
1031	Sr. Matthew Marie Beirne	02-02-1952
1032	Sr. Catharine Imelda Corr	02-02-1952
1033	Sr. Catharine Martin Smith	08-15-1952
1034	Sr. Thomas Patrick Dooley	08-15-1952
1035	Sr. Barbara Ann Rioux	08-15-1952
1036	Sr. Collette Bauer (Colette Marie)	08-15-1952
1037	Sr. Margaret Thomas Casey	08-15-1952
1038	Sr. Ruth Connors (Edward Joseph)	08-15-1952
1039	Sr. Therese Ann Wass	08-15-1952
1040	Sr. Columcille Foy	08-15-1952
1041	Sr. Ann Davette Moran	08-15-1952
1042	Sr. Joan Michael McVeigh	08-15-1952
1043	Sr. Eleanor Fabrizi (George Michael)	08-15-1952
1044	Sr. Grace Marie Pettepit	08-15-1952
1045	Sr. Rita Carr (Margaret Rita)	08-15-1952
1046	Sr. Mary Karen Laville	08-15-1952
1047	Sr. Lois Pineau (Rita Clare)	08-15-1952
1048	Sr. Mary Trinette Nolan	08-15-1952
1049	Sr. Mary Helen Thieneman (Martha Joseph)	08-15-1952
1050	Sr. John Michael Bahret	08-15-1952
1051	Sr. Patricia Hennessey (John Patrice)	08-15-1952
1052	Sr. Joseph Leo Pietrowski	08-15-1952
1053	Sr. Catherine Denise Doherty	08-15-1952
1054	Sr. Mary Otho Ballard	08-15-1952
1055	Sr. Thomas Joseph Nacy	02-02-1953
1056	Sr. Cornelia Marie Mahoney	02-02-1953

1057	Sr. Marjorie Edward Cummings	08-15-1953
1058	Sr. Collette Therese Higgins	08-15-1953
1059	Sr. Catharine Louise Harrington	08-15-1953
1060	Sr. Anne Marie Guthrie	08-15-1953
1061	Sr. Michelle Marie Hohlfeld	08-15-1953
1062	Sr. Dorothy Thomas Leahy	08-15-1953
1063	Sr. Ann Christine Ryan	08-15-1953
1064	Sr. Cecilia Marie Clinton	08-15-1953
1065	Sr. Michael Patrice Hellman	08-15-1953
1066	Sr. Thomas Francis Hartnett	08-15-1953
1067	Sr. Michael Brigid Driscoll	08-15-1953
1068	Sr. Mariona Ellard	08-15-1953
1069	Sr. Rose Leo Borgatti	08-15-1953
1070	Sr. Joan Marie Hill	02-02-1954
1071	Sr. Margaret William Buchanan	02-02-1954
1072	Sr. Maria Theresa Zayas	02-02-1954
1073	Sr. Mary Agnes Wilson	08-15-1954
1074	Sr. Alverda Bonifas (Alphonsine)	08-15-1954
1075	Sr. Nancy Rioux (Roberta Marie)	08-15-1954
1076	Sr. Helen Ann Marshall	08-15-1954
1077	Sr. Lorraine Ryan (John Mary)	08-15-1954
1078	Sr. Margaret Ruth Wimsatt	08-15-1954
1079	Sr. Joanne Gill (Michael Edward)	08-15-1954
1080	Sr. Mary Della Quinn (Clement Marie)	08-15-1954
1081	Sr. Eleanor Tierney (Richard Therese)	08-15-1954
1082	Sr. Jean Ann Goering	08-15-1954
1083	Sr. Rose Joseph Carroll	02-02-1955
1084	Sr. Joan Marie Dropski (David Marie)	02-02-1955
1085	Sr. Marilyn Callahan (Helen Joseph)	02-02-1955
1086	Sr. Louise Morris (Rose Nicholas)	02-02-1955
1087	Sr. Marie Francesca Cameron	02-02-1955
1088	Sr. Laurette Rivard (Yvonne Marie)	08-15-1955
1089	Sr. James Grace Richmond	08-15-1955
1090	Sr. Martha McNulty (Cecile Marie)	08-15-1955
1091	Sr. Joan Monica McGuire	08-15-1955
1092	Sr. William Mary Forster	08-15-1955
1093	Sr. Ruth Anne Rezek	08-15-1955
1094	Sr. Therese Mary Flynn	08-15-1955

1095	Sr. Grace Simms	08-15-1955
1096	Sr. Marjorie Quinlan (John Margaret)	08-15-1955
1097	Sr. Helen Cahill (Anne Margaret)	08-15-1955
1098	Sr. Jean Therese Grehan	08-15-1955
1099	Sr. Frederic Marie Simpson	08-15-1955
1100	Sr. Barbara Gianino (Dominic Mary)	08-15-1955
1101	Sr. Ann Daylor (Rose Cecile)	08-15-1955
1102	Sr. Lois Laronde (Therese Albert)	08-15-1955
1103	Sr. Marie de Montfort Geoghegan	08-15-1955
1104	Sr. Mary Leo Liston	08-15-1955
1105	Sr. Rita Imelda Sullivan	08-15-1955
1106	Sr. Patricia Rae McNamara (Marianela)	08-15-1955
1107	Sr. Joan Francis DeVriendt	08-15-1955
1108	Sr. Mary Cecilia Gauthier	08-15-1955
1109	Sr. Mary Laura Smith	04-03-1956
1110	Sr. Marion Jude Johnson	08-15-1956
1111	Sr. Jane Mattingly (Jane Agnes)	08-15-1956
1112	Sr. Walter Marie Henshaw	08-15-1956
1113	Sr. Mary Bernardine DeArio	08-15-1956
1114	Sr. Christine McManus (Ellen Peter)	08-15-1956
1115	Sr. Ruth Michael O'Toole	08-15-1956
1116	Sr. Sue Keene (Catherine James)	08-15-1956
1117	Sr. Joseph Marion Fredericks	08-15-1956
1118	Sr. Marjorie White	08-15-1956
1119	Sr. Margaret Louis Trudell	08-15-1956
1120	Sr. Patricia Kennedy (Catherine Edward)	08-15-1956
1121	Sr. Regina McCarthy (Edward Mary)	08-15-1956
1122	Sr. Mary Polycarp Hagan	08-15-1956
1123	Sr. Virginia Smith (Anne Francis)	08-15-1956
1124	Sr. Marie Jeanne Surette (Therese Martin)	08-15-1956
1125	Sr. Clair Mahan (James Rita)	08-15-1956
1126	Sr. Thomas Ann Ford	02-02-1957
1127	Sr. Bernadine Marie Egleston	02-02-1957
1128	Sr. Marie Francis Frank	08-15-1957
1129	Sr. Joseph Clement Hurley	08-15-1957
1130	Sr. Mary Carmel Gerrior (Melmarie)	08-15-1957
1131	Sr. Kathleen Corrigan (Edmund Marie)	08-15-1957
1132	Sr. Martin Damien Miguelon	08-15-1957

1133	Sr. Mary Jude Waters	08-15-1957
1134	Sr. Catherine Mahady (Mary Killian)	08-15-1957
1135	Sr. Rosemary McLoughlin (Mary Elaine)	08-15-1957
1136	Sr. Mary Regina Ready	08-15-1957
1137	Sr. Marie Cleary (Bernard Marie)	08-15-1957
1138	Sr. Appoline Simard	08-15-1957
1139	Sr. Lois Ann Pfiester	08-15-1957
1140	Sr. Corinne Caulfield	08-15-1957
1141	Sr. Charlene Vogel (Charles Ann)	08-15-1957
1142	Sr. Marie Elizabeth Chambers	08-15-1957
1143	Sr. Ann Bernardine Shaw	08-15-1957
1144	Sr. Joan Dunning (Anne Therese)	08-15-1957
1145	Sr. Marilyn Masura	08-15-1957
1146	Sr. M. Joanna Costello	08-15-1957
1147	Sr. M. Alan Fagan	08-15-1957
1148	Sr. Lillian Crowley (Ellen Daniel)	08-15-1957
1149	Sr. Catherine Philip Maher	08-15-1957
1150	Sr. Jo Ann McMaster (Anthony Marie)	08-15-1957
1151	Sr. Ann Dolores Shea	08-15-1957
1152	Sr. Marie Seamann (Joan William)	08-15-1957
1153	Sr. Margaret Therese Collins	08-15-1957
1154	Sr. Julie Marie Amicangelo	08-15-1957
1155	Sr. Mary Carmelita Falcon	08-15-1957
1156	Sr. Joann Luttrell (Jane Frederic)	08-15-1957
1157	Sr. Marilyn Pierson (Michael Marie)	02-02-1958
1158	Sr. Mary Ann Budka (Mary Helena)	02-02-1958
1159	Sr. Eileen Linehan (Maurice Marie)	08-15-1958
1160	Sr. Mary Beverly Cluff	08-15-1958
1161	Sr. Mary Richard Stubbing	08-15-1958
1162	Sr. Paula Marie Donahue	08-15-1958
1163	Sr. Nancy Ring (Mary Lyda)	08-15-1958
1164	Sr. Mary Costello (Mary Matthew)	08-15-1958
1165	Sr. Mary Clement McLaughlin	08-15-1958
1166	Sr. Elinor Greenhalgh (John Ellen)	08-15-1958
1167	Sr. Margaret Mahoney	08-15-1958
1168	Sr. Patricia Kelliher (Mary Thomas)	08-15-1958
1169	Sr. Mary Louis Shepard	08-15-1958
1170	Sr. Cathleen Condon	08-15-1958

1171	Sr. Odelia Seidel	08-15-1958
1172	Sr. Mary David Nadolski	02-02-1959
1173	Sr. Catherine Gallagher (Maria Ancilla)	08-15-1959
1174	Sr. Eleanor Shanahan (Mary Liam)	08-15-1959
1175	Sr. Eileen Maura Hourihan	08-15-1959
1176	Sr. John Louise Wall	08-15-1959
1177	Sr. Mary Ursula Doherty	08-15-1959
1178	Sr. Marilyn Mangan (Mary Mark)	08-15-1959
1179	Sr. Helen McCarthy (Kevin Marie)	08-15-1959
1180	Sr. Ruth Augustine Rassenfoss	08-15-1959
1181	Sr. Doris Huber (Mary Demetria)	08-15-1959
1182	Sr. Mary Elina Bernazani	08-15-1959
1183	Sr. Sharon Ann Wills	08-15-1959
1184	Sr. Maureen Flanagan (William Edna)	08-15-1959
1185	Sr. Pauline LaMothe (Marlita)	08-15-1959
1186	Sr. Ann Patrice Fagan	08-15-1959
1187	Sr. Ernestine Marie Russo	08-15-1959
1188	Sr. M. Clarellen McGinley	08-15-1959
1189	Sr. Francis Regis Donahoe	08-15-1959
1190	Sr. Maria Isabel Delgado	08-15-1959
1191	Sr. Catharine Gannon (M. Bartholomew)	08-15-1959
1192	Sr. Christine Marie Loughlin	08-15-1959
1193	Sr. Mary Gabriel Sullivan (Gloria)	08-15-1959
1194	Sr. Catherine Therese Stackpole	08-15-1959
1195	Sr. Mary Claire Kirkpatrick (Carleen)	08-15-1959
1196	Sr. Mary Ann Hagan (Veronica Mary)	08-15-1959
1197	Sr. Barbara Ann Sullivan (Anne Cecilia)	08-15-1959
1198	Sr. Barbara Marie Hughes	08-15-1959
1199	Sr. Catherine Siena Whitehouse	09-12-1959
1200	Sr. Mary Gregory Lyons	02-02-1960
1201	Sr. Marietta MacDonald	02-02-1960
1202	Sr. M. Winifred Miller	02-02-1960
1203	Sr. Mary Christoffel (Gertrude Mary)	02-02-1960
1204	Sr. Elizabeth Hanlon (Immaculae)	02-02-1960
1205	Sr. M. Lourdette Gangemi	02-02-1960
1206	Sr. Mary Janet Riggs	08-15-1960
1207	Sr. Elaine Shaw (Mary Malcolm)	08-15-1960
1208	Sr. M. Juanita Carrigan	08-15-1960

1209	Sr. Mary Brennan (Geralda)	08-15-1960
1210	Sr. M. Juliette Meehan	08-15-1960
1211	Sr. Barbara Ann Fava (Paul Dominic)	08-15-1960
1212	Sr. Mary Eileen Trecartin	08-15-1960
1213	Sr. Mareese Ballard	08-15-1960
1214	Sr. Mary Carol Feeney (Eugene Marie)	08-15-1960
1215	Sr. Ann Michelle Gergen	08-15-1960
1216	Sr. Robert Ann Lusk	08-15-1960
1217	Sr. Betty Ann Hesse (Thomasetta)	08-15-1960
1218	Sr. Patrick Mary Powers	08-15-1960
1219	Sr. Ann Byrne (Vincent Mary)	08-15-1960
1220	Sr. Julia Grey (Francis de Sales)	08-15-1960
1221	Sr. Lois McGovern (James Louise)	08-15-1960
1222	Sr. Dominica Damato	08-15-1960
1223	Sr. Ellen Miriam Nyquist	08-15-1960
1224	Sr. John Cecilia Doherty	08-15-1960
1225	Sr. Therese Connolly (Edwardine)	08-15-1960
1226	Sr. Angela Mary White	08-15-1960
1227	Sr. Kathleen Marie Coakley	08-15-1960
1228	Sr. Doris Lee Mingus (Mary Basil)	08-15-1960
1229	Sr. Catherine Galaskiewicz (Mary Lucy)	08-15-1960
1230	Sr. Michelle Sherliza	09-12-1960
1231	Sr. Alphonse Marie DeGirolamo	02-02-1961
1232	Sr. Gladys Perez (Marie del Socorro)	02-02-1961
1233	Sr. Deborah Ann Brown	02-02-1961
1234	Sr. Diane Marie Curran	02-02-1961
1235	Sr. Joyce Montgomery (David Ann)	08-15-1961
1236	Sr. Linda Ann Gahafer (Fidelis)	08-15-1961
1237	Sr. Barbara Lavin (Mary Kenneth)	08-15-1961
1238	Sr. Merici Bucci	08-15-1961
1239	Sr. Catherine Mary Albright	08-15-1961
1240	Sr. Marleen Mohatt	08-15-1961
1241	Sr. Marie Marguerite Beaven	08-15-1961
1242	Sr. Carolyn Smith (M. Eucharia)	08-15-1961
1243	Sr. Elizabeth Nally (Martine Marie)	08-15-1961
1244	Sr. Nora Rita Mudd (Ann Richard)	08-15-1961
1245	Sr. Janice Koss (James Francis)	08-15-1961
1246	Sr. Emil Clare Walters	08-15-1961
1247	Sr. Sheila Coughlin (Constantia)	08-15-1961

1248	Sr. Ellen Joyce (Joyce Marie)	08-15-1961
1249	Sr. Frances Belmonte (Rosaire)	08-15-1961
1250	Sr. Barbara King (Catherine Jeanette)	08-15-1961
1251	Sr. Nadina Barreto-Perez (Mary Paul)	08-15-1961
1252	Sr. Rita Marie Goodall	08-15-1961
1253	Sr. Rose Marie Cummins	08-15-1961
1254	Sr. Claire McGowan (Joan Vincent)	08-15-1961
1255	Sr. Anne Martin Petway	08-15-1961
1256	Sr. Joan Walsh (David Edward)	02-02-1962
1257	Sr. Rosemary Rule (Louis Bernard)	02-02-1962
1258	Sr. Robert Mary Barton	02-02-1962
1259	Sr. Ruth Therese Bender	08-15-1962
1260	Sr. Rosemary Cina (Miriam Loretto)	08-15-1962
1261	Sr. Roberta Anne Semper	08-15-1962
1262	Sr. Susan Morris (Francis Therese)	08-15-1962
1263	Sr. Theresa Fox (Mary Charles)	08-15-1962
1264	Sr. Helen O'Sullivan (Michael Ann)	08-15-1962
1265	Sr. Nancy Sumner (William Margaret)	08-15-1962
1266	Sr. Therese Edward Sparaco	08-15-1962
1267	Sr. Marie Patrice Tuohy	08-15-1962
1268	Sr. Elaine Kassian (Kenneth Marie)	08-15-1962
1269	Sr. M. Felice Schneider	08-15-1962
1270	Sr. Irene Whelton (Elizabeth John)	08-15-1962
1271	Sr. Mary Rene Pinsonnault	08-15-1962
1272	Sr. Margaret Xavier Lehr	08-15-1962
1273	Sr. Anne Cody (Raymond Anne)	08-15-1962
1274	Sr. Margaret Duggan (Mark Daniel)	08-15-1962
1275	Sr. Mary Letha Kosmicki (Mildred Paul)	02-02-1963
1276	Sr. Mary Jordan Herin	08-15-1963
1277	Sr. Mary Albert Pera	08-15-1963
1278	Sr. Isabel Callahan	08-15-1963
1279	Sr. Mary Delia McMahon	08-15-1963
1280	Sr. Mary Providence Malnick	08-15-1963
1281	Sr. Janet Pohlmeier (Margaret Mary)	08-15-1963
1282	Sr. Mary Andrea Brooks	08-15-1963
1283	Sr. Paulellen Hagan	08-15-1963
1284	Sr. Marie Seaman	08-15-1963
1285	Sr. Siobhan Oliva	08-15-1963
1286	Sr. Bernadette Coleman (Mary Judea)	08-15-1963

1287	Sr. Stephanie Rogers (Virginia)	08-15-1963
1288	Sr. Mary Jo Owens (Joanita)	08-15-1963
1289	Sr. Teresa Tuite (Mary William)	08-15-1963
1290	Sr. Dianna Illiano (Mary Joel)	08-15-1963
1291	Sr. Noelle Cameron	08-15-1963
1292	Sr. Maryann Tarquino (Mary Dismas)	08-15-1963
1293	Sr. Gilmary Loughlin	08-15-1964
1294	Sr. Carole Rossi (Phyllis)	08-15-1964
1295	Sr. Ollie Thibodeaux (Paul Therese)	08-15-1964
1296	Sr. Michael Mary Weiler	08-15-1964
1297	Sr. Mary Healy (Agnita)	08-15-1964
1298	Sr. Monica Marie Long	08-15-1964
1299	Sr. Felice Remsing (Gerard)	08-15-1964
1300	Sr. Mary Leah Turbeyville	08-15-1964
1301	Sr. Mary Elizabeth Thompson	08-15-1964
1302	Sr. Pieta Goldstein	08-15-1964
1303	Sr. Patricia Anne Regan (Camilia)	08-15-1964
1304	Sr. Mary Carolyn Clark (Sadoc)	08-15-1964
1305	Sr. Joan Scanlon (Joan of Arc)	08-15-1964
1306	Sr. Thomas More Deeney	08-15-1964
1307	Sr. Irene Mary Moore	08-15-1964
1308	Sr. Lawrence Marie Adams	08-15-1964
1309	Sr. Julianne Collins	08-15-1964
1310	Sr. Rosaire Hickey	08-15-1964
1311	Sr. Evelyn Marie Lyons	08-15-1964
1312	Sr. Mary David Palcich	08-15-1964
1313	Sr. Florita McLaughlin	08-15-1964
1314	Sr. Catherine Johnson (Sylvester)	08-15-1964
1315	Sr. Mary Louise Edwards (David Mary)	08-15-1964
1316	Sr. Barbara Harrington (Caritas)	08-15-1964
1317	Sr. Linda Gleason (Verita)	08-15-1964
1318	Sr. Barbara Dubois (Francesca)	08-15-1964
1319	Sr. Sheila Kingsley (Benedicta)	08-15-1964
1320	Sr. Virginia Marie Primrose	08-15-1965
1321	Sr. Norah Guy	08-15-1965
1322	Sr. Michael Francis Shea	08-15-1965
1323	Sr. M. Dolores Johnson	08-15-1965
1324	Sr. Barbara Sowers (Laetitia)	08-15-1965
1325	Sr. Elaine Smith (Terence Marie)	08-15-1965

1326	Sr. Kathleen Knowles (Marcella)	08-15-1965
1327	Sr. Mary Ann Cavagnaro (Josephine)	08-15-1966
1328	Sr. Jean Berney (Ann Lawrence)	08-15-1966
1329	Sr. Miriam Hixenbaugh (Margaret Leo)	08-15-1966
1330	Sr. M. Huberta Maloney	08-15-1966
1331	Sr. Catherine Jones (Joseph Catherine)	08-15-1966
1332	Sr. Mary Blaise Flynn	08-15-1966
1333	Sr. Margaret Jones (Dorothy Ann)	08-15-1966
1334	Sr. Mary Joy Prato	08-15-1966
1335	Sr. Jane McCarthy (Anne Maura)	08-15-1966
1336	Sr. Jean Hayes (James Bernice)	08-15-1966
1337	Sr. Carolyn Thomas (Thomasina)	08-15-1966
1338	Sr. Rita Petrusa (Maria Anthony)	08-15-1966
1339	Sr. Maria Mercedes Cruz	08-15-1966
1340	Sr. Michaelita McGurn	08-15-1967
1341	Sr. Corita Chester	08-15-1967
1342	Sr. Carolee Collins (Ann Harold)	08-15-1967
1343	Sr. Mary Damien Campbell	08-15-1967
1344	Sr. Charlene Moser (Charlesetta)	08-15-1967
1345	Sr. Anne Jaochim MacKay	08-15-1967
1346	Sr. Jacqueline Kirk	08-15-1967
1347	Sr. Joye Gros (Frances Elizabeth)	08-15-1967
1348	Sr. Brenda McCarthy (Maura Richard	08-15-1967
1349	Sr. Nancy Chausse (Mark Marie)	08-15-1967
1350	Sr. Gloria Jean Walters	08-15-1967
1351	Sr. Marybeth Irvine	08-15-1967
1352	Sr. Glenda Hutton (Robert Marie)	08-15-1967
1353	Sr. Mary Ann Choyeski (James Louise)	08-15-1967
1354	Sr. Catherine John Branicky	08-15-1967
1355	Sr. Cecilia Rose Spurlin	08-15-1967
1356	Sr. Maria Minerva Estremera (Regina del Carmen)	08-15-1968
1357	Sr. Pauline Dufresne (Lorraine Regis)	08-15-1968
1358	Sr. Julia Marie Vierk	08-15-1968
1359	Sr. Barbara Rapp	08-15-1968
1360	Sr. Jane Louise Meringleo	08-15-1968
1361	Sr. Lucille Marie Fiandaca	08-15-1968
1362	Sr. Michael Luke Hagelston	08-15-1968
1363	Sr. Eileen Francis Riddell	08-15-1968

1364	Sr. Josefina Ortega	08-15-1968
1365	Sr. Isabel Maria Perez	08-15-1968
1366	Sr. Judith Marie Morris	08-15-1969
1367	Sr. Carmen Leticia Maldonado (Maria Elenita)	08-15-1969
1368	Sr. Christine Connolly	08-15-1969
1369	Sr. Dianne Hagan (Anthony James)	08-15-1969
1370	Sr. Harriet Agnew	08-15-1969
1371	Sr. Mary Ann Kenney	08-15-1971
1372	Sr. Alice Green	08-15-1971
1373	Sr. Eileen Haklitch	08-15-1972
1374	Sr. Joan Petersen	08-10-1974
1375	Sr. Mary Lynne Magrino	09-01-1979
1376	Sr. Gail Mackin	08-30-1980
1377	Sr. Mary Cleary	09-12-1982
1378	Sr. Hue Thi Le	07-08-1984
1379	Sr. Donna Sullivan	08-20-1988
1380	Sr. Tuyet Ngoc Tran	06-24-1989
1381	Sr. Hoang Thi Luu	06-17-1990
1382	Sr. Huong Thi Nguyen	08-04-1990
1383	Sr. Mary Phuc Nguyen	09-01-1991
1384	Sr. Binh Thanh Nguyen	07-05-1992
1385	Sr. Nang Thi Nguyen	12-21-1996

Kentucky Dominican Associates: 1981-1997

Carmen Acevedo
Maria A. Acevedo-Perez
Rosa J. Aviles-Perez
Ann Ahern
Karen E. Albright
Julia Anderson
Kay Anderson
Louise Anderson
Lea Arthur
Agnes Austin

Amy Banks
Susan Barefoot
Jean Bartley
Jim Bartley
Mary Bastin
Jeanne Beatty
Elizabeth Benecke
George Benecke
Gayle Benson
Irene Beyer
Beatrice Birmingham
Cynthia Boulton
John J. Brennan
Doris Brusa
Ann M. Buescher
Nora Burlone

Isabelle Cadrett
Dorothy Cannon
Joan Carr
Myrna Cerezo
Sue K. Clements

Anne V. Coleman
Walter Coleman
Edna Cosette
Dianne Curley
Joseph R. Curley
Debbie Cusick

Patricia M. Daly
Jeanne DeVriendt
Raye Anne Dickerson

Catherine Edelen
Joseph Eiden
Markey Eiden

Raghda Fakhoury
Rev. Albert Faretra
Paula Finnegan
Carol Friedholm

Frank Giacoppo
Rose Giacoppo
Annabel Girard
Janet Glaser

Peggy Haines
Dorothy Hamilton
Clare Hamilton
Evelyn Harmeier
Margaret Mary Harr
Elinor Hartnett
Terry Harvey
Guimo Havansek

Christine Heckmeyer
Miriam Heine
Eleanor Higgins

Mary Beth Irvine

Marion Jordan
Rev. John Judie

Mae Kelly
Maureen Kelly
Diana King
Henry S. Klosky

Arthur Lorden
Edna Lorden
Patricia Lyons

Rev. John Mahoney
Joyce Maness
Cecelia Marsland
Frank Martinez
Madeline Mason
Jeanne Masse
Sabrena Masse
Donna Sue Medley
Tirsa Mendez
Lori Mikulis
Laura Miller
Agnes Mindrup
Rosemary Mitcheson
Sally R. Moll
Amelia Moody
Edna Moss

Corrine McCann

Bob McClellan
Ellen McClellan
Mary McDonald
Eileen McGee
Benedict McGrath
Dorothea McGuire
Nancy Guthrie McKay
Thomas McLaughlin
Rosemary McLaughlin
Elizabeth McNiff
Joan McSherry

Flaget Montgomery Nally
Angela Nance
Mary Neault
John J. Neuschel
Frances Nowack

Joan O'Connor
Mabel O'Toole
William O'Toole
Rosemary Ozanne

Betty Pate
Beatrice Peirce
Rosa A. Perez
Maria Perez-Areizaga
Jessica Perreault
June Peters
Joanie Petersen
Marilyn Priebe

Clemencia Ramos
Judith Rhodes
Yvette Richard
Margaret Riedel

Elaine Riley
Alma C. Rivera
Jane Bruce Roby
Catherine B. Rose
Margaret Mary Rose

Dr. Cathleen Schanger
David Seng
Gwendolyn Seng
Paulette Seng
Barbara Sharp
Patricia L. Sheppard
Alice Soucy
Jean Helen Stevens
Elsie Sullivan

Constance Tanzi
Harlean Ann Thissen
Clare Tiffany
Rosalie Tremblay

Terry Donovan Urekew

Arlene Waldron
Jane Wallace
LaGretta Walker
Marguerite Walker
Emilia E. Warner
Mary Watts
Bonnie Weskamp
Rosalie Weskamp
Mary Margaret Whelan
Jack Wimsatt
Martha Wimsatt
Agnes Windrup

Chronological Sequence

+1822-1904   St. Catharine Motherhouse, Siena Vale, KY
+1905-   St. Catharine Motherhouse, Siena Heights, KY

+1823-1971   St. Catharine Academy, KY
+1823-1951   St. Catharine Elementary, KY
+1833-1834   St. Catharine Boys School, KY

  1851-   St. Agnes Academy, TN, Memphis

  1852-1885   St. Peter Orphanage, TN, Memphis

+1864-1899   LaSalette Academy, TN, Memphis

  1865-1924   St. Peter Parochial School, TN, Memphis

  1866-1967   St. Louis Bertrand, KY, Louisville

  1867-1997   Holy Rosary Academy, KY, Louisville

  1869-1873   Immaculate Conception Academy, TN, Jackson

  1873-1875   Holy Saviour, IL, Jacksonville
                    (became the Springfield, IL foundation)

  1874-1880   St. Mary, TN, Memphis

  1875-1878   St. Brigid, TN, Memphis

  1877-1914   Holy Rosary, KY, Rosary Heights, Springfield
  1930-1966

  1878-n.d.   St. Patrick, TN, Memphis

1880-1951   St. Agnes, KY - Washington County School

1881-1888   Cecilville, KY - Washington County School
1919-1951

1881-1888   Smith School, KY - Washington County School
1919-1951

1882-1888   St. Dominic, KY, Springfield
1929-1988

1882-1970   St. Joseph, IL Mattoon

1884-NIA   St. Charles, IL, Marshall

1885-1888   St, Mary, IL, Paris

1886-1887   St. Bridget, KY, Louisville

1886-1889   Holy Trinity, KY, Fredericktown
1908-1910

1888-1991   St. Patrick, MA, Watertown
1891-1989   St. Patrick High School, MA, Watertown

1888-1895   School for Colored Children, TN, Memphis

1889-1989   St. Michael, MA, Lowell

1891-1992   St. Francis de Sales, MA, Charlestown

1895-NIA   Sacred Heart, IL, Effingham

+1898-1912 Infant of Prague, MA, Waverley

+1914-1962 St. Dominic School for Boys, MA, Waverley

+1901-   Spalding Academy, NE, Spalding

1904-NIA   St. Joseph, IL, East St. Louis

1904-1905   St. Rose of Lima, IA, Dennison

1906-1912   St. Patrick, NE, North Platte

1906-1970   St. Patrick, MA, West Lynn

1907-1912   St. Bavo School, IN, Mishawaka

1907-   St. John Berchmans, IL, Chicago

1907-1940   St. Stephen Grade School, NE, Exeter

+1909-1931   Immaculate Conception Academy & College, NE, Hastings

1910-1911   St. Catharine Grade School, MA, Charlestown

+1911-1986   Rosary Academy Elementary, MA, Watertown
+1911-1981   Rosary Academy High School, MA, Watertown

1912-1991   St. Cecilia Elementary, NE, Hastings
1931-1991   St. Cecilia High School, NE, Hastings

1912-1969   Sacred Heart Elementary, MA, East Boston
1956-1969   Sacred Heart High School, MA, East Boston

1912 1970   St. Anthony, NE, Cedar Rapids

1913-1923   St. Mary, NE, Dawson

1913-1987   St. John Grade School, MA, North Cambridge

1914-1941   St. Patrick, NE, Fremont

1915-   St. Mary, NE, Omaha

1915-1967   St. James, NE, Kearney

1916-1934   St. Patrick, NE, Havelock

1916-1969   St. Patrick, IA, Missouri Valley

1918-1970   St. Brendan, WV, Elkins

1918-1983   St. Patrick, NE, McCook

1919-1932   St. Mary, IA, Red Oak

1921-1939   Sacred Heart, IN, South Bend

+1921-1970   St. Catharine Hospital, NE, McCook

1921-1978   St. Bartholomew, IL, Chicago

1921-1957   St. John High School, MA, North Cambridge

1922-1964   St Augustine, KY, Reed

1922-1967   St. Mary of the Woods, KY, McQuady

+1922-1972   St. Agnes/Siena College, TN, Memphis

1923-1973   Our Lady of Peace, IL, Chicago

1924-1989   Sacred Heart Elementary, NE, Greeley
1924-1970   Sacred Heart High School, NE, Greeley

1925-1992   Resurrection, NY, Brooklyn

1925-1969   St. Augustine, IN, Jeffersonville

1926-1974   St. James Elementary, WV, McMechen

1927-1931   St. Mark, IN, Gary

1927-1981   SS Simon and Jude, NY, Brooklyn

1930-1988   St. Teresa, NE, Lincoln

+1931-   St. Catharine College, KY

1932-1994   Our Lady of Lourdes, NY, Queen's Village

1932-1985   St. Vincent Ferrer, NY, Brooklyn

1934-1937   Visitation, NE, O'Connor

+1936-1950   St. Catharine House of Studies, DC, Washington

1936-1952   St. Michael, AR, West Memphis

1938-1970   St. Francis, AR, Forrest City

1938-1982   St. Philip Neri, NE, Omaha

1940-1970   St. Luke, MA, Waverley

+1941-1969   Mount Trinity Academy, MA, Watertown

+1944-1970   St. John Hospital, NE, Spalding

+1944-1980   Mary Immaculate Hospital, KY, Lebanon

1945-1958   Nativity, TN, Memphis

1946-1956   St. Patrick, LA, Montgomery

1946-1966   Boys' Guidance Center, MA, Boston

1947-1955   St. Edward, KY, Fulton

1947-1962   Nativity, LA, Campti

1947-1970   SS Peter and Paul, KY, Hopkinsville

+1948-1968   Rosary Hospital,KY, Campbellsville

1948-1976   San Carlos, PR, Aquadilla

1948-1983   St. Mary, NE, Bellevue

1948-1993   St. Catharine Convent, NE, McCook

1948-1970   Our Lady of Perpetual Help, KY, Campbellsville

+ 1949-1960   Dominican Postulate, MA, Plainville

1949-1965   St. Mary, NJ, Williamstown

1949-1970   St. John, TN, Memphis

1949-1982   St. Michael, IL, Orland Park

1950-1960   St. Stephen Priory, MA, Dover

1950-1970   St. John, Oh, Lima
1950-1956   St. John High School, OH, Lima

1950-1970   St. Agnes, MA, Reading

1950-1971   St. Stephen Martyr, KY, Louisville

1950-1971   St. Joseph, MA, Belmont

1951-1969   St. Rose, KY, Springfield

+1951-1976   Dominican Academy, MA, Plainville

1952-1965   Our Lady of the Hills, KY, Finley (public school)

1952-1975   Blessed Sacrament, NE, Grand Island
1952-1970   Blessed Sacrament High School, NE, Grand Island

1952-1987   SS Simon and Jude, KY, Louisville

+1953-   St. Mel, MA, Gloucester

1954-1991   Sacred Heart, IN, Jeffersonville

1954-1971   St. Luke, NE, Ogalalla

1954-1978   Our Lady of the Wayside, IL, Arlington Heights

1955-1972   St. Michael, NE, Hastings

1955-1978   Catholic University, PR, Ponce

1955-1990   Immaculate Heart (West End Catholic), KY, Louisville

1955-1980   Bishop Donahue High, WV, McMechen

1956-1989   Central Catholic High School, NE, Grand Island

1956-1987   St. Pius X High School, NE, Lincoln

+1956-   St. Dominic School for Boys. TN, Memphis

1957-1988   North Cambridge Central High School, MA, North Cambridge

1957-1976   St. Louis, TN, Memphis

1959-1960   Camp Marymount (Summer Camp), TN, Kingston Springs

1959-1985   Our Lady of Mt. Carmel, KY, Louisville

1960-1974   St Albert the Great, KY, Louisville

1961-   Kearney Catholic, NE, Kearney

+1961-   Sansbury Memorial Infirmary, KY

+1963-1980 Marian Manor Nursing Home, KY, Lebanon

+1966-1971 Our Lady of Spalding Manor, NE, Spalding

1967-1969   Catholic High, KY, Owensboro

1967-1971   Popes John and Paul Consolidated, KY, Louisville

1967-1973   St. Ann, NE, Lexington

+1976-1990   Dominican Center, MA, Plainville

+1983-1991   Womancenter, MA, Plainville

+1989-1990   Celeste House, MA, Plainville

+1992-   Crystal Spring, MA, Plainville

+Indicates community-owned institutions; the remaining data relates to parish missions.

In some instances, withdrawal date is when the Congregational commitment ceased. Individual sisters may have contracted to remain at a mission. The individual contracting system began after the Chapter of 1969.

AAB	Archives, Archdiocese of Baltimore, MD
AAJN	Archives, American Journal of Nursing, New York, NY
AAO	Archives, Archdiocese of Omaha, Omaha, NE
ADL	Archives, Diocese of Lincoln, Lincoln, NE
AEPD	Archives, Elkins Park Dominicans, Elkins Park, PA
AFRD	Archives, Fall River Dominicans, Fall River, MA
AGBD	Archives, Great Bend Dominicans, Great Bend KS
AGOP	Archives General, Order of Preachers, Rome, Italy
AHD	Archives, Houston Dominicans, Houston, TX
APF	Archives, Propaganda Fide, Rome, Italy
ASCD	Archives, St. Cecilia Dominicans, Nashville, TN
ASD	Archives, Sinsinawa Dominicans, Sinsinawa, WI
ASE	Archives, San Estaban, Salamanca, Spain
ASL	Archives, Sisters of Loretto, Loretto, KY
ASRD	Archives, San Rafael Dominicans, San Rafael, CA
AST	Archives, San Tomas, Manila, Philippines
AUS	Archives of Ursuline Sisters, Maple Mount, KY
BAA	Boston Archdiocesan Archives, Boston, MA
BGC	Billy Graham Center Archives, Wheaton, IL
CAA	Cincinnati Archdiocesan Archives, Cincinnati, OH
CAH	Comission on Archives and History, Baltimore, MD
FCA	Filson Club Archives, Louisville, KY
FKPA	Friends of Kentucky Public Archives, Frankfort, KY
ISHA	Illinois State Historical Archives, Springfield, IL
LCNA	Library of Congress National Archives, Washington, DC
MSA	Maryland State Archives, Annapolis, MD

NAW   National Archives, Waltham, MA
NAC   Nazareth Archival Center, Bardstown, KY
OMIA   Oblates Mary Immaculate Archives, Washington, DC
OPUS   Order of Preachers United States, OPUS Project,
         Chicago, IL

SAAA   St. Agnes Academy Archives, Memphis, TN
SCA   St. Catharine Archives, St. Catharine, KY
SHDA   Sacred Heart Dominicans Archives, Springfield, IL

SJPA   St. Joseph Province Archives, Providence, RI
SMSA   St. Mary of the Springs Archives, Columbus, OH
UGA   University of Georgetown Archives, Washington, DC
UNDA   University of Notre Dame Archives, Notre Dame, IN

Libraries

Boston Public Library, Boston, MA
Centre College Library, Danville, KY
Cossett Library, Memphis, TN
Harvard University Libraries, Cambridge, MA
McCook Public Library, McCook, NE
Omaha Public Library, Omaha, NE
Peabody Library, Memphis, TN
St. Catharine College Library, St. Catharine, KY
Springfield Public Library, Springfield, KY

Ahlstrom, Sydney
A Religious History of the American People Vol. 1
Doubleday, NY 1975

Allen, William B.
A History of Kentucky
Bradley and Gilbert Publishers, Louisville, KY 1872

Aorist, Ralph K.
Andrew Jackson: Soldier and Statesman
Harper and Row, New York, NY 1963

Ashley, Benedict, OP
The Dominicans
The Liturgical Press, Collegeville, MN 1990

Billington, Ray A.
The Protestant Crusade
Quadrangle Paperbacks, Chicago 1964

Boorstin, Daniel J.
The Americans
Vantage Bks, NY 1965

Brady, Sr. Imelda, OSD
The Harp of Dawn and Other Poems
The Literary Society of St. Catharine of Siena, Springfield, KY
    1924

Burton, Katherine
Make The Way Known
Farrar, Straus and Cudahy, New York, NY 1959

Caroli, Betty Boyd
First Ladies
Oxford University Press, Oxford, England 1987

Casper, Henry W., SJ
History of the Catholic Church in Nebraska
Bruce Press, Milwaukee, WI
   Vol. I   1838-1874   1960
   Vol. II 1865-1910   1966
   Vol. III 1870-1874   1960

Chandler, David Leon
The Binghams of Louisville
Crown Publishers, NY 1987

Chinnici, Joseph P.
Living Stones
Macmillan Co., NY 1989

Code, Joseph B.
Great American Foundresses
Macmillan, NY 1929

Coffey, Reginald M.
The American Dominicans
Mt. Vernon Publishing Co., Washington, D.C. 1970

Cogley, John
Catholic America
Dial Press, NY 1973

Crews, Clyde F.
An American Holy Land: A History of the Archdiocese of Louisville
Michael Glazer, Inc., Wilmington, DE 1987

Curry, Sr. Lois, OP
Women After His Own Heart
New York City Press, NY 1966

Devadder, Jan, CFX
  Rooted in History, Vol. I & Vol. II
  Xaverianenstraat, Belgium 1985
  De Broeders Xaverianen
  Xaverianenstraat, Belgium 1989

Dolan, Jay P.
The American Experience
Doubleday, NY 1985

Donnelly, Sr. Mary Louise
Imprints
Burke, VA

Dorcy, Sr. Mary Jean, OP
St. Dominic's Family
Tan Books and Publishers, Rockford, IL 1983

Eaton, Sr. Mary Francine, OP
*History of the Development of Spalding Academy, Spalding,
    Nebrasks, 1901-1951*
DePaul Univ., Chicago, IL 1951

Ellis, John Tracy
Catholics in Colonial America
St. Paul, MN 1965

Eno, Arthur L.
Cotton was King
Lowell Historical Society, Lowell, MA 1976

Esch, Cora; Thome, Marie; Ballweg, Mabel; Hookstra, Mary
    Helen
Early Days of Spalding
Bicentennial Book Committee, Spalding, NE 1976

Esch, Cora; Langer, Helen; Glesinger, La Von
1886 St. Michael's Parish, Spalding, NE
N/A Publisher 1986

Ewens, Mary, OP
The Role of the Nun in 19th Century America
Arno Press, NY 1978

Faherty, William B.
American Catholic Heritage
Sheed & Ward, Kansas City, MO 1991

Fenwick, Benedict Joseph, SJ
Memoirs to Serve for the Future
U.S. Catholic Historical Society, Yonkers, NY

Filson, John
The Discovery and Development of Kentucke
University Microfilms, Inc., Ann Arbor, MI 1966

FitzGerald, Constance, OCD
The Carmelite Adventure
Published by Carmelite Sisters, Baltimore, MD 1990

Fogarty, Gerald P.
Patterns of Episcopal Leadership
Macmillan Co., NY 1989

Foote, Shelby
The Civil War: A Narrative Vol. I
Vintage Books, New York, NY 1986

Freidel, Frank and Brinkely, Alan
America in the Twentieth Century
Alfred Knopf, NY 1982

Garraty, John A.
Things Every American Should Know
Forbes Inc., New York, NY 1989

Gosen, Sr. Loretta, CPPS
*History of the Catholic Church in the Diocese of Lincoln, Nebraska,
    1887-1987*
Wadsworth Publishing Co., Marceline, MO 1986

Graham, James M.
Dominicans in Illinois — A History of Fifty Years 1873-1923
The Edward Hartman Co., Springfield, IL 1923

Green, Nathaniel E.
The Silent Believers
West End Catholic Council of Louisville, KY

Green, Sr. Mary Patricia, OP
*The Third Order Dominican Sisters of the Congregation of
    St. Catharine of Siena, St. Catharine , KY: Their Life and
    Constitutions 1822-1969*
Private Pub. 1978

Hannefin, Sr. Daniel
Daughters of the Church
New City Press, NY 1989

Harrison, V.V.
Changing Habits: A Memoir of the Society of the Sacred Heart
Doubleday, NY 1988

Hinnebusch, William A., OP
    Dominican Spirituality-Principles and Practice
    The Thomist Press 1964
    The History of the Dominican Order, Vol. I
    Alba House, NY 1965
    The Dominicans, A Short History
    Alba House, NY 1975

Hoffman, Msgr. Mathias
Franciscans Under Fire, Twenty Nuns, A Girl and a Dog
Foundation Books, Lincoln, NE 1990

Huettel, William L.
A Saint for St. Peter's: The Story of Brother Joseph Dutton
Unpublished Manuscript

Jarrett, Bede, OP
Life of St. Dominic
The Newman Press, Westminster, MD 1955

John Paul II
The Dignity and the Vocation of Women (Mulieres Dignitatem)
Vatican City, Rome 1988

Joseph, Sr., Mary, OP
Artistry Indeed
N/A Press 1975

Jourdan, Elise Greenup
    *The Land Records of Prince George's County, Maryland
        1702-1709*
    Family Line Publications, Westminster, MD 1990
    *The Land Records of Prince George's County, Maryland
        1710-1717*
    Family Line Publications, Westminster, MD 1990

Kalmer, Leo, OFM
Stronger Than Death
Publisher N/A

Kenneally, James K.
The History of American Catholic Women
Crossroad, NY 1990

Kennelly, CSJ, Editor
American Catholic Women-A Historical Exploration
Macmillan Publishing Co., New York, NY 1989

Kiefer, Sr. Monica, OP
  At the Springs: Part II
  Springs Press, Columbus, OH
  The Beginnings of St. Rose, Springfield, KY
  Springs Press, Columbus, OH
  A Chronicle of Courage
  Springs Press, Columbus, OH
  In the Greenwood
  Springs Press, Columbus, OH
  Log Cabin Days
  Springs Press, Columbus, OH
  O Lumen Ecclesiae, Doctor Veritatis
  Springs Press, Columbus, OH
  Undimmed Lamps
  Springs Press, Columbus, OH

Kelly, Msgr. George A.
The Battle for the American Church
Doubleday, Garden City, NY 1982

Lancaster, Samuel V.
The Lancaster Family of Maryland and Kentucky
N/A Publisher

Lehner, Francis C., OP
Saint Dominic Biographical Documents
The Thomist Press, Washington, D.C. 1964

LeMarie, Charles
translation from French by Srs. Wedding, SCN and Willett,
  SCN
A Biography of Benedict Joseph Flaget
Three Volumes, Bardstown, KY 1992

Liptak, Dolores
Immigrants and Their Church
Macmillan Co., NY 1987

MacCaffrey, Rev. James
History of the Catholic Church in the Nineteenth Century
B. Herder, St. Louis, MO 1910

Mackin, Sr. Aloysius, OP
  To Others: Sketches of a Catholic Educator in Tennessee
  St. Cecilia Congregation, Nashville, TN 1991
  Ventures Rewarded
  Williams Printing Co., Nashville, TN 1986

Maher, Sr. Mary Denis
To Bind Up the Wounds: Catholic Sisters in the Civil War
Greenwood Press, New York, NY

Masserano, Sr. Rose Marie, OP
The Nashville Dominicans
Roslyn Heights, NY 1985

Mattingly, Sr. Mary Ramona
The Catholic Church on the Kentucky Frontier
Catholic University of America, Washington, D.C. 1936

Maynard, Theodore
  The Story of American Catholicism
  Macmillam Co., New York NY 1941
  Great Catholics in American History
  Hanover House, Garden City, NY 1957

Meany, Sr. Mary Ignatius, CSJ
By Railway or Rainbow
The Pine Press, Brentwood, NY 1964

Merrill, James M.
William Tecumseh Sherman
Rand McNally, NY 1971

Minogue, Anna C.
Pages From A Hundred Years of Dominican History
F. Pustet & Co., NY 1921

Misner, Barbara
*A Comparative Study of the Members and Apostolates of the First
    Eight Permanent Communities*
University Microfilms, Inc., Ann Arbor, MI 1981

Nevins, Allan
Ordeal of the Union
Scribner, NY 1947

O'Brien, David
Public Catholicism
Macmillan Co., NY 1989

O'Connor, John B., OP
St. Dominic and the Order of Preachers
No Publisher given 1916

O'Connor, Sr. M. Paschala, OP
*Five Decades: History of the Congregation of the Most Holy Rosary,
    Sinsinawa, Wisconsin, 1849-1899*
The Sinsinawa Press, WI 1954

O'Daniel, Victor F., OP
    The First Two Dominican Priories in the United States
    Rosary Press, Somerset, OH 1947
    A Light of the Church in Kentucky
    Rosary Press, Somerset, OH 1932
    The Right Reverend Edward D. Fenwick, OP
    Pustet, NY 1920
    The Father of the Church in Tennessee
    Pustet Inc., NY 1926

O'Rourke, Alice, OP
Let Us Set Out: Sinsinawa Dominicans 1949-1984
Union Hoermann Press, Dubuque, IA 1986

Panas, Leo & Quinn, Ann
The Irish Came to Lowell
Lowell Historical Society, Lowell, MA 1985

Parable Publications, River Forest, IL
  O.P. Letters of Distinction, 1986
  Common Life in the Spirit of St. Dominic, 1990
  Dominicans at Prayer, 1983

Peden, Henry C., Jr.
Marylanders to Kentucky
Family Line Publications, Westminster, MD 1991

Peplinski, Sr. Josephine Marie, SSJ-TOSF
A Fitting Response
Pub. Sisters of St. Joseph, TOSF, Inc., South Bend, IN 1982

Petit, Loretta, OP
Friar In the Wilderness
OPUS Project, Willard Graphics, Chicago, IL 1994

Putz, Louis J.
The Catholic Church U.S.A.
Fides Publishers, Chicago, IL 1956

Reher, Margaret Mary
Catholic Intellectual Life in America
Macmillan Co., NY 1989

Sargent, Jean A.
Stones and Bones
P.G. Co. Genealogical Society, Bowie, MD 1984

Schauinger, J. Herman
  Cathedrals in the Wilderness
  Bruce Pub. 1952
  Stephen T. Badin
  Bruce Pub. 1956

Schweri, Sr. Helen Margaret
Under His Mighty Power
Louisville, KY 1983

Smaridge, Norah
Hands of Mercy: The Story of Sister Nurses in the Civil War
Benziger Bros., New York, NY 1960

Spillane, Sr. James Maria, SCN
  Kentucky Spring
  Abbey Press, St. Meinrad, IN 1968
  Summer Winds
  Abbey Press, St. Meinrad, IN 1991

Stepsis, Ursula, CSA & Liptak, Dolores, RSM
Pioneer Healers
Crossroad, NY 1989

One Hundred Twenty-Five Years of St. Louis Bertrand Parish,
  Louisville, Kentucky 1866-1991
New Hope, KY

Stritch, Thomas
The Catholic Church in Tennessee
The Catholic Center, Nashville, TN 1987

Szmrecsany, Stephan
History of the Catholic Church in Northeast Nebraska, 1891-1969
Catholic Voice Publishing Co., Omaha, NE 1983

The Canon Law Society
The Code of Canon Law
William P. Eerdmans Publishing Co., Grand Rapids, MI 1983

The Records Committee
Index to the Probate Records of Prince George's County, Maryland
  1696-1900
P.G. Co., Genealogical Society, Bowie, MD 1988

Thomas, Sr. Mary, OP
*The Lord May Be in a Hurry: Dominican Sisters, Kenosha,
    Wisconsin*
Bruce Publishing Co., Milwaukee, WI 1967

Townsend, Anselm, OP
Dominican Spirituality (translated from the French)
Bruce Publishing Co., Milwaukee, WI 1934

Tuchman, Barbara W.
The March of Folly
Knopf, Inc., NY 1984

Tugwell, Simon, OP, Ed and trans
    Jordan of Saxony: On the Beginnings
    Dominican Publications, Dublin, Ireland 1982
    Early Dominicans-Selected Writings
    Paulist Press 1982
    *Henry Lacordaire-On the Re-Establishment in France of the Order
        of Preachers*
    Dominican Publications, Dublin, Ireland 1983

Vicaire, M.H., OP
Saint Dominic and His Times
Aly Publishing Co., Green Bay, WI 1964

Waldo, Anna
Sacajawea
Avon Books, NY 1978

Ward, Geoffrey; Burns, Ric; Burns, Ken
The Civil War; An Illustrated History
Alfred Knopf, NY 1990

Watson, James Douglas
Prince George's County: Past and Present
Federal Lithograph, Washington, D.C. 1962

Webb, Hon. Ben J.
The Centenary of Catholicity in Kentucky
Charles A. Rogers, Evansville, IN 1884

Wilcox, Shirley Langdon, CG
  Prince George's County Land Record 1696-1782
  P.G. Co., Genealogical Society, Bowie, MD 1976
  1828 Tax List: P.G. Co., MD
  P.G. Co., Genealogical Society, Bowie, MD 1985
  1850 Census: P.G. Co., MD
  P.G. Co., Genealogical Society, Bowie, MD 1978

Winterbauer, Sr. Thomas Aquinas, OP
Lest We Forget
Adams Press, Chicago, IL 1973

Wittburg, Patricia, SC
Creating a Future for Religious Life: A Sociological Perspective
Paulist Press, Mahwah, NJ 1991

Wolff, Florence, SL
From Generation to Generation
Louisville, KY

Wright, F. Edward
Maryland Militia: War of 1812, Vol. 5
Family Line Publications, Silver Springs, MD 1983

Painting of St. Catharine of Siena by Sr. Dorothy Briggs